Sturdy Black Bridges: Visions of Black Women in Literature

ABOUT THE AUTHORS

Roseann P. Bell received her B.A. from Howard University and her M.A. and Ph.D. from Emory University in Atlanta, Georgia. She has taught Black American and Black African literature at Spelman College, Georgia State University, and Cornell University. She now lives in St. Croix, Virgin Islands, and produces radio programs on Afro-Caribbean literature and culture.

Bettye J. Parker grew up in Mississippi. She was actively involved in the Civil Rights Movement there in the 1960s and received her B.A. degree from Tougaloo College during that time. Since then, Dr. Parker has taught African literature and has directed nontraditional education programs. Currently, she directs a bachelor of arts degree program for adult learners at Northeastern Illinois University in Chicago. She holds a Ph.D. in literature.

Beverly Guy-Sheftall was born in Memphis, Tennessee. She received her B.A. from Spelman College in Atlanta and her M.A. from Atlanta University, and is currently pursuing her Ph.D. in American Studies, with special emphasis on black women in America and other aspects of women's studies, at Emory University. Ms. Guy-Sheftall has taught at Alabama State University and at Spelman College.

Sturdy Black Bridges: Visions of Black Women in Literature

Edited by ROSEANN P. BELL
BETTYE J. PARKER *and*
BEVERLY GUY-SHEFTALL

ANCHOR BOOKS
Anchor Press/Doubleday
Garden City, New York
1979

The Anchor Books edition is the first publication of *Sturdy Black Bridges.*

Anchor Books edition: 1979

We gratefully acknowledge Leo Carty and Richard Powell for the use of their drawings and the following people for permission to reproduce their photographs: Dawoud Bey/First Image, Nikki Grimes, Gail A. Hansberry, Gloria I. Joseph, Ed Leek, Judy Mutunhu, and Joan Stephens.

Library of Congress Cataloging in Publication Data

Main entry under title:

Sturdy black bridges.

Bibliography: p. 379.

1. Women, Black, in literature—Addresses, essays, lectures. 2. Women authors, Black—Addresses, essays, lectures. 3. Women, Black—Literary collections I. Bell, Roseann P. II. Parker, Bettye J. III. Guy-Sheftall, Beverly.
PN56.3.B55S86 810'.9'352
ISBN: 0-385-13347-2
Library of Congress Catalog Card Number 77-16898

To the memory of
Willanna Courtney Pope Wells—
the composite woman—
and to that of Rosalie,
the child/mother

R.P.B.

To Mother Thelma

For whipping some
sense in me with
her love

B.J.P.

In memory of
Grandmother,
Grandaddy,
Aunt Pearl,
Uncle Willie,
and
Cleone

B.G.-S.

Editors' Note and Acknowledgments

When we consider that it took Ralph Ellison a score of years to write *Invisible Man,* and Alex Haley twelve to write *Roots,* the four years of labor poured into *Sturdy Black Bridges* seems almost insignificant. However, *Sturdy Black Bridges* is a different kind of experience from that of *Roots* or *Invisible Man,* not in quality or even concept, but in its eclectical commitment. That eclecticism, represented in works as diverse as Margaret Walker's classic poem "Lineage" and Mae Jackson's "Cleaning out the Closet," has been at times frustrating; more often it has led to valuable exposures—encounters with people, places, and ideologies which have enhanced our own and others' lives.

The shape of this anthology is incomplete and fluid—all collections are which purport to be fundamental. But the work is generically incomplete, for such are the lives of people, and Black women, among others in the First World, are people, creating and destroying with regular frequency ideas and even dogmas. Hence, the unfinished song of *Sturdy Black Bridges*.

This collection adopts a broad attitude which may require substantiation in the "programmed" expectations of instructors or lay readers. Why, for instance, should Iva Carruthers' "War on African Familyhood" be included?—it is not a "literary" piece. The inclusion of Carruthers' essay is a more potent statement than our own which would simply explain that we believe and respect the verity that all aspects of human existence are interrelated: This includes the pure and social sciences as well as the humanities and other learning constructs academically located under "disciplines." In many of the literary selections chosen, the creative impetus has been fed by economics, biogenetics, political science, history, sociology, the performing arts. Thus, in order to combat a telescopia

—a narrow rigidness of vision—we have gone beyond boundaries traditionally prescribed for us in search of more functional and more comprehensive truths.

There were hundreds of people involved in this project, starting with the mothers, sisters, aunts, cousins, and friends situated in our homes: Mississippi, Tennessee, and Kentucky. Study and gradual comprehension of novel precepts charted our way to Kenya, Tanzania, Ghana, Nigeria, Togo, Benin, Ivory Coast, Senegal, Haiti, Barbados, Puerto Rico, St. Thomas, St. John, St. Croix, St. Kitts, Antigua, Tortola, Curaçao, Trinidad, Jamaica, Aruba, Guyana, Louisiana, Georgia, Alabama, Detroit, New York, San Francisco, Chicago, Connecticut—together or separately we went anywhere there were Black people in large numbers. Once based, for a week, month, or year, we tried, more than most "Yankees," to be as inconspicuous as possible and to become immersed in the societal fabric. With language and cultural differences being objective realities, we experienced difficulties primarily engendered by our predecessors who, in many cases, "dug up the ground" during the "roots-seeking" sixties, in search of a phenomenon called a Black Aesthetic.

The savage zeal with which many attacked this mission often caused irreparable damage as thousands of students, teachers, and professional researchers clogged the airways with strange and expensive appendages hanging from necks and shoulders—objects that took unrequested photographs or taped conversations which were later used commercially, without adequate or cordial concern for the temporary disruptions in the lives of those persons intruded upon.

Thus, much of what one comes to expect in a Black anthology is absent from *Sturdy Black Bridges:* the classic photographs of African women with babies on their backs; southern Black sharecropper women with six to thirteen children peering from a dark, rickety, dust-ridden shack; and Caribbean women with Afro/Spanish/Indian blood, sauntering under regal coconut palms down unpaved forbidding roads that lead nowhere but to the sea.

Instead of the stereotypes, we have substituted character studies—what we perceive to be real people instead of their reflections.

Whatever we have accomplished in this effort is the result of collective beliefs that the work should be done—a focus shared in by even those who could not and never intended to be able to read the book: The promise that *somebody* might tell a real tale is awesome, and it is also a harbinger of change.

In 1973 Richard Carroll, chairman of the Spelman College English Department, was among the first to encourage this project. A physically small man who looms majestically over many comrades because of his visionary acumen, Dr. Carroll unselfishly spent hours with two of the editors, suggesting approaches, reminding us of the history we had denied or ignored, or would destroy by using insensitive research tactics. His perspectives, along with those of Millicent Jordan, also a senior faculty member at Spelman, were best categorized as germinating seeds. Joining Professors Carroll and Jordan in providing encouragement were the other members of the small, close-knit English faculty: Mrs. Juanita Toomer, Mrs. Helen Brooks, Mrs. Rhoda Hendrikson, Dr. June Aldridge. And elsewhere in Atlanta, we benefited immensely from talks with Dr. Richard Long, the director of African Studies at Atlanta University; Toni Cade Bambara, writer-activist (see Beverly Guy-Sheftall's interview with her in Part Two); Dr. Carolyn Fowler, critic and professor of Black literature at Atlanta University; Dr. Richard Barksdale, co-editor with Richard Kinnamon of *Black Writers in America* and former Humanities professor at Atlanta University; Dr. George Napper, author of *Blacker Than Thou* and an eminent criminologist; and Dr. Gloria Gayles, whose unwavering commitment to struggle and truth requires and rewards struggle and truth (see her introduction to the book and her poetry in Part Three).

When faculty development funds became available at Spelman under the administration of President A. E. Manley, the general committee at Spelman validated our project by making a small grant available to do preliminary research. Our travels began and so did our encounters with a series of people—all, ironically, women–who had the skills and patience to type, edit, and reproduce our ideas so that we could "see" where we were going. In this cadre are Mrs. Quincy Tillman, Humanities secretary at Spelman, and later, what seems to be an army of women volunteering to suffer through typewriters that did not type, tape recorders that did not record, copy machines that did not copy, and postal services that were no service at all.

Daisy Rowe and Janice Steele Anderson come to mind immediately. Both were secretaries at Cornell's Africana Studies and Research Center, where two of the editors were based, and where we received another small grant for clerical and communication expenses. Both Mrs. Rowe and Mrs. Anderson spent countless hours not only typing the endless drafts but commenting on the ideational value of pieces which fascinated or bored them (we excised all the boring works). Their input was valuable for many reasons, but most especially because it was a constant reminder that Black women everywhere have *a* shared experience which can and should be utilized for many purposes. June Wall, an administrative secretary at Cornell, a collector of rare Black dolls, a griot of Ithaca, and a poet who writes poetry that yearns ("thank de lawd, i'se gon' sit quiet a spell"), was also a moving force, along with Barbara Murapa, a writing instructor who helped out with the clerical work. In the Caribbean we discovered Mrs. Urla Isaac, a fast, efficient, and pleasant person, whose joint New York–St. Croix persuasions and dedication to deadlines helped immensely.

And then there were other colleagues and friends whose regular inquiries and revelations on the book prohibited our giving up the idea because it often seemed too big: the distinguished professor J. Saunders Redding; the accomplished writers Etheridge Knight, Haki Madhubuti, Toni Morrison, Michael Echeruo in Nigeria, Timothy Callendar and Elton Motley in Barbados, Ama Ata Aidoo and Efua Sutherland in Ghana; Zulu Sofola in Ibadan, Nigeria; Ngugi Wa Thiongo in Kenya; Michael Harper at Brown University in Rhode Island; Drs. John Henrik Clarke and Josef Ben Jochannan, whose interpretations of Black history are monumental and culturally accurate; Professors Robert Harris, Jr., Bill Cross, Hamida Maalim, Ron Bailey, Maryemma Graham, Rukudzo Murapa, Tendai Mutunhu, Pierre Michele-Fontaine, Congress Mbata, June Brewer, Phyllis Thompson, Robert Johnson, Jr., Vincent Richards.

A successful project of this kind requires the co-operation of trained librarians who must also have an appreciation of the ethic producing the book. We were fortunate in working with such persons at the Spelman College Library; Atlanta University's Trevor Arnett Library; the Beinecke Library, Yale University; Olin Library, Cornell University; the University Library at Ibadan, Nigeria; the general library at the University of Ghana, Legon; Butler Library, Columbia University; the Moorland-Spingarn Special Collection at Howard University; the Caribbean Collection, Williams Library, Christiansted, St. Croix; and the impressive reservoir of Black culture located at the Arthur A. Schomburg Collection, New York Public Library. We are especially grateful to Mr. Ernest Kaiser at the Schomburg for giving so much assistance on the Caribbean bibliography. And we want to thank Marie Dutton Brown, who was sensitive enough to put us through a seasoning process, patient enough to put up with our individual and collective neuroses, and courageous enough to publish us.

There are people whose names we do not know. Cab drivers, restaurant personnel, passengers on buses, trains, and planes. People we've talked with or just overheard, talking about Black women in many parts of the world. Our ignorance of their names does not detract from our gratitude for our own enrichment, and that we hope to share with the readers of *Sturdy Black Bridges*. Rather, we appreciate that these conversations, participated in and observed, are the contents of this and similar learning adventures.

R.P.B.
B.J.P.
B.G.-S.

Preface

A PERSONAL RESPONSE . . . A CELEBRATION

By definition (or is it tradition?), a preface to a book should measure the weight of the book, recording pounds per segment and holding each segment close to the light of truth so that distortion, irrelevance, and confusion will be revealed. It should locate the book's deserved place on the broad spectrum of historical truths, pulling those truths and the truth of the book into close communion. And a preface, at least a good one, should add to the total significance of the book, for at the moment that it assesses the book, it enhances our understanding of the basic ideas and ideals the book addresses.

I cannot write such a preface. Even after a third reading of *Sturdy Black Bridges,* I cannot push myself or pray myself into the academic distance such a preface demonstrates. Stubborn, with a mind and will of its own, *something* pushes me into the center of the vision of this work, making it breathe for me. Perhaps that *something* is the persistence of a song I learned as a child from women who were the words and the melody; or the pressure of their hands designing beauty on my soul, aware of a sore that would mark me, never healing; or the deep simplicity of their sermons, preaching a text never changing. As I try to examine this book critically, I see only the towering grandeur of those women, three sturdy black bridges I crossed over on.

I am mindful of Ralph Ellison's observation that sometimes we hold our blackness too tightly around us and thus do we choke on that which should define and liberate us. I confess that I hold my identity as a black woman very tightly around my vision of reality, around the vision of this book, but I feel no suffocation. Instead, I feel a dance of jubilation coming on and twirling me through a rich history that bears the distinct imprint of positive forces who are/were black women. Let me explain this dance of jubilation.

Sturdy Black Bridges has been in the making for several years. I witnessed its various stages of becoming. I spent hours listening to the editors explain their vision—how they would give it voice and form, and what they hoped the sound and flesh of it would do for us in this country and elsewhere throughout the Diaspora. Weighted down by the responsibilities of wifehood and motherhood, doctoral studies and heavy teaching loads; enduring the sorrow of family illnesses and family deaths; stockpiling letters that are assembly-line productions of an institution that will not significantly underwrite research conducted by black women—through all this, Roseann Bell, Beverly Guy-Sheftall, and later, Bettye Parker unearthed images of black women in literature, fingering their positive beauty one by one, until this book, itself a bridge, was completed. Having witnessed their labor, I read *Sturdy Black Bridges* and know that I am witnessing birth. I do what one always does when the first sounds of life, of creation, are heard, strong and distinct. I rejoice. I celebrate. I dance with my soul.

There is reason to celebrate the publication of this work, for our lives have been touched in various ways by black women who are real-life models for images in literature. As mothers, grandmothers, sisters, aunts, lovers, wives, children. As people who were and are major architects of the black experience. It is a special book, because it refuses to pay homage to the "system's" distortions of black women and to our refusal too long to correct those distortions. It is a bridge we have needed to cross over on into a deeper understanding of and more sensitive appreciation for *our* women as positive forces in our experience.

The journey into that understanding includes in *Sturdy Black Bridges* three well-marked and converging paths: (1) what has been happening critically with images of black women in literature, (2) the astute perceptions of those who have been a vital part of that happening, either as image makers or as critics of images made, and (3) an experience with fresh and powerful images that further inform the why of sturdy black bridges as we continue to cross over on into ourselves.

Part One, "The Analytical Vision," is a necessary first step in the journey, for we must know *those* visions if we are to understand the why of this book. The introduction to this section by Bell and Parker, as well as Parker's general introduction to the book, establishes the fertile mind-set for a creative experience within this section and the entire book. Bell and Parker analyze and raise questions about those visions, juxtaposing them to the historical reality of black women. The major task for all of us, Parker writes, "is to raise images (of black women in literature) to a level commensurate with historical truths," and we do that by moving "beyond fragmented judgments historically practiced by white Western critics" and beyond a momentary pause on the achievements of black women artists and critics.

Preparation for this task demands a richly textured and sensitive approach to the study of analytic visions, and thus is Part One a variegated garden of visions. Gloria Hull's compact but comprehensive study, "Black Women Poets from Wheatley to Walker," names poets, examines their work within a historical context, and places them prominently in the vision that *is* this book. And there are Mary Helen Washington's and Chester Fontenot's studies of Alice Walker as artist, thinker, woman, and image herself—studies surpassed in intimacy and depth only by Walker's own "In Search of Our Mothers' Gardens." There are other articles equally impressive in defining visions of the black women in literature.

Perhaps two essays in this section should be set apart for comment: Daryl Dance's "Black Eve or Madonna?: A Study of the Antithetical Views of the Mother in Black American Literature" and Hortense Spillers' "The Politics of Intimacy: A Discussion." Dance's work is a critical study of images of the black mother as they are found in works by Amiri Baraka, John O. Killens, John Williams, Douglas Turner Ward, and other male writers. Spillers' work analyzes issues related to the intimate life of black women, with special focus on the relationship between black men and black women as it is treated in the fiction of James Baldwin.

There is no question that the subject of each essay is vital to the vision of the entire project, for how can one begin to talk about images of the black woman in literature without placing in bas-relief the identity of mother and other identities that involve the black woman in relation to men. That Dance and Spillers examine works by black men writers might make the essays seem anomalies in *Sturdy Black Bridges*. But on a higher level, where visions live and thrive, the essays are synchronic; they are essential to this experience. For getting to the center of images of black women involves the seeing of those who, with us, define the black experience. As Parker explains, *Sturdy Black Bridges* "does not suggest that black women writers be treated as a separate entity of the Black literary experience" or that black men writers be seen as aliens to those images. They cannot be, for on one level, what black women are is reflected in what happens between them and black men. While it is necessary to go to women for definitions of *our* visions, it is equally necessary to go to men if we would see ourselves as they see us, and if we would correct and/or deepen that seeing.

Reading Part Two is like being with black writers and critics—Toni Cade Bambara, Arthenia Bates, Gayl Jones, Ann Petry, Toni Morrison—all are here, speaking to us in close quarters, making the printed page a canvas of sharp and moving portraitures. The women writers explain how they deal creatively with their double identity (or is it triple identity?), how they envision literature as a vital medium for clear reflections of women, and how what they create as artists finds its way into literary criticism. In the interviews we are in touch with introspections, revelations, judgments, prophecies, and dreams. We read them and we find ourselves standing in a gallery. We see individual women writers emerge from well-wrought frames as women we know and have always known in our reality—as women to whom we have trusted and will continue to trust the painting of large portraits that include us and those who named us "black women."

Let me hasten to add that not all the interviews in Part Two are conversations with black women. Addison Gayle is here and so is George Kent. In particular, Roseann Bell's interview with George Kent deserves special notice, but not because it is more important than the other interviews. How can it be when those other interviews reveal such significant black women writers to us? Rather, the Kent interview is notable because it symbolizes the kind of indepth interchange that should take place between black men and black women in the world of criticism. What emerges from this interview is a rather unique picture of a black woman educating a black man on her visions of herself as a black woman, visions that include all of us. From a posture of warm admiration and deep respect, Bell leads Kent gently into areas he has not yet explored or at least not put into print. She raises questions and she suggests answers. Kindly, but firmly, she asks Kent about the low profile black women writers have in his brilliant scholarship.

And Kent educates Bell. He is open in his comments on black women writers, displaying that honesty and commitment which make him one of Bell's most intriguing interviewing experiences. Of black women writers he has read, Kent says that their works lack depth, and he measures those works against the depth of works by black male writers, Ernest Gaines in particular. He says that all too infrequently in works by black women does the black man occupy the same space together with the black woman. His comments on Zora Neale Hurston are insightful. When they are placed in the larger context of women writers defining themselves away from themselves, Kent's observations are priceless. It does not matter that Bell takes issue with several of Kent's judgments. What matters is that Bell and Kent, in the same space together, raise penetrating questions that will not lie still until they are soothed by profound answers.

In Part Three, "The Creative Vision," the journey ends and, on another plane, it begins again. This section includes poems, plays, short stories, and monologues on black women written by women and men, by well-known and upcoming writers, by artists born in the United States, the Caribbean, and in Africa. The images here are rich and moving representations of black women from different places, different circumstances, in different roles, and carrying the faint or strong aroma of different experiences: Bessie Head, South Africa; Lorna Williams, Jamaica; Paule Marshall, Barbados; Jacquelyn F. Hunter, Trinidad; Carolyn Rodgers, Chicago; Lynn Suruma, Hartford.

The photographic essays, as photographs and essays, speak authoritatively and powerfully, moving gracefully and majestically as they replicate the *modus operandi* of the book. It is not enough to speak of Judy Mutunhu's coptic vision; of Nikki Grimes's range and eclecticism; of Ed Leek's double vision; of Gloria Joseph's and Gail Hansberry's mellow intrusions into delicate unstaged moments. The photographs are worth millions of words—they elicit much more than verbal response.

Among the illustrators, Richard Powell is a beacon. His careful and spiritual artistic development, beginning somewhere on Martin Luther King Drive in Chicago, continuing at Morehouse College, Howard University, the Smithsonian Institution, the Metropolitan Museum, and now, Norfolk State College, is exhibited here. Already a master of detail in his youth, Mr. Powell is especially adept at capturing the versatility evident in black female forms. Leo Carty utilizes a different sensuality and maturity in his drawings. From his early work, such as the 1964 *Freedomways* drawing, "Women at the Well" (and featured in *Sturdy Black Bridges*), to the two most recent ones which depict a moving, aware Caribbean female experience, touched by a black past, present, and future, Carty is consistently able to summon that inner world which profound artists have—to do their bidding.

Finally, there are the three bibliographies—gold mines for scholars in African-American, African, and Caribbean studies—paths that lead to others. This book was originally designed for scholar and layman. The inclusion of the inexhaustive though impressive bibliographies proves that the original intention was a serious one come to fruition.

Sturdy Black Bridges is already a classic.

Gloria Gayles
Talladega College
Talladega, Alabama

Contents

Part Three: THE CREATIVE VISION

Sturdy Black Bridges: Visions of Black Women in Literature

Introduction

BLACK WOMEN IN AND OUT OF FICTION: TOWARD A CORRECT ANALYSIS

Sojourner Truth was old and tired with years. Her breasts sagged from the weight of too much sucking of babies born to those other than herself. As she stood at the rostrum echoing the condition of her people, a young white doctor rose in the audience and interrupted the old woman's speech.

"There are those among us," he began in a tone characteristic of institutional training, "who question whether or not you are a woman. Some feel that maybe you are a man in a woman's disguise. To satisfy our curiosity, why don't you show your breasts to the women in this audience?"

The old woman walked down from the stage and stood directly in the path of the man-child's eyes. In them she saw the wrongs heaped upon her people. She smelled the infectious stench from the overcrowded slave ships, and heard the bellows of auctioneers and the cries of families split and sold. She felt the crack of the whip and noticed that callouses on his hands were still visible. Her body shuddered from memories of the rapes and she felt the null drippings from his pale body into her precious naked womb. The palms of her hands itched but she stood queenly and erect. And this time when she spoke, her tone was not as evangelical as before.

"I'm not afraid to prove to you that I am a woman," she whispered. "I'll show my breasts to all who are present here. You see, it is not my shame that I do this, but yours."

She unbuttoned her dress and exposed her breasts and in the

eyes of the young white doctor, who claimed knowledge in the field of anatomy, she saw the cycle of oppression continue to revolve.

Now clearly, this level of dehumanization did not begin with Sojourner Truth. Most certainly, it did not end when she was forced to perform this horrendous act. Rather, the process began with the first Asian and European intrusions on African civilization. And, unfortunately, these seeds of degradation have weaved their way into the present.

The process of transforming the image of Black women from respectable and honorable members of African societies to sinister and repugnant creatures has been both premeditated and continuous. If history is correct in its assurance that Black women have a legacy of worthy and positive attributes, then the primary questions become: How can this history be used to eradicate the stereotypes created by invaders and interlopers so that the Black woman can lay this weighty burden down? Additionally, what ingredients can be put into what cauldron to ward off the demons inferred by Aunt Jemima, whore and emasculator, so that the Black woman can smoke a peace pipe with herself? How can the negative images of the Black woman and her family in the visual media and creative literature be arrested so that Black people can carry on the tradition of complete familyhood, an accomplishment first heralded by African man and woman in partnership?

Historical evidence such as that recently presented by the famed historian and scholar John Henrik Clarke serves to legitimize the Black woman's claim to a rich and lucrative past. He reminds us that history has long recorded the "impressive strides" made by Black women "during the rise of great dynasties in Egypt, Kush and Ethiopia."[1] For example, Dr. Clarke notes that:

> In ancient Afrika, she [the Afrikan woman] often ruled society with unquestioning power. Many Afrikan women were great militarists, and on occasion led their armies into battle. The Afrikan had produced a civilization where men were secure enough to let women advance as far as their minds or their royal lineage and prerogatives would take them.[2]

He continues by relating the accomplishments of Queen Hatshepsut, who reigned over Egypt about fifteen hundred years before the birth of Christ; Queen Nefertiti, who ruled Egypt almost singlehandedly after the death of her husband; Queen Makeda, better known as Queen of Sheba, who is mentioned in the Bible and the Koran for her skillful reign; and of course, Cleopatra, who is well known for her astute political maneuvers. The surety and adoration to which Black women were accustomed before European and Asian invasions diminished once the scramble over Africa began.[3]

While it is evident that sound historical analysis is coming into its own, attempts to reach the roots of the problem are also surfacing in the area of sociology. One of the most prized examples of sensitive research is Joyce Ladner's study *Tomorrow's Tomorrow*. Dr. Ladner contends that the only rational way to assess the Black woman is by examining the historical conditions that have shaped her. She states:

> It would seem impossible to understand what she [the Black woman] is today without having a perspective on what her forebears were, especially as this relates to the roles, functions and responsibilities she has traditionally held within the family unit. . . . Only by understanding these broader sociohistorical factors can we properly interpret her role today.[4]

It is evident by the current discussions among Black women that the task at hand is to raise the images to a level commensurate with historical truths. Paradoxically, however, efforts such as those suggested by Dr. Ladner have consistently been dominated by more obscure visions. For example, amid the emergence of historical reinterpretations by white "researchers" continue trying to control the images of Black life. This insistence is demonstrated in Gerda Lerner's involved research on Black women. Highly critical of this historical study, *Black Women in White America,* Jacquelyne Jackson comments:

> . . . her extremely superficial and sophomoric work appeared to fall within the genre of hasty and inefficient work developed quickly to capitalize on "blackness." Her work suffers considerably from inadequate conceptualizations of questions confronting historians investigating Black women, as well as

> from a predominantly monolithic and contradictory treatment of Black women. . . .[5]

Notably, continued distortions influence the patterns and behavior of Black women in and out of fiction. And, to be sure, growing accounts of sophisticated studies—i.e., suicide, sex, matriarchal, and others–are indicative of the incessant trend to shape and reshape the ways of Black womanhood.

Only slight critical attention has been given to Black women in creative literature, thus evoking grave concern among female artists and scholars. Recently, a number of Black anthologies and major critical works have been published. It is unfortunate, however, that in most cases, attention accorded Black women writers is sparse. Some of these works are very traditional in scope and have emulated the general American trend of including those one or two Black women writers who could not possibly be omitted. Margaret Walker, Gwendolyn Brooks, and sometimes Zora Neale Hurston are heralded as fitting and proper profiles. And even though these three writers have made giant strides in the growth and development of Black literature, sex notwithstanding, they are often treated scantily by anthologists.

The failure to regard Black writers as part of literary analysis in the move toward a correct interpretation of Black arts is a serious problem, indeed. If Black criticism is to adequately function on a level proportionate to our total literary experience, then the Black critic, both male and female, must move beyond the type of fragmented judgments historically practiced by white critics. Significantly, responding to a question about the function of the Black critic, Ngugi Wa Thiongo, the East African novelist, stated in an interview:

> We want the kind of critic who can really see the significance of those involved in the struggle. . . . The critic should review, comment on every work from the point of view of how far it is to a particular point of the struggle of the people for the full realization of themselves as a people and how far that work returns that realization.[6]

Deliberating on the plight of Black writing and criticism, during an interview conducted for this book, Addison Gayle offers the following explanation for the neglect of Black women in criticism:

> . . . We can go back to the eighteenth century in English literature when criticism first begins its large impetus and males always wrote condescendingly about women writers. That is historic among Black male critics and, I think, all males have probably done so. I suppose the big chance will come when women begin doing critical works of their own on women writers.[7]

It is important to note that a major source of literary criticism on Black women is the papers presented at recent conferences and institutes. In some cases, these papers have been collected and published. Also, scholarly journals such as *Black World* (now *First World*) and *The Black Scholar* have published special issues on Black women. Included in these issues are topics of literary concern.

Without a doubt, it is significant that Black women engage in serious research. However, the task of research, especially by Black female scholars, is slow and painful and often void of support from foundation grants and academic tenure that provide money and leisure to research. So, because of the contexts out of which we operate, negative images continue to emerge and the task becomes more difficult.

Sturdy Black Bridges does not suggest that Black women writers be treated as a separate entity of the Black literary experience. And, certainly, it is not intended to imply that the problem of critical negligence can be arrested here. Rather, the idea has been to subscribe to wide-range ideas and creative contributions by and about a specific group of Black writers who have never been accorded the literary courtesy that they are due.

The first part of this book, "The Analytical Vision," is an attempt to formulate a diasporic nexus of critical thought. Thus, included in this section is a collection of shared visions by African, Caribbean, and African-American writers. Some of the essays in this section were written expressly for this book. Some have been extracted from speeches made at various conferences and institutes. Others were borrowed from journals. "The Analytical Vision" takes a critical look at Black women as writers and characters.

Part Two, "The Conversational Vision," has been compiled with the conviction that knowledge and experience are prerequisites to wisdom and that to understand the revelations and ethics of Black life, it is as essential to examine ideas of the folk element as it is to subscribe to educated concepts. In observing this view, Part Two bears a composite of interviews ranging from such profound scholars and artists as George Kent and Arthenia Bates to the wisdom gathered from a select group of Mississippi mothers. Except for James Ivy's interview of Ann Petry and the interviews with Mississippi mothers, these conversations were arranged especially for this book.

The general plan of Part Three, "The Creative Vision," is to harmonize the theories visible in the first two sections with representative artistic achievements in poetry, fiction, and drama. Contributions received for the section far outnumber those submitted in Parts One and Two. The selections included were carefully chosen from both established and novice authors and they reflect positive images of Black women. However, our listing is by no means exhaustive or conclusive of positive expressions. Several of these selections were written particularly for *Sturdy Black Bridges.*

From the onset, a function of the book has been to furnish our audience with exemplary selections that will enable them to acquire a certain familiarity with the history and contributions of Black women writers. Three bibliographies—African-American, African, and Caribbean—have been provided. It is hoped that this feature will make the book more definitely suited to be included in course outlines and will serve as a resource for those interested in the research and development of Black women writers.

Finally, headnotes are included in Parts One and Two to assist in the identification of both individuals and concepts. These statements, some of which are quoted directly from the essays, are presented in accordance with the authors' intents and purposes and furnish either the main drift of the essay or specific biographical information.

NOTES

1. John Henrik Clarke, "The Black Woman: A Figure in World History," *Essence,* May 1971, p. 28.
2. Ibid.
3. Ibid., p. 29.

4. Joyce Ladner, *Tomorrow's Tomorrow* (Garden City, N.Y.: Doubleday & Company, 1971), p. 4.
5. Jacquelyne Jackson, in *Journal of Social and Behavioral Sciences,* Winter 1975, p. 71.
6. Bettye Parker, interview with Ngugi Wa Thiongo, Nairobi, Kenya, 1975.
7. Roseann P. Bell, interview with Addison Gayle, New York, 1975.

Part One The Analytical Vision

Introduction:

THE ANALYTICAL VISION

by ROSEANN P. BELL and BETTYE J. PARKER

For the most part, available literature on Black women is replete with distortion and is distinguished chiefly by either pathos, with which it dispatches apologetic overtones, or questions that lead to irrelevant conclusions. Unfortunately, the problems and pleasures of Black life have been defined, ill-defined, and redefined, explained and re-explained, sawed and chewed and twisted, more often than not, by persons severely limited in their abilities to understand the intricacies of Black love, laughter, and hard times. Nevertheless, the recently increased volumes of material on Black women writers allow us to observe, if not certain common motifs, at least certain common motives: curiosity and disquietude about a subject primarily ignored historically in literary criticism, or an opportunity to reap academic (and economic) harvests from an issue suddenly mushrooming in popularity.

From our vantage point, the selections in Part One, "The Analytical Vision," were chosen out of an explicit loyalty and sensibility to truth and scholarship. Our need to express a historical integrity around which much of the critical focus revolves led to the inclusion of Iva E. Carruthers' article, "War on African Familyhood." Although devoid of literary content, her Afrocentric historical focus corresponds to that of Dr. John Henrik Clarke in a three-part historical study on African women that is referred to but not included in this book. The significance of historical perimeters is evident, especially as we delve into the exotic and intriguing power of African literature.

Four authors infuse a vital understanding of history and literature in their critical perspectives. Andrea Benton Rushing's "Images of Black Women in Modern African Poetry" briefly discusses the proverbial "Mother Is Gold/Mother Is Supreme" photograph which dominates modern African poetry. Rushing identifies the social, economic, and political factors partially responsible for this monolithic image of African women, and for the absence of "poems . . . about women working, living alone, rejecting polygamy, deciding to have small families [or none], agonizing over the crises of romantic love, snapping their ties to the extended family, playing critical roles in past and present liberation struggles."

That Ama Ata Aidoo *does* write about African women who are inside and outside of the unidimensional African mother type gives credence to this observed attitude and advice for all Black women writers: The only way that undesirable/unlifelike images change is that Black women must themselves write about themselves. Karen Chapman's introduction to Aidoo's exciting play, *Dilemma of a Ghost,* raises for us a number of liberating inquiries: Why are there so few African women writing as Aidoo writes—unfettered and undenying of her cultural history and kinships? Why is the collective identity which formulates for Aidoo a holistic entity critically minimized? These questions among others are not answered in Chapman's introduction alone, but her article as well as those by Marie Linton-Umeh, Sonia Lee, Carruthers, and Benton is drawn from the matrix of an interdisciplinary sensibility: Separately and in concert, all of these critics impose fresh and informative insights on the meaning and responsibilities of "The African Diaspora," especially in shaping viable images of Black women in literature, and in answering signficant cultural questions. For example, Marie Linton-Umeh's revelations on the African heroine express the view that African history can and does provide seminal, largely unexploited literary material, while Sonia Lee's limited explorations into the heroine creations of Ousmane Sembene are insightful and important.

The similarities between the African and Afro-Caribbean writers and characters are astounding. Eintou Apandaye, a member of the National Joint Action Committee in Trinidad, offers an overview of Afro-Caribbean women's writings in several genres. More significant, however—from a theoretical stance—is the ending of this summary article, which outlines answers to some of the questions that haunt us: questions about why African and Afro-Caribbean women writers and characters are underexposed; questions about the history, psychology, and sociology of Blackness and the women's impact on literature and the art of writing. A suitable complement to Apandaye's report is the Selected Bibliography of Caribbean Women Writers and General Caribbean Literature included in this text.

The critical assiduousness accompanying works by Black American women writers is, by comparison to African and Caribbean women writers, encouraging, though the quality of the criticism has left much to be desired. The eight treatises on Afro-American literature are pregnant with heretofore unexplored reflections on a few specific creations, but the over-all thrust recognizes a continuum in Black literary criticism and Black life.

"Black Women Poets from Wheatley to Walker" by Gloria T. Hull furnishes not only an impressive catalogue of Black female poetry from Lucy Terry's "Bars Fight, August 28, 1946," to Margaret Walker's collection of poems, *For My People* (1942). It also "gives a necessary perspective on the present poets by placing them in their appropriate rich tradition."

Hortense Spillers' origination of "the politics of intimacy" is efficiently applied to a fertile source—the writing of James Baldwin, and specifically to the novel *If Beale Street Could Talk.* Spillers' adeptness at handling the powerfully subtle intricacies of myth and language establish her as a major critic. Her choice of Baldwin is especially interesting since her investigation is one of the few in the text which specifically and logically *examines* (as well as alludes to) female characterizations fomented by men.

"Images of Self and Race in the Autobiographies of Black Women" is another adventure beyond narrowly compartmentalized "disciplines." Mary Burgher steps into political, economic, historical, and sociological avenues as she proves that "autobiographies of Black women are rich and valid sources for further studies of the Black woman and for critical inquiries into how she has viewed herself historically despite labels, myths, and ideas about her place and role."

In a studied and controlled essay, Daryl Dance recapitulates and then analyzes the antithetical views of the mother in Black American literature. She looks at the primary sources—the literature of Imamu Amiri Baraka, Jimmy Garrett, Maya Angelou, Ernest Gaines, Margaret Walker, John A. Williams, among others, "not as mere fiction, but rather as an interpretation and compilation of history, anthropology, sociology, psycholgy, and a host of other areas." From these interpretations and compilations, Dance posits interesting alternatives to the traditional ways we "see" Black American mothers: "Is she a destructive Eve offering the poisonous apple or a Madonna bringing hope and salvation?"

There are two selections on the contemporary popular writer, Alice Walker. Mary Helen Washington, who has paid considerable attention to Walker's poetry, short stories, articles, and long fiction in this text and in other media, suggests that Alice Walker is "the apologist for Black women" whose main concern is "for the lives of Black women." (For further comment and discussion on Alice Walker, see the interviews with Addison Gayle, George Kent, and C. L. R. James in Part Two, "The Conversational Vision.") Using another approach, Chester J. Fontenot delineates the cultural kinship between Walker's "Diary of an African Nun" and W. E. B. Du Bois' classic theory on double consciousness.

Critics Blyden Jackson and Louis D. Rubin note that "there is a general way in which women do tend to know women and also a general way in which they tend to know men, largely because our culture makes it so. Miss [Gwendolyn] Brooks, whether she is talking of women or men . . . constantly speaks as a woman." Nowhere is this observation more lucidly supported than in Brooks's "women of Bronzeville." Beverly Guy-Sheftall writes of the urban impact juxtaposed against Brooks's sexual and racial identity.

The resurgent (and insurgent) interest in Zora Neale Hurston as scientist (anthropologist and folklorist) and fictionist finds its expression in "The Influence of Voodoo on the Fiction of Zora Neale Hurston" by Ellease Southerland. The utilization of charms, numbers, spells, chants, sacrifices—the whole range of Black occult connectives practiced in Hurston's Eatonville, Florida, in Haiti, and in the Honduras—sheds an imposing light on the life of the enigmatic artist, Hurston, and on her equally mysterious but fulfilling work.

Jerry Ward's "Bridges and Deep Water" impressed us first with its abrupt and magnetic title. The contents comprise an appropriate footnote as well as an extended celebration of Carolyn Rodgers' poem from which the title of this book was taken.

The war on African familyhood probably began with the issuance of a series of papal bulls in 1493 which divided colonial possessions. The East went to Portugal and the West went to Spain, but this decision was later compromised in the Treaty of Tordesillas to permit the Portuguese tenure of Brazil.

Thus, the rape of Africa began in the name of progress and imperialism, and the system most widely employed to reap the harvests of the plunder was *slavery*. Slavery, as Dr. John Henrik Clarke recounts (see "The Black Woman: A Figure of World History," *Essence*, July 1971), "had been the basis of Greek economy, and had built up the Roman Empire. It made the American South and the Caribbean Islands. It created the raw materials for the mills of New England. It was, and still is, a system without heart or sentiment. It laid the foundation for a still-prevailing evil called racism."

As a direct result of slavery, African families shipped to the "New World" began their "new" life without benefit of familial attachment, care, and sustenance. Information on the breeding and selling practices among slaveholders is legion, and this data partially explains the moral, physical, economic, and psychic damage suffered by Black people from the eighteenth century to the present.

Dr. Iva Carruthers' treatise adds to the body of literature which brings the "odious resource" (slavery) to task because its wide-ranging effects are continuing to be discovered and felt, especially in an area which is central to our sense of selfhood and peoplehood: Black familyhood.

War on African Familyhood

by IVA E. CARRUTHERS

The struggle for African independence throughout the world is inextricably connected to the battle for definition and control of black familyhood. By familyhood, we include all those expressions and manifestations of individual/community/national life and organization which emerge from the African world view of relationships between Man, Woman, and the Universe. Implicit in the definition of familyhood is thus the African conceptualization of the Creator, the Creation, and the dictates for Procreation. The questions which necessarily follow relate to explaining the cosmic/natural and right and the sociopolitical/natural and right order of the universe, the origins of races and civilization. With that body of knowledge as a foundation, all African institutional development will re-emerge as a universal expression of Africanity directed at assuming our rightful place in the world.

The articulation of an Afrocentric understanding of familyhood has yet to be completed, though we are guided by the unparalleled works of Diop, Obenga, Delaney, Williams, Jochannan, James, and Jackson. The works of these scholars must be lauded because they were able to circumvent the trappings of Eurocentricism which is embedded in most explanations of "truth" offered by both Aryan and black scholars. Our task requires two directions: one which explains the history, tradition, and necessary foundation for natural African family community and life, and the other which falls under Aryanology and identifies and explains the nature of those forces which have operated to the detriment of African familyhood. Obviously, these two foci of our research cannot in reality be separated, but we must clearly see the distinction between the two in order to deal with our oppression by first denouncing the myth of university. This paper will focus primarily on the latter methodological challenge, providing an analytical framework to discuss the destiny of African familyhood.

Today one of the most serious assaults to African familyhood is being forged by the white feminist movement; the theory for which is emerging from a predominantly Jewish elite group and its organizational aspect characterized by white and black female organizations. The blacks in these organizations either (1) dismiss race as unimportant or secondary to their "sexually inferior status" or (2) claim autonomy and independence from the white feminists but form cautious alliances with them in the interest of black womanhood. Further examination of the evolution of the Aryan family reveals the insidious nature of the feminist movement, its relationship to contemporary Aryan population patterns, and its irrelevance to the real needs of black women.

Beginning with the premises embodied in the Cress theory of white supremacy,[1] and the more exhaustive work of Cheikh Anta Diop, identifying the opposing cradles of civilizations, we can establish that the Aryan race, Asiatics and Europeans, were biological mutants, whose environmentally induced abnormal struggle for survival would totally prescribe their institutional and social organizations. According to Diop,

> The ferocity of nature in the Eurasian steppes, the barrenness of those regions, the overall circumstances of material conditions, were to create instincts necessary for survival in such an environment. . . . Here, nature left no illusions of kindliness . . . he must learn to rely on himself alone; . . . he would conjure up deities maleficent and cruel, jealous and spiteful. . . . All the peoples of the area whether white or yellow, were instinctively to love conquest because of a desire to escape from those hostile surroundings . . . they had to leave it or succumb, try to conquer a place in the sun in a more clement nature.[2]

Professor Diop is cautious concerning the cause of this syndrome. He argues environmental determinism, but nothing refutes a biological imperative.

A European theoretician, Thorstein Veblen, asserted that the present European types are indeed hybrid derivations of an original blond mutant and that the commonality of these types is evidenced by their Aryan speech and culture. According to Veblen, Aryan culture was a pastoral-predatory one with appropriate institutions and manners. It was "substantially patriarchal, with a well-defined system of property rights, a pronounced subjection of women and children."[3]

The evolution of the Aryan family as a patriarch is very interesting and raises pertinent questions about our present struggle. Keep in mind that for European scholarship, patriarchal family structure represents a move toward a more "civilized" form of social organization, as opposed to the nonpatriarchal form which they define as matriarchy.

Supporting Lewis, Morgan, Marx, Lenin, and Engels assert that the Eureopean family evolved in three stages. The savage stage was characterized by group marriages, i.e., each and every woman belonged to every man. The second stage was the barbaric stage, characterized by pairing in which within the group two people mated and related on a consistent basis, and by men having female slaves; polygamy was also practiced. The last stage of Aryan development instituted monogamy with prostitution, as a patriarchal form—the male is undisputed head.[4] It is this final form of family organization which temporarily resolved the struggle between Aryan sexes, the males winning out. It is this form of family organization which today the Aryan woman is rebelling against. The point here is that being at war with nature, or all that is natural, including the basic male-female relationship, is apparently endemic to these nomadic, predatory types.

The patriarchal revolution was preceded by some critically relevant practices on the part of the Aryan family. The period of female dominance, still evident in seventeenth-century Europe, brought forth feminine phallus worship. Catholic women, like their earlier Roman predecessors, would sit on the erect penis of a saint in desire of fertility—or gratification. Among the Aryan priestesses, feminine phallus worship led to male castration as a religious rite.[5] It was, in fact, the practice of circumcision, originating with African Egyptians, learned by the Jews, and taken to other Aryan tribes, which would replace physical castration practiced among Aryan women phallus worshipers.

As one may have anticipated, the introduction and further evolution of the patriarchal system called for innovative evidences of Aryan male dominance of their women. The practice of female infibulation or the use of chastity belts was introduced to ensure absolute control. The desire for certain hymenal types was so prevalent among the elite that selection of mates was based on the lack of hymen development. For example, the reason Queen Elizabeth I was called Virgin Queen was not because she never went to bed with a man, but because none of her partners were able to penetrate her too tight vagina. This was reputed to have resulted from hereditary hymen development, and of historical incestual relationships among Europe's nobility.[6]

Thus, today's feminist movement is but an extension of the continued struggle for dominance between Aryan sexes, representing the decaying social organization of a group prescribed by defective birth and its inseparable culture. At the center of their war between the sexes is the need for the obsession with conquest and dominion.[7] On the other hand, black problems of family organization today are but an extension of the continued struggle for survival and the effort to retake our rightful place in the world since our first meeting with the Aryan and his institutions. The greatest vulnerability of a people is to allow the impregnation of aliens into one's family.

> The record of 5,000 years that ended with the European conquest of the whole continent in the 19th century shows that every African state remained relatively secure and independent as long as it maintained a strict policy of excluding foreigners from settlement within its borders; and that same record makes clear that wherever this policy was abandoned and whites were admitted under any pretext whatsoever, the eventual doom of that state was certain.[8]

Our first mistake, then, was to recognize these aliens as a part of the human family, i.e., like us. We educated them, they destroyed and claimed our civilization, and have ever since sought to use us as the necessary nerve force for their survival—our land, our ideas, our sperm, our womb, and our bodies. Now, let's examine ourselves to view what Aryans defined as a semibarbaric, uncivilized form of family organization, generally found among peaceful sedentary peoples—the African matriarchy.[9]

The concept of African matriarchy is a misnomer in that it is merely antithetical to another Aryan concept, patriarchy. That is to be expected because Aryan observations and characterizations emerge from the Aryan world view; a view when superimposed on African reality inevitably creates Aryan explanations of African behavior, thus leading to lies, misrepresentations, and confusion. The effect of this scientific and intellectual tyranny and its attendant policies upon the black family has been devastating. In attempting to examine African familyhood on its own terms we see that African family tradition reinforced familyhood, not malehood or womanhood. There was no endemic antagonism between the sexes but rather a holistic approach to community organization out of which both men and women would find self-definition, security, and continuity. African women are the Mothers of Civilization and community life, and African men are the Fathers of

Civilization and community life. This traditional harmonious relationship was especially revealed between mother and son.

> The bearing of a son toward his mother is a combination of deference and affection. To him swearing, undressing or conducting himself in an immodest manner in her presence, brings about direct punishment by ancestors. He will be publicly rebuked and can be forced by the family council to pay a fine. It is expected that his mother will scold him, should he neglect his duties as a son, a husband or a father and he must not reply to her angrily.[10]

What greater service to, or for that matter, influence on, a community could a woman have than to be the barometer and perpetuator of a son's development as a child, husband, and father? As a complement, African man was the protector, provider, and giver of the life that nutured the community. Thus was the egalitarian and harmonious African traditional family and community from which emerged such leaders and care defenders as Hatshepsut, Nzingha, Chaka, Taa Asantewa, Osei Tutu, Dessalines, Harriet Tubman, Marcus and Amy Garvey.

Aspects of the traditional African kinship system are still evident today and by Eurocentric definitions can at best be characterized as matrilineal. To be sure, prior to Aryan intrusion, African familyhood was vital to the world view characterized by collective identity, i.e., the community and oneness with nature, i.e., the Creator and the universe. It is precisely for that reason that the Aryan has always directed special attention to destroying African familyhood, because from family flows life, community, institutions, and civilizations. It is our ability to survive all these assaults that attests to the correctness of our traditional way. Our recent history reveals an amazing capacity to adapt our families, but we must not let that blind us to the necessity to control our families.

Diop points out that the role of Islamic, Christian, and European influences on the transformation of African tradition must be emphasized. He asserts that

> polygamy was customary . . . in Egypt among the family of Pharaohs and dignitaries of the court. . . . But monogamy

> was the rule at the level of the mass of the people. . . . It seems that this was true until the extension of Islam to the native populations. Polygamy tended in this way to become general without ever ceasing to be a sign of social rank. Thus it is not rare to see members of the lower classes who, seeking to deceive themselves about their own social rank, marry several wives.[11]

Likewise, homosexuality was alien to African traditional family, introduced through Arab conquest. The corps of African eunuchs was the vehicle to becoming a slave with privileges instead of a mere slave.[12]

The lust for the African woman was evidenced in African antiquity; by example, tawny Cleopatra's shrewd use of Julius Caesar and Mark Anthony in an effort to save Egypt from total Roman control.[13] The institution of the Hebraic law that a traditional Jew must be born from a Jewish mother[14] in fact may be related to the attempt to discourage the obsession with African women that the Semite men seemed to have had.[15]

The early plague to the African family posed by the white woman is evident in the Aryan phallic worship of Dionysus (Greek version of the god of renewal and fertility, i.e., Egyptian Osiris). The Greeks killed all women caught worshiping this Egyptian god.[16] The occasion of the Arabian Nights was marked by the Arabs' return from a hunt, to find their wives in bed with the black slaves.[17]

We now see the historical precedents to major problems confronting African traditional family today: sex ratios, homosexuality, and interracial sex. This leads us to seriously question the preponderance of black scholarship on the black male/female relationship today. Unfortunately, all too many of our most gifted minds are responding to white definitions of our condition. They either have never had or have given up on the idea that we can *re-create* and *control* our families, our communities, and ultimately the world. Thus, the literature on the black family concentrates on *analysis* of *adaptations* as opposed to *analysis of control*. Often we begin to destroy white analysis, only to resurrect it in a renewed form.

The refutation of the black matriarchy concept put forth by

Moynihan and attacked by Billingsly, Staples, Hare, and others merely evoked the fallacious tendency for us to blackenize the true Aryan family model. The question of where are the men does not speak to any new phenomenon. The boys, fathers, and husbands are defending themselves and adapting to the same Aryan plague that the daughters, mothers, and wives of Africa confront. The assertion that black females are the most oppressed group in the world order, A over B model, and/or that the feminist movement may have some benefits for black women if approached cautiously, is leading us further down the path of Aryan control of our families. The simplistic analysis pointing to polygamy as the futuristic family model ignores our history and the real nature of our struggle. It submits to the mentality of adaptation, not control, because communities can never be built around a begrudging female who feels she's gotta take what she can get because she can't do any better.[18]

In short, we either answer the wrong questions or use alien approaches to answer the right questions. Ignoring our historical past which reveres collective and biological motherhood to the extent that all women are called Mother and some mothers called Mother of so and so, Cress concludes that the black man who calls his woman Mama is manifesting some inferiority complex.[19] Such is the danger of using alien sciences to understand ourselves.

Analysis of our present problems of male-female roles and relationships cannot be separated from the development and nature of Aryan family organization and the consequential population genetics that has emerged from the biological imperative. European population growth is at a critical level not just because of birth declines but because the crude death rate continues to decline despite decreased mortality.[20] This increase in numbers of death is caused by apparent increased vulnerability of the European to influences of the aging process. Thus, the emergence of aging as a disease and eugenics have become of overwhelming concern to Aryan scholarship. The proceedings of a conference held ironically by the South African Institute of International Affairs in Johannesburg in summer 1970 reflect the following concerns:

> European population represented 17.5% of the world population in 1920 and is projected to drop to 8.6% by 2000.

> The populations of Western Europe are old. The birth rate has fallen by about 10% and it has not yet been proved that this is due to any marked behaviour change . . . the use of the pill is not enough to explain the drop. We must ask ourselves will birth rate and fertility go on falling and [what] will be the political repercussions? . . . We have not dealt here with population genetics . . . but biological discoveries may well pose completely new problems.[21]

In attendance at the conference were representatives from Israel, Japan, Australia, France, Britain, Germany, and the Netherlands and such Aryan notables as Spengler from Duke University, Organski of the University of Michigan, and Enke from General Electric Company. Organizational sponsorship included Ford and General Motors companies, Goodyear, Volkswagen, Holiday Inn, and IBM.

On the contrary African populations world-wide are projected to more than triple by 2000, essentially due to the age structure distribution;[22] thus, the Aryan schemes for population control and biological warfare. Our challenge is both clear and at hand. We must by all means avoid those models of destruction from the Aryan temple which even now is crumbling and about to fall on the heads of all who worship there. We must return to our history and traditions as the model and source for controlling our families and communities.

NOTES

1. See Francis Cress Welsing, "The Cress Theory of Color Confrontation," 1970. Independently published.
2. Cheikh Anta Diop, *African Origin of Civilization: Myth or Reality* (Westport, Conn.: Lawrence Hill & Co., 1974), p. 112.
3. Thorstein Veblen, *Veblen on Marx, Race, Science and Economics* (New York: Capricorn, 1969), pp. 457, 477.
4. Karl Marx, Frederick Engels, V. I. Lenin, and Joseph Stalin, *The Woman Question* (New York: International Publishers, 1951), p. 67.
5. Elizabeth Gould Davis, *The First Sex* (New York: Penguin, 1971), p. 99.
6. Ibid., p. 163.
7. Michael Biddis, ed., *Gobineau: Selected Political Writings* (New York: Harper & Row, 1970), p. 126.

8. Chancellor Williams, *Destruction of Black Civilization* (Chicago: Third World Press, 1971), p. 79.
9. George Murdock, *Social Structure* (New York: Macmillan, 1949).
10. Cheikh Anta Diop, *The Cultural Unity of Negro Africa* (Paris: Présence Africaine, 1963), p. 70.
11. Ibid., p. 126.
12. Bernard Lewis, *Race and Color in Islam* (New York: Harper & Row, 1971), p. 84.
13. John H. Clarke, "Black-White Alliance: Historical Perspective," *Afrocentric World Review,* 1, No. 2 (Spring 1975), p. 19.
14. Ernest Van Den Haag, *The Jewish Mystique* (New York: Dell Publishing Company, 1971), p. 185.
15. Davis, p. 102.
16. Diop, *Cultural Unity,* p. 174.
17. See *Arabian Nights.*
18. See Jacquelyne J. Jackson, "But Where Are the Men?" *Black Scholar,* December 1971; Barbara Sizemore, "Sexism and the Black Male," and Mae C. King, "The Politics of Sexual Stereotypes," *Black Scholar,* March–April 1973; Joseph Scott, "Polygamy: A Futuristic Family Arrangement Among African Americans," *Black Books Bulletin,* Summer 1976.
19. Francis Cress Welsing, "The Mother Fucker and the Original Mother Fucker in the White Supremacy System and Culture," *Black Books Bulletin,* Fall 1976.
20. John Barratt and Michael Louw, *International Aspects of Overpopulation* (London: Macmillan, 1972), p. 4.
21. Ibid., Chap. 12.
22. Ibid., p. 214.

Without destroying the credibility of the "Mother Is Gold" mythic structure, Andrea Benton Rushing examines some of the reasons why most portraits of Black women in African poetry emanate from that source. These reasons are succinctly understated in the early part of the essay, but that technique serves to heighten our critical perceptions as we move through the graceful poetry of authors whom Rushing has chosen to illustrate her various salient points. African women outside the mother structure in poetry—those who are barren, or are prostitutes, workers, traditional singers and dancers, or who are fortunate enough to carry the title "beloved"—are also seriously considered.

An important feature of this essay is the interweaving of "disciplines" within a literary mode.

Images of Black Women in Modern African Poetry: An Overview

by ANDREA B. RUSHING

It is tempting to erect a study of the images of black women in African poetry on the foundation of existing literary models like Ferguson's categories, based on Euro-American women, in *Images of Women in Literature* (the submissive wife; the mother angel or 'Mom'; the dominating wife; the bitch; the woman on a pedestal; man's sex object; the woman alone; the liberated woman), or on those based on Afro-American women that Mary Helen Washington mentions in her introduction to *Black-eyed Susans*. Neither construct will do justice to the images of black women in African poetry because they derive a wholly different set of economic, political, and cultural imperatives. A few facts throw the poetic image of African women into sharp relief: First, *the* role for a traditional African woman is mother. While it is true that women have had political power as queen mothers and as chiefs, have power in their age-grade associations, and have power (especially in West Africa) as traders, the primary means of achieving status has been as mother. Second, pre-conquest Africa allowed women political, economic, and social power that Europeans (having no parallels in *their* sexist cultures) ignored when they replaced traditional African social structures with colonial institutions. Third, post-independence civil legislation has changed traditional practices about polygamy, bride price, how old women must be to marry, who inherits a man's property when he dies (his wife and children or his family of origin). Fourth, the colonial view was that the impact of Western civilization liberated oppressed African women; the revisionist view is that it cut women loose from their cultural moorings and provided no replacement for the institutions it destroyed. Fifth, 60 per cent to 80 per cent of the agricultural labor in Africa is *currently* done by women. Sixth, women's literary rates lag behind men's. Seventh, urbanization, which has obviously affected the lives of those women who live in cities, also affects the lives of women in rural areas because men often leave wives and children behind to scour for work in urban centers. The best place, then, to begin our examination is within African culture. The Yoruba proverb says, "Mother is gold," and portraits of black women in African poetry seem to radiate from that hub.

Achebe writes, "For it is to a mother to whom you turn, of whom you speak when nostalgia grips you, when distress clouds the vision of the moment. . . . When there is sorrow and bitterness . . . The mother is there to protect you. . . . And that is why we say that mother is supreme." A social scientist postulates, "The African woman is associated with core values that tend to be among those resistant to change. A theme throughout African literature depicts the woman as guardian of traditions, the strong Earth-Mother who stands for security and stability." All three formulations about mother are brilliantly exemplified in Birago Diop's classic poem "Viaticum," where the mother is pictured invoking the power of the ancestors to protect her son as he leaves home. Other views of mother in modern African poetry include David Diop's portrayal of his mother nursing him through recurrent bouts with tuberculosis in "For My Mother"; the anguished, bereaved mother in Wole Soyinka's "A Cry in the Night—Burial of a Still-Born"; and the unnatural urban mother who discards her child in a garbage can in Mtshali's scathing "The Abandoned

Bundle." In frequency and in emotional intensity images of women as mothers dominate portraits of women in modern African poetry and almost always partake of traditional culture's reverence for motherhood, the strong affective bonds fostered by breast feeding children for two or three years and maintaining strong ties with them throughout adulthood.

Cultures which enshrine motherhood are, though, no place for childless women to be, and we see that vividly in Kottobbe's stern "To the Childless," which begins:

> You are the cold nests
> In which the migrant bird lays no eggs
> In which it never enters to brood

Similarly, Ntiru's "Rhythm of the Pestle" portrays a woman tormented not because she is oppressed by the strictures of traditional culture, but because of her failure to marry and have the twins she dreamed of; and in two poems (one by Soyinka and John Pepper Clark) on the "abiku," the child born over and over to the same grieving mother only to die in early childhood.

African women are also portrayed as workers, and when they are (with the exception of poems about prostitutes) the emphasis is on the tedium of menial labor as in Mtshali's poem about a washerwoman and Ntiru's "Rhythm of the Pestle." The most poignant and startling vision of African women at work is by a woman (Marina Gashe) in "The Village."

> . . .
> Old women dark and bent
> Trudge along with their hoes
> . . .
> Young wives like donkeys
> From cock crow to setting sun
> Go about their timeless duties
> Their scraggy figures like bows set in a row
> Plod up and down the rolling village farms
> With loads on their backs
> And babies tied to their bellies
> . . .
> Stirring up the soil with hands and knives
> Like chickens looking for worms

James Olney has said that the "dominant characteristic of the African world, in contrast to the Western world, is its unity, its indivisible coherence and singleness, its non-compartmentalized texture." Both that view and Senghor's observation (". . . We are the men of the dance, whose feet take on new strength from stamping the hard ground") inform our understanding of another important set of images of African women: those that connect them with song and dance. In poems like both David Diop's "To a Black Dancer," which begins:

> Negress, my warm rumour of Africa
> My land of mystery and my fruit of reason
> You are the dance by the naked joy of your smile

and John Pepper Clark's "Agbor Dancer" poets see the dancing African woman as a symbol of the contours of traditional African life and for the unselfconscious union of body and mind which distinguishes African and European ideas of being. Although one critic finds Diop's poem frankly sensual, that view reflects a mindset which is alien to traditional African views of female sexuality rooted as they are in the language of fertility which makes woman (as mother) and land metaphors for each other. In that context, a reference to a woman's hips or breasts is not an isolated mention of her sexual being, but rather an emblem of her highly valued childbearing abilities. The idea of motherhood as the role for women informs almost poetic images of women in African poetry—even when the poems, like the ones about dancers, do not have mother as their subject. What is being hymned is woman's closeness to the earth (the repository of the spirits of the ancestors), her biological connections to the rhythms of birth, growth, and death, and her proximity to traditional African culture in a world increasingly besieged by Western mores.

There are two complications to examining the image of the beloved in African poetry. On the one hand, what Soyinka says of Senghor is often true of other poets: The objects of their lover sooner or later become identified with homeland; on the other, romantic love is a European concept which is only now gaining a foothold in Africa. David Diop's poem "Rama Kam" celebrates the beauty of the beloved comparing her to mango and pimentos and focusing on her blackness and the "warm rhythm of her hips," and Cissoko (another *négritude* poet) glorifies "the blue palm tree of your lashes" and lips like "fleshy dates." P'Bitek has his Acoli heroine, Lawino, mock her husband's latest love, the westernized Clementine:

Her lips are red-hot
Like glowing charcoal
She resembles the wild cat
That has dipped its mouth in blood,
Her mouth is like an open ulcer,
Like the mouth of a friend!

Tina dusts powder on her face
And it looks so pale
She resembles the wizard
Getting ready for the midnight dance.
. . .
She looks as if
She has been ill for a long time!
. . .
She does not eat
She says she fears getting fat,
. . .
She says a beautiful woman
Must be slim like a white woman.

The poetry of Dennis Brutus contains compelling images of the beloved, including the sensuous bathing woman in "Gaily Teetering":

Gaily teetering on the bath's edge
one long bare arm outflung to balance
the sweep of sting flanks and thews,
face-level the brown triangular fuzz
grey glistening with a hoar of drops,
. . .
Etched aloft against the prison-grey light
that filtered through the plastic curtaining
the smooth flesh surging tautly over
the thoracic cage to where the nipples gazed
in blandly unselfconscious innocence
. . .

and the beloved who combines the qualities of diamond and mother and affords a refuge from South African oppression in an untitled poem:

Kneeling before you for a moment
Slipped quite unthinkingly into this stance
—for heart, head and spirit in a single movement
responded thus to some stray facet
of prismatic luminous self
as one responds with total rhythm in the dance—
I knelt
And answering, you pressed my face against your womb
and drew me to a safe and still oblivion,
shut out the knives and teeth; boots, bayonets and knuckles:
so, for the instant posed, we froze to an eternal image
became unpersoned and unageing symbols
of humbled vulnerable wonder
enfolded by a bayed and resolute maternalness

but there are, finally, only a handful of poems which both have the beloved as subject and refract her attributes within the poem.

Part of the legacy of traditional African attitudes toward women is the dearth of negative images of African women in modern African poetry which seems to have absorbed the positive images of women in oral literature and ignored the negative ones. In contemporary poetry the tone is usually serious and the only negative images are of women who have discarded the roles of wife and mother which traditional culture esteemed. P'Bitek writes, with irony, about prostitutes and the westernized Clementine. Ntiru writes a ditty about the miniskirt and, in "The Roses Are Withering," laments the urbanized African women who sit on bar stools, make love on car cushions, and lift "fallen breasts with textile props," but most other images of women are laudatory.

This is in sharp contrast to the many negative images of European-American women (the shrew, the bitch, the dumb blonde, the old maid, the "Mom"); to the negative images of Afro-American women (the "bad-busting Mammy," Sapphire, Caldonia, the sex kitten); and to the negative images of women in Afro-Caribbean poetry where, according to Young, they are portrayed as primitive, superstitious, and hip-swinging (especially mulatto women) temptresses surrounded by snake imagery.

Unlike the images of African women in contemporary West African fiction, very few poetic images mirror the social change stalking Africa. One looks almost in vain for poems (like the short stories in Ama Ata Aidoo's *No Sweetness Here*), about urban women working, living alone, rejecting polygamy, deciding to have small families, agonizing over the crises of romantic love, snapping their ties to the extended family, playing critical roles in past and present liberation struggles. On the one hand poetry, with its terse and vivid imagery, is the wrong place to go for full-scale realistic and naturalistic representations. On the other, almost all modern African poetry is written by men, and poems which distill the kaleidoscope of women's lives on the African continent and create images of black women with the vigor of those rooted in the religious and cultural matrix of precolonial days may not emerge until African *women* write the poetry which speaks their days and dreams for our hearing.

One of the youngest writers to come out of Black West Africa is Ghana's Christina Ama Ata Aidoo. While still in her twenties, Ms. Aidoo wrote the play *Dilemma of a Ghost,* which was first performed at her alma mater, University of Ghana, Legon Campus, and later at several experimental theaters in New York. *No Sweetness Here,* an iconoclastic collection of short stories, followed.

Aidoo is joined in her fervent intentions to "Africanize" African literature by several other notables, among them, Ayi Kwei Armah and Efua Sutherland, her countrymen, and Wole Soyinka of Nigeria. Their works skillfully combine the paradoxical realities of the present with the ancient sustaining patterns of the African past, especially in the use of proverbs and indigenous customs. See the bibliography of Selected African Women Writers for more information on Christina Ama Ata Aidoo.

"Introduction" to Ama Ata Aidoo's "Dilemma of a Ghost"

by KAREN C. CHAPMAN

Christina Ama Ata Aidoo (b. 1942) is best known for her poems and short stories, which have been much anthologized in Africa and elsewhere. She wrote *Dilemma of a Ghost,* her first play, while she was still an undergraduate at the University of Ghana (Legon)—an institution that has a school of drama (one of only four on the African continent) and a writers' workshop, founded by Efua Sutherland, Ghana's leading woman of letters. Miss Aidoo graduated in 1963, and she now teaches at the University College, Cape Coast. Her second drama, *Anowa,* has recently been published.

Dilemma of a Ghost was first produced in 1964 and was published in 1965. Such an achievement from such youth would be astonishing anywhere; its having happened in Ghana may be an augury.

Black African theater (and also film), still young and still forming, is a first fruit of Independence; few of its makers are yet middle-aged. More than any other literary form, theater requires for its life a physical continuity of institutions and audience, an atmospheric "place" where talent (and learning) congregates, collides, and grows old in the practice of skills; not less important, it requires a supportive community physically hooked on theatergoing. Until 1960, a gifted African writer had no such place to go, no theatrical world of ongoing work in which to immerse himself authentically. He was caught between two worlds, the colonial-academic and the tribal-mimetic. If he wrote plays at all, he soon abandoned this form, in which he was sure to be either too literary or not literary enough; instead, he sought the audience-at-large of novels or tales, poems, and essays, not to mention polemic broadsides. The merest glance at acknowledged classics of Black African achievement, written in either French or English, reveals few plays (other than some recent ones) that even approach the excellence achieved in other forms.

As for brilliance detoured or denied, one thinks perhaps of Ezekiel Mphahlele (a South African, now in exile), who, early in his career, wrote two plays in English on Bantu themes, or of Bernard Dadié, a French writer from the Ivory Coast, who began a career in theater, discovered its prematurity, and did not return to playwriting until, significantly enough, after Independence. In Africa, as elsewhere, creative winds blow as they will—unpredictably; nothing can be more futile than a singled-minded effort to define their life by cause-and-effect relations that are politicosocial in slant. Yet the fact remains that Independence witnessed a turning point in the theater of many African countries. Also, it coincided not only with the rise of a new generation of literary talent but also with a new sense of practical, shared enterprise—a sense of collective identity that not only yearned to but was able to explore itself freely and be explored.

As has been remarked many times, French was the first language of African genius—one thinks, almost at random, of *Batouala,* Senghor, Césaire, *négritude*. Before World War II, Paris was the international capital of the whole modernist movement in literature and the arts, including African modernism; after the war, it was only natural that French-speaking writers should be looked to for the leadership they gave. From 1945 to 1960,

French-speaking writers and intellectuals dominated literary Black Africa to an extraordinary degree, in fiction, poetry, and—especially after the founding of Présence Africaine—in criticism. As so often in Europe's own experience of the two languages, French led while English waited for time's ripening: French occupied the vanguard brilliantly, fantasizing new worlds and advancing ideas; English, although rich in individualists such as Mphahlele, Ekwesi, and Achebe, had no organized center.

Politics and literature, never far apart in Africa, were intensely allied in the pre-Independence writers working in French; even for some of the most gifted—for example, Ferdinand Oyono and Mongo Beti—the end of political struggle with France seems to have also ended their inspiration to write. Camara Laye remains active, but *Dramouss* (1966) lacks the power of earlier novels. Perhaps only Bernard Dadié continues in full vigor. Among the new generation writing in French, Yambo Ouologuem and Ousmane Sembene are both novelists (the latter also a filmmaker) so brilliantly inventive as to prove the risk of all generalizations about genre, language, or times. Indeed Africa is so big and so regionally diverse that to speak of "African" anything is risky. Nevertheless it is true that, in theater, English-speaking West Africa has stolen the lead. It is not cynical to add that funds from the Rockefeller Foundation and other foundations, and also Anglo-American fellowships and prizes, have assisted; theater costs money.

Nigerian theater is the most celebrated and best documented, because from it have emerged Wole Soyinka and John Pepper Clark, both of them major poets whose plays have already earned an international audience. Behind them, however, lies a richly active theatrical world, which includes the experiments of James Ene Henshaw in the 1950s, the vernacular folk operas (in Yoruba) of Kalu Ogunmola and the recently translated Duro Ladipo, the traveling theater of Herbert Ogunde, and the plays, mimes, or television scripts of such lesser-known writers as Obi Egbuna, Ernest Edyang, and Nkem Nwankwo.

Theater in Ghana, however, has been almost as active, if less acclaimed. The government has officially encouraged and subsidized theater groups of a great variety, both amateur and professional, especially through the Institute of Art and Culture, founded in Accra in 1962, and the African Studies program at the

University of Legon. Ghanaian theater has aimed self-consciously at preventing segregation in the arts; drama, music, mime, dance, painting (including mask and costume), are seen, as in traditional ceremonies, as organically related in the African spirit. But it is the leadership of Efua Sutherland, perhaps more than all else, that has matured Ghanaian theater—in her own plays, in founding the Drama Studio in Accra, in helping to establish *Okyeame* (Ghana's literary magazine), and in designing an open-air theater more suited to African forms derived from tribal and folkloric materials. In addition, Ghanaian theater has made special efforts to achieve a simplicity of style and language more accessible to a popular audience whose fluency in English, though growing, is still elementary.

To such a heritage, Miss Aidoo brings a special gift for characterization in simple domestic situations. The central theme in most of her writing is familial love, its pains and sacrifices between brothers and sisters, and particularly between mothers (almost always strong characters) and their children—as, for example, in the stories *No Sweetness Here* and *A Gift from Somewhere*. Frequently, in both her fiction and poetry, this theme is explored against a backdrop of conflicts between new and old, European and African. In a poem such as "The Last of the Proud Ones," to give but one illustration, the pathos of growing old in an alien new world, intensely realized, is no more intense than the almost tragic dignity of the mother who, knowing her world is finished, refuses to yield her pride:

> You sneer, little thing?
> Youth, do not lift your brows,
> nor raise those lids
> and curl your mouth;
> for I will not—
> though I want to—
> talk of the good old days.
> But what will you have me do
> with bread and cheese?
> Cheese, hah!
> This stuff you say
> comes from milk
> but reeks, reeks
> the odour of stinking fish.

There were plantains
and yams,
meat from rams
and......
But I will not talk
of the good old days
when there were rains.
. . .
And come, take away
your breads and cheeses.
A little while and I'll faint,
faint to look at them:
though I want to go
I'll hate to shove from such
as these.

I will sit here, with my stick,
watching the fire
no one needs,
and when its last flicker is gone,
I too, with cold and hunger
and my Pride
may go
there
where
is neither bread nor cheese.[1]

Nana, in *Dilemma of a Ghost,* derives from her past the same strength; but what tragedy there is, is softened in the play by her effectiveness in passing on within the family the values of that past.

Dilemma of a Ghost received mixed reviews. Among the technical faults: Playing time is less than an hour for the five acts into which the play is broken; the issues raised in the play, complicated as they are, tend to disintegrate and lose climactic rhythm, especially in the last two acts; points are raised, then left hanging; and characters appear or reappear without clear dramatic reasons—some disappear altogether, just at the point when the audience begins to identify with them sympathetically. Given such filmlike moving in and out of characters, and the speed with which acts are terminated, the play might have worked better as a series of tableaux—or as an intense short story. Yet, despite these probably youthful faults in technique, Miss Aidoo has treated human problems with an understanding unavailable to many dramatists twice her age. There is no romanticizing of *négritude* or violence. In her writing, none of the tedious, quasi-anthropological, quasi-sociological treatment of Africa's past (or future) geared naïvely to attract anti-white audiences. She is soberly aware of human truths. While her play is firmly wedded to the social world it embodies—today's fragmented Africa—it is always reaching toward something more universal and, as such, beyond the color barrier.

The plot is, at bottom, a simple one. Ato Yawson, a young Ghanaian who has been studying in the United States, returns home with his strong-willed, Black American wife from Harlem, Eulalie, whom he has married without forewarning his tradition-conscious family. The cultural differences between the American Black and the African village folk threaten to become irreconcilable. Ato, whose role it should be to work for an understanding between his wife and family, fails miserably. When all seems hopeless, it is Ato's mother, the uneducated mother of an older generation, who bridges the gap. In the end, Ato remains what he was throughout the play: a desperate drifter who, in wandering between worlds, has lost touch with the truth that the people in them share the same basic needs.

The background of conflict in the play, therefore, is that of opposing cultures or life-styles: Black American on one hand, Black African on the other. The experience of a Black American is inevitably different from that of an African, despite their common ancestry. In the eyes of many Africans, particularly those in the countryside, Black Americans have more in common culturally with white Americans than with Africans. The American Black has been removed from Africa for a long time. Contrary to what many romantically inclined Garveyites would like to believe, to return to the "source" is a much more difficult task than its fascination may suggest, for it would mean returning to a culture never experienced in fact.

Eulalie brings with her to Ghana some of the storybook myths of primitive Africa. She dreams of "belonging" to a heroic, hallowed land, only to discover—with some pain—that Mother Africa is not all colorful birds, wild fruits, or peaceful rhythms of deep, mysterious rivers; nor is the African drum-playing always jazzlike. The welcoming embrace Eulalie hopes to encounter on her return "home" does not, as she herself realizes in more sober moments, happen automatically. Eulalie is an outsider—a Black *American,* or, in the words of Langston Hughes, "Chicago and Kansas City and Broadway and Harlem." An embrace, if it is to come, must be somehow transcultural. Denied the guiding hand of Ato, unable on her own to make the home so yearned for and needed, Eulalie turns to drink. When finally it does happen, the long-sought-after embrace derives its life not from myths of bookish "ideas," or from some real or imagined miracle, but from the elemental wisdom and strength of an actual mother.

The two life-styles juxtaposed in the play, American and African, are concretely described. First of all, there are the outward manifestations of Eulalie's "Americanness": cigarettes, clothes, liquor, and the countless machines that do her work—all trappings of a way of life that Eulalie, for reasons confused and complicated by her love-hate relationship with it, is determined not to renounce. At the same time, Eulalie's attitudes toward Africa and its people range from innocent and pathetic to decidedly contemptuous. "So at last here am I in Africa," she tells herself early in Act II, ". . . I am finding all this rather cute . . . I never knew there is a Coke in these parts . . . I've come to the very source . . . Native Boy is the Blackest you ever saw. . . ." By the end of the play, her youthful if misguided enthusiasm has turned to contempt. Africans are not only "stupid" and "narrowminded," they are "more savage than dinosaurs." On first reading, one may feel annoyed by Eulalie's steady inveighing against African manners and customs, by her hostile stereotypes. But in time, one realizes that the stereotypes characterize her: Her hostility masks an innocence as desperately hungry for guidance as it is in need of sobering.

In counterpoint to Eulalie's Americanness are the ways of the African village folk, their rituals and family gatherings, and—even more important in terms of the play—their intimate relationship with their ancestors and their unfailing reverence for children. As is usual in African thought, the ancestors in *Dilemma of a Ghost* not only are alive and in possession of great wisdom but are also, from time to time, rather intimidating as they hover protectively over the heads of those still on earth. Significantly, what quickens

Esi Kom's support for Eulalie in the end is precisely the knowledge that the ghost of Eulalie's dead mother must be watching over everything that happens to her. By far the dominant theme in the play, however, and perhaps the ultimate source of all misunderstanding, is the meaning of childbearing. Despite an awareness of the importance of children in African life, and despite momentary lapses into "womanly" feelings, Eulalie, with Ato in full agreement, decides to postpone all thoughts of having a family. Contraception is, of course, contrary to African mores and values; abundance of children is not only the joy of womanhood but also the source of all family pride. Ato's family cannot understand why his marriage has produced no children—"For men and women marry because they want children," as Ato's Uncle Petu says in Act IV. What is interpreted by Ato and Eulalie as family planning is misinterpreted by the Africans as barrenness. When an herbal concoction is brought to wash Eulalie's "barren" stomach, Ato, at a moment when a satisfactory explanation indeed seems called for, merely mumbles an impotent series of "nothings." As a result, he provokes, if not anger, then at least bitter disappointment on the part of both his family and Eulalie; at the same time, he increases the distance already separating them from him.

The seriousness with which Africans regard both childbearing and barrenness is underlined throughout the play by the conversations of two women gossips; one a mother, the other not. While the mother would, at times, gladly give up some of the problems associated with a household "teeming with children," the childless one would sacrifice all to know them. In Act IV, in one of several intensely lyrical passages in the play, the barren woman, believing that Eulalie might share her fate, recalls her own past:

> If it is real barrenness,
> then, oh stranger-girl,
> Whom I do not know,
> I weep for you.
> For I know what it is
> To start a marriage with barrenness.
>
> My people have a lusty desire
> To see the tender skin
> On top of a child's scalp
> Rise and fall with human life.

Your machines, my stranger-girl,
Cannot go on an errand
They have no hands to dress you when you are dead . . .
But you have one machine to buy now
That which will weep for you, stranger-girl
You need that most.
For my world
Which you have run to enter
Is most unkind to the barren.

Yes, my young woman, I shall remember you.
I shall remember you in the hours
  of the night—
In my sleep,
In my sleepless sleep.

Barrenness becomes linked in the play with "modern," "educated" ways of life. Eulalie, the wayfarer, has no "home" in America, no family; nor can she find them in Africa. She brings to Africa only her habituations—to cigarettes, Coca-Cola, machines, and wishes. When she is received into the African family at the end of the play, she begins, for the first time, to belong somewhere—to find again "Mother Nature," which, in the Western world, was only a voice from the dead. *From a subhuman world of deprivation and excess, therefore, she has journeyed toward a human world of natural instinct and fertility.* Ironically, Eulalie has been a slave to her cigarettes and machines—signs of the Western "emancipated woman"—but in the end, or so the play implies, she may find a truer freedom and womanhood within the African collectivity. African ways are envisioned as life-giving.

The play's similarities to classical Greek theater are striking. Miss Aidoo focuses on one house, one family. Apparently, the family is an important one in the village, for the clan house is referred to, by Ato's grandmother, as "sacred precincts," and the people in it are addressed as "Royal Ones." Preoccupation with ancestors and their mysterious workings of the gods, who may choose to either bless or curse a house. The tone of many speeches is oracular and brooding. Moreover, the two women gossips function as a chorus, commenting, warning, fearing, often sharing in the grief that threatens the Odumna Clan. Miss Aidoo makes use of the familiar dramatic technique of an exchange of roles—effected in *Dilemma of a Ghost* between Eulalie and Ato. Throughout most of the play, members of the African family refer to Eulalie as a "stranger," a "Black-white woman," a "wayfarer" come to the "sacred precincts." Even though Eulalie, as an outsider, disrupts life within the clan house, she is, nevertheless, finally admitted into the family. In the end it is Ato, the wanderer who lost his way home, who becomes the stranger and outcast.

The significance of the play's title becomes clear in Act III. The act opens with two young children, heretofore unseen, who, in the mood for games, sing a popular song about a ghost who found himself at a road junction, but could not decide whether to go to Cape Coast or Elmina. The young boy, as Miss Aidoo explains in her list of characters, is the ghost of Ato's former self—the ghost of a *living* past, therefore, not an ancestral ghost. The song awakens Ato from an afternoon sleep; whether it is a dream or not at this point, the dilemma of the ghost at Elmina Junction haunts Ato throughout the remainder of the play. In the end, the ghost's dilemma becomes Ato's. The closing scene shows him in the dark, flitting back and forth indecisively between the new wing of the clan house, where he lives with Eulalie, and the old wing belonging to his family. The ghost, an amorphous counterpart of Ato himself, functions therefore as an African symbol of "lostness."

The reincarnation of the ghost's dilemma at the end of the play is prepared for early in Act I. Ato's grandmother, sitting in the dark of evening and waiting for her family to appear, hears a stumbling noise: "One day the people in this house will commit murder. Do they not know that if the heavens withdraw their light, man must light his own way? But no. They will let us all lie in darkness. How will he find his way around this dark place should the ghost of one of our forebears pay us a visit?" Darkness becomes a symbol not only of blind misunderstandings between cultures–and to some extent between the living and the dead—but also of a confusion in Ato's own mind. Significantly, in the closing scene, set at midnight, the two women gossips who see Ato stumbling around in the dark mistake him for a ghost. Nana's musings are therefore a foreboding of things to come, of a gathering power of darkness in the play. Ato loses all light, reality, and hope of direction in his life. But the evil ghost that haunts him is not that of a forebear or of some foreign culture; rather, it is one within his personal past—the demon of his own self-conjured failures to "light his own way."

Dilemma of a Ghost begins with a Greek-like prologue by the so-called Bird of the Wayside, a many-sided symbol that recurs throughout the play—one easy to feel but difficult to define, and therefore, perhaps, successful. A bird of the wayside is insubstantial, fleetingly ironic, and "outside." In the opening monologue of the play's prelude, for example, it speaks of itself not only as "the trunkless head of shadow in the corner" (establishing a link with Ato in the end) but also as "a pair of women . . . chattering their lives away" (a link with the two wandering gossips, who, having their own homes, also seek another). It is "an asthmatic old hag . . . whose soup . . . nourished a bundle of whitened bones" (like Nana, whose family world is threatened by Ato's regard for "a white man's world," when he marries an *American* Black). Throughout the play, the Bird of the Wayside is associated with strangers or wayfarers in life, and also with today's young people, who, in the words of one of the women gossips, are "strange . . . very strange"—to which her fellow gossip replies, "If you meet them, jump to the wayside." A Bird of the Wayside is ominous in African eyes, for, as Ato's Uncle Akroma remarks, "We can soon know the bird which will not do well, for his nest hangs by the wayside." Most comprehensively perhaps, the symbol defines a process of coming and going in the collectivity of life itself—here one minute, gone tomorrow, some being born, others dying. The Bird of the Wayside springs from a spirit of life/death continuum in African thought, in which the pastness of the present and the presentness of the past may yield ironic discrepancies.

In the final act, for example, Eulalie calls Ato "Moses": "Poor darling Moses," "Damned rotten coward of a Moses." Ato's family, especially his mother, has suffered and sacrificed to make him a scholar; but this Moses, who should lead his people to a promised land of prosperity and "civilized life," cannot. Ato is an ironic hero. One is left wondering whether Ato—again like Moses—may never see the true promised land, which, in terms of the play, is that of understanding among people.

The Bible is an evident shaping-force throughout African literature and style. There are frequent biblical allusions in *Dilemma of a Ghost,* all of them placed judiciously and skillfully, to reinforce Miss Aidoo's dramatic vision. They bring the universal applications of the play's dilemma into sharp relief. In the opening speech, for example, the Bird of the Wayside echoes I Corinthians 2:9 when it says: "Look around you / For the mouth must not tell everything / Sometimes the eye can see / And the ear should hear." And toward the end of the prelude, one finds echoes of the Book of Ruth: Eulalie asks, "Ato, can't your Ma be sort of my Ma too? . . . And your Pa mine? . . . And your gods my gods?" Ato replies: "And all my people are your people . . ." Later, in Act II, one of the two women gossips echoes Luke 6:42: "But those days are over / When it was expedient for two deer / To walk together / Since anyone can see and remove / The beam in his eye with a mirror."

Miss Aidoo's control of language is her forte, and is perhaps a most interesting feature of the play. The dignity of her characters is defined, to a degree, by their idiom. The intensely poetic passages belong to respected elders, mostly Nana and the two women gossips. What they say is redolent of the mysteries in life and death, and of the weight of suffered experience—as, for example, in the first gossip's speech, in Act II, to Mother Nature:

> Oh, Eternal Mother Nature,
> Queen Mother of childbirth,
> How was it you went past my house
>   Without a pause
>   Without a rest?
> Mighty God, when shall the cry
>   of an infant
> Come into my ear;
> For the sun has journeyed far
> In my sky.

A blend of poetry and often lyric prose belongs to Esi Kom and to the other members of the African family. For example, Esi Kom says: "Keep quiet, my son, and let me speak now, for something has pricked my wound. My knees are callous with bending before the rich. . . ." Other speeches capture the spirit of tribal wisdom couched in strangely graphic proverbs. Uncle Petu, for example, commenting on confusion within the family after Ato announces his American bride, says: "One must take time to dissect an ant in order to discover its entrails." Ato's younger sister, Monka, remarks later: "If nothing scratched at the palm fibre, it certainly would not have creaked." And toward the end of the last act, Esi Kom, reproaching Ato for his failure to lead his people and Eulalie into understanding, says:

> You have not dealt with us well.
> And you have not dealt with your
> wife well in this. Tomorrow, I
> will tell your grandmother,
> and your uncles and your aunts
> about all this, and I know they
> will tell you that.
> . . .
> Before the stranger should dip
> his finger
> Into the thick palm nut soup,
> It is a townsman
> Must have told him to.

The weakest language in the play belongs, rightly, to Ato. Much of the time he is speaking in banal phrases, or mumbling "I don't know." Eulalie speaks in a jazzy slang befitting her role as outsider from the Harlem ghetto—a slang somewhat forced at times, however, as if Miss Aidoo were unsure of its nuances.

On balance, *Dilemma of a Ghost* has elements of both the tragic and the comic. Esi Kom's embrace of Eulalie suggests a possible happiness or rebirth to come; cultural differences do not necessarily mean defeat. Ato, however, may possibly continue haunted, unable to decide "which way to go" or to synthesize his two upbringings. As for the true hero of the play, it is neither Ato, who is unmasked, nor Eulalie, who is only disabused of follies; rather, one suspects, it is Esi Kom, Ato's mother. It is she alone who remains steadfast in patiently trying to "do right" and it is she who brings about such reconciliation as the play allows. As in Miss Aidoo's short stories, the African woman-mother has a strength denied to others.

Christina Ama Ata Aidoo's gifts are evident, particularly in her evocation of local color and manners, her controlled lyricism, and her skill in tracing the curve of delicate human emotions. She herself is no wayfarer, no bird of the wayside. She is committed to African situations, but she is creatively flexible in her forms. Her voice is distinctly African, and now that African theater is a fact, her voice will surely be heard.

NOTE

1. The poem in its entirety appears in *Okyeame,* 2, No. 1 (1964), 9–10.

"The Brave African Huntress" created by Amos Tutuola is not the image usually conjured up when African heroines are portrayed. Indeed, they are so rarely presented at all that whenever they do appear, they are surrounded with a mystical schema that makes their credibility almost unfathomable. Marie Linton-Umeh delves into some of the historical precedents for "real" African heroines—those with the charisma, courage, and fortitude which help to create and sustain a people's culture. Though limited in her scope to nonvernacular writing, because of the obvious language difficulties experienced in investigating indigenous literature, Mrs. Linton-Umeh makes sufficient descriptive comments about historical events which are ultimately responsible for the actual as well as fictional treatments of several African heroines.

The African Heroine

by MARIE LINTON-UMEH

The fact that the masses of women in traditional African society cared for the children and tended the farm need not suggest that the society prevented African women of exceptional abilities from playing other significant roles similar to those played by Queen Nzingha, Queen-Pharaoh Hatshepsut, and Moremi. Whether it was as diviner, huntress, or warrior, African women often accomplished great feats in their communities.

In African creative writing, a heroine is one whose outstanding and admirable achievements are diverse, and one who can be defined as having leading roles assigned to her because of her superior gifts of body and/or mind. Another characteristic of the heroic figure is that the community which one attempts to serve acknowledges that the person possesses a number of qualities that most members of the community lack. Just as there is more than one kind of human excellence, there is more than one kind of heroine. Thus, the uniqueness of the individual is a reflection of different episodes in African history and points of view which the conception of a heroine presupposes.

In modern African fiction there are few images of African women portrayed as heroic characters. Peter Abrahams, in his prophetic novel *A Wreath for Udomo,* counteracts the flat, stereotyped image of the African woman as wife and mother. The fact that the author has lived in Africa, England, and the West Indies is apparent. Unlike most African male writers, Abrahams depicts a female character who does not play a minor role in the novel. Selina, one of his main characters, is described as a clever and wealthy market woman who is politically aware. As a result, she acts out an important role in the development of the plot and leaves a positive impression of a heroic African woman.

As soon as Selina is introduced in the novel, she is recognized as an extraordinary being whose personal characteristics are rare. She meets Udomo on the boat en route from London to Panafrica, a fictitious African country, where he hints of his plans to fight for the freedom of his country. Upon learning this, Selina tells Udomo not to forget the women.

After Udomo has been working for a newspaper for a while and is ready to start a revolution, it is to Selina he turns for help. When she learns of his plans, she becomes animated and agrees to help him in the struggle to free Panafrica from British colonial rule. According to C. M. Bowra, author of an essay, "The Hero," heroic characters "devote their talents to some concrete cause which provides scope for action and an end to which they can direct their efforts."[1] Selina aptly fits into this category. The cause which Selina serves is the emancipation of her people from British imperialism. She is totally involved in changing her society and liberating her people from the colonization system which is essentially one of economic exploitation and political oppression. Her responsibility toward her people is demonstrated in her launching the Africa Freedom Party with Dr. Adebhoy. Abrahams writes:

> Selina offered them Udomo as leader, chairman and president of the party for the rest of his life. Then she led them in a pledge of loyalty to Udomo and the new party. Suddenly, in all parts of the great gathering, flaming torches sprang alight. Tall young men held them high overhead.
>
> "We, the people of Panafrica—" Selina said.
> "We, the people of Panafrica—" the great throng echoed.

"Swear undying loyalty to the Africa Freedom Party—"
"Swear undying loyalty to the Africa Freedom Party—"
"And to its great and beloved leader—"
"And to its great and beloved leader—"
"Udomo!"
"Udomo!"[2]

It is at this point in the novel that Selina becomes a political heroine. Abrahams makes it abundantly clear that colonization was loathed by African women as well as by African men. Udomo's decision to select her as one of his major allies in his struggle for freedom guaranteed his success. She is one to whom men report and whom people follow. Throughout the book, her leadership capabilities are demonstrated. For Selina, the love of Mother Africa and her country's independence are the driving forces.

Dexterity and stratagem, other qualities of heroic figures, are also Selina's gifts. Her ability to clandestinely distribute tens of thousands of copies of Udomo's newspaper, which prevented the British from confiscating that particular issue, points not only to her intelligence but also to her influence and loyalty to the masses. At another time, when Mhendi (a political refugee) wants to travel secretly to Pluralia—that is, South Africa—it is Selina who smuggles him through the jungle to Pluralia. The density and peril of the jungle were believed to make any kind of penetration impossible. However, Selina and her comrades are able to outsmart the colonialists. It is indicated that Mhendi's trip via the jungle to Pluralia is partly Selina's brain child.

There are some who feel that independence from colonial rule and the flourishing of traditional African values need not be separated. Selina believed that freedom meant the triumph and superiority of Africa's great past as well as the modernization and development of her country. However, Udomo had his own ideas about what independent Panafrica should embrace and discard. As he saw it, the new nation's enemies were the colonialists, poverty, and tribalism. This clash in their ideologies is what causes the chasm in the bond between Selina and Udomo. At a confrontation with Selina and Dr. Adebhoy, Udomo reveals his ultimate goals to eradicate traditional African customs such as the ritual of juju, blood ceremonies, and worshiping at the shrines of the ancestors. Upon learning of Udomo's hatred for Africa's traditional *modus vivendi,* Selina accuses him of betraying her. It is at this point that another characteristic of her heroic nature asserts itself. Heroism is oftentimes accompanied by tragedy. Usually one who allows pride to enter into his very being feels, all too easily, any wrong done to him and becomes frustrated to the point of killing those who surpass him. Selina tells Udomo:

> "You are destroying our ways, Udomo. The old ways are dying at your hands. We were slow to see. We thought: he knows what he does; he's our man. So I said, 'Let him be. Give him time. He's matching white cunning with black cunning.' She turned to him then. Her face now ablaze with bitter hatred. But you fooled me. You fooled Selina."[3]

Then she has Udomo killed, in tribal fashion, demonstrating not only her superiority but also the power of the tribal gods. This act underlines Selina as a heroic figure in the novel. She triumphs in her vengeance.

The heroine in Amos Tutuola's novel *The Brave African Huntress* is Adebisi. Her motivation, determination, and communal consciousness enable her to destroy the vicious animals of the jungle that threaten the happiness of the people in her village as well as those in the neighboring communities. The novel opens when Adebisi, at the age of eight, learns that she had four brothers who never returned to their village after a hunting trip. With this information, Adebisi vows not only to free her people of the terrors of the jungle but also to search for her lost brothers. She thus acquires the skills of a hunter by practicing daily the stoning of animals and the shooting of objects without missing. Once she considers herself a skilled huntress, she pleads with her father to allow her to enter the dark jungle in search of her brothers. Her father, a melancholy man since he lost his sons, is reluctant to grant Adebisi her wish because he has already forfeited his sons and wants to have his only child, Adebisi, remain with him. However, Adebisi's constant pressure and pleading force him to permit her to inherit the hunting profession of the family and enter the fearful jungle. Equipped with a gun, a hunting bag, a cutlass, and juju, she sets off on her trip. She announces to her people before leaving:

> Now, old women and men and children. I am leaving you all this afternoon for the jungle of the pygmies! Though I am young and I am a lady but for the benefit of our town and many others, I shall go there and I shall see that I kill or drive the whole pygmies away from that jungle and I shall kill the whole wild animals of that jungle before I will come to you or die in the jungle if I cannot bring back those hunters, etc., who were in the custody of the pygmies for a long time.[4]

The significance of this book is that Tutuola creates a female protagonist who is not characterized in the traditional role as a wife and mother. More important, the author presents a multidimensional character who is community conscious. What prompts Adebisi to act is her concern for the well-being of her people. Thus Adebisi transcends another of the stereotyped versions of the African woman and accepts the challenging profession of a huntress. Her decision is the product of years of meditation on how best to continue her family tradition of great hunters and protect her clan from the fearful creatures in the jungle.

The heroine in the novel possesses both supernatural and intellectual gifts, which assures her success in all her endeavors. In Tutuola's world, juju plays an important part in the achievements of the brave huntress; the emphasis on human strength is secondary. This fact neatly weaves itself into the novel primarily because Adebisi is a young girl of eighteen who, although skilled in her profession, would need some aid—if not an army of warriors, then some supernatural powers to assist her in difficult times. In various episodes, Adebisi is able to escape death by the power of her juju: Although the pygmies of the jungle beat her mercilessly and bash her head against mighty rocks, she still lives. And when poisonous snakes bite her ankles, she survives but the snakes fall down dead. All of this is attributed to the powerful medicines which protect her from bodily harm.

What adds to Adebisi's heroic character is her enduring attitude and fortitude. Inspired by a great cause to which she devotes all her energies, she destroys the horrendous beasts of the forests, vanquishes all the pernicious monsters, and eradicates the cruel tyrants, namely the pygmies. These spectacular feats associate her with heroic African women to whom history accords great importance, Queen Nzingha and Moremi, to name only two. Like Queen Nzingha, Adebisi is accorded the heroic qualities of a warrior.

Intellectual acumen is another of Adebisi's heroic qualities. A case in point is her ability to outsmart the chief keeper of the pygmies, who employs her to clean his office. Adebisi states:

> As I was enjoying my life quite well in this office it was so I was thinking in mind how I could ruin these pygmies. One day, as I was going round this custody, I saw in a certain part of it a substance with which to make gun powder. Immediately I discovered this thing it came to my mind to make a lot of native gun powder from this substance. And having made a lot of native gun powder, then when it was midnight I dug several holes round the wall [rock] of this custody. I filled each of them with this gun powder and I covered it with sand and refuses. Then I put in mind that perhaps one day the gun powder would be blown off and then we the captives would be able to come out and then escape for our lives. It was like this, I buried the gun powder everywhere in this custody.[5]

When the opportunity arises, Adebisi sets fire to the oil wells in the center of the town and kills thousands of pygmies. Then the hunters which the pygmies held captive for years are able to flee from the village of the pygmies. Unlike Selina, in *A Wreath for Udomo,* Adebisi's accomplishments bring her peace. She is able to locate her brothers after she destroys all the dangerous creatures in the jungle, and thus she returns to her community where she is joyously received. Once her task is completed, her truly heroic character is recognized by her community. All of her efforts lead to glory and fame.

Ousmane Sembene's novel *God's Bits of Wood* reports a railway strike by both African men and women in Senegal between October 1947 and March 1948. In an attempt to secure adequate wages and fringe benefits from colonialists in power at that time, Senegalese railway workers formed a union to determine the course that should be followed in order to obtain equality and respect. Women play an important part in the development of the plot. Sembene's characterization of heroic African women whose efforts are unselfishly devoted to promoting the rights and opportunities of their fathers, husbands, and sons is significant. The title of the book, *God's Bits of Wood,* typifies the courageous actions of the African women who support their men in the face of much sordidness and suffering. Their strength of character and will, which enables them to withstand devastating conditions, is equated with the hard, fibrous substance which forms a tree. Thus, the women are referred to as "bits of wood." The colonialists, in their efforts to force the strikers back to work, prevent the entire community from purchasing rice and having access to drinking water. However, the endurance and resourcefulness of the women thwart the plans of the colonialists and enable the men to continue pressing for their demands.

Sembene's Marxist viewpoint is made explicitly clear in the book. In an interview with the critic Guy Flatley, Sembene states that he "would like to be a Marxist but that it is not easy to be one in a society like Africa, where liberty is limited and the economy is controlled by the United States, France, England, Spain, Portugal and Germany."[6] On the other hand, in *God's Bits of Wood,* he exalts the participation of women in the struggle for liberation. According to Marxist principles, creative artists are active participants in bringing about a cultural revolution. Art and politics must be completely integrated if the level of consciousness of the masses is to be raised so that they will be able to identify the national enemy of the people and assist in the struggle. Thus women and men become allies in the party.

One of the most complex female characters in the novel is Penda, whose rejection of European exploitation and debasement of both Senegalese men and women bring about her death. The French colonialists regard the wives of their employees as concubines. Their disdain for polygamy is reflected in the low wages they pay the railway workers. The fact that the typical laborer has more than one wife is used by the French to justify the argument that an increase in their salaries still would not enable them to provide better housing and provisions for their enormously large families. From Sembene's point of view, just as the colonialists eagerly recruit the sons of the so-called concubines for the Europeans' wars, they should be just as enthusiastic to provide adequate allowances to their employees to take care of their wives and children. It is unfair practices such as these that Penda fights against.

At the beginning of the novel, she is depicted as an independent woman who isolates herself from the community and their ways of life. Her sexual escapades (weeks at a time) make her notorious throughout the village. A. C. Brench, author of *Writings in French,* contends that responsibility prompts the characters in the novel to act. The present state of affairs in the community impels Penda to act heroically. An impartial woman is needed to distribute small rations of food equally to all members of the community, as food is scarce. Penda volunteers to do so and this task goes under way relatively smoothly. Penda's forceful character and ability to lead enables her to act as a unifying force in the emergency. In order to feed the children, as well as the entire community, Penda conceives a plan to steal rice from a Syrian merchant who has been forbidden by the French to sell rice to the villagers. One afternoon, Penda, accompanied by a few children, goes into the shop pretending that she wants to purchase some muslin. While negotiating with the shopkeeper, the children empty a large sack of rice into their bags and exit from the shop. Thus, the community is able to feast on the rice for a couple of days. Penda's heroic act becomes the talk of the community for weeks.

After meeting with the colonialists, the Senegalese union representatives are unsuccessful in procuring better wages and benefits for their families. To help bring the strike to an end, Penda puts forth the suggestion that all capable women march from Thiès to Dakar to convince the *toubabs* (white Frenchmen) that the women are behind their men and that the strike will continue until all grievances are met. The march is successful. Penda's tact and skill in handling the various problems that arise during the march demonstrate her ability to organize and lead. In spite of this fact, once the group reaches the outskirts of Dakar, the colonialists, confused and scared, fire shots to prevent the women from entering the city and they kill Penda.

In 1857 the Ama-Xosa of South Africa engaged in a cattle-killing craze which caused the starvation and death of over twenty thousand men, women, and children. Herbert I. E. Dhlomo reports this historical incident in his drama *The Girl Who Killed to*

Save: Nongqause the Liberator, where he gives a rationale for the tragedy.

Nongquase, the heroine in the play, is a well-known prophetess. A quality of a heroine can be intimacy with the gods. The gods either directly assist the heroic figure to do something or they call for some act or idea. As a medium, Nongqause is highly regarded for her ability to communicate with ancestral spirits in the hope of bringing prosperity and good fortune to the group. Nongqause's gift makes her quite visible and wins her much respect among the Ama-Xosa.

In obedience to her father, Mhlakaza, a great Xosa witch doctor, Nongqause informs the clan of a vision Mhlakaza and Chief Kreli fabricate without consulting her. One day while walking along the river with her father and the chief, Nongqause hears strange noises. Mhlakaza interprets the sounds to be the voices of their ancestors. Nongqause is then told that their dead ancestors want all the cattle slaughtered and the grain destroyed. It is only when this is accomplished that prosperity will once again predominate throughout the community and the Europeans will be blown into the sea. The playwright suggests that Mhlakaza and Chief Kreli are villains who hope to starve the people into fighting the Europeans. Thus, Nongqause becomes a tool and fakes a vision whenever they request. Some village elders who are hesitant to destroy their cattle and provisions are brought to Nongqause's hut. The following act occurs:

> (Nongqause, feigning to be seized with a hysteromania-like trance, laughs, cries, spins around and falls down on her knees and hands—and acts out what took place at the river, with additions proposed by Mhlakaza.)
>
> *Nongqause.* Nice water. Let me drink a little. What's that? Who are singing? (She makes a noise like the lowing of cattle.) (Jumps up, afraid.) Cattle lowing from under the ground! What can it mean? (She makes a great noise in imitation of horses carrying warriors.) What is this great cloud of dust? Who are these warriors riding past and vanishing? Oh! I am afraid, afraid! What? Who is speaking? Who are these? Ndhlambe, Hintsa, Eno Eno, Mushane, Gaika! Marvellous! Amazing! Triumph! Yes, I shall run now and tell it

to father and to the Great One, the Lion—the Chief . . . The Ama-Xosa will win!

Visitors. Wonderful! Great! It is true!
We believe, we believe!
Hail Kreli! Long Live the Lion!
Victory! Salvation![7]

It is Nongqause's assurance that their ancestors will replenish the earth once they carry out the prophecy that prompts them to slaughter their cattle; here Dhlomo makes Nongqause responsible for the actions of the group.

As a result of her prophecy, tens of thousands die. After the killing of cattle and the burning of grain, the ancestors fail to furnish the clan with cattle and supplies of grain. Nevertheless, Nongqause's innocence and good faith toward her people bring her even closer to them after the trauma. According to Dhlomo, the episode is regarded as a positive event which leads the Ama-Xosa to Christianity and progress. Instead of condemning Nongqause for her inaccurate prediction, the Ama-Xosa esteem her as the Europeans supply food and shelter for those who were able to survive the tragedy.

From a purely conventional point of view, Nongqause's capabilities are far from outstanding. She is in a way an inversion to all that we commonly identify with heroism. The qualities of a diviner—knowledge and certainty—are lacking. After all, her prophecy brought about a catastrophe. On the other hand, it is the result of the cattle-killing drama that enables Nongqause to maintain her respect among the people. She is able to give her people something else to believe in, namely, Christianity. Thus, the Nguni, according to the writer, regard her as the force that led them to interact with the West and gave rise to the demise of those aspects of tribalism which impeded progress. It is in this way that she is heroic.

Olagoke Ariwoola, in *The African Wife,* states that "what a man can do a woman can also do."[8] In a short story entitled "Girls at War" Chinua Achebe exalts an Igbo woman who heroically sacrifices her life in an attempt to help a disabled soldier escape death

At the beginning of the story, Gladys is described as a militia girl who is devoted to the Biafrans' cause. Her duty to her country and fellowman supersedes all other concerns. A case in point is when she tactfully and thoroughly inspects a Minister of Justice, Reginald Nwankwo, who is annoyed upon being asked to be searched. During the emergency, those traveling from one point to another throughout Iboland are carefully checked. Ignoring the fact that Mr. Nwankwo is a minister, Gladys completes a thorough examination of his car and thus impresses the curt minister. At this point in the narration, Gladys is characterized as a fully conscious woman who actively participates in the struggles of her people. Her dedication and loyalty for the well-being of all the members in her community is further dramatically demonstrated in the story.

According to Nwankwo, much squalor prevails in Iboland as the civil war continues. The narrator reports,

> Death and starvation having long chased out the headiness of the early days, now left in some places blank resignation, in others a rock-like, even suicidal, defiance. But surprisingly enough there were many at this time also who had no other desire than to corner whatever good things were still going and to enjoy themselves to the limit. For such people a strange normalcy had returned to the world. All those nervous check-points disappeared. Girls became girls once more and boys boys. It was a tight, blockaded and desperate world but none the less a world—with some goodness and some badness and plenty of heroism which, however, happened most times far, far below the eye-level of the people in this story—in out-of-the-way refugee camps, in the damp tatters, in the hungry and bare-handed courage of the first line of fire.[9]

When Nwankwo meets Gladys eighteen months later, she has undergone a complete metamorphosis. In the name of survival, Gladys sleeps with any man who provides her with food and shelter. Nwankwo, too, becomes one of her lovers, although at the same time he laments the degeneration of his society. However, beneath Gladys' apparent loss of morality remains her undying commitment to her people. Her heroic virtue is illustrated at a time when the difference between men and mice are determined.

While driving Gladys home after they have spent a few days together, Nwankwo hastens his driver to pick up a soldier in need of a ride. Thirty minutes later, bombs explode. As Nwankwo, Gladys, and the driver run for their lives, the maimed soldier cries, "Please come and open for me!"[10] It is Gladys who stops and returns to help the soldier. Another bomb goes off. Some hours from this time Nwankwo finds the dead bodies of Gladys and the soldier entangled. Thus, her final concern for the immediate needs of the soldier marks her individual integrity and selflessness and crowns her as one of the most memorable heroic characters in African literature. Unlike Gladys, Nwankwo, for all his solipsisms about the decadence of his society, is unable to transcend the limitations of mere thought and act courageously.

The lack of heroic female characters in East African literature need not suggest that African women in traditional African society in East Africa did not play prominent roles in their societies. Iris Berger's essay "Rebels or Status-Seekers? Women as Spirit Mediums in East Africa" discusses the significant roles East African women played in Uganda, Rwanda, Burundi, and northern Tanzania before colonial penetration. Accounts emphasize that a large number of East African women were respected mediums in their societies. Hence, the myopic vision of the male writers in various disciplines in regard to the influence East African women wielded through ritual and cult associations is responsible for the omission of accurate portrayals of African women in many studies. Berger states that although East African women's

> exercise of power and authority was restricted to ritual situations, they could acquire wealth from their positions and apparently commanded respect at all times because of their religious powers. And here, as in the elitist cults, smaller numbers of women achieved institutionalized high positions either as national figures or, more frequently, as local religious leaders. Yet this religious form arose largely in the most highly stratified societies of the region.[11]

South African women also acquire prominence through spirit-possession associations. E. Jensen-Krige speaks of the respect the Rain-Queen of Lovedu commanded not only from her clan but also from neighboring ethnic groups. And as a result of her study of the Bantu peoples of South Africa, Laura Longmore asserts that in traditional African society South African women were in every way as economically important as their husbands.[12]

In conclusion, then, the small representation of heroic female figures in African literature merely points to the shortsighted conclusions presented in the accounts of many writers who ignore and minimize the significant contributions African women in traditional African society have made. As I have attempted to show, the near invisibility of the image of the African woman as heroine cannot be attributed to the mores of traditional African society, but instead to the colonial impact which, far from liberating African women, only diminished their inalienable rights and prerogatives.

NOTES

1. C. M. Bowra, "The Hero," in Victor Brombert, ed., *The Hero in Literature* (Greenwich, Conn.: Fawcett World, 1969), p. 24.
2. Peter Abrahams, *A Wreath for Udomo* (New York: Collier Books, 1956), p. 203.
3. Ibid., p. 391.
4. Amos Tutuola, *The Brave African Huntress* (London: Faber & Faber, 1958), p. 20.
5. Ibid., p. 92.
6. Guy Flatley, "Senegal Is Senegal, Not Harlem," New York *Times,* November 2, 1969, p. 17.
7. Herbert I. E. Dhlomo, *The Girl Who Killed to Save: Nongqause the Liberator* (Lovedale, South Africa: Lovedale Press, 1935), pp. 6–7.
8. Olagoke Ariwoola, *The African Wife* (London: Kenion Press, 1965), p. 80.
9. Chinua Achebe, *Girls at War and Other Stories* (Garden City, N.Y.: Doubleday & Company, 1973), p. 112.
10. Ibid., p. 129.
11. Iris Berger, "Rebels or Status-Seekers? Women as Spirit Mediums in East Africa," in Hafkin and Bay, p. 181.
12. Laura Longmore, *The Dispossessed* (London: Jonathan Cape, 1959), p. 120.

African literature in general has not been versatile in its re-creating of female characters. A startling departure from the flat, traditional female stereotypes is the work of Ousmane Sembene, Senegalese novelist, short story writer, script writer, playwright, and cinematographer. Creator of the celebrated films *Black Girl* and *Dock Worker,* among others, Sembene is majestically at ease in the print medium as well. In works such as *White Genesis* and especially *God's Bits of Wood* this artist (who brings to mind Ngugi Wa Thiongo's equally powerful and lucid portraits of real African women) merges artistic theory and praxis: If a people are to change, grow, and prosper in ways that are human-oriented instead of machine-motivated, all the people must participate in fighting for and maintaining needed change in the society. The presence of roles designated by biological custom in no way alleviates one's responsibilities to the total community. In many of Sembene's works, we observe African women "pulling the double shift" without whining and, it seems, without a modicum of care for self. However, Sonia Lee's discussion focuses on this dimension, the supposed negation of self as it is seen in the West, and the interpreted differences in this concept *for the sake of the total community* wrought by the pen of Sembene.

The Awakening of the Self in the Heroines of Ousmane Sembene

by SONIA LEE

Most African writers of French expression have been educated in the best French schools. Such education has placed them at the crossroads of two cultures and is both a valuable tool and a source of anguish. Through writing, however, the African intellectual can renew contact with Africa and its culture, a vital aspect of which is the African woman. The image of the woman in the African literature of French expression is an exclusive creation of the male psyche, since French-speaking Africa does not count, as yet, any women writers. Therefore, the feminine protagonist throughout the African novel presents a certain homogeneity of character which can be attributed to a basic similarity in the man's view of the woman. For example, the feminine protagonist is always seen from the standpoint of her traditional role, which in turn is frequently used by the writer to illustrate a particular social thesis. Through the role of the woman the writer may be re-examining man's role in his changing society. Consequently, the heroine often has a didactic function which deters her from psychological development. Furthermore, the feminine character often plays a secondary role in the novel, frequently being placed in the fixed context of the village where she illustrates traditional life. In the changing contemporary society she seems to remain the constant factor because the social changes imposed upon traditional life by modern times are seen almost exclusively in the life drama of the male protagonist. An exception can be seen in the character of the young girl who in most instances appears in an urban context, where she illustrates the problems facing the African woman in contemporary society.

Although she is stereotyped, the female protagonist is always a positive character. The male writer shows the African woman in a very favorable light and expresses repeatedly his deep admiration and appreciation for what she is and what she stands for. Such a positive vision of the woman stems from the undeniable respect which the writer has for the role of the African mother. The maternal image has an obsessive presence in the French African novel, seeming to dominate the vision which the writer has of the woman. Despite all her qualities, the heroine is always a tragic figure and her life brings her more sorrows than joy. This unhappiness, however, is very often a result of the selfishness and lack of understanding of the male. The male writer seems to be questioning the traditional misogyny of the African male and trying to bring about a change of attitude not only befitting but also necessary to new African society. Such a critical attitude as well as a deep interest in the situation of the African woman is particularly noticeable in the works of Ousmane Sembene, a Senegalese author of several novels and short stories who is also a successful filmmaker. In 1966 he won a prize for his short story "Véhi-Ciosane" at the Festival of Black Arts in Dakar. His work is often characterized as socially *engagé;* his Marxist viewpoint is evident in the way he examines his traditional Moslem society and in his desire to enlarge the role and the position of the woman in contemporary African society.

Sembene's literary works abound in female characters. Although they are never the main protagonists, they often play an important role in the development of the plot and, moreover, leave a deep impression on the reader. The four heroines discussed here, each taken from a major work and representative of Sembene's image of woman, encompass at least two generations of Africans and reflect the changes which have taken place not only in their society but also in their awareness of themselves as human beings. The first two heroines belong to what could be called traditional Africa—the Moslem-Wolof tradition. The traditional woman becomes aware both of the injustice of her position and of the decomposition of the social structures, once used to justify the very position which she now questions.

The first heroine struggles with the problems of polygamy. Sembene is neither the first nor the only writer who is challenging the validity of Africa's traditional institution of marriage, but he is the only one who does so from a feminine point of view, with much compassion and understanding. If Sembene concentrates on the woman's plight, he does so also in order to demonstrate the male's selfish attitude. The young woman, Noumbe, is the main protagonist of "Ses Trois Jours," a story in the collection *Voltaïque* (1962). Noumbe is the third wife of Moustaphe, who has very recently taken a fourth wife. Following the law of the Koran, the husband must treat his four wives equally in all ways and spend the same amount of time with each of them. But Sembene confronts us with reality: Husbands do not treat their wives with equal fairness, and the new wife is almost always the favorite. It is Noumbe's three days, that is, the time during which the husband becomes her husband. Moustaphe, no longer eager to visit his wife, arrives late, and the whole story tells of Noumbe's painfully long wait and of what goes through her mind as she hopes for the arrival of the husband. Still young but fatigued by a heart condition and by five children whom she bore too quickly, Noumbe knows that she is no longer in favor. Yet she is counting on her three days to recapture Moustaphe's heart, please him, seduce him, show him that she can still delight him with her body.

Noumbe remembers how it was to be the favorite and remembers also how she kept the husband beyond her own three days just as the new wife is doing now. She remembers how she cheated the other wives, how she tried to drain the husband of his strength so he would be "no good" to the next woman whom he was to visit. Now it is her turn, and she sees for the first time the viciousness of the competition. Noumbe realizes that she and the other wives are fighting a losing battle and that the husband is always the winner. Their happiness is of short duration; his is constantly renewed. Finally, Noumbe asks herself: "Why do we accept to be man's play thing?"[1] Her questioning does not go much further. There are neither possibilities for changing things nor even a conscious desire to do so, but merely a vague feeling that it would be nice if things were different. Noumbe knows nothing else but the tradition in which she has been raised and which has taught her that after Allah the husband is her master. However, she senses that something in her is changing, and she can no longer close her eyes to the reality of her life, the emptiness of her heart, the constant fear of being abandoned, the humiliation of being ever eager to please and to be used. After two days of waiting, Noumbe knows that the only thing left to cling to is her dignity. Finally when the husband comes, she sees him in a new light, like "a beast of prey."[2] She greets him with contempt and sarcasm; it is her only defense, her only way to protest her fate, her only way to say no more of this! Her heart can no longer bear the strain, and she collapses. Furious, the husband leaves, cursing women and thinking he has been wronged.

The female character in "Véhi-Ciosane" expresses her revolt in the most tragic manner. The story takes place in a small village in Senegal which is slowly dying because its young men are leaving for the city. It is the end of the world; Sembene, however, makes us understand that the decomposition of traditional life is caused principally by the moral impotence of men. The story is an act of accusation through which Sembene not only reproaches his contemporaries for the stagnation and the breakdown of ancestral values but also for the oppressive situation of the woman.

The heroine of the story is both a character and a symbol, and Sembene confronts us with her plight, which he identifies with contemporary Africa. As a character in the story, she portrays the maternal role which has been lived traditionally by millions of African women. Although she is given a particular name, Ngone War Thiadum, she represents the African mother living and reacting to the events of everyday life as she has been taught to by the ancestral customs. In the story the mother is confronted with an extraordinary event, incest, which is usually judged and punished immediately by the elders of the village. Unfortunately, in this instance, the men will not react since they have lost the ancestral sense of honor and have retained only the traditional privileges given to their sex. Confronted by lethargy and wounded in her honor as a wife and mother, Ngone War Thiadum is obliged to react and break away from tradition.

Ngone, wife of the village chief, is of noble birth; at dawn she lies in bed trying to come to grips with a terrible reality. Her husband is guilty of incest with their only daughter, who is now bearing his illegitmate child. Ngone feels stricken and wounded in her honor by her husband's unspeakable act. At the thought of his horrible deed, "She moaned like a frustrated lioness."[3] Frustrated because she sees herself deprived of her dignity and of the respect which is due her now that she has fulfilled her woman's destiny: being a good wife and mother. She did not choose her life; it was chosen for her even before she was born—she simply fulfilled the role which tradition had imposed upon her and fulfilled it well. But the wife-mother role included respectability and dignity since ancestral Africa had always been proud of its honor. Now she feels nothing but shame, disgust, confusion, and also anger for a lifetime of submission and resignation to the will of her husband, her master, the one who was to help her enter Allah's paradise and whose slightest wishes were laws. For the first time in her life she is questioning the rigidity and the validity of her traditional role and challenging the undisputed authority of her husband:

> Tortured, her will broken, inclined to semi-emotional predispositions, today's act was forcing her to doubt what was yesterday her reason for being. Like a tear, a very small hole, which she herself unconsciously kept enlarging, she was coming to this discovery—a new stage—namely, to judge all events from her own feminine selfhood. This new acquisition (responsibility) in a human being who up to now had never been allowed to think for herself was devastating to her.[4]

Such a sudden self-consciousness of a woman of Ngone's generation comes too late and is too terrible an experience, but perhaps it will serve the new generation. Acting on her own and going against the tradition for the first time in her life, Ngone leaves her family jewels to the child about to be born and also names it Véhi-Ciosane (White Genesis), which means the birth of a new world where the moral defects of the old one will no longer exist. Even though Ngone is hoping for a boy, since in her world it is always better to be a man, the future is given to a woman: The illegitimate child is a girl.

Burdened by her new lucidity, Ngone can no longer survive her humiliation and the disintegration of her world; she commits suicide. By her act of revolt, she transcends her traditional role since she refuses to accept and to resign herself to a destiny which is no longer valid. Such awareness in a traditional feminine character is unique in French African literature; for Sembene, apparently, the traditional feminine role must change. In his story, Ngone is an admirable vision of a past which now is no more than a myth. The traditional woman is a character who no longer has a place in modern society; she is that frustrated lioness who has not yet accomplished her true destiny. On the other hand, one may think that Ngone's daughter, alone with her child, outcast, without a husband, without a family, without bonds and particularly without a destiny, will perhaps succeed in avoiding her mother's frustration and be able to realize to the fullest her life as a woman. Such a new breed of African women is illustrated by two other female protagonists: N'Deye Touti and Tiombe.

In his novel *Les Bouts de Bois de Dieu* (1960) Sembene fictionalized the actual struggle of the railroad workers of the Dakar-Niger and the story of their long strike to obtain social justice. The women participated actively in the conflict, and Sembene shows how important the women can be in the shaping of social and political events. Among a great variety of female characters portrayed in the novel, the young N'Deye Touti illustrates the alienation of a new generation of African women who, because of their education, feel out of place in their own traditional milieu. She is also a transitional character in the evolution of the feminine consciousness and bridges the gap between the frustrated awareness of the traditional woman and the total self-realization of the emancipated one.

N'Deye Touti lives in Dakar, where she is a student at the École Normale. She is painfully aware of the distance which separates her from the other girls, the ones who did not go to school but followed the customary feminine destiny: marriage and motherhood. Because of her French education she is now torn between two worlds without belonging to either. She no longer wants to be like her contemporaries, old before their age, with their drooping breasts, numerous children, and hard and thankless lives. N'Deye Touti dreams of a different life, a life like the one she has seen in the movies and read about in books. She dreams of love; for her the ideal man would be a doctor or a lawyer, someone to take her away from her part of town and toward the European district. She cannot help feeling contempt for her own kind because of their "lack of civilization."[5]

For N'Deye Touti, self-awareness will come with the shattering of her first love. The object of her affection is Bakayoko, a union leader, militant and totally dedicated to the social problems of his society. He is already married, and although N'Deye Touti is against polygamy, she asks to become his second wife because she cannot bear the thought of losing him. Mostly because of his Marxist principles, Bakayoko cannot accept her offer; his rejection completes N'Deye Touti's emancipation and social awakening. She slowly realizes that her education must be used to serve, guide, and comprehend her own society and not to scorn it. She understands that she must help men like Bakayoko in their struggle toward justice and social progress. She will abandon her selfish dream in order to participate in the common cause: the building of the new society.

With Tiombe, the young female character of *L'Harmattan* (1964), Sembene finally portrays his ideal woman. From the beginning of the novel she is a totally aware and mature young woman who does not need anyone to tell her what to do. When choosing between her love and the country's political struggle for independence, she will choose the latter, understanding fully the extent of her sacrifice. Her act is not prompted by despair or revolt or any outside influence; it is a mature, responsible, and thoroughly free decision.

Tiombe is her own person, and she controls her own destiny. Her maturity and self-awareness, however, did not come without great effort. All her life she had to fight for the right to be her own self. She had to struggle against the paternal tyranny and turn herself away from her mother, whose traditional ways she could no longer accept. Breaking away from the old world was heartbreaking for her. She knows that her mother does not understand her behavior and sees her as an object of shame and endless sorrow. Tiombe does not want to get married, at least not in the immediate future; she is a teacher, a Marxist, and an activist in the struggle for independence. Her lover is a young Guinean who decides to go back to his country, which has just obtained its freedom. Tiombe will not go with him despite his request and her love for him. She knows she must stay in her own country (a fictitious land in the novel) in order to liberate it from colonialism: "For Tiombe love and Africa could not be separated, one did not go without the other."[6] The political involvement does not stop her from being a woman:

> Do you think that I am different from other women? I am like all of them. In our apparent diversity, we all welcome love in the same way. But what separates us is our window on the future. How many times alone after meeting or class, all alone, I have questioned my behavior! I am a woman, even if I wanted to forget it, I could not.[7]

For Tiombe to be a woman is to be free, free to choose her life and her destiny; it means awareness of the human condition and the desire to improve it. For her, to be a woman means to have a future, a life where nothing is preordained and where everything is yet to be done.

In the works of Ousmane Sembene, then, the awareness of the self in the woman seems to be symbolic of the self-awareness of Africa. In turning in on herself the female character discovers not only a whole variety of unsuspected feelings and emotions but also the revelation of the outside world which she now perceives with a critical eye. Coming to terms with oneself and one's cultural background is often a shattering experience but an indispensable step toward social progress. Although Sembene is particularly sensitive to the dilemma of the woman, he always sees her through the prism of her social and political context. One cannot help wondering which of these two fascinates him more—the context or the woman. Sembene makes clear, nevertheless, that as far as he is concerned the future destiny of Africa will not unfold without the woman.

NOTES

1. Ousmane Sembene, *Voltaïque* (Paris: Nouvelles Éditions Latines, 1962), p. 58. My own translation is provided for all the passages quoted in the essay.
2. Ibid., p. 59.
3. Ousmane Sembene, *Véhi-Ciosane ou Blanche-Genèse Suividu Mandat* (Paris: Présence Africaine, 1965), p. 35.
4. Ibid., pp. 32–33.
5. Ousmane Sembene, *Les Bouts de Bois de Dieu* (Paris: Presses Pocket, 1960), p. 100.
6. Ousmane Sembene, *L'Harmattan* (Paris: Présence Africaine, 1964), p. 291.
7. Ibid., p. 298.

A perusal of the Selected Bibliography of Caribbean Women Writers indicates that the excuse ". . . But they don't write anything . . ." does not obtain. The facts are the same ones which do and have applied to all oppressed people everywhere: Publishing outlets and opportunities are controlled and limited by those with the economic and political clout (neither status has been enjoyed by Caribbean women), and role expectations have been imposed and observed with the severest strictures so that the status quo can be maintained.

However, things are changing. On June 30, 1975, at Howard University, Washington, D.C., a conference, "The Caribbean Woman: Her Needs in a Changing Society," was held in honor of International Women's Year, under the auspices of the Caribbean American Intercultural Organization. Not unlike many revolutionary movements which have led to permanent political change, this conference identified its priorities as education, social sciences, health, and economics. One of the two male participants (who also, incidentally, compiled a short bibliography of literature in English by Caribbean women) succinctly categorized some of the reasons why literature by Caribbean women has *not* flourished, though that was not his purpose.

> It is quite clear that what the
> Caribbean woman and man need most to
> effect unity is a REVOLUTION—a
> revolution where the women ensure that
> the governments do not continue to
> measure the progress of the people in
> general governmental advances—GNP—
> international fame while the bases of
> prosperity and advancement for an
> agrarian people, clean air, good food,
> cooperative economics, are destroyed.*

Obviously the speaker does not expect *just* the women to effect the changes he signals, but the point is that women as

* Gene Emanuel, "Caribbean Women: A Male Perspective" (Paper delivered at a conference on "The Caribbean Woman: Her Needs in a Changing Society," Washington D.C., May 1977).

well as men in their communities must deliver and extract from their people qualitative responsibilities that lead toward concepts worth writing about.

Some male West Indian writers have charged that there is an absence of history in the Caribbean, and hence, a vacuous, fragmented base that depresses and debilitates the creative powers. The muted, though certainly present woman's voice speaks otherwise. Using the positive *and* undesirable influences of the Chinese, East Indian, Arab, European, Amerindian, and African fusions as their historically based subject matter, they call upon their realities to create the fantastic in the world of imagination. But there is much to be done, theoretically and practically, as Eintou Apandaye relates in this piece abbreviated from a longer article.

The Caribbean Woman as Writer

by EINTOU APANDAYE

In every society, as a people become conscious of themselves, there emerges the creative artist who transposes the essence of the society into dance, song, painting, and, in fact, all the other art forms. Creative writing is one of these. It is important, because it can help people to understand themselves by looking at themselves, as it were, living in the pages of a book.

In a society in which education and the printed word are given such importance, the culture, ranging from spiritual and material forms to life-style, are seen to be given greater validity, by being depicted in print.

The first piece of creative writing by a Caribbean woman that I have been able to locate is Alice Duries' "One Jamaica Gal," published in the *Jamaica Times* in 1939 and eighty pages long. Ada Quayle's *The Mistress* (1957) is next. The works themselves were unavailable for scrutiny so I cannot comment on them.

The writings of two white West Indian women, Phyllis Allfrey and Jean Rhys ("Wide Sargasso Sea") are set in the immediate post-emancipation period. Allfrey's "Orchid House" is set in the twentieth century. Though far apart in time span, both reflect the

"White minority's sensations of shock and disorientation as a massive and smouldering Black Population is released into an awareness of its power" (Kenneth Ramchand, West Indian novel).

Only two novels of note by Black West Indian women seem to have emerged in the sixties. One is Rosa Guy's *Bird at My Window;* the other is Sylvia Wynter's *Hills of Hebron.* The latter is humorous in parts but takes a very real look at the way our people grab at religion in an effort to fill the cultural and economic void in their lives. The belief that education is the cure for all the Black man's problems is also treated.

This novel is one of the few by women that examines in depth the African experience in the Caribbean, in terms of the effect on the psyche, the feeling of worthlessness, and the thorough destruction of the concept of self that the slave experience produced: The relationship between the Black man and the white man is also examined—the fawning, the self-contempt resulting in the aping of the very white man that dehumanised him. The exploitation of the Black woman's body, continuing the rape of slavery, is also viewed.

The plight of the Black woman struggling to survive and take care of her children, and the pressure to use her body and her good looks as her sole meal ticket or to supplement an inadequate income is highlighted. The tenacity with which she clings to religion, blindly using it as the opiate that eases her desperation and makes her frustration bearable, is treated. The dung heap of total poverty that is the economic reality for Black people in the Caribbean is projected. This contrasts the urgency with which those who make it economically try to integrate themselves into the same society that had hitherto spurned them. Wynter tries to suggest that the way for the African man in the Caribbean to find truth and self-realisation is to come to terms with himself as an African and to develop confidence in his own creativity.

Since 1970, our Trinidad women have given us quite a few novels. The most popular of these is Merle Hodges' *Crick Crack Monkey.* This is the story of two children growing up in Trinidad. It says very much about our life-style. It deals with the differences between the grass roots and the bourgeois with their pretentiousness, "good" English, table manners, and the scorn that is heaped upon grass-roots children in prestige schools.

The lack of relevance of our school curriculum is harshly dealt with. Merle's book has a lyrical quality about it. It brings back the memory of most of our childhoods—spending our school holiday in the country, and the smell and taste of toolum and sugar cakes as well as the tamarind whip descending mercilessly on our backs. But the strongest character and the most evocative is Tantie—she represents the strong mother, struggling to give her children the bare necessities and protecting them with a loving fierceness.

Another novel is Marion Jones's *Pan Beat.* This is a novel about the middle class written by a middle-class librarian. People always ask why Caribbean writers, almost all the time, write about the so-called lower classes. Marion Jones's novel, in a way, tells why she depicts the sterility and aridity of middle-class lives: their apartness from the turmoil that is going on in the society. For they are concerned merely with survival and, therefore, in maintaining the status quo.

Her novel deals with a group of young people all from "good homes" except for one, who lives with his mother, a prostitute, in Piccadilly Street. He is not one of them but has all their aspirations. The young people are linked by a love of pan. They form a middle-class steel band, then grow up and drift apart. They meet many years later and Marion examines what they had each done with their lives. She documents the empty, capitalistic lives they lead. Their self-seeking is seen to lead to both material and physical self-destruction.

Writings for Children

Recently there has been an upsurge of Caribbean literature for children. This has come from the realisation that both leisure and textbooks are too heavily European-centred. Therefore, there has been an effort to create writings which relate to both the history and present-day environment of our children. Our women have played their part here. From Jamaica we have Louise Bennett's "Anancy stories" and from Trinidad Eaulin Ashtine, Enid Kirton, and Therese Mills all writing stories for children. Guyana is foremost in the Caribbean as far as producing relevant writings for children, and sisters there have made contributions. Among them are Evelyn Wallace, Yvonne Wray, and Maureen Newton.

Rick Powell

Rick Powell

Rick Powell

Rick Powell

Writings for children have a significance at this period which cannot be overemphasised.

Let us look at one text, Therese Mills's *Great West Indians*. In it we have the lives of Butler, Kofi, Nanay Seaeste, Paul Bogle—all figures who exemplify the spirit of fight in Caribbean people. Think of what that can do, in terms of building an image of oneself and redefining our history for Black children. For have we not been painted as happy-go-lucky and shiftless? Do we not subscribe to Thomas Carlyle's image of ourselves as all "lazy Negroes, unmotivated by the whip of slavery, lulling aimlessly under pumpkin leaves"?

The children before this present generation grew up on literature as remote from themselves as Snow White and Peter Pan, unrelieved by any imagery related to their own environment. Their dreams literally and figuratively could therefore only be centred on things and people alien. Not only this, but by reading only of the environment of the white man, one could have no real concept of him as the one who has disinherited us.

Apart from biographical and historical material, the importance of the rebirth of the Anancy stories must also be recognised, since its links are so direct with a past we have been taught to despise. To go from Brer Anancy of the Caribbean to the Kwaku Anancy of the African continent is to begin to recognise the fact of our denied cultural richness, and to begin to dig for our roots.

There is still the problem with the availability of these writings for children. Too few copies are being printed. Many of those out are not properly illustrated and there is also not enough publicity given them so that parents and teachers hardly even know of their existence.

Poetry

Let us take a look at some other fairly recent publications. Louise Bennett's *Jamaica Labrish* stands as an exceptional work. It is a collection of poems and songs in the Jamaican dialect. It ranges from politics to the "emigration to Metropolis syndrome," "the Rastas," to "high cost of living"—almost every facet of Jamaican life is treated. Most of us will remember her "Capital Site," a satire on the jostling between the different islands of the abortive

Federation, to be the site of the Federation's capital. On the emigration syndrome:

Dem a pour out of o' Jamaica
Everybody future plan is fe
get a big time job
An settle in the mother lan.

Louise Bennett's work satirizes all aspects of the Jamaican society. Her importance largely relates to her use of the dialect.

Her works fulfill three important functions: (1) the documenting of the dialect, (2) the striking of a blow for the pride of the grass-roots Jamaicans in themselves, for this must happen when they see themselves reflected in the printed word, and (3) the ability to take punches at the untouchables of Jamaican society, be they in the political arena or in high social circles, as though coming from the mouth and mind of the disinherited grass-roots element.

In Bennett's works, as well as in the writings for children, there is an identity at work, be it conscious or unconscious. It is an ideology of belief in one's environment; in the striving for self, for knowledge of past, for a truth that would give relevance and direction to one's existence and a wish to share one's own strivings with the rest of the community, and, perhaps, help to give some direction to the entire society.

Another poet, but not of dialect, is Barbara Jones. Her *Among the Potatoes* is a very introverted collection and does not really reflect the concern for an involvement with the society she is supposed to have felt. A strong love of nature and philosophy come through. Her poem "The Chant of the Blacks" has gained more popularity recently.

There are at least three other poets whose writings, when published, will be very interesting to look at for an understanding of women at this time in our history. One is Cheryl Byron. Her poetry is as strongly introverted as Barbara's. But all through one can feel the pulse of a woman dedicated to her people. Where and how does she fit in? What kind of a woman should she be? What makes the society tick? Why should my people suffer so? These are some of the questions Cheryl tries to answer in her writings.

Cheryl also writes songs and paints. Her best known poem is

"Money," which, like much of her poetry, can be done to music, particularly the flute and drums. This is partly because she, like Louise Bennett and Marina Maxwell (another unpublished poet and playwright), are involved in the theatre.

Cheryl is one of our new young Black women who was involved in, and strongly affected by, the events of 1970. She does not see her writing as "art" per se, but understands fully its social and political importance, and sees herself as an example of the change in ideology and attitudes among our young people.

One of the other poets is Hilda Bynoe. Her poetry has largely been written during her stay as governor in Grenada. It will reveal some of what she must have felt during that traumatic period.

Another sister, whose consciousness came to birth in 1970, is the National Joint Action Committee's (NJAC) Onika Kimati. Her poetry expresses the Black Power ideology of NJAC to which she is committed. She understands the relevance of her work but she knows that understanding at this point is not where the Black woman should stop. She feels that active participation and commitment to the struggle for change within the society is the point to which "consciousness" should inevitably lead. So she fuses her art and her politics, and the one feeds on the other.

Why, we might ask, in a society that in some way or other has been trying to grapple with identity problems since 1838 have we so few women writers? Are our women not the backbone of the society? Should they not then be best guided to analyse and give direction through the printed word?

There are several answers to this. I can only put forward a few:

Lack of proper educational direction is one. It is only quite recently that Caribbean parents seek as avidly for the education of their daughters as they have been doing for their sons for about a century.

The view we held of ourselves is another reason for lack of Black women writers in the world.

Many of our women regard their education as giving them a headstart over other women in the race for a husband.

Many of our women who may feel inclined to write never bother to take time off from diapers and stoves to try.

Our slave experience has left us rooted to the concept of ourselves as work horses only. On the other side, however, is the intellectual and so-called liberated woman of this generation who scorns her traditional role and seeks to compete with men, ending up making it professionally and creativity-wise, but seldom finding real happiness and fulfillment. As new Black women, we must seek to establish a median range.

Because of the limited ideas that we have of ourselves and our roles, another real handicap is lack of publishing facilities in the area. Although this has improved a great deal in the last three years, getting anything published is still something of a hassle. So even when our women do write, many of us hide it away in a corner, unsure, and many of those who may have the self-confidence to expose their work never really think in terms of having it published.

The need for our women to write is very real, but maybe the most significant reason that we don't is our lack of awareness of self. Our women, caught up in a morass of false and imported values, swing this way and that to white propaganda. We hardly ever take time out to try and understand our society and the role we can play. Most of us are caught up in the rat race for survival, eking out an existence in a society where our bodies and labour are still being heavily exploited. How then can we find the time and knowledge of self which will help us to analyse and guide our society either through the printed word or otherwise?

But the Black woman is strong and a fighter. That consciousness will come, must come. . . .

Fore day morning come—
And nite slips away. . . .

NOTE

From *Black Woman! A Magazine of the Black Woman in the Caribbean,* 1, No. 1 (November 1975). Published by National Joint Action Committee. Printed by Scope Publishing.

In 1927 Countee Cullen included Anne Spencer's work in his anthology *Caroling Dusk*. For the biographical section, Spencer wrote this, among other things, about herself:

> I write about some of the things
> I love. But have no civilized
> articulation for the things I
> hate. I proudly love being a
> Negro woman—it's so involved
> and interesting.

Gloria Hull's well-written essay gives us a glimpse of the involved and interesting saga of Black women poets from Lucy Terry and Phillis Wheatley in the eighteenth century, to Margaret Walker Alexander and Gwendolyn Brooks in the twentieth. Hull's apprehension of historical nuances widens this overview so that we have more than a cataloguing of names, titles, and dates. Within her text is also a deft critical stance which makes the information she provides on the lives and works of Terry, Wheatley, Harper, Brooks, Dunbar-Nelson, and the female members of the Harlem group exceptionally valuable.

Black Women Poets from Wheatley to Walker

by GLORIA T. HULL

In certain ways, the often garish spotlight which has been focused on contemporary Black women poets such as Nikki Giovanni, June Jordan, and others has, ironically, tended to obscure the already shadowy literary past by suggesting that Black female poets are something new. Granted that they are among the strongest voices in this current explosion of Black poetry, and that it is normal for contemporary readers (and sometimes even scholars) to be more familiar with modern writers. Yet, despite the implications of this present emphasis, the tradition of Black women poets goes back much further than the 1960s. In fact, Black American literature begins with a female poet, and an imposing line of her successors stretches from that time forward.

These women who wrote before the modern period have received neither the popular nor the critical attention which they deserve—even though growing interest in the field makes knowing what has gone before that much more imperative. Studying them teaches us that significant numbers of Black women have always written poetry and accords this earlier work its rightful esteem. It also gives a necessary perspective on the present poets by placing them in their appropriate, rich tradition. In this way, a body of literature, which is too often perceived as isolated and fragmented, assumes a coherent shape; and this, in turn, works to correct the myopic view taken toward Black women writers and Black poetry in general.

Even before a formal literary history began, slave women were, no doubt, helping to produce the earliest Black poetry—the spirituals and secular songs. One of the curious and distinguishing characteristics of this folk poetry is its lack of an identifying sexual framework—that is, a reader cannot tell if the consciousness or voice behind the song is male or female. Yet, surely, women are to be counted among the "Black and unknown bards."

This beginning period, rich in oral literature, is correspondingly sparse in formal, written poetry. However, the eighteenth century brought the first poem by a Black American and the emergence of the first widely known Black American poet. Both of these writers were women. Lucy Terry, a sixteen-year-old slave girl, witnessed an Indian raid on her village of Deerfield, Massachusetts, and left behind the best account of the massacre in fourteen naïve tetrameter couplets called "Bars Fight, August 28, 1746." The work was not published until 1893 and survives today because of its historical importance.

Phillis Wheatley, on the other hand, is the major Black writer of the period. Quite a bit has already been written about her. Students of literature are familiar, if only in outline, with her genius and remarkable history: how she was kidnaped from the African coast of Senegal when she was five or six years old and brought to America, where, in the nurturing atmosphere of the Wheatley household, she learned to speak and read English in sixteen months and to write creditable poems in six years. And they also know of her abstract elegies and occasional poems modeled after the English neoclassic poets. The table of contents of her 1773 *Poems on Various Subjects, Religious and Moral* is illustrative of this preoccupation and influence:[1] "Thoughts on the Works of Providence," "An Hymn to the Morning," "On Recollection," "On Imagination," and then in a particularly calamitous time, these four poems: "To a Lady on her coming to North America with her Son, for the Recovery of her Health"; "To a Lady on her remarkable Preservation in a Hurricane in North Carolina"; "To a Lady and her Children on the Death of her Son, and their Brother"; and, finally, "To a Gentleman and Lady on the Death of the Lady's Brother and Sister, and a Child of the Name of Avis, aged one year"—very complete and descriptive titles, typical of their day.

Almost equally well known is the common criticism of Wheatley for her lack of race consciousness—at least of a kind which would have led her to personally empathize with the average slave or protest against the institution of slavery in her writings. All of these bits and pieces form a prevailing idea of her which one critic has summed up in this way: "Phillis Wheatley was a pathetic little Negro girl who had so completely identified herself with her eighteenth century Boston background that all she could write was coldly correct neo-classical verse on dead ministers and even deader abstractions."[2] There is truth in this common view, but there are also corrective observations which need to be made.

The first is that her poetry is not as imitative and moribund as most commentators make it sound. Some of her images and conceits display an originality which shows that many of her thoughts are fresh ideas of her own even if her rhythm is almost always Pope's—for example, these lines from the hurricane poem just mentioned:

> Aeolus in his rapid chariot drove
> In gloomy grandeur from the vault above:
> Furious he comes. His winged sons obey
> Their frantic sire, and madden all the sea.

Secondly, Phillis Wheatley was conscious of herself as a poet, a Black poet, a Black female poet, as the numerous references to herself in her poems attest—their stylization notwithstanding. One should also remember that she was a thorough New England Puritan, and it is partly her Christianity which compels her to look upon deliverance from her native land as the blessing which she describes it to be in one of her best-known poems, "On Being Brought from Africa to America." Furthermore, her personality was naturally delicate and reticent. After being feted on both sides of the Atlantic, she and an infant child died in the squalor of a cheap Boston boardinghouse—a circumstance which is of course another tragic writer's tale, but also a chilling commentary on the precariousness of Wheatley's status as a Black female poet.

The period from 1800 to 1865 was a time of antislavery agitation and utilitarian literature. All resources, including the pens of writers, were marshaled for the abolitionist cause. Understandably, the slave narrative, the speech, and the essay flourished to the relative neglect of more belletristic literary genres. However, the poetry which was written shows its political involvement. George Moses Horton, who earned from twenty-five to fifty cents each for the eighteenth-century-style love lyrics which he wrote for University of North Carolina students, also complained against his slavery and entitled the 1829 volume of his poems *Hope of Liberty*. A second major poet, James M. Whitfield, added Byronic misanthropy to his forceful denunciation of America.

The key female poet of this period (there is only one other), Frances Harper, is a better technician than Horton and ranks well with Whitfield. In addition to her abolitionist themes, she has subjects and moods which give her greater variety and also reveal her special qualities as a woman writer. The editors of *The Negro Caravan* call her "easily the most popular American Negro poet of her time."[3] This popularity stemmed from the fact that she took her poetry to the people—just as did the young Black poets of the 1960s and '70s. As a widely traveling lecturer of the Anti-Slavery Society, she spoke to packed churches and meeting halls, giving dramatic readings of her abolitionist poems which were so effective that she sold over fifty thousand copies—an unheard-of figure —of her first two books, mostly to people who had, in the words of her fellow abolitionist William Still, "listened to her eloquent lectures."[4]

Essentially this poetry is message verse, dependent on an oratorical and histrionic platform delivery for its effect. Harper leans heavily on the poetic and emotional appeal of sensory imagery, as can be seen in these characteristic lines from "Bury Me in a Free Land":

> I could not rest if I heard
> the tread
> Of a coffle gang to the
> shambles led,
> And the mother's shriek of
> wild despair
> Rise like a curse on the
> trembling air.

Harper's speaking and writing did not end with 1865, for the fight against slavery was only one of the many battles which engaged her during her lifetime. She was also deeply involved in religious, feminist, and temperance movements—with no apparent conflict or lack of energy—which is comparable today to being in the Black Liberation, the Women's Liberation, the Jesus, and the ecology/health-food movements. She combined these interests in her writing as well as in her life to produce a fairly extensive body of quite readable poetry.

From her feminism comes "A Double Standard," a poem spoken by a seduced and abandoned young woman who addresses the reader or listener in these terms:

> Crime has no sex and yet today
> I wear the brand of shame;
> Whilst he amid the gay and proud
> Still bears an honored name.

The social double standard is directly condemned in the final lines:

> And what is wrong in woman's
> life
> In man's cannot be right.

She also wrote about Vashti, the Persian Queen in the Bible who gave up her throne rather than shame her womanhood. And included in her corpus are temperance poems like "Nothing and Something"; a mother, confident that her son would not ". . . tread / In the downward path of sin and shame," was not alarmed about alcohol, but she became quite concerned when that only son ". . . madly cast in the flowing bowl / A ruined body and sin-wrecked soul." In her forms (as is obvious), Harper relies mainly on the ballad stanza and rhymed tetrameters.

Her last volume of poems, *Sketches of Southern Life,* 1872, presents a Black heroine, Aunt Chloe, who is very well drawn and is firmly set in the folk-life milieu which would furnish the dialect poets with their materials. Its "Learn-to-Read" epitomizes Harper's manner and catches up most of her themes. Although the "Rebs" hated the schools established for ex-slaves—education of Blacks ". . . was agin' their rule"—Aunt Chloe is determined to learn to read:

> So I got a pair of glasses,
> And straight to work I went
> And never stopped till I could read
> The hymns and Testament.

She also moves into her own "little cabin," where she feels ". . . as independent / As the queen upon her Throne."

After Mrs. Harper herself, there were no more queens on her poetry throne for a long while—nor kings either, for that matter. A. A. Whitman wrote extremely long versified romantic tales à la Scott and Byron which were very popular with both Black and white readers near the end of the nineteenth century (William Cullen Bryant, for instance, liked him). And, during the same period, Henrietta Ray published her mannered, bookish poetry. On the whole, the Reconstruction-backlash period from 1865 to 1915 was not congenial to Black literary activity. But near the end of the century, a crop of writers auguring the Renaissance began to spring up—chief among which were Dunbar and the whole slough of dialect poets

When Gwendolyn Brooks was a little girl writing verses, her mother encouraged her by predicting that she would be "the lady Paul Laurence Dunbar."[5] In his own time, however, Dunbar had no such female counterpart. But even before that, not one of the dialect poets who are usually encountered is a woman. This is a significant—and in certain ways, a gratifying—fact, but one is not altogether sure of what it means. There does not seem to be anything inherently masculine in either the content or the manner of this largely plantation-and-minstrel-tradition-based dialect verse. Conceivably, women could just as easily have imagined or reminisced about cooking, kissing, and raising children in the ante bellum South as the men did about eating, courting, and coon-hunting. Or a woman poet could have followed the lead of Harper in her Aunt Chloe poems and given realistic and human depictions of folk life as Dunbar does in the best of his dialect work. But none of them did.

At any rate, there is no major female poet in this period—although Dunbar's wife, Alice Dunbar-Nelson, produced some poems, one of which, "Sonnet," is almost always anthologized. But the most arresting poem which she wrote is a three-stanza lyric called "I Sit and Sew," in which she protests against her apparently petty occupation when real work is needed for the war. The poem could read as a rebellion against the chafing confinement of a "woman's place." She writes:

> But—I must sit and sew.
> The little useless seams,
> the idle patch;
>
> . . .
>
> It is no
> roseate dream
> That beckons me—this pretty
> futile seam,
> It stifles me—God,
> must I sit and sew?[6]

The picture presented by the Harlem Renaissance years—roughly from 1915 to 1930—is, of course, very different from that of the preceding period. Black literature flourished. The major writers were poets—Johnson, McKay, Cullen, Hughes. And there were women poets, too, seven of whom are worthy of note—Angelina Grimke, Anne Spencer, Georgia Douglas Johnson, Jessie Fauset, Effie Lee Newsome, Gwendolyn Bennett, and Helene Johnson. But none of them is considered "major." A serious investigator naturally wonders why and tries to determine if this is a valid judgment. The answer which emerges after a closer study of their poetry and their lives is a mixed one. First the poetry.

The most prolific writer was Georgia Douglas Johnson. Between 1918 and 1938, she published three volumes of poems. (Four years before her death in 1966, she brought out a final book.) This was enough to make her the first Black woman after Harper "to gain general recognition as a poet."[7] However, a modern reader does not usually find her efforts very impressive—mainly because of the sameness of her themes and manner, and her conventional style. She writes either melancholy love lyrics or muted, attenuated poems of racial protest. Illustrative of the first type is this stanza from her poem "Welt":

> Would I might mend the
> fabric of my youth
> That daily flaunts its
> tatters to my eyes,
> Would I might compromise
> awhile with truth
> Until our moon now waxing,
> wanes and dies.

This lyric gathers up the themes of youth, aging, time, love, and death, which recur in these poems.

The personae and characters are usually women (such as the suffering outcast in "Octoroon"), and her poetry almost always has a definite feminine voice. For example, in her first book, *The Heart of a Woman* (1918), she talks about a "woman with a burning flame" which was kept covered and hushed until death, and in the title poem, she likens the heart of a woman to a bird which "goes forth with the dawn" but

> falls back with the night,
> And enters some alien cage
> in its plight,
> And tries to forget it has
> dreamed of the stars,
> While it breaks, breaks,
> breaks on the sheltering bars.

Representative of her handling of the race theme is "The Suppliant":

Long have I beat with timid hands
upon life's leaden door,
Praying the patient, futile prayers
my fathers prayed before,
Yet I remain without the close,
unheeded and unheard,
And never to my listening ear
is borne the waited word.

Soft o'er the threshold of the years
there comes this counsel cool:
The strong demand, contend, prevail;
the beggar is a fool!

Almost all of her poems are in the ballad stanza, which she sometimes stretches out into heptameter couplets. The diction is predictably poetic with, every now and then, a fresh word or image. She uses parallel and balanced phrases for rhythm and development of thought (especially in her heptameter racial poems), and resorts to inversion for the sake of meter and rhyme.

A better and more interesting poet is Anne Spencer. When asked by Cullen to write her biographical notice for his 1927 anthology, *Caroling Dusk,* she responded with the following paragraph:

> Mother Nature, February, forty-five years ago forced me on the stage that I, in turn, might assume the role of lonely child, happy wife, perplexed mother—and, so far, a twice resentful grandmother. I have no academic honors, nor lodge regalia. I am a Christian by intention, a Methodist by inheritance, and a Baptist by marriage. I write about some of the things I love. But have no civilized articulation for the things I hate. I proudly love being a Negro woman—it's so involved and interesting. We are the PROBLEM—the great national game of TABOO.[8]

Her civilized articulation about things that she loves includes poems as varied as their titles: "Before the Feast of Shushan,"

"At the Carnival," "The Wife-Woman," "Dunbar," "Letter to My Sister," "Lines to a Nasturtium," "Neighbors," "Questing," and "Creed." Her forms are an eccentric mixture of free verse and rhymed, iambic-based lines. The result works, but it defies precise categorization. She also exhibits something of a predilection for casting herself into roles. For instance, "Shushan" is a dramatic monologue spoken by a King (the material is the same biblical story treated by Harper in "Vashti"). In trying to make love to Vashti, he calls her Sharon's Rose and then says:

And I am hard to force
the petals wide;
And you are fast to suffer
and be sad.
Is my prophet come to teach
a new thing
Now in a more apt time?[9]

Not surprisingly, Spencer liked Browning. She even wrote a light poem about him, bemoaning the fact that "Life-long, poor Browning never knew Virginia"—which is her native state. It is full of biographical references and allusions to his work ("Pippa Passes," for example) which show her familiarity with him. This kind of dramatic distancing is surprising, appearing as it does during a time of intensely self-centered lyric poetry.

Spencer also has a sense of woman-self and a female identity which comes through in her poems, notably in her "Letter to My Sister," in which she gives advice about how a woman must live; although

It is dangerous for a woman
to defy the gods;
To taunt them with the
tongue's thin tip,
Or strut in the weakness
of mere humanity,
it is even worse if you
Dodge this way or that,
or kneel or pray,
Be kind, or swear agony drops
Or lay your quick body over
your feeble young.

Even though Spencer's poetic instincts are not unerring (she can be obvious and predictable), her work is attractive because of the originality of her material and approach, and because of her terse—almost elliptical—style, apt or unusual diction, vivid images and metaphors, and the occasionally modern lines, which stop the reader with their precise wording and subtly pleasing sounds and rhythms. It is difficult to choose one poem which adequately conveys Spencer's essence. "At the Carnival" might, or "The Wife-Woman," but both of them need to be quoted entirely, yet are too long. "For Jim, Easter Eve," then, best serves the purpose. The persona, after comparing her garden "with old tombs set high against / The crumbled olive tree—and lichen" to Gethsemane, continues:

> what is pain but happiness here
> amid these green and wordless
> patterns,—
> indefinite texture of blade and
> leaf:
> Beauty of an old, old tree,
> last comfort in Gethsemane.

Spencer wrote before the Harlem Renaissance (note that she was forty-five years old in 1927), but was first published during that era. Her uniqueness was apparent even then. Editors who printed her work used phrases like "independent, unconventional style"[10] and "first Aframerican woman poet to show so high a degree of maturity,"[11] and Sterling Brown called her "the most original of all Negro women poets."[12] Not enough is known about her, and the biographical basis of her poems remains a tantalizing question. She is still alive, over ninety years old, in Lynchburg, Virginia, where she has spent almost all of her life.

Anne Spencer did not write racial protest poems. However, the same statement cannot be made about the last Renaissance poet who will be looked at in detail, Helene Johnson. The youngest of the Harlem group, she took "the 'racial' bull by the horns,"[13] and she also wrote poems in the new colloquial-folk-slang style popular during that time. Of all the women poets, her work most reflects the themes which are commonly designated as the characteristic ones of the Renaissance. Her "Sonnet to a Negro in

Harlem" is pro-Black and militant and calls to mind the work of Claude McKay. In "Poem," she gushes over the "Little brown boy / Slim, dark, big-eyed" who croons love songs to his banjo down at the Lafayette:

Gee, brown boy.
I loves you all over.
I'm glad I'm a jig.
I'm glad I can
Understand your dancin'
and your
Singin', and feel all the
happiness
And joy and don't care in you.[14]

"Bottled" presents her notion that a Black man dancing on Seventh Avenue in Harlem has been bottled just as has some sand from the African Sahara sitting on the shelf of the 135th Street public library. Finally, she has a poem which expresses a pro-African primitivism which should be better known than it is, since it is superior to some of the more frequently encountered works on this theme. It is entitled "Magalu" and seems to be a fantasy about meeting Magalu, "dark as a tree at night, / Eager-lipped, listening to a man with a white collar / And a small black book with a cross on it." She enters the scene and ends the poem like this:

Oh Magalu, come!
Take my hand and I
will read you poetry
Chromatic words,
Seraphic symphonies,
Filled up your throat with laughter
and your heart with song.
Do not let him lure you
from your laughing waters,
Lulling lakes, lissome winds.

The bulk of Helene Johnson's poems are more conventional lyrics. In them, she uses much descriptive imagery and frequently treats young love and youthful sensuality.

Now, briefly, a word about each of the four remaining poets. Angelina Grimke wrote commonplace lyric poetry before the Renaissance, but first saw it published then. Her strength lies in her notable use of color imagery. The poem of hers most often reprinted, "Tenebris," envisions a huge black shadow hand plucking at the blood-red bricks of the white man's house. Jessie Fauset, though primarily a novelist of four published books, is usually represented in poetry anthologies by her love poems. Some of these are distinguished by the French titles which she gave them and her sometimes humorous and ironic cast of mind. Effie Newsome wrote primarily children's verse based on nature lore. And, finally, there is Gwendolyn Bennett, whose poetry is rather good. She was, by occupation, an artist, and consequently in her work she envisions scenes, paints still lifes, and expresses herself especially well in color.

Looking back over this group of seven female poets of the Harlem Renaissance and assessing their impact and collective worth, we can begin to see why they are not better known or more highly rated. In the first place, they did not produce and publish enough: Grimke no book, Spencer no book, Fauset no book, Newsome no adult book, Bennett no book, Helene Johnson no book —which means that six of the seven did not collect a single volume of their work. And the one who did, Georgia Johnson, is not the best poet—though she was the most popular. And even here, her popularity is uncharacteristic of the new themes and forms of the Renaissance. Except for Helene Johnson perhaps, this same factor was operative in the cases of the other six writers.

Furthermore, since the Renaissance was a predominantly masculine affair, these poets did not benefit from being insiders. Though Fauset held her quiet literary gatherings, these women—as women—did not fraternize with the male writers and artists. Nor did they have much opportunity to do so. Fauset lived in New York, and Bennett and Helene Johnson were there for a while—but, on the whole, they were not based in the city which was the cultural center of the Renaissance. In fact, most of them were at one time or another a part of the Washington, D.C., social and literary circle which revolved around Georgia Johnson, whose husband had a government appointment in the Capitol. Thus, they were out of the mainstream in more ways than one.

For these reasons, then, these poets represent a group of talented individuals who did not produce enough, or, in a worldly-wise fashion, parlay their talent into "fame." So, lamentably, they end up being "interesting," "minor"—a kind of secondary wave which helped to make up the Renaissance tide.

After this glorious and busy period, the country and Black literary activity went into a slump. What poetry there is, is tinged with depression, socialism, and sometimes protest. Between 1930 and 1945, the major poet was Margaret Walker and the most important poetic event the appearance of her 1942 volume *For My People,* brought out as No. 41 of the Yale Series of Younger Poets, making her the first Black poet to appear in that prestigious group. At the time of its publication, Walker was a twenty-seven-year-old professor of English at Livingston College in Salisbury, North Carolina, her first teaching position after she had received a master of arts degree from the University of Iowa's School of Letters two years earlier.

For My People is divided into three sections. The first seeks to define the poet's relationship to "her people" and her native Southland, and it begins with the well-known title poem, a work which anticipates the material and the manner of the rest of the section:

> For my people everywhere
> singing their slave songs repeatedly:
> their dirges and their ditties
> and their blues and jubilees,
> praying their prayers nightly
> to an unknown god, bending their
> knees humbly to an unseen power.[15]

The form of "For My People" is the most immediately striking thing about it. Drawing on free-verse techniques, on the Bible, on the Black sermon (her father was a preacher), Walker fairly overwhelms the reader with her rhetorical brilliance. She continues this same method and approach in the poems in the collection—reciting her heritage of "Dark Blood," tracing Black people's blind belief in gods from Africa to America, singing of her "roots deep in southern life," and decrying the fact that she is not as strong as her grandmothers were in "Lineage," one of the simplest and nicest poems in this group:

My grandmothers are full of
memories
Smelling of soap and onions
and wet clay
With veins rolling roughly
over quick hands
They have many clean words to say.

Part II of *For My People* is made up of ballads about Black folk heroes known and unknown, famous and infamous. Traditional subjects are "Bad-Man Stagolee" and "Big John Henry." But no less worthy are "Poppa Chicken," the "sugah daddy / pimping in his prime"; the "Teacher," who was a "sap" about women; and "Gus, the Lineman," who "had nine lives / And lived them all." Two of the best of these ballads have heroines as their central figures—Molly Means, "a hag and a witch: / Chile of the devil, the dark, and sitch," and Kissie Lee, a tough, bad gal, whose account ends like this:

She could shoot glass doors
offa the hinges,
She could take herself
on the wildest binges.
And she died with her boots on
switching blades
On Talladega Mountain
in the likker raids.

In these tall tale and ballad narratives, Walker adheres pretty closely to the traditional ballad stanza, varying it with four-beat couplets and spicing it up with dialect speech which she is successful at orthographically representing.

The final section, composed of only six poems, is much shorter than the first two. These are sonnets (with the form freely handled) in which Walker gazes back on her childhood, writes about experiences she has had since leaving the South (such as talking to an Iowa farmer), and expresses needs and struggles common to all human beings. Her craftsmanship is not always smooth in this section, but some of her best lines conclude the poem entitled "Whores":

> Perhaps one day they'll all
> die on the streets
> or be surprised by bombs
> in each wide bed;
> learning too late in
> unaccustomed dread
> that easy ways, like whores
> on special beats,
> No longer have the gift
> to harbor pride
> or bring men peace,
> or leave them satisfied.

On the whole, *For My People* is a good book. Unlike many volumes of poetry, one can read it from cover to cover without getting bored or inattentive—probably because of the narrative interest of Part II. Walker is best with these poems and with her unique "for my people" style, but not as sure or deft in her handling of the sonnets.

The volume was (and is) significant for many reasons. First, its mood coincided with the Depression and hard times of the 1930s, and also with the social consciousness and militant integrationism of that and the following decade. In style, it was different in a worthwhile way from what had been written during the Renaissance. Her attention to Black heroes and heroines was also timely and helped to communicate the *négritude* of the volume and the delving for roots which is one of its major themes.

After Margaret Walker's *For My People,* Gwendolyn Brooks published *A Street in Bronzeville* in 1945 and went on to win the Pulitzer Prize (the first Black to do so) in 1950 for her 1949 volume *Annie Allen.* From this point on, Black women are well represented in poetry. In the 1950s and early '60s, Margaret Danner, Naomi Madgett, and Gloria Oden are significant. In the 1960s, poetry exploded (as did Black America) and in this second Renaissance, women were not left out. Walker, after a twenty-eight-year poetic silence, published two more books of poems. Brooks, also of an earlier period, has gone through changes and remained current, productive, and good. And important new names have appeared, including Audre Lorde, Sonia Sanchez, Lucille Clifton, Nikki Giovanni, Mari Evans, June Jordan, and Alice Walker. These writers show all of the characteristics of the poetry of the Black sixties while revealing, at the same time, their wonderful woman/human selves. They are a large and exciting group and, as a group, are of a higher order or quality and achievement than the comparable group of Black male poets.

Whereas, in the thirty years from 1915 to 1945, one could name only about fourteen female poets, the number swells to near fifty for the almost thirty years following—and it is constantly growing. When proportionate figures are compared, more of the Black women who are writers are primarily poets as compared to the men, showing that more women than men have turned to this form of creative and literary expression. In it, they have wrought well.

NOTES

1. Phillis Wheatley, *Poems on Various Subjects, Religious and Moral* (London: Bell, 1773). Quotations from her poems are from this first edition.
2. Arthur P. Davis, "Personal Elements in the Poetry of Phillis Wheatley," *Phylon,* 14 (1963), 192.
3. Sterling A. Brown, Arthur P. Davis, and Ulysses Lee, eds., *The Negro Caravan* (New York: Arno Press and the New York *Times,* 1969), p. 293.
4. Quoted from William H. Robinson, Jr., ed., *Early Black American Poets* (Dubuque, Iowa: Wm. C. Brown, 1971), p. 27. Quotations from Harper's poetry are also taken from this collection.
5. Gwendolyn Brooks, *Report from Part One* (Detroit: Broadside Press, 1972), p. 56.
6. Robert T. Kerlin, ed., *Negro Poets and Their Poems,* 2nd ed (Washington, D.C.: Associated Pubs., 1938), p. 146.
7. James Weldon Johnson, ed., *The Book of American Negro Poetry,* rev. ed. (New York: Harcourt, Brace & World, 1931), p. 181. All quotations of her poems are from this work except "The Suppliant," which is taken from Langston Hughes and Arna Bontemps,

eds., *The Poetry of the Negro, 1746–1970* (Garden City, N.Y.: Doubleday & Company, 1970), p. 76.

8. Countee Cullen, ed., *Caroling Dusk: An Anthology of Verse by Negro Poets* (New York: Harper & Brothers, 1927), p. 47.
9. Johnson, p. 214. All other quotations of her work come from Hughes and Bontemps.
10. Kerlin, p. 158.
11. Johnson, p. 213.
12. Sterling Brown, *Negro Poetry and Drama* (1937) (New York: Atheneum Publishers, 1969), p. 65.
13. Johnson, p. 279.
14. Ibid., p. 280. "Magalu" is quoted from Hughes and Bontemps, p. 263.
15. Margaret Walker, *For My People* (New Haven: Yale University Press, 1942), p. 13. This is the source for all citations of her poetry.

Intensely flammable and articulate, James Baldwin was for years *the* Black writer in the United States. He attained that dubious status by converting the psychic wounds he suffered during childhood and adolescence into powerful and aesthetically impressive art. A brilliant essayist, novelist, dramatist, and lecturer, Baldwin, who resides most of the time in Paris, but who has declared his intentions to return to the United States to live, has been "an honest man and a good writer," a goal he first stated in 1955.

Baldwin's titles, outside scores of reviews, articles, and stories, include *Go Tell It on the Mountain, Notes of a Native Son, Nobody Knows My Name, No Name in the Street, The Fire Next Time, Giovanni's Room, The Amen Corner, Another Country, Blues for Mister Charlie, Nothing Personal, Going to Meet the Man, Tell Me How Long the Train's Been Gone, A Rap on Race* (with Margaret Mead), *If Beale Street Could Talk,* and *The Devil Finds Work.*

If Beale Street Could Talk is the corpus from which Hortense Spillers makes her thesis—about Baldwin, about Tish and the other female characters in the novel, vis-à-vis the males, and about the power of language and myth in and out of the homiletic mode.

The Politics of Intimacy: A Discussion

by HORTENSE SPILLERS

This essay is an attempt to suggest a working model for a literary analysis of issues specifically related to the intimate life of Afro-American women. I suggest literary criticism as a model because its rhetorical resources, at best, reveal both semantic and poetic meaning. As I see it, the debate that women engage requires both the spare-bone sharpness of systematic thinking and the compassionate grasp of issues which define men and women as human sympathetic endeavor. In short, I'm trying to enter an already established conversation, offering a few basic suggestions: (1) that literary criticism, not the only, or even pre-eminent, instrument at our disposal, gives us a clue to the text of our own experience and (2) that the "politics of intimacy" can recover its lost ground only when we understand that its present diction is demonstrably outmoded; we need new notations for our time.

Definition cannot be avoided, and I know that "politics" and "intimacy" pose a sharp contradiction. The stipulated term brings together extremes of human purpose and function, but the combination suggests itself because it reverberates the elements of both power and compassion which cluster around relationships. As I use it, I mean primarily the intricate fabric of feeling drawn out in fictional situations between men and women. By focusing on its grammar, we may discover more precisely how woman-freedom, or its negation, is tied to the assertions of myth, or ways of saying things.

The grammar of fictional situations is the easiest one to manipulate because the characters are beyond change or corruption. They are free. They stay still. They contain a contradiction more readily than we do because their lips are not their own, but these unchanging characters may ultimately yield up some bright secret about our own dynamic experience. I choose Baldwin as an example because he offers a landscape of black characters in powerful intimate situations, but more than that, he is the culmination of a tradition of language whose roots are histrionic and religious. We need to watch the ways of its charm: That it rehearses a rhetoric of "received opinion" is both its danger and its apparent timelessness. I also intend to follow a hidden theme in certain fiction, particularly Baldwin's, which suggests that repetition (dramaturgic and rhetorical) breeds anticipation.

Fictional character is the upshot of certain formalistic and thematic strategies aligned in final ways. If the strategies are shifted around, then character changes decisively. That observation alone is nothing new. In fact, we can even look forward to it as a leading proposition of the woman critic's vigil of male writers, but my deeper point is to try to demonstrate the impact of the grammar of male and female relationships as the crucial component of the "politics of intimacy." A contract is implicit; the partners either share power or engage a heirarchy of motives, but relationships, whether they end or not, have an outcome—thus the motive of power. To say that relationship boils down to nothing but the assumptions which operate behind the façade of language is to be reductionistic, perhaps, but it is clear that the terms of relationship, even in fictive situations, are historically based and lend their characters an attitude, more or less suitable to them. In other words, once it is clear how fictive situations may pursue a locking of female and male destiny, then it will be clearer, perhaps, how everyday language and its situation create an attitude of containment or liberation.

Perhaps it can be fairly argued that all myth, specifically its translation into notions of social hierarchy and political status, is concealed in eternal valuation. So robbed of their historical detail, men and women in intimate situations appear wild and colorful: man against woman, the battle of the sexes; try as we will, it is not always so easy to avoid these configurations of thought, and I must admit a certain profound pleasure in entertaining this dream of history. Indeed, we could go so far as to say that a certain quality of mental and imaginative life is inconceivable without the dreaming, mythic mind, but reality intrudes on myth and seeks to plunder it. The burden of consciousness appears to be the negotiation between myth and reality.

The "exotic" engenders no such negotiation and like an eternity, which it imitates, is the same, everywhere, for all time. "Heritage," one of the Countee Cullen's poems from the 1920s,[1] embodies the Exotic Ideal in U.S. poetry. The world view out of which the poem is made has no live notion of "Africa" as a continuous series of cultural movements, but has it as symbolism, a status which can be achieved, not unlike the Calvinist Heaven, by blessed election. The subject becomes, as a result, an essence whose mystery is inherent. "Feminine mystique," "feminine intuition," "male logic," "strong black woman" belong to this category of a historical notation.

Baldwin's long-suffering females show this symbolic value as a consistent thematic feature of the writer's career from *Go Tell It on the Mountain* to *If Beale Street Could Talk*. Not unique among American writers in this respect, Baldwin is certainly the most eloquent. His women characters usually occupy a central place in his fiction, and as tragic heroines, their foretaste of disaster gives them a dignity and largeness of movement which outsize life. The weight of lamentation falls most strikingly on them because they have no language relevant to their specific condition, generating humor, variety, and above all, personal moral choice. Florence Grimes, the sister of Baldwin's preacher in *Go Tell It on the Mountain,* is a child of Mother Legend, expanding the tale of Emancipation to its northern border. Proud and brooding, Florence comes North, haunted by ancient enmities, her own sickness unto death. When she confronts the altar on the night of the saints, tears coming down like "burning rain," she stands in fear of death and pride of heart. Serpent-eyed death teases her: "God's got your number, knows where you live, death's got a warrant out for you."[2] As appealing as this Old Testament drama may be, the reader wants Florence to be rid of her demons. Against serpent-eyed death, tears won't do. True to the logic of interdiction and divine justice, Florence will be sacrificed. Gabriel Grimes's wife, Elizabeth, is kin to Florence in her pride and trouble. Also the tale of an odyssey from South to North, Elizabeth's plot line bears the specter of father-riddle—abandonment and unfulfilled love. As pitiless as a stone, gripped by erratic fears, Grimes has only compounded Elizabeth's grief.

With none of the ferocious dignity of Florence, nor the slow halting sadness of Elizabeth, nor yet the strange atavistic mournfulness of Deborah (Gabriel's first wife and God's Holy Fool), Esther is Gabriel's third victim—his illicit lover with whom he has a foredoomed son, Royal. However, Esther is a breath of fresh air in her boldness and charm. A man's woman—sensuous, short-skirted, and teasing—Esther and her mother belong to the swinging, the foxy, and the ruined, and Gabriel is her downfall.

This sketchy summary of Baldwin's women, in what is, perhaps, his finest fiction, reminds us not only of the terms of his statement but also of the moral universe to which he addresses himself. *Go Tell It on the Mountain,* though set in Harlem, occurs outside a specific time and place. As allegory, the entangling takes work well, for all the characters move along a spiritual trajectory whose material correspondence goes from the valleys and back roads of the South to the light of the Northern Temple of the Fire Baptized. In this context, unspeakable suffering is an instrument of enlightenment rather than a brutal or maudlin contrivance of "facts." Baldwin's social facts are only shadows of an infinite reality.

Baldwin's characters, especially his women, are rammed through the try-works too often for us to believe that their world is anything other than an extension of Heaven and Hell. They are so close to fire and brimstone that all they have to do is roll over, go right on to heaven without dying. They need not earn their death, since their time and eternity coexist. We therefore regard their suffering, male-originated, as another instance of God-mischief. What have they done to be so black and blue? We don't know. We're not told, and being able to make no sense of it, we can only grieve for their absurdity or tragedy.

The pattern of female suffering in the novel has its counterpart in the tale of Juanita of *Blues for Mister Charlie*. Richard's lover and a potential liaison of both Meridian Henry (Richard's preacher father) and Parnell James (liberal white editor of the Mississippi newspaper), Juanita represents, we can safely assume, women loyalty. In love with Richard for all time, Juanita is willing to bear any burden as her testimony would have it. On the witness stand, as Lyle Britten is brought to trial for the murder of Richard, she thinks:

> . . . Mama is afraid I'm pregnant.
> Mama is afraid of so much. I'm not
> afraid. I hope I'm pregnant. I
> hope I am! One more illegitimate
> black baby—that's right, you
> jive mothers! And I'm going to
> raise my baby to be a man. A
> man, you dig? (Baldwin) Oh, let
> me be pregnant, let me be preg-
> nant, don't let it all be gone![3]

Right before this, Juanita recalls the last time that she and Richard made love:

> . . . My God. His chest, his belly,
> the rising, the falling, the moans.
> How he clung, how he struggled—

> life and death! Why did it all
> seem to me like tears? That he
> came to me, clung to me, plunged
> into me, howling and bleeding,
> somewhere inside his chest, his
> belly, and it all came out, came
> pouring out, like tears. My God,
> the smell, the touch, the taste,
> the sound, of anguish.[4]

This grim lyricism is the victim's voice, left with its pain and what it anticipates for the future. Is it possible for a black woman to assert another kind of consciousness? The question is relevant if we are looking for responsive strategies to any new historical situation, specifically, the woman as a stranger in urban/industrial experience without man or father to define her. We could put the question another way: What are the terms of definition for women outside the traditional hierarchies? Is female status negated without a male-defining principle?

Two important elements are opposed in the question, and Baldwin's *Beale Street* embodies both in the love story of Clementine Rivers and Alonzo Hunt. It is clear that the opposition between obedience and liberty is the crucial thematic component of this tale, and it is precisely this opposition which women seek to restore as a dialectical notion. In *Beale Street,* obedience (female) and liberty (male) are irreconcilable opposites in this family drama set in modern Harlem.

Baldwin's metaphor for young Afro-American manhood, Fonny Hunt, is ingenious and imaginative; his plot line reflects the urban experience of black males like himself. His encounter with a white cop leads to his arrest for the alleged rape of a Puerto Rican woman. Fonny is framed by Officer Bell for reasons which are historically and psychologically profound—white male lust for black flesh. Ostensibly, Fonny is thrown in jail because he defends Tish against the sexual advances of an Italian thug on the streets of the Village; not only does Fonny successfully defend Tish against her assailant, but he is also defended in the process by an Italian woman (the owner of the vegetable stand where Tish is shopping), who has witnessed the incident and speaks up in

Fonny's behalf. Officer Bell, the aggregate white cop and the defender of white America's doubtful virtues, is mad in the deepest springs of his emotions. Because he is in trouble, Tish and Fonny are endangered. This is the central story of *Beale Street,* predicated on the American myth of race, and from it unfolds the moving love story of Tish and Fonny, the children of the Hunt and Rivers clans, who endure their separation with heroic love and honor.

Baldwin's themes are familiar, and we've encountered them time and again in his essays and the two works already mentioned here. The unspeakable cruelty of white men is his *cause célèbre,* and in its name infinite horrors are committed. "Uptown" would not be what it is without the awful white menace. To it are conjoined the heroic qualities of black men, their love and honor in the face of terror, but together these contrapuntal forces engender a world essentially joyless, one group living in perpetual and numbing fear of the other. Why and how the promise of new life under these conditions breeds rejoicing strikes this reader as perverse sentimentality. Tish is pregnant (as Juanita of *Blues* hopes she is), Fonny is in jail, Frank Rivers, Fonny's father, will kill himself by carbon-monoxide poisoning, and the woman who can save Fonny, Victoria Alvarez, is hiding out, hysterical, in the mountains of San Juan. Fonny did not rape her; everybody knows it, but Victoria is too confused and terrified to reconsider her allegations, yet, despite all this, the novel ends in diapason celebration:

> . . . You see Fonny today? (Sharon)
> Yes. (Tish)
> And how was he?
> He's beautiful. They beat him up,
> but they didn't beat him. He's
> beautiful . . . Fonny is working on the
> wood, on the stone, whistling, smiling.
> And from far away, but coming nearer,
> the baby cries and cries and cries
> and cries and cries and cries and
> cries and cries and cries like it
> means to wake the dead.[5]

We appreciate, perhaps, the irony of Baldwin's closure as a believable imitation of life rhythm, but the situations of the novel are suspect primarily because the moral obligation of racial continuity devolves on the women. This is not a tragedy, if the women choose it as their "program of action," but the novel, as I read it, poses the problem of choice as one of fate—a locking of destiny wherein the females are doomed to play out time and again the fated conclusiveness of their peculiar emotional temperament—to yield to their love for men—and its inevitable biological destiny, to have children, despite hell.

Because Baldwin has toned down his grammar—exuberant metaphors, biblical allusions, impacted sentences, and the evocation of powerful natural forces—black church ritual and its telluric drama of weeping, moaning, praying saints recede in significance. Since the tale has been removed from out the center of the Eye of God, the novel follows a less convoluted design than *Go Tell It on the Mountain.* Tish's narrative style is, therefore, an easy, graceful informality of tone, and she is charming, generous, and slow to anger with her antagonists, but her acceptance of the terms of obedience (patience, waiting, living for her man) is reminiscent of the Old World sorrow tales of Florence and Elizabeth.

Love in the novel is achieved variously: Tish and Fonny as sexual partners; Sharon and Joseph Rivers as parent-lovers; Ernestine and Tish as sister-lovers; Joseph and Frank as brother-lovers; Frank and Fonny as father and son reconciled. Love within this circle is sufficient to its own ends, and the novel suggests that continuity, or the passion for survival, is most probable under conditions of courage. This is all very nice, but the love between man and woman here is predicated on the surrender of the female's imagination. Baldwin, interestingly enough, puts the words in Tish's mouth:

> He [Fonny] was a stranger to me, but joined. I had never seen him with other men. I had never seen the love and respect that men can have for each other . . . It can be a very great revelation. And, in this fucked up time and place, many women, perhaps most women, feel, in this warmth and energy, a threat.[6]

About a quarter of the way through the text, this passage is central to the novel's logic and order. We would do well to brood over it, for it also contains more than one element crucial to Baldwin's metaphysics. We cannot miss the high moral seriousness of the passage which resembles the essay in its claim to truth. Suddenly, we're in the midst of a righteous divination from the controlling drama with Tish as something of a mountebank. Tish will not be this "sensible" and high-toned again. In fact, we are not used to this kind of penetration from her, since, in a few pages, she will relinquish this delicious understanding in a put-down of Fonny's mother and sisters. This elevated vision, not of her own doing, we suspect, is Baldwin usurping her role in order to re-enforce his moral point. Its careful elaboration has its complement elsewhere, particularly *Notes of a Native Son* and *The Fire Next Time*.

The word "stranger" has an interesting echo here in calling up what we imagine to be the historical alienation between men and women, but note that the burden of sensation falls on Tish—*she* senses his strangeness to her as though he is some half-fabulous creature from another world whose essence is eternally concealed from her eyes. The rest of the passage supports the mystery. The "love and respect" that men "can have for each other" is somehow quite different from the passion between the sexes and, perhaps, more desirable in its "warmth and energy." It seems to me that this desirable thing, from which women are excluded by virtue of natural law, should not be threatening, but a matter of envy, a goal to be attained, woman to woman. To see it as threat is to evaluate it through male eyes, since the proposition assumes that women don't have it and experience, therefore, an absence or lack of genuine camaraderie. But note: It is only because the "time and place" are "fucked up" that women perceive "love and respect" among men as a threatening thing. It is just possible that disorder is a human product and has something to do with a man's insistence that he is a "stranger" to a woman and she, therefore, eternally "the other."

This brotherhood which Baldwin perceives has its own language, its singular idiom, which women can neither manipulate nor even decipher. According to Tish, maleness is a hieroglyph of experience, based on nothing more concrete than the accident of birth. This is not unlike a Calvinist election in which case only God knows why some are more equal than others, and its mysterious celebration reverberates racial dogma where white is simply right. One is more than others just because.

Whether or not men can grow up without women is quite beside the point. In our time, they usually don't (and vice versa). Under special historical circumstances—wars, migration movements spurred by unemployment when both men and women tend to move singly or in packs, or under special sociohistorical arrangements like monasteries and abbeys—the sexes may undergo temporary isolation from each other, but otherwise, men and women are neighbors, both subject to mutability and death. If Baldwin means that men and women grow up knowing or anticipating quite different experience, then we can vouch for him, since they clearly inherit "received opinion" radically different from each other in its thrust and emphasis. An aspect of woman legacy is: "You're a girl. You can't do what your brothers do," and this is later conjoined with sentiments like Tish's: Men are strangers.

"Mystery and terror" are quite appropriate to the figure of thought that Tish outlines, since both terms speak, by implication, to issues which are older than a modernist vocabulary. "Bottomless terror," the woman's archetypal nightmare of male manipulation or rejection, belongs to this category of nighttime things. It is precisely the nighttime of the human race that "bottomless terror" belongs to because it is irrational and profoundly concealed. But "terror" is an important word for Baldwin, even seminal and ubiquitous, from the awful dread of John Grimes in the face of his father's divine wrath to the sorrow of Jaime, one of Baldwin's Puerto Rican characters in *Beale Street*. Jaime's "terror" is unutterable," just as "terror" in Baldwin, in line with his metaphysics, is always unutterable. In fact, I cannot think of a single character, male or female, in Baldwin's works, who has been freed from these Awful Unspeakabilities. That the latter are rarely specified relegates them to a Heideggerian category of primordial dread, and the characters' most persistently remarkable feature is their inability to speak their trouble, but in a Manicean order, personality is immersed in chaos, a dark sweltering density of confusion where the same nightmare keeps repeating itself, time and time again. Since action is predicated on the chaos of experience, then character is stalled in a preconscious intent where John may as well be Dick or Tom, swimming around in the nightmare of the race. On this level, the sexes, ironically enough, are equal—both confused, both benighted.

Fonny, however, has been given intelligence, even art, and purpose: He is Baldwin's sculptor, spending long hours fashioning objects of art from wood. For Tish, this "other life" of Fonny's is his defining passion. At what will be their loft back in the Village, Tish recounts this scene:

> . . . he moved away from me; his heavy hands seemed to be attempting to shape the air—"I live with wood and stone. . . . all I'm trying to tell you, Tish, is I ain't offering you much. . . . you gone have to work, too, and when you come home most likely I'll just grunt and keep on with my chisels and shit and maybe sometimes you'll think I don't even know you're there. But don't ever think that, ever. You're with me all the time, all the time. Without you I don't know if I could make it at all, baby, and when I put down the chisel, I'll always come to you. . . .[7]

There follows from the proposition a telluric love scene, complete with the rupture of Tish's hymen and the powerful flow of blood and seed:

> Well, we were something of a sight. There was blood, quite a lot of it—or it seemed like a lot to me, but it didn't frighten me at all, I felt proud and happy—on him and on the bed and on me; his sperm and my blood were slowly creeping down my body, and his sperm was on him and on me; and, in the dim light and against our dark bodies, the effect was a strange anointing. Or, we might have just completed a tribal rite. . . .[8]

This stirring rites of passage, carried out against the background of Fonny's workshop, defines both the dramatic and the rhetorical significance of Tish's story: She not only yields to the terms of relationship as Fonny has imagined them but also sanctifies her complicity in notions which disguise her wonderful passivity. "Strange anointing," "tribal rite," "proud and happy," are offered with not a trace of irony or second thought; Tish, true to romantic deception, is swept away by what her imagination has made a powerful eventfulness, hinting of first and last things. Her situation is precisely passionate, even agonistic, and whether or not it destroys her will depend a great deal on Fonny's generosity.

She has already told us earlier that a woman exists at the *mercy* of a man's imagination, and since the contract is merciful, then we need not wonder for long why Tish's love for Fonny is devout and all-consuming. She had *better* keep it together, being at his mercy, not unlike the weeping saints of the Temple, who kneel around God's altar. Baldwin would have us believe, however, that Fonny is more human and enlightened than the God of Darkness, even grants certain concessions to the woman: "I'll always come to you, I'll always come to you." But at the other end of this beneficent gesture is, of course, the waiting, patient female, who has no chisels and stone and wood to *live with*. What she does have is a dream of her strong man, and one's strong man can change his mind, as he often does, despite his promises, so for the woman, trust gets to be risky business. The man, after all, is at liberty, and in Fonny's case, plans to organize his love and work around a central place, the loft. Exactly what Fonny needs Tish for may be rather precisely guessed by anybody, since art is his "real life," but Tish, in love and trouble, seeks to contain the contradiction. To Fonny's apologia, she responds: "'Of course it's alright with me,' I said. I had more to say but my throat wouldn't open." We're very close to enthusiasms here with this otherwise articulate woman (she "tells" the whole book) struck dumb.

We already know Who calls people by the Thunder—and it is not Fonny—and Who, also, has people in His Hands, by God, and we also know how the elders say "I felt a change" when God converts one's life, but Baldwin has his tribal rite working here, and the juxtaposition of mystical language and sexual intent is not an error. Tish's love is transcendent, and we can nearly smell her demon-possession:

> All that I could do was cling to him. . . .
> everything was breaking and changing and
> turning in me and moving toward him. . . .
> I heard, I felt his breath, as for the first
> time. . . .[9]

Tish *receives* Fonny's breath like a mystic might feel divine afflatus, but better than the mystic-lover is able to achieve, Tish has a demigod and man all wrapped up into a single living visible enigma. Baldwin, rather cunningly, has spliced together sacral impulse and secular practice into a swift concord of passion and purpose. This is heady stuff, and we should know, having been there before in our own naïveté and enchantment, but the kind of love projected in Tish and Fonny's story is not of this earth which insists that the gift of love, not even promised, must be earned through responsibility and error. The scene portrayed in these pages is love falling down, or spewing up, sacerdotal and whole, from some supernatural source. We are not far from the divine ground of being when lover becomes a presence: "It was a strange weight, a presence coming into me—into a man I had not known was there. . . ."[10]

The passage, by implication, is a revisitation of the myth of hyperbolean phallic status, the powerful male member which "stiffens and grows and throbs" and brings Tish to "another place." One laughs and cries, then both together, then calls out the lover's name. When men and women in church "get happy," they do the same thing, and it is all very well, but the potential problem for Tish is that Fonny has an option not allowed her or any of the other women in the novel. Fonny can return to his "real life," leaving Tish with the memory of their passion, waiting until he comes again (pun intended).

Baldwin is on the verge of something other than female sorrow in this novel, but he draws back from that something else, leaving his females in an essential state of emotional dependence. More precisely, the expense of female energy here is man-compelled, man-obsessed. When the women act (and they are probably his most active heroines) their action flows from the law of love; therefore, they exist for others. By contrast, or at least such contrast is implied, the men act on their own authority, a sometimes contradictory, curious mix of freedom and gallantry.

Since all the characters are black and, therefore, exaggeratedly vulnerable to the political power of white, none of them is free in the sense that Sartre might have meant it—being for oneself—but Baldwin has them moving in that direction, a forecast which decisively marks off the emphasis of this text from others written in the sixties. Perhaps a transition, *Beale Street* stands at mid-ground between Baldwin's religious dramas and his brave new world, and his characters talk, then, out of both sides of their mouths, or perhaps the writer does. The women can take things in hand—Sharon Rivers goes to San Juan alone, without Spanish, to bring back Victoria Alvarez in person, but at the same time, she and her daughters, even Ernestine, perhaps the freest woman here, subscribe to traditional forms of behavior. After the stirring love scene, Fonny takes Tish home in order to explain to her parents why he has had her out so late. In the process, we imagine, he will assure Joseph (Tish's father) that his intentions are honorable. Fonny and Joseph go to another room of the house as the three women—Ernestine, Sharon, and Tish—await the outcome. That left-alone room-locked men often embroil the world in trouble—and call it "responsibility" for women—is no longer a secret, but the real point is that the powerful myth of brotherhood is a symptom of status and secrecy from which the exclusion of women is a dangerous re-enforcement of difference, but more than that, such exclusion magnifies the prerogatives of power in its negation of individual conscience. In the conference of the like-personalities, loyalty is a decisive motive and whether or not loyalty is responsible is a principal question of peace settlements and all historical movements. That these notions echo in Baldwin's pages re-enforces to my mind the decidedly hierarchical motions of this story.

Men are, in fact, men, and what they decide unto themselves is beyond the ken of women-reason. Why, in this case, Joseph and Fonny have to isolate themselves momentarily appears to be the chasing after taboo. Tish believes that their doing so is most eventful primarily because she accepts the terms of secrecy, wants to have it, wishes to believe that there is, indeed, some cause or reason more ultimate than her own to be assigned to Joseph and Fonny. Again, it is the accretions of mythical belief subtly playing over the surface of Tish's mind: By substitution, Fonny and Joseph are the custodians of a hieroglyph of experience to which access is granted only the priest, or the prince, or the warrior. This is a currency of belief I'd associate with medieval life, and not recent Harlem. It certainly opposes notions of tedious democratic order where the principals work through the substance and formality of problems.

This detail has its complement earlier in the text when the women are left alone, but, not as brotherly to each other as the men, the women hassle. We don't wonder that the men split: The women together have no sense. They call each other names, and before it's all over (about six agonized pages later), Ernestine spits in Mrs. Hunt's (Fonny's mother) face. Mrs. Hunt is the mad puritan, coming to visit the Rivers women and to condemn Tish's "lustful action":

> I always knew that you would be the destruction of my son. You have a demon in you—I always knew it. My God caused me to know it many a year ago. The Holy Ghost will cause that child to shrivel in your womb. But my son will be forgiven. My prayers will save him. . . .[11]

The men leave, and what follows is an elaborately clinical scene, reminiscent of the T-group when participants confront each other with an unstinting rehearsal of their individual weaknesses, but there is nobody here to dispense the Kleenex or "resolve the conflict." Mrs. Hunt is as ridiculous and isolated and pathetic as the moment she walks in the house. Now she gets insulted.

Whether or not she brought on her own nemesis by cursing the unborn is quite beside the point, nor is it very interesting that she is a "dried-up yellow cunt" versus dark, sensuous folk, but it is certainly remarkable that her parody is unrelieved and that these otherwise compassionate women have no tricks up their sleeves to calm her. The one thing they agree on is that Fonny must be free, so their essential fight is not that the child has been cursed, but how will Fonny be possessed, and by whom. Mrs. Hunt is supposed to be the typically covetous hen, clucking over her brood, threatened by the advancing guard of hens, but none of them appears to notice that they engage a false motive, disguising from themselves their genuine fear—Fonny is potentially free and at will to choose both his love and his work. That they cannot perceive the common enemy (the woman's fear to risk aloneness or a self-imposed silence) but choose, instead, the noise and clamor of vain gestures, betrays the writer's mockery of their pain. If everybody really is so offended beyond the common domestic courtesies, then why not have them fight it out? At pitch anger, can women only spit in each other's face? To "take it to the whoop," as men might say, would draw out the worth of the issue. After all, one fights for his life, or decides not too slowly that his life is not at stake. We could call it interestedness, but less than that, one dances in an attitude of interestedness without risking the dangers of decision. The women are safe from each other because they are selfless, in the shadow of the men and their time.

Living for their men, the women are an extension of the men's integrity. We may, therefore, regard their existence as inauthentic. Though such an evaluation is borrowed from the objective world, it is useful, by analogy, in exposing the opposition between symbolic behavior and freedom. The latter takes its chances in the world, risks the possibility that its status is sliding and relative, in tension with its environment and other human beings; the former, on the other hand, seeks a role to play, minimizing the spontaneity and danger of freedom. In objective time, neither symbolic behavior nor freedom exists in unalloyed autonomy, and we slide rather more subtly from role to freedom from it, back again. The fictional character, however, names his or her destiny in the very fact of characterization and is determined by laws of fiction as inexorable as fate. "Acting out of character," "inconsistent with character," describe our reaction to characters in real life or fiction who behave in a way that shocks or negates our expectations. In fact, our rebellion is often directed toward breaking from a role which others have imposed on us when we least suspected, or one that we have adopted ourselves to facilitate or appease or disguise some human process. But role moves toward mystification of personality, and, as a borrowing from the language of the theater, suggests stylization of personality as well. This happens in relationships when men and women insist that their functions are fixed and symbolic.

It is precisely this fixing or symbolification that Frank implies in *Beale Street* when he tells his daughters that they should be out on the streets "selling pussy" in order to raise enough money for the defense of Fonny, their brother. Since Frank has the idea, perhaps he should sell whatever the male equivalent of "pussy" would be in order to free his son. Because "pussy-selling" is alleged to be the traditional response of women trapped by circumstance, Frank is able to make his daughters feel guilty about their womanhood. Frank would have them assume a symbolic task—perhaps it has nothing to do with whom or what they think they are, but everything, in his eyes, with what woman is.

There are societies where the symbolic personality is paradigmatic,[12] but in our situation with its emphasis on freedom and responsibility, self-reliance and individual esteem as variations of existentialia, the rhetorical personality tends to be an exaggeration or a distortion. New World history has moved decisively toward "I" as the dominant mode of all ethical consideration. The argument is not whether this is best, but that our circumstances militate against conservatism of motive as a strategic response to experience: Women work outside the home, very often away from their families, and they seek, therefore, a new centrality around which to build their lives. In other words, the vision of paternity, or father as central authority, has receded. In the absence of the father, the lone woman may seek to restore the notion of responsibility and authority by investing it anew in another male, but the challenge, not to be put off, is that the woman seek reconciliation by seizing her own potential.

In this sense, vocation, or relationship to the world of work, dictates a shift in the woman's metaphysical landscape. Where there was father protection, or parental authority of some kind, there is now risk, and the woman is thrown back on her own reserves. Nothing stands now between her and the world, lest intellectual, artistic, or political activity fill up the vacuum. Under new historical conditions, based in the division of labor as the central mode of discourse, and the rise and expanse of the professions, life issues are seen to emanate from concrete sources. Now status, or standing, is the right not only to earn one's own money but to dictate also how one will organize her own consciousness of time as an instrument of creative endeavor.

The impression that freedom is always antagonistic to role-playing is false, although we may simplify the analysis by opposing them. This theoretical opposition by way of fictive characterization moves us into the right ball park, so to speak, but it does not exhaust the game or the "program of action" which women engage in in their own "politics of intimacy." Outside fiction, the question is: What are the terms of relationship to be worked out between partners when the social and moral condition, given a change of slope in the landscape, conforms to other than traditional life patterns? By implication, the man is also drawn into the inquiry, and whatever changes of status the woman sustains will also affect him in dynamic ways. These changes in the propositions of relationship, the soil from which they spring, lead us to perceive the "politics of intimacy" as a dialectical encounter rather than an antagonism of opposites—in other words, the situation requires *conversation,* the act of living among others, in all the dignity and concentration that the term implies. It is this tension in our dynamic experience which shocks mythic expectations.

As we have seen in *Beale Street,* love between Tish and Fonny is noumenal—something God-given, the marriage made in Heaven, not quite of this earth—and therefore, it escapes the dynamic character of reality. This escape names the common attitude of both characters—their perceptions, their values, their activity, are colored by these symbolic assumptions which they take on as a function of legacy. In having achieved the perfect symbolic union, they demonstrate the paradox of motion—touched by death, moving on this earth, in this time at once. Their situation is closed.

In objective experience, this attempt to block the corruption of time and mutability in intimate encounter often leads the woman to error. First, she imbues the male with an extraordinary dimension, as Tish gives Fonny "strangeness." This kind of fantastic investment often amounts to confusion of the sex act with the commitment of love. (Tish makes the sexual encounter a "tribal rite.") Men appear less confused about it, but it is very likely that our own susceptibility to the assumptions of European courtly love tradition and, closer, the Puritan equation between love, sex, and duty leads to this confusion of historical necessity. The truth is that we may not need this baggage of inherited belief in order to express love and companionship. Again, love and companionship for one's mother (whose entire life was sacrificed to her children) must be understood in light of the daughter's different situation.

Secondly, the woman in love tends to assume that *all* the particular males of her race "belong" to her—"our men." These males become, then, an extension of her own ego, while she, ironically, gives up her authority to them in intimate encounter. The perception of love as possession is a distorted feature of the woman's urge for permanence, but it is particularly dangerous to locate that urge in a man, since he is not the object of her own personal history, but the primary subject of his own. One possesses objects; even better, one tries to create them. Toni Morrison's *Sula* is a compelling recent fiction whose heroine eloquently demonstrates this issue:

> In a way her strangeness, her naivete, her craving for the other half of her equation was the consequence of an idle imagination. Had she paints, or clay, or knew the discipline of the dance or strings; had she anything to engage her tremendous curiosity and her gift for metaphor, she might have exchanged the restlessness and preoccupation with whim for an activity that provided her with all she yearned for. And, like an artist with no art form, she became dangerous. . . .[13]

Morrison's message is clear—and it is my own: Women must seek to become their own historical subject in pursuit of its proper object, its proper and specific expression in time. In that sense, male absence or mutability in intimate relationship is not the leading proposition of a woman's life, but a single aspect of an interlocking arrangement of life issues. Through the discipline and decorum exacted by form, the woman's reality is no longer a negation, but a positive and dynamic expressiveness—a figure against a field—shaped by her own insistence.

Thus, the grammar subsumed by the theme of intimacy and its accompanying attitudes and hidden assumptions are parodic unless they reflect a situation whose contradictions have been heightened. The new grammar has no particular standard or rule, unlike the dictates of courtly love or the laws of "seduction and betrayal," but will be shaped by the specific environment of relationships. Under the impetus of alternative—one of them contraceptive and chemical—women, in short, introduced a new dynamic to the old equation of love. From the fragments of the myth of male dominion, we seek to structure a new way of saying things, one apposite and graceful to the new situation. The urgency is to acquire a language which expresses the woman's grasp of reality as present and immediate; even in love, such urgency must not be suspended.

NOTES

1. This much-anthologized poem is perhaps best identified by its opening six lines:

    What is Africa to me?
    Copper sun or scarlet sea,
    Jungle star or jungle track,
    Strong bronzed men, or regal black
    Women from whose loins I sprang
    When the birds of Eden sang.

   Arna Bontemps, ed., *American Negro Poetry* (New York: Hill & Wang, 1963), p. 83.
2. James Baldwin, *Go Tell It on the Mountain* (New York: Alfred A. Knopf, 1953), p. 91.
3. James Baldwin, *Blues for Mister Charlie* (New York: Dial Press, 1964), Act III, p. 125.
4. James Baldwin, *If Beale Street Could Talk* (New York: Dial Press, 1974), pp. 196–97.
5. Ibid., pp. 58–59.
6. Ibid.
7. Ibid., pp. 76–77.
8. Ibid., p. 81.
9. Ibid.
10. Ibid., p. 79.
11. Ibid., p. 68.
12. Intended to be read by Lionel Trilling at the Jane Austen Bicentennial Conference at the University of Alberta, October 1975, "Why We Read Jane Austen" was not delivered by the author, who was too ill to attend. Trilling died in November 1975. Picking up observations made by Clifford Geertz, the distinguished anthropologist, Trilling shares many insights into the epistemology of culture with a discussion of Javanese and Balinese societies as an aspect of his own argument (*The Times Literary Supplement*, March 5, 1976, pp. 250–52). The essay is unfinished.
13. Toni Morrison, *Sula* (New York: Alfred A. Knopf, 1974), p. 105.

Images of Self and Race in the Autobiographies of Black Women

by MARY BURGHER

Prior to the surge of interest in Black culture during the late sixties, few critical examinations of the Black woman's past and of her cultural and creative spirit were available to readers of Black American literature. Most critical anthologies either did not examine specifically the works of Black women or they tucked brief analyses of a few "representatives" within the corners of a section or near the end of an essay. The effect was twofold: Black women writers were the stepchildren of Black American literature—an indistinct adjunct to the mainstream of Black writing—and stereotypes of Black femininity and myths about the Black woman's role were left largely unquestioned.

The scene has changed. Toni Cade (*The Black Woman,* 1970), Mary Helen Washington (*Black-eyed Susans,* 1975), and this volume as well as others by Black female critics and scholars have been focusing increasingly on the cultural impact and the artistic merit of the literature of Black women. With sensitive yet objective eyes, they have begun to reveal the multiplicity and diversity among Black literature's long-neglected "stepchildren." They have begun to explore the realities of Black feminine experience and to define the roles and the images of Black women as reflected in their literature and their lives.

The autobiographies of Black women are rich and valid sources for further studies of the Black woman and for critical inquiries into how she has viewed herself historically despite labels, myths, and ideas about her place and role. If any form of literature is capable of aiding in the Black woman's attempts to correct the record, it is autiobiography, for nowhere does one find literature as a celebration of life more than here. Even when the writer is not an artist and although actual events and highly personal experience often abound, the life stories of Black women are poignant and sensitive definitions of self and compelling expressions of the unchanging needs and ideals of the Black race.

Images of the Black Woman as Slave

Black women were brought to the United States to breed slaves, attend to the personal needs of slaveholders, care for their families, and—if they were strong enough—work in the fields, too. Breeder, concubine, mammy, mule. The ante bellum ideals of womanhood—delicacy, shrinking mannerisms, sexual innocence, and social grace—were luxuries slave women could seldom aspire to. The few extant narratives by slave women indicate that most often they measured their worth in self-respect, moral courage, strength of mind, and, most important, in their capacity to love. Obviously unable to ignore the role forced on them by their masters, they blended the external shields of strength and tenacity required of them with an inner core of tenderness and compassion.

To illustrate, at the age of seven Harriet Tubman was compelled to become a child's nurse as well as a field hand. Being too small to hold the child while standing, Tubman often was placed in a chair where she remained rocking the child until her mistress returned hours later to lift it from her arms. By the age of eleven years, she had an adult's sense of responsibility and the calloused, work-hardened hands of a field slave, yet all her life she was able to express love and understanding toward those placed in her care, and to have faith in their knowledge—and hers—that she was a different woman inside than her crude men's clothing and deep, urgent voice made her appear outside. Although Harriet Tubman was illiterate, her oral accounts of her experiences as a slave and as a freedom fighter for her people indicate that she had amazing physical strength and moral courage. She walked, ran, hid, coaxed, cajoled, and prayed until through her efforts three hundred Black people had been rescued from a lifetime in chains. Her activist role forced her to be strong, seemingly invincible, but her persevering love of freedom and of Black people was her true strength, the hidden life force that defined her as a woman. The tenacity of spirit that enabled her to rescue so many Blacks from slavery also rescued her, inwardly, from total brutalization by a system that denied her and other slave women the luxuries of softness, grace, and prevailing notions of beauty.

Speaking from the floor at a Women's Rights Convention in

1853, another noted slave woman, Sojourner Truth, expressed the predicament of slave women in these words:

> . . . That man over there says that women need to be helped into carriages everywhere. Nobody ever helps me into carriages, or over mud puddles, or gives me any best place, and ain't I a woman? Look at me! Look at my arm! I have plowed and planted and gathered into barns, and no man could head me . . . and ain't I a woman? I could work as much and eat as much as a man (when I could get it), and bear the lash as well . . . and ain't I a woman? I have borne 13 children and seen them most all sold off into slavery, and when I cried out with a mother's grief, none but Jesus heard . . . and ain't I a woman too?[1]

This now classic statement is both a protest and an affirmation. It aggressively protests society's refusal to acknowledge Black women as women—even if such acknowledgment is condescending to feminists. Yet it quietly affirms the historical identity of Black women: strong, hard-working, unprotected, unpampered women who retain, nevertheless, a wealth of tenderness and compassion.

A slave for forty years, Sojourner Truth is described in her narrative as strong yet imaginative; she was a tall dusky woman who walked with great authority. Yet the tone of her numerous anecdotes of love and death, religious ecstasy, and physical punishment suggest that there was much compassion in her authoritative air, her fiery outbursts and protests, and there was gentleness beneath her physical vigor. In telling the story of her life as a slave and an advocate for the rights of Blacks and women, she creates vivid images of herself as a woman who views physical strength and native intelligence as life-sustaining forces and resiliency and moral courage as invaluable tools of progress and freedom, however unfeminine they might make one appear to others. Her first meeting with Sojourner Truth prompted Harriet Beecher Stowe to write, "her tall form, as she rose up before me, is still vivid to my mind. . . . She seemed perfectly self-possessed and at her ease; in fact, there was almost an unconscious superiority, not unmixed with a solemn twinkle of humor, in the odd, composed manner in which she looked down on me."[2]

Stowe's use of terms such as "unconscious superiority" and

"odd, composed manner" suggest a reluctance to accept these qualities as anything other than the special demeanor of exceptional Blacks. Yet slave women who were not "cultural heroes" like Tubman and Truth and whose life stories were recorded in the autobiographies of other slaves perceived themselves in much the same way and with a very wholesome self-esteem. In *Twelve Years a Slave* Solomon Northup describes Patsey, a field hand, as ". . . slim and straight. She stood erect as the human form is capable of standing. There was an air of loftiness in her movement, that neither labor, nor weariness, nor punishment could destroy," although she was often badly used by her master.[3] Her situation is parallel to Harriet Jacobs, who narrated to L. Maria Child her story of seven years of imprisonment to avoid concubinage. While Patsey's rejection of concubinage is not as aggressive as Jacobs', it suggests reliance on the same qualities: moral courage, self-respect, and refusal to become inwardly brutalized. Similar also is Henry Bibb's description of his wife, Malinda, and her struggles to retain self-respect and the love of her family. Unlike Patsey and Harriet, however, after years of abuse Malinda's spirit is broken and she succumbs to her master's idea of what her role should be, rationalizing that at least she was better used than ordinary slaves.

Older slave women like Frederick Douglass' grandmother, William Wells Brown's mother, and Harriet Jacobs' aunt are described traditionally in ante bellum literature as breeders and mammies, but if their actions are examined carefully, these silent, seemingly passive women consistently translated the Black slave woman's role as nurse and breeder into ethnically progressive and individually creative identities. According to the narrators of their stories, they instilled in their sons positive survival skills, aided in their development of self-awareness and created among the younger slaves, the group-mindedness and interdependence that even today are the mainstay of Black families.

The Black Woman-Child

Just as the ante bellum South's worship of helpless femininity clouded and debased the vigorous womanhood conceived and lived by Black women during slavery, contemporary ideas about the formation of feminine roles in childhood and the proper stages of growing up also have led to myopic interpretations of Black women. Most writers quickly recognize and acknowledge—often negatively—the womanly status the Black female assumes at an early age. But few reveal the special blending of adult responsibility with sensitivity and curiosity that make the Black woman forever youthful, vibrant, and creative. In *Tomorrow's Tomorrow,* Joyce Ladner says that the various myths which surround the Black community can be seen in microcosm in the Black female adolescent who, primarily because of the different prescriptions and expectations of her culture, reaches her status of womanhood at an early age.

The Black woman's need to grow up fast, bypassing a leisurely childhood, emanates from harsh environmental conditions coupled with strong interdependent and intraresponsible familial relationships. The collective consciousness inherent in "We're all in this together" and "We must do it for ourselves or do without" necessitates adult awareness, grown-up strength, and independence at a very early age. Thus, more often than not, the route to Black womanhood is fast and direct. Zora Neale Hurston's autobiography, *Dust Tracks on a Road,* illustrates this point. Written about her life during the first half of this century, it records a girl's robust and spirited search for a place in the world and it includes several chapters describing her childhood in the rural poverty of an all-Black town in central Florida. Remembering her early years, Zora Hurston says, "I was weighed down with a power I did not want [visions and dreams]. I had knowledge before its time. I knew my fate."[4] She is referring specifically to the visions and premonitions she claimed to have had at age seven, but her observations are also a comment on the flavor and direction of her life which seemed already determined. Her life demanded that she learn or create the appropriate techniques for coping with it and transcending its cruelties. Hurston learned and created, coped and transcended, and her experiences, particularly her use of dreams and visions as guiding forces in her life, were uniquely her own, but the urgency in her childhood and her early sense of "grown-upness" are not. They are the inheritance of the Black woman-child.

Hurston says that her "real childhood" ended with the coming of these visionary experiences, and on one level it did. She left home at age nine when her mother died, then after a little schooling and many house-cleaning and child-nursing jobs, she left Florida at the age of fifteen. For a time thereafter, she worked as a maid for a traveling show, a manicurist in a barbershop, and a servant to well-to-do Black families in Washington, D.C. Following the do-it-yourself-or-do-without pattern set by slaves before her, she became, of necessity, a hard-working woman long before her teen years were fully lived. Arriving in Harlem during the twenties, at the height of the Harlem Renaissance, Zora Hurston found herself with one dollar and fifty cents, no job, no friends, and a lot of hope, to become, not much later, a Black novelist, folklorist, and vivid interpreter of the fears and aspirations of Black people.

Dust Tracks is permeated with images of agony and urgency, yet Hurston never loses, until very near her death, the desire to experiment with life and try out its possibilities. This kind of optimism is a truer measure of youthfulness than frailty and innocence. Her autobiography excels in capturing this quality. Throughout the first half of her story she sees and defines herself as a symbol of the Black woman-child who accepts adult responsibility, yet remains forever youthful in her optimism and her curiosity about life. Clearly, then, if Hurston's story is at all symbolic, growing up quickly and becoming seemingly unfeminine in the pragmatic life-style they must adopt have not robbed Black women of youthfulness—a precious quality they retain and celebrate in their writing as well as in their lives.

More than a quarter of a century after Hurston's autobiography, Maya Angelou describes in *I Know Why the Caged Bird Sings* a similarly brief and painful-pleasurable childhood. Her autobiography reiterates and expands concepts of Black womanhood dramatized in earlier autobiographies by Black women. It also provides insight into the Black woman's migration from the southern rural environment with its hardening poverty and racial cruelty to the sobering realities of St. Louis, San Francisco, and other urban settings.

The Caged Bird moves swiftly from the tranquility of childhood to the horror of an eight-year-old girl being seduced and assaulted by her mother's friend. The lazy, slow-motion childhood Maya Angelou might have expected abruptly ends: "I was eight, and grown."[5] Of course she is not. One cannot survive the kind of experience Maya Angelou describes without losing a part of one's innocence and peace of mind. Yet she attempts to do so. With the same kind of push-pull ambivalence slave women exhibited toward ante bellum femininity, she both yearns for and rejects the adulthood that is thrust upon her.

After Maya Angelou's return to her grandmother's home in Arkansas, following her assailant's mysterious death, her world seems actionless and wordless. She wants Stamps, Arkansas, to be a cocoon whose "obscure lanes and lonely bungalows set back deep in dirt yards" allow her to be again a child. She wants "to be left alone on the tightrope of youthful unknowing" and to "experience the excruciating beauty of full freedom and the threat of eternal indecision."[6] But she has been shocked into awareness, and like other Black women in other places with other experiences, she cannot afford the luxury of "unknowing." Thus, within the next few years, her experiences include racing a car in Mexico, sleeping for a month in an abandoned automobile, working as a streetcar conductor in the predawn hours of San Francisco, giving birth to a healthy Black son, being a madame for two aging prostitutes, and being a prostitute herself. "I gave up some youth for knowledge," she remembers, "but my gain was more valuable than the loss."[7]

Doubtless, Maya Angelou, as well as Zora Hurston and other Black women autobiographers, write about experiences more varied, much harsher, and at times more beautiful than most others encounter. They create incisive and sensitive images of womanhood that are meaningful to all Black women who struggle to come to terms with the hardships and violence just beneath the surface in Black experience. *The Caged Bird,* like other autobiographies by Black women, is a valuable resource to the understanding of Black women because it reveals and symbolizes the Black woman's daring act of remaking her lost innocence into invisible dignity, her never-practiced delicacy into quiet grace, and her forced responsibility into unshouted courage.

Black women like Maya Angelou who write about their childhood with all its limitations and possibilities seldom do so with bitterness and despair. Ida B. Wells, born a slave in 1862, later dubbed "pistol-packing Ida," refused all of her life to succumb to adversity. From the time she finds herself, at age sixteen, and following her parents' death, the mother-father-big sister to other children in the family to her first act of defiance against racism in a segregated railroad car, she not only follows her own precedent of militant resistance to humiliating and degrading conditions but also retains the moral strength, physical vigor, and spiritual buoyancy characteristic of the Black woman-child. Similarly, Daisy Bates, remembering the capricious cruelty of the white South particularly during the violence of school desegregation in 1957, maintains a constant and identifiable level of spiritual buoyancy in her autobiography. As the autobiographies of these women suggest, the Black woman's positive sense of self and of race is not shattered by the experiences she has.

Yet many critics and anthologists give little attention to the bursts of joy mingled with protest in these works, or to the vibrant descriptions of Black men, present or missing, or the revelation of dreams whether fulfilled or not. While critics may point out the protest, the missing men, and the unfulfilled dreams, they seldom see that the Black woman's detailing of these painful experiences is a profound celebration of self: It is a way of saying I perceive all that is wrong, I see where my life has gone awry, but I have the sensitivity, the talent, the language—all obtained against great odds—to expose that which has gone awry and to celebrate what has not. Nikki Giovanni cryptically capsules the Black woman's dilemma in historical and critical literature when she notes in "Nikki Rosa," "they'll probably talk about my hard childhood and never understand that all the while I was quite happy."[8]

Images of Black Motherhood

According to their autobiographies, most Black women, when they were children, were happy and optimistic despite poverty or other forms of deprivation, including the double-edged burden of racism and sexism. Many, in fact, remember the ambivalent, good-bad years of their childhood as a brief but intense preparation for early adulthood, which they also describe ambivalently—probing into the traditionally unfeminine traits they acquired and survived on and using the act of writing about themselves or their female parents and relatives as a means for unveiling the complexities in the adult life of a Black woman.

Particularly meaningful and recurrent in the autobiographies of Black women is their concept of motherhood. It is seldom a monolithic view, easily categorized under a single, stereotypic label. Instead, Black women who focus on this aspect of their lives are more concerned with the multidimensional response of Black women to the honorific yet restrictive place motherhood assumes in life and in literature. Against a background of racial and sexual myths—breeder, provider of numbers for the race, stabilizer for the community, matriarch—Black women autobiographers consistently expand motherhood into a creative and personally fulfilling role.

In her autobiography or in her daughter's, the Black mother's knowledge and endurance of America's racial hostility and violence are envisioned as strengthening and motivating tools with which she prepares others of her race for self-sufficient and productive lives. In *I Know Why the Caged Bird Sings,* the first of three autobiographical works, Maya Angelou remembers her grandmother in this role. Mrs. Henderson is an ageless and timeless symbol to her grandchildren as well as to other Blacks and whites in Stamps, Arkansas. Maya writes: "a deep-brooding love hung over everything she touched," and "Just the gentle press of her rough hand conveyed her own concern and assurance to me."[9] Her mother, whom she struggles throughout her youth and early adulthood to understand, also emerges as a strong, culturally motivating force in her life. She is Vivian Baxter Jackson, "hoping for the best, prepared for the worst, and unsurprised by anything in between."[10] When Maya becomes a mother herself at age sixteen, Mrs. Jackson initiates her daughter into the natural, nonindividualistic consciousness of Black motherhood: "You don't have to think about doing the right thing. If you're for the right thing, then you do it without thinking."[11]

In the autobiographies of Black women, motherhood is a nonindividualistic, cultural force that is not based solely on procreation, breeding, or providing numbers. It means a great deal more. It means being individually creative in whatever task is before one. It means ordering the universe—or whatever small part of it one can claim—in the image of one's personal concept of beauty, and transmitting this conception along with a respect for strength to one's heirs. Alice Walker expresses this dimension of the Black mother's consciousness of self and race in an essay entitled "In Search of Our Mothers' Gardens." She says that it was to her mother that she went in search of the secret of what has fed that "muzzled and often mutilated, but vibrant, creative spirit" that is the Black woman's inheritance. She discovers that the Black mother, sometimes unconsciously and sometimes as a conscious artist or writer, hands on the creative spark, the legacy of Black strength, that ensures the progress of the race.[12] In autobiography and other forms of Black literature the Black mother is the actor or the doer in a subordinate sense. Primarily, she is the impetus or the catalyst which enables others to act or to do. Carolyn Rodgers' description of her mother as "the great Black bridge I crossed over on"[13] dramatizes the cultural weight Black mothers bear. Dynamic embodiments of cultural beliefs, aspirations, and fears, often they are seeds that flower only in their heirs.

Usually the strongest members of the community spiritually, Black mothers assume the responsibility of retaining and communicating values and ideals that support and enhance the Black community as a viable unit separate from but interrelated to the larger society which surrounds and seemingly suffocates the Black race. Values specifically attributed to Black mothers include the beliefs that there is a promised land beyond this life of bondage and oppression, that one has within oneself the natural wit and resourcefulness to find strength in apparent weakness, joy in sorrow, and hope in what seems to be despair, and that the love of a mother cannot always be determined by physical presence or material gifts. Frequently, the love and kinship of family and race grow out of hardship, or shared suffering, and out of the love and concern that harsh admonitions and beatings imply. In *His Eye Is on the Sparrow,* Ethel Waters describes a home life of poverty, violence, and crime, yet throughout her story, she stresses the love and concern communicated to her in her grandmother's insistence on daily baths, her loudly spoken rules on clean Christian living, and her beatings if Ethel forgot her prayers. Waters' image of Black motherhood is a strong, hard-working woman who does what is necessary—including stealing food and fighting with sinful relatives—to ensure the survival of her children. Although frantic with the defeats that have occurred through the years, the Black mother, according to Waters, never quits on you.[14] These values suggest that the Black mother, whether or not she is able to articulate it, sees herself not as a breeder nor as a matriarch but as a builder and nurturer of a race, a nation. Women, Sojourner Truth once said, are the mothers of creation. About her particular role as mother and crusader for truth and justice she said, "Why, I feel so tall within—I feel as if the power of a nation is within me!"[15] The proud sense of identity in this exclamation did not grow only out of Sojourner Truth's ability to bear children and protect and provide for them. Her statement is an affirmation of the essential role of Black women as seminal forces of the endurance and creativity needed by future generations of Blacks not merely to survive, but to thrive, produce, and progress.

Images of Black Women During the Seventies

The civil rights movements of the fifties and sixties produced a number of Black women activists whose stories about their lives present dynamic versions of Black women's concepts of self and race. One of these autobiographies, *The Long Shadow of Little Rock,* is an often shocking and bitter protest against white America's social and political oppression of Blacks. Yet the events and experiences Daisy Bates describes reveal a woman with an optimistic and progressive consciousness that reaches beyond the concerns of her own family into the needs and interests of the total Black community. Her sensitivity and creativity as a Black woman were formed by an awareness of beauty in the land and in the people around her, and even more important, by a personal buoyancy—a spirited perseverance—despite adversity and apparent ugliness. To illustrate, at the age of seven years, Daisy Bates learns from a routine trip to the grocery store that a Negro in her hometown had no rights that a white man was bound to respect and that for her father to question a white grocer about giving his child fat meat instead of the center cut pork chops she had ordered was to choose between living and dying. At eight years, she learns that her mother had been murdered years before by three white men and that her father, in helpless despair, had left her with neighbors to be raised as their child.

Like Black females before her, Daisy Bates had to grow up fast so that she could cope with and possibly transcend the sufferings so frequent in her life. In *The Long Shadow of Little Rock,* she says, "So happy once, now I was like a little sapling which, after a violent storm, put out only gnarled and twisted branches."[16] This estimate of herself is harsher than it need be, but seeing herself not as free, but as the seed of the coming free, she also sees that the pain in her growing up is not negative or defeating, but a strengthening force for her seminal role in the school desegregation crises of the 1950s. Her political awareness and her creative use of the strengths and coping techniques that began with slave women are preludes to the bold confrontations with the political nature of racism and sexism recorded in autobiographies written by Black women during the seventies.

Ideas and experiences vary, but Shirley Chisholm, Gwendolyn Brooks, Angela Davis, and other Black women who wrote autobiographies during the seventies offer similar but expanded visions of the Black woman's role in the struggle for Black liberation and of her positive, celebratory sense of Black womanhood. The idea of collective liberation prevails in Shirley Chisholm's *Unbought and Unbossed* and in *Angela Davis: An Autobiography*. This idea or ethos says that society is not a protective arena in which an individual Black can work out her own destiny and gain a share of America's benefits by her own efforts. Most Blacks simply do not feel they have that kind of autonomy; most know that individual control over what happens to one is almost impossible. Accordingly, survival, not to mention freedom, is dependent on the values and actions of the group as a whole, and if indeed one succeeds or triumphs it is due less to individual talent than to the group's belief in and adherence to the idea that freedom from oppression must be acted out and shared by all.

This is not an unexpected or startling idea, for Chisholm and Davis are recognized political activists. What is significant is their ability to use the movement of their personal lives as a dynamic expression of collective Black liberation. Chisholm relates instance after instance in which the needs of her people shape the actions of her life. "My role," she explains, "is more that of a catalyst. By verbalizing what is wrong, by trying to strip off the masks that make people comfortable in the midst of chaos, perhaps I can help get things moving."[17] Envisioning herself as a voice for her race's struggle for justice and equality, Chisholm seldom probes into the private, individual implications of her activities. In *Unbought and Unbossed,* her identity is clearly female and Black. Recognizing, however, that no one can be equal to the impossible task of representing all Blacks in the country and curing all the evils of hundreds of years of racism and sexism, her political vision is pragmatically optimistic and her sense of self, like less political Black women before her, is quietly and consistently humanistic and celebratory.

Angela Davis' autobiography also reflects the absence of self-interest and the increased political awareness of Black women in the seventies. Her political expressions in *An Autobiography* may not be agreeable to all, but her examination of the motives and experiences that led to her imprisonment in 1970 reveals a woman who is in control of her ideals and who possesses the intellect and the power to pull her readers and audiences away from personal survival techniques into an awareness of far-reaching political strategies—beyond those strategies for attaining day-to-day necessities and immediate satisfactions. As noted earlier, slave women and Black mothers traditionally found themselves bound by time and circumstances to instill a basic survival consciousness in their heirs. Black women activists like Davis strive to do more. To illustrate, Black women have viewed suffering as a redemptive tool that strengthens one, not so much for retaliation as for personal survival and racial growth. In *An Autobiography* Davis pushes the idea of redemptive suffering further. As the experiences in these writings suggest, because of her perception of what has happened and is happening to Black people, she refuses to accommodate to the constitutionalized "truths" of this country. Moreover, she does not write about her experiences to provide the victims (Blacks) of these "truths" with redemptive symbols, or to soothe the victimizers (white Americans) with hopes of a calm future. Reading *An Autobiography* is not a passive encounter. One sees and feels the torment of unfreedom and the meaning of perseverance in the face of seemingly overwhelming odds. About George Jackson's death she says, for example, "My tears and grief are rage at the system responsible for his murder." Compelling baptismal images follow her declaration of rage. "George's death would be like a lodestone, a disc of steel deep inside me, magnetically drawing toward it the elements I needed to stay strong and fight all the harder. It would refine my hatred of jailers, position my contempt for the penal system and cement my bonds with other prisoners."[18] The lumps and welts of unmerited suffering are there—exposed, unrepaired. The writer emerges unredeemed but cleansed by her strength and freed by her determination to act.

Whether or not one agrees with the political ideology in *An Autobiography,* one senses the liberating effect of her refusal to succumb to conditions and her refusal to accept prevailing notions about her capacities as a Black and as a woman.

Of all the qualities which may be explored in an attempt to understand the myth-ridden, stereotyped Black woman, the most revealing are that it is not she separately who is significant and it is not what she attains personally and immediately that matters; instead it is what the future brings from the ideas she expresses, the consciousness she reflects, and the actions she takes. In *Report from Part One,* Gwendolyn Brooks, who describes her new Black consciousness and her aesthetic and ideological alignment with young Black nationalist writers, expresses such a vision of herself. She says that "there *is* something different that I want to do. I want to write poems that will be non-compromising . . . that will be meaningful to those people I described a while ago, things that will touch them." Explaining that she is not writing poems with the idea that they will become "social forces," she also describes the political and cultural thrust of her writings, her ideas, and her actions: "I think I've had some hand . . . in spreading this new spirit [Black solidarity and pride in one's brothers and sisters]. I saw how proud and how strong Blacks were becoming. Their confidence in themselves was inspiring. They knew they were right; they had the essentials."[19] Whether or not she intentionally and primarily conveys a social message in her post-sixties poetry and her autobiography, the idea that stands out in these works as in her life is that amid the worst and best of circumstances—"Black people in taverns, Black people in alleys, Black people in gutters, schools, offices, factories, prisons, the consulate"—there is beauty in them and in oneself.

In the autobiographies of Black women, one finds the essence of Black experience, including the qualities that have ensured the survival and the growth of Black people. But this is not their uniqueness, for much of contemporary Black literature fulfills this cultural need for its Black readers. The uniqueness of the autobiographical literature of Black women is its powerful and poignant portrayal of both the anguish and the joy of Black life in a largely white world, and its poignant portrayal of what it feels like, inside, to be a woman in such a world. Not everything the Black woman writes or says about herself is positive; certainly, there is still some negativism in her concepts of self and race. Still, the Black woman's blend of physical strength and vigor with inner tenderness and compassion; her awareness that growing up too early does not have to rob one of youthfulness, curiosity, and optimism; her insistence that motherhood is a creative, nation-building role; and her awareness that to be Black and female is to be political are all authentic and vital dimensions of the Black woman's concept of herself and her race. For too long these vital dimensions have been ignored, lost, overlooked, or perverted by critics and scholars handicapped by preconceptions, biases, naïveté, and ignorance. It is time to recognize that while every Black woman wrestles, individually, with her own identity, most have taken at least part of the journey described in the autobiographies discussed in these pages. Black women have absorbed the vigorous and courageous self-concept of slave women and added proud, confident, activist roles to their lives.

NOTES

1. Sojourner Truth, *The Narrative of Sojourner Truth* (1878) (New York: Arno Press, 1968), pp. 120–21.
2. Ibid., pp. 151–52.
3. Solomon Northup, *Twelve Years a Slave,* in Gilbert Osofsky, ed., *Puttin' On Ole Massa* (New York: Harper & Row, 1969), p. 327.
4. Zora Neale Hurston, *Dust Tracks on a Road* (1942) (New York: Arno Press, 1969), p. 65.
5. Maya Angelou, *I Know Why the Caged Bird Sings* (New York: Random House, 1970), p. 70.
6. Ibid., pp. 74, 231.
7. Ibid., p. 217.
8. Nikki Giovanni, *Black Feeling, Black Talk, Black Judgement* (New York: William Morrow & Co., 1971), p. 59.
9. Angelou, pp. 47, 96.
10. Ibid., p. 244.
11. Ibid., p. 246.

12. Alice Walker, "In Search of Our Mothers' Gardens: The Creativity of Black Women in the South," *Ms.*, May 1974, pp. 68, 70.
13. Carolyn M. Rodgers, *How I Got Ovah* (Garden City, N.Y.: Doubleday & Company, 1976), pp. 11–12.
14. Ethel Waters, with Charles Samuels, *His Eye Is on the Sparrow* (Garden City, N.Y.: Doubleday & Company, 1951), p. 11.
15. Truth, p. 134.
16. Daisy Lee Bates, *The Long Shadow of Little Rock* (New York: David McKay, 1962).
17. Shirley Chisholm, *Unbought and Unbossed* (Boston: Houghton Mifflin, 1970), pp. 170–71.
18. Angela Davis, *Angela Davis: An Autobiography* (New York: Random House, 1974), pp. 319–20.
19. Gwendolyn Brooks, *Report from Part One* (Detroit: Broadside Press, 1972), pp. 152, 177.

It is partially because of the symbiotic nature of oppression that Black mother characters have been pushed through a sieve and been relegated to two cauldrons: Eve or Madonna. Daryl Dance scrutinizes the hazards and ironic benefits which inhere in these two (too) limited roles of the Black child-bearer, using masters familiar to aficionados of Black literature—Baraka, Baldwin, Killens, Ward, Wright—to prove her points and proffer a perennially logical posture.

Black Eve or Madonna?

A Study of the Antithetical Views of the Mother in Black American Literature

by DARYL C. DANCE

In the biblical story of the creation we find a situation not unlike that in accounts of the creation of the world in other ancient myths. We find that woman is half accountable for the sins of the world—for the downfall and destruction of mankind. It is Eve who succumbs to the temptations of the world and who also tempts Adam to eat the apple and thereby calls down the wrath of God upon the two of them as well as their children and all of their children's children, all succeeding generations.

But if it is woman in the person of Eve who gives birth to the sins of the world which destroy man, it is also woman in the person of Mary who gives birth to the Savior who brings redemption and salvation to man.

Within these two extreme views of woman—the mother who brings death and destruction versus the mother who brings life and salvation—where does the Black American mother stand? It seems to me that it would not be inappropriate to look at the literature, not as mere fiction, but rather as an interpretation and compilation of history, anthropology, sociology, psychology, and a host of other areas. Thus the true literary artist reveals life more accurately and with more insight than any historical facts and statistical details, because he deals with the truth of the human heart, with the realities of man in society. Therefore, let us consider what our literary artists have had to say about the role of the Black American mother.

A surface reading of Black literature may well lead one to the disturbing conclusion that the Black American mother is an Eve who has succumbed to the tempting allurements and wiles of the Devil—the Devil in this case being white American society—and that this Black Eve offers to her Black men the poisonous apple that will destroy him, that will repress his spirit and vitality, kill his pride in his Blackness, and render him impotent in a hostile white world. Such a curse cannot help but damn future generations of Blacks, and thus this threatening evil force must of necessity be hated, repelled, and, if possible, destroyed.

One of the most talented of our contemporary writers, LeRoi Jones, or Amiri Baraka, has written a morality play called "Madheart" in which one character, lest we miss the symbolism, is named Mother. Having eaten of the tree of white American life, Mother is a prostitute and a drunkard, intoxicated not only by wine but also by the lure of white society and its symbols. She loves and wants to protect white Devil Lady, who wishes to seduce and destroy Black men. She hates her Black men and is appalled and bewildered by the Black youths and their appreciation of their Blackness. As the major character, Black Man, views this old, diseased, broken woman and her "lost" daughter, he asserts, ". . . this can't go on, this stuff can't go on. They'll die or help us, be Black or white and dead. I'll save them or kill them."[1]

In his "Experimental Death Unit #1" Baraka portrays a vile, diseased, drunk, forty-year-old whore with drooping stockings, who tries to protect two repugnant white leeches from Black Revolutionary Soldiers, whose motives and actions bewilder her. The revolutionaries kill her and she falls, Baraka writes, "terribly surprised, ignorant."[2] While Baraka does not specifically portray her as a mother, he forces us to see this despicable creature in this symbolic role when he has one of his soldiers play the dozens with another whom he accuses. "That bitch looks just like your mother!"[3]

In another play by Baraka, "A Black Mass," with its constant references to the role of the Black woman as mother, a fertile life-giving force, one of the women, Tiila, is attacked by the horrible white monster who turns Blacks white. She is consequently transformed into an animalistic, white robot-type monster. Because she has been, in Baraka's words, "touched by this foulness,"[4] she must be cast off from her people. She is no longer a person. "She is," rather, as the wise character Nasafi indicates, "the void. The evil of blank cold licking the stars."[5]

Another young Black writer, Jimmy Garrett, wrote a play in which a young Black revolutionary is dying, but he does not wish to see his mother because he knows that having eaten of the apple of the tree of white American society, she uses her strength to emasculate her men. Nonetheless, the mother comes to him, and like Baraka's mother, she is too old to understand the militancy of Black youths and dismayed at their willingness to die for their freedom. She preaches instead love, religion, and respect for the white man, whom she would have her son emulate. Unable to accept this apple, the dying boy vehemently exclaims, "Motherfuck . . . Mama and all them house niggers. Death to the house niggers." Pointing his gun at his mother, he avers, "We're . . . new men, Mama . . . Not niggers. Black men." Then he kills her.[6]

Contrasting with these authors who apparently view the Black woman as a fallen Eve who must be destroyed before she corrupts others, numerous Black writers have paid tribute to the Black mother as a Madonna bringing salvation to her Black children. Such is the tribute recently paid to her by Maya Angelou, who avowed:

> There is a kind of strength that is
> most frightening in Black women.
> It's as if a steel rod runs right
> through her head down to the feet.
> And I believe that we have to thank
> Black women not only for keeping the
> Black family alive, but [also] the white
> family. . . . Because Black women have nursed
> a nation of strangers. For hundreds
> of years, they literally nursed babies
> at their breasts who they knew, when
> they grew up, would rape their daugh-
> ters and kill their sons.[7]

George Jackson has written, "The Black woman has in the past few hundred years been the only force holding us [the Black race] together and holding us up."[8]

When Black novelists have attempted the epic of their race, they have chosen the Black woman as the symbol of her people. In his saga of the Black race in America, Ernest J. Gaines has chosen Miss Jane Pittman as his Everyman—or should I say Everywoman? It is she who suffers the indignities of slavery; sets out on the quest for freedom; embodies the unfulfilled dreams, the suffering, the bitter struggles, the endurance, and the strength of her people; and who finally overcomes. Margaret Walker's Vyry in *Jubilee* also fulfills the role of a Black Everyman, though she lacks the strength of character and the broader vision of Miss Jane Pittman.

How, then, can we reconcile these antithetical views of the Black American mother? Is she a destructive Eve offering the poisonous apple or a Madonna bringing hope and salvation? Actually the paradox is not so great as these contrasting versions I have presented suggest. The writers who have dealt the Black mother a death blow as a dangerous Eve have, I believe, condemned her mainly for one sin—the emasculation of the Black man. If I may be permitted a bit of levity here I might suggest that this might at first be construed as the typical male tendency to blame women for their own shortcomings as suggested in this account of the creation.

Her Sphere

When wives were quiet unprecedented
In Eden, where that first tree grew
When Eve, that is, was just invented
And even Adam was rather new,
A good idea occurred to Adam,
A theory and a practice too;
"Your sphere," he said, "will be,
dear Madam,
To bear the blame for what I do."[9]

More seriously, it seems to me that these writers in their bitter attacks have been dealing in a symbolic way with only one aspect of the character of the Black mother and have been calling for the destruction, not of the Black mother, but rather of that aspect of her character that white racist society has forced her to develop—the repression of the spirit and vitality of her Black men, whether as a result of her blind acceptance of the dictates of white American society or her subservience to them. This emasculation of the Black male has been an obnoxious feature of American society from slavery to the present, and the Black mother has been unwillingly forced into the role of accomplice.

It is hardly necessary to recount the emasculating effects of slavery where a Black man could not even legally marry, or if he selected a woman as his wife, could in no way protect her. He had to stand powerless if any white man chose to beat her, abuse her, or take her to his bed. His children could be taken from him and sold at the will of his white slaveowner. He himself could be snatched away from his family at any moment, and sold like any chattel of the field. The despair and hopelessness he faced in these and similar degrading situations have been poignantly recorded by many former slaves in any number of slave narratives. The kind of psychological emasculation and dependence developed in the Black male during slavery continued after emancipation. This economic system denied him the opportunity to compete with white men for the kinds of jobs that would bring pride and relegated him to degrading tasks or total unemployment. For the ordinary Black man the same situation too often exists even today, and if his despair at his inability to fulfill his role as father and provider doesn't drive him away from home, the welfare laws will.

Because the Black man has historically been stripped by society of his authority, pride, and manhood, the Black woman has naturally been forced to assume a dominant role. It is she who has often been faced with the tasks not only of providing for her children but of shaping their characters and preparing them to live in this American society. As Doctors Grier and Cobbs point out in their perceptive psychological study of the Black psyche, accurately titled *Black Rage,* "This is every mother's task. But the Black mother has a more ominous message for her child and feels more urgently the need to get the message across. The child must know that the white world is dangerous and that if he does not understand its rules it may kill him."[10] Thus at every point in her child's development, the Black mother, cognizant of the slave master, the lynch mob, the present-day legal system, had to teach her child to mask and repress his normal masculinity and aggressiveness lest these put his life in danger. She had in other words to prepare him for his subordinate place in the world.

That Black sons often interpreted a mother's repression as a lack of love and developed hostility toward their mothers for inhibiting them is a psychological fact, but that their mother's repression saved them is also a fact—an unattractive reality of American life. Without that repression, this country's lynching statistics would be even more horrifying and our mental institutions would be even more crowded. If their mothers had not prepared them for the abnormal role forced upon them in American society, particularly in the South, many would have either been killed or lost their sanity. That a man could not walk into the southern Jim Crow system without a great deal of psychological preparation was attested to by New York author James Baldwin. Though he knew what to expect, he found in his first trip South that he was not psychologically prepared to deal with the insults and the humiliations without making the wrong step or wrong response that might jeopardize his life. The fear and tension of experiencing the life which Black Southerners daily endured thrust him into a complete collapse when he got back to New York, a collapse he described as a paralyzing "retrospective terror."[11]

And yet, despite the historical necessity for the Black mother's repression of her offspring, young Black boys have never understood her behavior until later, and this has had a profound psychological effect on the relationship between them and their parents. This may be seen in an incident which actually occurred in the life of Black novelist John Oliver Killens. The deep-rooted effect it had on him is attested to by the fact that he has written and rewritten the incident, both in autobiographical sketches and in fiction. In the novel *Youngblood,* Robby beats some white boys who were attempting to rape his sister. The sheriff naturally arrests the Black boy, for Blacks must never hit whites—regardless of the circumstances, and, of course, in any legal conflicts Blacks were automatically guilty. The mother is called to jail and given an ultimatum. Robby will be charged with assault and sent to the reformatory or she must beat him with a whip in front of white men. The mother, realizing the horrors of Black reformatories in the South, is thus forced to beat her son's naked back until it bleeds. The humiliation the boy feels in the presence of these whites and the hatred he feels toward his mother tear her heart to pieces, and the distraught mother realizes that whites are not only cruel to Blacks, they actually "turn your own children against you."[12]

Innumerable incidents of this nature abound in Black literature —of the Black boy who is punished for fighting whites, no matter what the provocation. Richard Wright recounts a similar incident in "The Ethics of Living Jim Crow," in which he fought back when attacked by whites who left a long gash in his neck that required three stitches; instead of offering sympathy, his mother beat him and lectured him in "Jim Crow Wisdom," warning him that "I was never, never, under any circumstances, to fight *white* folks again."[13]

A novel whose main thesis deals with the effect of living in white American society on the relationship of a Black mother and her children is John A. Williams' *Sissie,* titled after the dominating mother whose memory haunts her children's lives. As her two children, Ralph and Iris, relive their childhood on their way to Sissie's deathbed, they both feel a great deal of hostility and animosity—even hatred—for their Black mother. But Ralph finally reaches some kind of understanding and says to his sister, "Don't be too hard on her—she was strong in her way, stronger than any of us will ever be. I think she has to be."[14] Then later, considering his mother's love, he says, "Love? What is that? Giving love to children was a luxury she couldn't afford and when she could, she had got out of the habit. I don't mean that she didn't *have* the feeling. Love? You know, that's whipping the crap out of your children so that they don't crack their heads against the walls that make up the labyrinth, and if they don't they might live and make out somehow. That's a kind of love, isn't it . . . ?"[15]

That is indeed a kind of love—the deepest and strongest kind—the kind that must require a mother to hide her natural emotions and punish her child to save him; the kind that allows her to see the horrors that await her child in the northern ghettos and the southern race belts and still face that difficult task of teaching him to survive in them. Baldwin says of his mother, who raised them in a Harlem ghetto, "She was a very tough little woman, and she must have been scared to death all the years she was raising us." Further, he adds, "I think she saved us all" (the nine children).[16]

Indeed from a historical perspective the Black American mother emerges as a strong woman who, though she had from her beginnings in this country suffered rape, humiliation, and despair, has nonetheless successfully and continuously faced the difficult task of supporting and maintaining her children *and* preparing them to cope with the world, *and* to succeed in it. Unquestionably it is this—her love, her strength, her endurance, her ability to survive in the most ignominious circumstance—that has made possible the new militant who sometimes fails to appreciate the Black mother's role and many too hastily condemn her as a hated Aunt Jemima. He fails to appreciate her strength and endurance which are so necessary to the victory he desires and toward which she has been moving and moving him all along.

Many Black authors suggest the lack of understanding that has led youthful militants to reject the strength that lies behind the Black woman's apparent docility in certain instances. This is humorously treated in Douglas Turner Ward's *Happy Ending,* where the young nephew spurns his two motherly aunts because of their apparent love of and concern for their white folks. He accuses them of having no race pride and exclaims, "Never have I been so humiliated in all my life."[17] It turns out, however, that this young man's fine clothes, his delectable food, his comfortable home, and his generally prosperous way of life have been procured as a direct result of their apparent "bonuses" that make their lives comfortable—*bonuses* meaning the extra benefits they swindle from their employer. As a result of the nephew's new awareness, there is a happy ending in which he pays tribute to his "cagey aunts."[18] A similar situation is suggested in Ruby C. Saunders' "The Generation Gap." The narrator in the poem is an older Negro in a menial job, but one who always took up for "Colored" men, including Rap Brown, and one who keeps up with what "whitey" is doing. The poem concludes:

I don't wear my hair all nappy
Don't throw my fists up in the air
I can't wear them African garments
On my subway job no how.

> But I knows that
> You's in colleges and schools
> All over this land
> Got good jobs and houses, senators,
> Congressmen, the vote . . . plans!
> Now just because this is so
> And the white folks calls you news
> Remember, . . . Tom . . . and . . . Aunt Jemima
> Bent low to pay your dues.[19]

A similar appreciation of the role of the apparently unaware mother in laying the foundation for the forming of the more race-conscious and political contemporary Black is seen in Carolyn Rodgers' poem "It Is Deep," when she cautions, "don't never forget the bridge that you crossed over on." She goes on to picture the strong and loving mother, who, though unaware of the new Black pride and contemporary militant leaders, is nonetheless one who has "waded through a storm" and paved the way for her child.[20]

Indeed as we look back over the history of the Black American mother, we see that she emerges as a strong Black bridge that we all crossed over on, a figure of courage, strength, and endurance unmatched in the annals of world history. She is unquestionably a Madonna, both in the context of being a savior and in terms of giving birth and sustenance to positive growth and advancement among her people. It is she who has given birth to a new race; it is she who has played a major role in bringing a race from slavery and submission to manhood and assertiveness. It is largely because of her that we can look back on the past with pride and look forward to the future with courage.

NOTES

1. LeRoi Jones, *Four Black Revolutionary Plays* (New York: Bobbs-Merrill, 1969), p. 87.
2. Ibid., p. 15.
3. Ibid.
4. Ibid., p. 36.
5. Ibid., p. 37.
6. Jimmy Garrett, "We Own the Night," in LeRoi Jones and Larry Neal, eds., *Black Fire: An Anthology of Afro-American Writing* (New York: William Morrow & Co., 1968), p. 540.

7. Maya Angelou, quoted in *Jet*, 45 (December 13, 1973), p. 48.
8. George Jackson, *Soledad Brother: The Prison Letters of George Jackson* (New York: Coward, McCann & Geohegan, 1970), p. 24.
9. Alice Miller, *Women Are People* (New York: n.p., 1917), p. 52.
10. William H. Grier and Price M. Cobbs, *Black Rage* (New York: Basic Books, 1968), p. 61.
11. James Baldwin, *No Name in the Street* (New York: Dial Press, 1972), p. 57.
12. John Oliver Killens, *Youngblood* (New York: Trident, 1975), p. 211. Writing of a similar incident in his own life, Killens comments: "every Black American must learn . . . that he has no inalienable right to defend himself from attack by Mister Charley . . . the cruelest aspect of this story is how they used Black mothers to drive this lesson home." See John Oliver Killens, *Black Man's Burden* (New York: Simon & Schuster, 1965), pp. 104–5.
13. Richard Wright, *Uncle Tom's Children* (New York: Harper & Brothers, 1940), p. 4.
14. John W. Williams, *Sissie* (New York: Farrar, Straus, 1963), pp. 38–39.
15. Ibid., p. 41.
16. James Baldwin, "Disturber of the Peace: James Baldwin," an interview, in C. W. E. Bigsby, ed., *The Black American Writer* (Baltimore: Penguin, 1971), Vol. 1, 211–12.
17. Douglas Turner Ward, in William Couch, Jr., ed., *New Black Playwrights* (New York: 1971), p. 33.
18. Ibid., p. 46.
19. Ruby C. Saunders, in Orde Coombs, ed., *We Speak as Liberators,* (New York: Dodd, Mead, 1970), p. 165. Quoted by permission of the author.
20. Carolyn Rodgers, in Richard A. Long and Eugenia W. Collier, eds., *Afro-American Writing: An Anthology of Prose and Poetry* (New York: New York University Press, 1972), Vol. 2, 780–81.

When the first draft of *Sturdy Black Bridges* was complete in 1976, Alice Walker had, by then, created twenty-five distinctly different Black women in her poetry and fiction. Those volumes include *Once* (1968), *Revolutionary Petunias* (1973), *The Third Life of George Copeland* (1970), *In Love and Trouble* (1973), and *Meridian* (1976).

Walker is a prolific and imaginative artist who, within a relatively short space of time, has become a touchstone in Black literature, especially that created by female writers. Hardly any conference or seminar on Black American literature can be called viable without proper attention being paid to Walker's visionary plots, her laconic style impacted with a premature wisdom, her fervent regard for history (especially) that associated with the Civil Rights era), or her perceptive and fertile analyses of continuing social dramas.

Mary Helen Washington's "Essay on Alice Walker" grew from a larger project—her doctoral dissertation. In addition to the standard primary and secondary works on Walker, Dr. Washington had access to special materials and experiences generously furnished by the author herself. Thus, Washington's descripion of Walker as a "poet, novelist, short story writer, critic, essayist, and apologist for Black women" is profound and apt.

An Essay on Alice Walker

by MARY HELEN WASHINGTON

From whatever vantage point one investigates the work of Alice Walker—poet, novelist, short story writer, critic, essayist, and apologist for black women—it is clear that the special identifying mark of her writing is her concern for the lives of black women. In the two books of poetry, two novels, one short story collection, and many essays and reviews she has produced since she began publishing in 1966, her main preoccupation has been the souls of black women. Walker herself, writing about herself as writer, has declared herself committed to "exploring the oppressions, the insanities, the loyalties, and the triumphs of black women."[1] In her first four published works—*Once,*[2] her earliest book of poetry; *Revolutionary Petunias,*[3] also poetry; *The Third Life of Grange Copeland,*[4] her first novel; *In Love and Trouble,*[5] a collection of thirteen stories—and her latest novel, *Meridian,*[6] there are more than twenty-five characters from the slave woman to a revolutionary woman of the sixties. Within each of these roles Walker has examined the external realities facing these women as well as the internal world of each woman.

We might begin to understand Alice Walker, the apologist and spokeswoman for black women, by understanding the motivation for Walker's preoccupation with her subject. Obviously there is simply a personal identification. She says in her interview with John O'Brien, "I believe in listening—to a person, the sea, the wind, the trees, but especially to young black women whose rocky road I am still traveling."[7] Moreover her sense of personal identification with black women includes a sense of sharing in their peculiar oppression. In some length she describes her own attempts at suicide when she discovered herself pregnant in her last year of college and at the mercy of everything, especially her own body. Throughout the interview with this writer in 1973,[8] Ms. Walker spoke of her own awareness of and experiences with brutality and violence in the lives of black women, many of whom she had known as a girl growing up in Eatonton, Georgia, some in her own family. The recurrent theme running throughout that interview and in much of her other pieces on women is her belief that "Black women . . . are the most oppressed people in the world."[9]

In one of her earliest essays, "The Civil Rights Movement: What Good Was It?"[10] she herself recalls "being young and well-hidden among the slums,"[11] knowing that her dreams of being an author or scientist were unattainable for a black child growing up in the poorest section of rural Georgia, that no one would encourage a black girl from the backwoods to become an artist or writer. In the same essay she recounts an episode in her mother's life that underscores her sensitivity to the peculiar oppression of black women. She saw her mother, a woman of heavy body and swollen feet, a maid in the houses of white women for forty years, having raised eight children in Eatonton, Georgia, turn to the stories of white men and women on television soap operas to satisfy her yearnings for a better life:

> My mother, a truly great woman who raised eight children of her own and half a dozen of the neighbors' without a single complaint—was convinced that she did not exist compared to "them." She subordinated her soul to theirs and became a faithful and timid supporter of the "Beautiful White People." Once she asked me in a moment of vicarious pride and despair, if I didn't think that "they" were "jest naturally smarter, prettier, better."[12]

Walker understands that what W. E. B. Du Bois called double consciousness, "this sense of always looking at one's self through the eyes of others, of measuring one's soul by the tape of a world that looks on in amused contempt and pity,"[13] creates its own particular kind of disfigurement in the lives of black women, and that, far more than the external facts and figures of oppression, the true terror is within; the mutilation of the spirit *and* the body. Though Walker does not neglect to deal with the external *realities* of poverty, exploitation, and discrimination, her stories, novels, and poems most often focus on the intimate reaches of the inner lives of her characters; the landscape of her stories is the spiritual realm where the soul yearns for what it does not have.[14]

In the O'Brien interview Ms. Walker makes a statement about Elechi Amadi's *The Concubine,* a Nigerian novel, and in that statement there is an important revelation about Walker's own writings. She sees Amadi as unique among black writers because through his book he exposes the subconscious of a people; that is, he has written about the dreams, rituals, legends, and imaginings which contain the "accumulated collective reality of the people themselves."[15] It would be possible to apply that same description to Walker's writings about black women, particularly the stories in *In Love and Trouble,* through which we can see a conscious effort by Walker to explore the imaginings, dreams, and rituals of the subconscious of black women which contains their accumulated collective reality. We begin this analysis of Walker's writings with a discussion of her personal identification with the lives of black women because it is that internal personal sharing that has put

Walker in touch with this selective reality. Speaking of her short story "The Revenge of Hannah Kemhuff," Walker says:

> In that story I gathered up the historical and psychological threads of the life some of my ancestors lived, and in the writing of it I felt joy and strength and my own continuity. I had that wonderful feeling writers get sometimes, not very often, of being *with* a great many people, ancient spirits, all very happy to see me consulting and acknowledging them, and eager to let me know, through the joy of their presence that indeed I am not alone.[16]

One vital link to those "historical and psychological threads" of her ancestors' lives is the stories passed on to her by her mother, stories which Walker absorbed through years of listening to her mother tell them. The oral stories are often the basis for her own stories, as are the lives and stories of people she grew up with in Eatonton, Georgia. Once when questioned about the violence and pain in the lives of so many of her women, she recounted an incident from her childhood which was the basis for the story of Mem in Walker's novel *The Third Life of Grange Copeland*. When she was thirteen, a friend's father killed his wife, and Walker, a curious child, saw the mother's body laid out on a slab in the funeral home:

> . . . there she was, hard working, large, overweight, Black, somebody's cook, lying on the slab with half her head shot off, and on her feet were those shoes that I describe—hole in the bottom, and she had stuffed paper in them . . . we used to have, every week, just such a murder as these (in my home town), and it was almost always the wife and sometimes the children.[17]

The true empathy Alice Walker has for the oppressed woman comes through in all her writings—stories, essays, poems, novels. Even in a very brief review of a book of poetry by a woman who calls herself "Ai," Ms. Walker exhibits, almost with conscious design, her instinctive concern for the experiences of women. The choice of *Ai* as a pen name appeals to Ms. Walker because of the images of women it suggests:

> And one is glad she chose "Ai" as her name because it is like a cry. If I close my eyes and say the word (the sound) to myself, it is to see a woman raising an ax, to see a woman crying out in childbirth or abortion, to see a woman surrendering to a man who is oblivious to the sound of her true–as opposed to given—name.

Raising an ax, crying out in childbirth or abortion, surrendering to a man who is oblivious to her real name—these are the kinds of images which most often appear in Ms. Walker's own writing and have prompted critic Carolyn Fowler to say that Walker has the true gift of revealing the authentic "Heart of Woman" in her stories.

What particularly distinguishes Alice Walker in her role as apologist[18] and chronicler for black women is her evolutionary treatment of black women; that is, she sees the experiences of black women as a series of movements from women totally victimized by society and by the men in their lives to the growing developing women whose consciousness allows them to have control over their lives.

In historical terms the women of the first cycle belong to the eighteenth and nineteenth centuries and the early decades of the twentieth century. Although only one of Walker's characters is a slave, the institution of slavery set up the conditions and environment for the period immediately following, extending from the end of the Reconstruction Era to the first two decades of the twentieth century. Borrowing the term first used by novelist Zora Neale Hurston, the black women of this period are "the mules of the world," carrying the burdens heaped upon them by society and by the family, the victims of both racial and sexual oppression. Walker calls them her "suspended" women: a concept she develops in an important historical essay entitled "In Search of Our Mothers' Gardens: The Creativity of the Black Woman in the South," published in *Ms.* magazine in May 1974. Walker explains this state of suspension as caused by pressures in society which made it impossible for the black women of this era to move forward:

> They were suspended in a time in history where the options for Black women were severely limited. . . . And they either

> kill themselves or they are used up by the man, or by the children, or by . . . whatever the pressures against them. And they cannot go anywhere. I mean, you can't, you just can't move, until there is room for you to move *into*. And that's the way I see many of the women I have created in fiction. They are closer to my mother's generation than to mine. They had few choices.[19]

Suspended in time and place by a century, an era that only acknowledged them as laborers, these women were simply defeated in one way or another by the external circumstances of their lives. For such women—the great-grandmothers of the black women of contemporary times—pain, violence, poverty, and oppression were the essential content of their lives. Writer June Jordan calls them "black-eyed Susans—flowers of the blood-soaked American soil."

If these were the pressures and obstacles against the ordinary black woman who existed in the eighteenth and nineteenth centuries, what, then, did it mean for a black woman to be an artist, or want to be an artist in such times? Walker poses the question: "How was the creativity of the Black woman kept alive, year after year, century after century, when for the most of the years Black people have been in America, it was a punishable crime for a Black person to read or write?"[20] If the freedom to read and write, to paint, to sculpt, to experience one's creativity in any way did not exist, what became of the black woman artist? Walker says it is a question with an answer "cruel enough to stop the blood."

> For these grandmothers and mothers of ours were not "Saints," but Artists; driven to a numb and bleeding madness by the springs of creativity in them for which there was no release. They were Creators, who lived lives of spiritual waste, because they were so rich in spirituality—which is the basis of art—that the strain of enduring their unused and unwanted talent drove them insane. Throwing away this spirituality was their pathetic attempt to lighten the soul to a weight their work-worn, sexually abused bodies could bear.[21]

Of course, in spite of these many circumstances in which the art of the black woman was denied or stifled, some evidences of the creative genius of the black women of that age still remain. Walker cites the poetry of Phillis Wheatley, the quilt making of so many anonymous black women of the South, the wise woman selling herbs and roots, as well as the brilliant and original gardens designed and cultivated by her own mother, as evidence that the creative spirit was nourished somehow and showed itself in wild and unlikely places. Though Ms. Walker is the first writer to define and develop the concept of the black women of the post-Reconstruction period as "suspended," as artists "hindered and thwarted by contrary instincts," the suspended black woman is a recurrent theme in the writers who deal with black women. Many of the black women characters in women writers from Frances Harper to Toni Morrison, as well as the women of Jean Toomer's *Cane,* are suspended women, artists without an outlet for their art or simply women of deep spirituality who "stumble blindly through their lives . . . abused and mutilated in body . . . dimmed and confused by pain, unaware of the richness of their gifts but nonetheless suffering as their gifts are denied."[22]

So we have part one of Walker's personal construct of the black woman's history—the woman suspended, artist thwarted and hindered in her desires to create, living through two centuries when her main role was to be a cheap source of cheap labor in the American society. This is the construct developed mainly in Walker's interviews and essays: How, then, does this construct fit in the fiction of Alice Walker?

Most of Walker's women characters belong to the first part of the cycle—the suspended woman. Three women from her first novel, *The Third Life of Grange Copeland,* and seven of the thirteen women from her short story collection, *In Love and Trouble,* are women who are cruelly exploited, spirits and bodies mutilated, relegated to the most narrow and confining lives, sometimes driven to madness. They are the contemporary counterparts of the crazy, pitiful women Jean Toomer saw in the South in the early 1920s.

In "Roselily," the opening story of *In Love and Trouble,* the main character, Roselily—young, black, poor, trapped in the southern backwoods, unmarried, the mother of three children, each by a different man—is about to give herself in marriage to a Muslim man. His religion requires a set of customs and beliefs that control women and subordinate them to men. She will have to wear her hair covered, sit apart from the men in church; her required place will be in the home. There will be more babies regardless of her wishes. She also senses another kind of oppression, dictated not by his religion, but by his condescension. He is annoyed by country black folk, their way of doing things, the country wedding. Roselily knows that in his eyes her three illegitimate children, not all by the same man, add to her lowliness. He makes her feel "ignorant, wrong, backward." But he offers her a chance that she must take. A chance for her children. A chance for her to be "respectable," "reclaimed," "renewed." And it is a chance she cannot afford to miss because marriage is perhaps her only way out of brutal poverty.

The excerpt from Elechi Amadi's *The Concubine,* a prefatory piece to *In Love and Trouble,* is a particularly interesting one for the light it throws on Roselily's situation. This excerpt depicts a woman named Ahurole who is given to unprovoked sobbing and fits of melancholia. An intelligent woman, Ahurole is generally cheerful and normal, so her parents blame her fits on the influence of an unlucky and troublesome personal spirit. At the end of the excerpt, it is revealed that "Ahurole was engaged to Ekwueme when she was *eight days old.*" Walker sees Roselily, like Ahurole, as a woman trapped and cut down by archaic conventions, by superstition, by traditions that in every way cut women off from the right to life. Their personal and inner rebellion against the restrictions of their lives is reduced to the level of an unlucky spirit.

Roselily, too, has no way to explain her troubled and rebellious spirit. She has married off well, she will give her children a better life; but she is disturbed by what she senses will be an iron shackle around her life and her self. All of the fleeting images that inadvertently break through her consciousness are premonitions of what is to come: *quicksand, flowers choked to death, cotton being weighed, ropes, chains, handcuffs, cemeteries, a cornered rat.* The very robe and veil she is wearing are emblems of servitude that she yearns to be free of.

Mrs. Jerome Franklin Washington III, a beautician, another of Walker's suspended women, not unlike Roselily, is caught in a marriage that destroys her little by little. When she discovers how very little she means to her husband, she burns herself up.

Ms. Washington (we know her in this story only through her

husband's name) is an unlovely, unloved woman: big, awkward, with rough skin, greasy, hard pressed hair. She is married, because of a small inheritance, to a quiet, "cute," dapper young schoolteacher whom she adores. She buys him clothes and cars, lavishly spending money on him, money she has earned in her beauty shop by standing many hours on her feet. It is not long before he is beating her and ridiculing her coarseness; for he considers himself one of the elite, the "black bourgeoisie," and his wife is so obviously, in spite of her hard-earned money, a woman of no learning, no elegance. In short, she is devoid of any black middle-class pretensions. Even her pretensions are clearly indicative of her lower class. She tells her customers as she does hair behind dark glasses, "'One thing my husband does not do, he don't beat me.'" She discovers Jerome's infidelity is his dedication to some sort of revolutionary cadre. He has hidden it from her no doubt because she is ignorant, but it is a revolution financed by her money and her devotion to him. She sets fire to their marriage bed, and she herself is caught in the blaze.

The physical and psychic brutality that are part of the lives of several other women in Walker's *In Love and Trouble* are almost always associated with poverty. Rannie Toomer, in "Strong Horse Tea," for example, struggling to get a doctor for her dying child, is handicapped by poverty and ignorance as well as by the racism of the southern rural area she lives in. No "real" doctor will come to see about her child, so she gives in to the "witche's" medicine of Aunt Sarah and goes out in the rain to catch horse urine, which is the "strong horse tea" the old rootworker has requested. Her child dies while she is out filling up her shoes with the tea. In his death, all of the elements seem to have conspired—the earth, the "nigger" magic of Aunt Sarah, the public and private racism of the South. One wonders what desperate hysteria allowed Rannie Toomer to stomach the taste and smell of horse urine.

In "The Child Who Favored Daughter," the father presides over the destruction of three women in his family: his own wife, whom he drives to suicide after beating and crippling her; his sister, named Daughter, whose suicide is the result of the punishment her family exacts after she has an affair with a white man; and his own daughter, whom he mutilates because she will not renounce her white lover. To understand the violence of this man toward these three women in his family, author Walker makes us know that it is the result of an immense chaos within—the components of which are his impotent rage against the white world which abuses him, his vulnerable love for his child and his sister, both of whom chose white lovers. He is so threatened by that inner chaos that the very act of violence is a form of control, a way of imposing order on his own world. By killing his daughter, he has at once shut out the image of Daughter which haunts him, he has murdered his own incest, and he has eliminated the last woman who has the power to hurt him. His brutality toward women foreshadows other Walker characters—Grange and Brownfield in *The Third Life of Grange Copeland,* the farmer who cripples his wife in "Really Doesn't Crime Pay?," Hannah Kemhuff's husband ("The Revenge of Hannah Kemhuff"), and Ruth's father in "A Sudden Trip Home in the Spring."

It is Walker's own documentation and analysis of the historical struggles of the black women that authenticates the terrible and chilling violence of these stories. These are stories about several generations of black women whose lives were severely limited by sexual and racial oppression. First slaves, then sharecroppers, then part of the vast army of the urban poor, their lives were lived out in slow motion, going nowhere, a future not yet within their grasp.[23]

Such were the women Jean Toomer discovered in *Cane,* and the similarity between Toomer's women and the women of Walker's first cycle (the suspended woman) is striking:

> To Toomer they lay vacant and fallow as Autumn fields, with harvest time never in sight: and he saw them enter loveless marriages, without joy; and become prostitutes without resistance; and become mothers of children, without fulfillment.[24]

Both Toomer and Walker have explored the tragedies in the lives of Black women—the tragedy of poverty, abuse from men who are themselves abused, the physical deterioration—but there is greater depth in Walker's exploration because not only does she comprehend the past lives of these women but she has also questioned their fates and dared to see through to a time when black women would no longer live in suspension, when there would be a place for them to move into.

In the second cycle of Walker's personal construct of the history of black women are the women who belong to the decades of the forties and fifties, those decades when black people (then "Negroes") wanted most to be part of the mainstream of American life even though assimilation required total denial of one's ethnicity. Several literary critics have labeled this period in black literature a period of "mainstreaming" because of the indications in literature that writers such as Willard Motley and Frank Yerby and even one novel of Zora Neale Hurston were "raceless." And what of the black women during this period, particularly the woman who had some chance at education? Walker writes of her as a woman pushed and pulled by the larger world outside of her, urged to assimilate (to be "raceless") in order to overcome her background. In Walker's historical construct, these black women were, ironically, victims of what were ostensibly greater opportunities:

> I have this theory that Black women in the '50's, in the 40's—the late 40's and early 50's—got away from their roots much more than they will probably ever do again, because that was the time of greatest striving to get into White Society, and to erase all of the backgrounds of poverty. It was a time when you could be the Exception, could be the One, and my sister was The One. But I think she's not unique—so many, many, many Black families have a daughter or sister who was the one who escaped because, you see, that was what was set up for her; she was going to be the one who escaped, and the rest of us weren't supposed to escape, because we had given our One.[25]

The women in this cycle are also victims, not of physical violence, but of a kind of psychic violence that alienates them from their roots, cutting them off from real contact.

The woman named Molly from Walker's poem "For My Sister Molly Who in the Fifties" is the eldest sister in a poor rural family in Eatonton; she is, in fact, Alice Walker's sister and Walker is the child narrator of the poem mourning the loss of her talented and devoted "Molly." When Molly first comes home on vacation from college, she is very close to her brothers and sisters, teaching them what she has learned, reading to them about faraway places like Africa. The young narrator is enraptured by Molly, spellbound by the bright colorful sister who changes her drab life into beauty:

Who in the Fifties

Knew all the written things that made
Us laugh and stories by
The hour. Waking up the story buds
Like Fruit. Who walked among the flowers
And brought them inside the house
And smelled as good as they
And smelled as good as they
And looked as bright.
Who made dresses, braided
Hair. Moved chairs about
Hung things from walls
Ordered baths
Frowned on wasp bites
And seemed to know the endings
Of all the tales
I had forgot.[26]

As a writer especially concerned with the need for black people to acknowledge and respect their roots, Walker is sensitive to these women who are divorced from their heritage. As she describes them, the Chosen Ones were always the bright and talented ones in the family. They were the ones selected to go to college if the family could afford to send only one; they were meant to have the better life, the chance at success. And they learned early the important lesson that to be chosen required them to feel shame for their background, and to strive to be as different and removed as possible from those not chosen. But being a child, the narrator does not realize or suspect the growing signs of Molly's remoteness. Molly goes off to the university, travels abroad, becoming distant and cold and frowning upon the lives of the simple folks she comes from:

Who Found Another World

Another life With gentlefolk
Far less trusting
And moved and moved and changed
Her name
And sounded precise
When she spoke And frowned away
Our sloppishness[27]

From her superior position she can only see the negatives—the silent, fearful, barefoot, tongue-tied, ignorant brothers and sisters. She finds the past, her backward family, unbearable, and though she may have sensed their groping after life, she finally leaves the family for good. She has, of course, been leaving all along with her disapproval of their ways, her precise speech, her preference for another world. The tone of the last two lines suggests the finality about her leaving, as though Molly has become too alienated from her family to ever return:

For My Sister Molly Who in the Fifties

Left us.

The women of the second cycle are destroyed spiritually rather than physically, and yet there is still some movement forward, some hope that did not exist for the earlier generation of American black women. The women in this cycle are more aware of their condition and they have greater potential for shaping their lives, although they are still thwarted because they feel themselves coming to life before the necessary changes have been made in the political environment—before there is space for them to move into. The sense of "twoness" that Du Bois spoke of in *The Souls of Black Folk* is perhaps most evident in the lives of these women; they are the most aware of and burdened by the "double consciousness" that makes one measure one's soul by the tape of the other world.

In June of 1973 in an interview with this writer, Ms. Walker made one of the first statements about the direction and development of her black women characters into a third cycle:

> My women, in the future, will not burn themselves up—that's what I mean by coming to the end of a cycle, and understanding something to the end . . . now I am ready to look at women who have made the room larger for others to move in. . . . I think one reason I never stay away from the Southern Movement is because I realize how deeply political changes affect the choices and life-styles of people. The Movement of the Sixties, Black Power, the Muslims, the Panthers . . . have changed the options of Black people generally and of Black women in particular. So that my women characters won't all end the way they have been, because Black women now offer varied, live models of how it is possible to live. We have made a new place to move. . . .[28]

The women of the third cycle are, for the most part, women of the late sixties, although there are some older women in Walker's fiction who exhibit the qualities of the developing, emergent model. Greatly influenced by the political events of the sixties and the changes resulting from the freedom movement, they are women coming just to the edge of a new awareness and making the first tentative steps into an uncharted region. And although they are more fully conscious of their political and psychological oppression and more capable of creating new options for themselves, they must undergo a harsh initiation before they are ready to occupy and claim any new territory. Alice Walker, herself a real-life prototype of the emergent black woman, speaks of having been called to life by the civil rights movement of the sixties, as being called from the shadows of a world in which black people existed as statistics, problems, beasts of burden, a life that resembled death; for one was not aware of the possibilities within one's self or of possibilities in the larger world outside of the narrow restraints of the world black people inhabited before the struggles of the sixties. When Walker and other civil rights activists like Fannie Lou Hamer[29] began the fight for their lives, they were beaten, jailed, and, in Fannie Lou Hamer's case, widowed and made homeless, but they never lost the energy and courage for revolt. In the same way Walker's own characters, through suffering and struggle, lay the groundwork for a new type of woman to emerge.

The process of cyclical movement in the lives of Walker's black women is first evident in her first novel, *The Third Life of Grange Copeland*. The girl, Ruth, is the daughter of Mem Copeland and the granddaughter of Margaret Copeland—two women whose lives were lived out under the most extreme forms of oppression. Under the pressure of poverty and alienation from her husband, Margaret kills herself and her child; and Mem, wife of Brownfield Copeland, is brutally murdered by her husband in one of his drunken rages. Ruth is brought up by her grandfather, Grange, who in his "third life" attempts to salvage some of his own wasted life by protecting Ruth. Ruth emerges into a young woman at the same time as the civil rights movement, and there is just a glimpse at the end of the novel of how that movement will affect Ruth's life. We see her becoming aware, by watching the civil rights activists—both women and men—that it is possible to struggle against the abuses of oppression. Raised in the sixties, Ruth is the natural inheritor of the changes in a new order, struggling to be, this marking the transition of the women in her family from death to life.

Besides political activism, a fundamental activity the women in the third cycle engage in is the search for meaning in their roots and traditions. As they struggle to reclaim their past and to re-examine their relationship to the black community, there is a consequent reconciliation between themselves and black men.

In Sarah Davis, the main character of Walker's short story, "A Sudden Trip Home in the Spring,"[30] we have another witness to the end of the old cycles of confusion and despair. Her search begins when she returns home to the South from a northern white college to bury her father. She is an artist, but because of her alienation from her father, whom she blames for her mother's death, she is unable to paint the faces of black men, seeing in them only defeat. It is important for her, therefore, to answer the questions she is pondering: What is the duty of the child toward the parents after they are dead? What is the necessity of keeping alive in herself a sense of continuity with the past and a sense of community with her family? Through a series of events surrounding her father's funeral, Sarah rediscovers the courage and grace of her grandfather and re-establishes the vital link between her and her brother. Her resolve at the end of the story to do a sculpture of her grandfather ("I shall soon know how to make my grandpa up in stone") signifies the return to her roots and her own personal sense of liberation. This story, more than any other, indicates the contrast between the women of the second cycle who were determined to escape their roots in order to make it in a white world and the emergent women of the third cycle who demonstrate a sense of freedom by the drive to re-establish those vital links to their past.

In Walker's second novel, *Meridian,* the cyclical process is clearly defined in the life of the main character, Meridian Hill, who evolves from a woman trapped by racial and sexual oppression to a revolutionary figure, effecting action and strategy to bring freedom to herself and other poor disenfranchised blacks in the South. Again, as with other third-cycle women who are depicted in the short story collection, the characters in the two novels—*Grange Copeland* and *Meridian*—follow certain patterns: They begin existence in a numb state, deadened, insensible to a life beyond poverty and degradation; they are awakened to life by a powerful political force; in discovering and expanding their creativity, there is a consequent effort to reintegrate themselves into their culture in order to rediscover its value. Historically, the second novel, dealing with a woman who came of age during the sixties, brings Walker's women characters into the first few years of the seventies.

NOTES

1. John O'Brien, ed., *Interviews with Black Writers* (New York: Liverwright, 1973), p. 192.
2. New York: Harcourt, Brace & World, 1968.
3. New York: Harcourt Brace Jovanovich, 1973.
4. New York: Harcourt Brace Jovanovich, 1970.
5. New York: Harcourt Brace Jovanovich, 1973.
6. New York: Harcourt Brace Jovanovich, 1976.
7. O'Brien, p. 211.
8. Interview with Mary Helen Washington, Jackson, Mississippi, June 17, 1973. I traveled to Jackson in June of 1973 in order to meet, talk with, and interview Ms. Walker.
9. "Interview with Mary Helen Washington," Part 1, p. 7.
10. *American Scholar,* Winter 1970–71.
11. Ibid., p. 551.
12. Ibid., p. 552.

13. W. E. B. Du Bois, *Souls of Black Folk* (New York: Blue Heron Press, 1953), pp. 16–17.
14. Carolyn Fowler, "Solid at the Core," *Freedomways,* 14 (First Quarter, 1974), p. 60.
15. Alice Walker, "Interview," in O'Brien, p. 202.
16. Reid Lecture at Barnard College, November 11, 1975.
17. "Interview with Mary Helen Washington," p. 6.
18. *Apologist* is used here to mean one who speaks or writes in defense of a cause or a position.
19. "Interview with Mary Helen Washington," p. 6.
20. "In Search of Our Mothers' Gardens," *Ms.,* May 1974, p. 66.
21. Ibid.
22. Ibid., p. 69.
23. Ibid., p. 66.
24. Ibid.
25. "Interview with Mary Helen Washington," Part 1, p. 1.
26. *Revolutionary Petunias* (New York: Harcourt Brace Jovanovich, 1973), p. 17.
27. Ibid., p. 18.
28. "Interview with Mary Helen Washington," Part 2, p. 2.
29. The identification of Hamer as a model for the emergent woman is developed in Walker's review of a biography of Hamer by June Jordan. The review appeared in *The New York Times Book Review,* April 29, 1973.
30. In Mary Helen Washington, ed., *Black-eyed Susans: Classic Stories by and About Black Women* (Garden City, N.Y.: Doubleday & Company, 1975).

Traditionally, when nonwhites have been "studied"—especially nonwhites of African descent—there has been a lack of scientific objectivity employed in the applied techniques and the resulting conclusions. One man, William Edward Burghardt Du Bois, did more to correct and change this process than anyone else in the twentieth century.

Poet, philosopher, historian, social scientist, dramatist, *Moon, Crisis,* and *Phylon* editor, social activist, and "race" man for many decades, Du Bois spent his ninety-five years in prolific and significant activity. He died in his adopted Ghana after having joined the Communist party of the United States in 1961, and after having renounced his United States citizenship.

Chester Fontenot's decision to locate an analysis of Alice Walker's short story within one of the landmark ideological statements of this century sharply conveys the perennial timeliness of the "double consciousness" theory in Black colonial and neocolonial situations. Du Bois was the architect of that theory which defined Black double consciousness as "this sense of always looking at one's self through the eyes of others, of measuring one's soul by the tape of a world that looks on in amused contempt and pity. . . ." Fontenot skillfully demonstrates the impact and the legacy of Du Bois' genius, especially for young talented writers like Alice Walker and her ilk.

Alice Walker: "The Diary of an African Nun" and Du Bois' Double Consciousness

by CHESTER J. FONTENOT

Faced with the demands of Anglo-American literary critics to make Black writers cast their experiences in the universal mode on one hand, and the demands of Black political activities and literary scholars to make Black literature and artists more directly responsive to the needs of the Black masses on the other, Black writers, during the sixties, created a "fighting revolutionary literature." This literature was characterized by the abandonment of conventional literary forms and techniques, by the return to the forms of Black cultural expression as poetic material, and by the emphasis on direct social statements. Since that time, Black literature has been pigeonholed into what one critic has called "masturbatory literature"—literature which attacks white people through the use of such language as "honky," "white bastards," "racist crackers," and other terms. And this conception of Black literature has, in a sense, won the opinions of many Black and white critics, leading them to categorize the subject as second-rate literature, as a body of literature which is inferior to that written by Anglo-American writers.

These critics have ignored that there are some Black writers who do not conform to this conception, but who seek to write about the Black experience through the aesthetic mode. These artists often find themselves caught between the purely literary expectations of formalist critics, and the sociological demands of the Black masses; they experience—through creative writing—the double consciousness which Du Bois speaks of in *Souls of Black Folk.* "The Negro is a sort of seventh son," writes Du Bois, "born with a veil and gifted with second-sight in this American world—a world which yields him no true self-consciousness, but only lets him see himself through the revelation of the other world." This double consciousness, "this sense of always looking at one's self through the eyes of others, of measuring one's soul by the tape of a world that looks on in amused contempt and pity,"[1] produces two warring factions; to be an American and a Black person. The struggle between these two unreconciled strivings threatens to plunge the Black American, in particular the Black artist, into a sort of halfway house, where the artist is accepted neither as a part of the American literary tradition nor as a Black artist worthy of critical attention.

One Black writer who has successfully coped with these two warring factions is Alice Walker. Though much of her writings demonstrate that she is attempting to work through this problem, "The Diary of an African Nun"[2] is a supreme statement of the dilemma. Though this short story is only six pages in length, it contains material for a novella. It is divided into six parts and is set in an African mission school in Uganda, where an African woman has rejected her traditional tribal religion for Christianity. Walker begins Part 1 by introducing things which not only are foreign to African culture but also suggest tension between the "true" spirituality of African culture and the materialistic underpinnings of European culture. The mission is both a school by day and a resting place for travelers by night. The travelers are struck, first, by the African nun's beauty; this leads them to question her commitment to the Catholic Church: The Americans cannot understand her humility—"I bring them clean sheets and towels and return their too much money and candid smiles" (p. 113); the Germans "do not offer money but praise. The sight of a Black nun strikes their sentimentality" (p. 113); the French are patronizing and wish to paint a picture of her; the Italians ignore her except when they need her to make their material surroundings more livable.

Just as the Europeans question her commitment to the Catholic Church, so does the Black nun feel uneasy about her rejection of African traditional religion and values. She repeats her vows to the Catholic Church, but cannot help remembering the colonization of her people by Europeans. She says that "I was born in this township, a village 'civilized' by American missionaries" (p. 114). Walker's use of quotation marks around the word "civilized" emphasizes the irony in her using the term. The things which one would call civilized are all materialistic. The first part of the story ends as the nun gazes at the Ruwenzori Mountains; she tells us that they "show themselves only once a year under the blazing heat of spring" (p. 114). It is at this time that the snow, which is a false covering, melts and reveals the true nature of the mountains. The nun, like the mountains, is within a sort of superstructure which inhibits natural growth.

Part 2 seems to suggest the ultimate irony of an oppressed group—that is, the oppressed sees himself or herself through the eyes of the oppressor and seeks to assimilate into the society the oppressor has set up. Once the oppressed achieves this goal, he or she realizes two things: (1) The alien society does not want him or her to be a part of it, and it will never provide the means by which the oppressed can function as a full member of that society, and (2) the oppressed realizes that he or she really doesn't want to become a part of the dominant society. This leaves the oppressed in a sort of halfway house, or as Fanon says, "a zone of non-being, an extraordinary sterile and arid region, an utterly naked declivity where an authentic upheaval can be born."[3] The oppressed is halfway between the world of the oppressed and that of the oppressor, yet belongs to neither. But the important thing to consider is that to reach a vantage point from where the oppressed can become conscious of his or her predicament requires that the oppressed distance himself or herself from the sociocultural milieu which confronts him or her. The African nun reaches this ironic stance when she recalls the way she became a nun. At the age of twenty, she says,

> I earned the right to wear this dress, never to be without it, always to bathe myself in cold water even in winter, and to wear my mission-cropped hair well covered, my nails clean and neatly clipped. The boys I knew as a child are kind to me now and gentle, and I see them married and kiss their children, each one of them so much what our Lord wanted—did he not say, 'Suffer little children to come unto me'?—but we have not yet been so lucky, and we never shall. (p. 114)

The "we" in the above quotation refers to the African people who have not been able to succeed in becoming part of European society and culture (which is here symbolized as the kingdom of God). And the nun's last words in this quotation, "and we never shall," leads one to question her position toward her new-found faith and culture.

Part 3 further develops this problem. It begins with images of African tribal life—drums, smell of roasting goat's meat, chants. Walker shifts her tone—she speaks as if she is part of the Christian (European) world, and the Africans are the "others." The nun listens to the rhythm of the festive chants, and sings her own chants in response to theirs. Her chants, however, are those of the Catholic Church, which, she says, are less old than those of the African's. Walker's language suggests a tension between Christianity and African pagan worship. This tension leads her to question her position in the mission school and finally toward her belief in Christ. She asks: "Must I still ask myself whether it was my husband, who came down bodiless from the sky, son of a proud father and flesh once upon the earth, who first took me, and claimed the innocence of my body? Or was it the drumbeats, messengers of the sacred dance of life and deathlessness on earth?" (p. 115).

Moreover, she contrasts the down-to-earth sensuality of African tribal religion with the aloofness of Christianity. The nun longs to be "within the black circle around the red, glowing fire, to feel the breath of love hot against my cheeks, the smell of love strong about my waiting thighs! Must I still tremble at the thought of passions stifled beneath this voluminous rustling snow!" If we compare the imagery of snow which covers up the natural passions to the habit the nun wears which covers up her body, we can see that the contrast between the snow and habit on one hand and the mountains and the nun's body on the other further develops this tension. Walker concludes this part of the short story in an almost blasphemous manner. She adopts an ironical tone toward the stereotypical way in which we think of Christ. The nun, thinking about the price she pays for rejecting the sensuous African rituals, tries to move Christianity in the direction of African tribal religion. She asks of Christ: "How long must I sit by my window before I lure you down from the sky? . . . Will you not come down and take me!" (p. 115).

Part 4 is dominated by the life and vitality of the African people. Walker begins this section by reversing African stereotypes. She speaks of the Africans "cutting the goat's meat in sinewy strips. Teeth will clutch it, wring it. Cruel, greedy, greasy lips will curl over it in an ecstasy which has never ceased wherever there were goats and men" (p. 116).

Walker contrasts the African images of sexuality—through describing the ritual lovers' dance—with the *a*sexual nature of Christianity. Perhaps this suggests that European civilization is somewhat artificial. There are sins on both the Christian side, which sins against the flesh in preference of a transcendental existence, and on the African side, which sins against the eternal, spiritual world in preference of a continued re-enactment of the creation. The lack of sexuality indicates that the European values are a superstructure which covers the African nun, like the snow covers the mountains, until spring, which represents a psychological revival.

Part 5 reveals the nun's psychological plight. Walker revives the metaphor of spring as the vitality of African culture as opposed to the harshness of European culture (symbolized as winter snow). Perhaps this imagery also suggests the fixed nature of African culture—its durable quality in contrast to the temporary or superficial nature of European culture (the snow melts every spring). It seems that the nun isn't really talking about Christianity as a belief, but as a way of attaining certain things which she couldn't get through African pagan worship. The nun says, "Leave me alone; I will do your work; or, what is more likely, I will say nothing of my melancholia at your lack of faith in the spring. . . . For what is my faith in the spring and the eternal melting of snows (you will ask) but your belief in the Resurrection? Could I convince one so wise that my belief bears more fruit?"

The nun sees Christianity as a sort of material salvation for her people. She knows that it is spiritually decadent, yet the African people must function in a Christian world. Hence, Christianity becomes a way of teaching her people a conscious lie to further their own ends—survival.

The last section of the short story reveals the nun's paradoxical stance toward what she is doing. She feels that she must adopt the "enlightened" stance of the Europeans in order to make an "objective" analysis of the social conditions in which her people find themselves. This position removes her from mundane reality and places her outside the world she has always been a part of. Yet, to do this is contrary to her heritage, to her culture, and to her goals. In short, she must walk the tight rope between the two worlds without becoming a part of either, for to become a part of the European world is to die a spiritual death, and to become a part of the African world condemns her to a material death.

If we allegorize the story, we can say that the plight of the African nun is that of the Black intellectual or middle class (Fanon calls them "newcomers"), who find themselves caught between two worlds which are at once complementary and contradictory. The conclusion the nun comes to is that one must be aware of the situation in which one places himself or herself by assuming an alien perspective which contradicts that of his or her native culture. "Civilizaton" can become something that Blacks can utilize in their struggle for independence, but to do so, they need leaders (much like Du Bois' talented tenth) who can teach the masses to put the intricacies of civilization to constructive use. In this way, Black people will be able to see their involvement with American civilization as simply a way of surviving. The adoption of American values by Black Americans on one hand, and of American literary conventions by Black artists on the other, can be seen by analogy as the snow which covers the mountains and as the African nun's habit. This process would move the problem from a psychological predicament to a conscious manipulation of American civilization, and could, therefore, make progress toward lessening the agony Black Americans feel in having to deal with a double consciousness.

NOTES

1. W. E. B. Du Bois, *Souls of Black Folk* (1953) (New York: New American Library, 1969), p. 45.
2. Alice Walker, *In Love and Trouble* (New York: Harcourt Brace Jovanovich, 1973), pp. 113–19. All subsequent references are to this edition.
3. Frantz Fanon, *Black Skin, White Masks* (New York: Grove Press, 1967), p. 10.

Professor George Kent, eminent critic of Black American Literature and American Literature at the University of Chicago, is preparing a full-length study on the works of Gwendolyn Brooks. That study will be welcomed, for therein will lie acute introspection and interpretations of the works of the 1950 Pulitzer Prize winner and poet laureate of Illinois.

Gwendolyn Brooks is one of the most consistent and prolific poets of her generation (see bibliography of African-American Women Writers) and she has taught those in others the importance of craft. She defines her genre, poetry (though she is an accomplished and impressive prose artist), as "a distillation of life." Beverly Guy-Sheftall examines a small segment of the distilled life of Mrs. Brooks apprehended three decades ago, but for a more comprehensive statement on the significance of Gwendolyn Brooks, we recommend the poet's autobiography, *Report from Part One,* and the introductory remarks to the anthologized work of Brooks in *Black Writers of America,* by Richard Barksdale and Kenneth Kinnamon.

The Women of Bronzeville

by BEVERLY GUY-SHEFTALL

An obvious difference between Gwendolyn Brooks and male writers such as Richard Wright and Ralph Ellison who have used the urban environment as the setting for their works is the greater amount of attention she devotes to the experiences of females. While women are not absent from Wright's or Ellison's ghetto worlds, they remain background figures who are of secondary importance, at best, to the central actions of their novels. Like Ann Petry, Brooks focuses on the impact of the urban experience on females as well as males. Her sexual identity as well as her racial identity has molded her vision of the city. Though this aspect of her work has been generally ignored by critics, occasionally one can find comments about the value of the insights she has gained as a result of her sex.

> . . . The life of women, particularly Negro women, and the life of Negroes, particularly those who have grown up since World War I in the North, where America's big towns are, figure prominently in Miss Brooks' poetry. Moreover, it does seem true that she is a woman writing, although not in the manner of the damned mob of scribbling women who so distressed Hawthorne—nor because of any mysterious and occult woman's intuition which seems to guide her inner labors . . . Miss Brooks is a woman, and yet not one in an ignoble way. . . . There is a general way in which women do tend to know women and also a general way in which they tend to know men, largely because our culture makes it so. Miss Brooks, whether she is talking of women or men . . . constantly speaks as a woman. . . .[1]

Though one might disagree with this assessment of her as a woman writer, it is difficult to ignore her numerous portraits of the women who inhabit Bronzeville,[2] the setting for much of her poetry.

Like Richard Wright, she explores the tragic aspects of black ghetto life, but she also probes beneath the surface in order to illuminate those areas of the slum dweller's life which often go unnoticed and should not be seen as ugly or horrifying. Ironically, then, her poems reveal both the destructive and the nurturing aspects of the black urban environment. Brooks's paradoxical vision is perhaps best revealed in a statement which appears in the appendix of her autobiography concerning her plans for *In the Mecca.*

> . . . I wish to present a large variety of personalities against a mosaic of daily affairs, recognizing that the *grimiest* of these is likely to have a streak of sun.
>
> In the Mecca were murders, loves, lonelinesses, hates, jealousies. Hope occurred, and charity, sainthood, glory, shame, despair, fear, altruism. (pp. 189–90)

A central paradox of her composite portrait of Bronzeville is the ability of its residents to transcend, if only temporarily, the sordid conditions of their lives. They are not dehumanized or paralyzed by the poverty which engulfs them. It is against this backdrop of

Brooks's over-all vision of Bronzeville that her images of urban women as they appear in selected poems from *The World of Gwendolyn Brooks* will be examined. Though a discussion of the urban women in *In the Mecca, Riot,* and *Family Pictures* will not be included, it would be interesting in a more comprehensive study of Brooks's women to compare the images projected in her pre-1967 poems with these later ones.

The diverse nature of Brooks's females enables her to reveal the many facets, complexities, and paradoxes of the urban black experiences. They range from the death-in-life figure of a woman in "obituary for a living lady"[3] to the life-in-death figure of a woman in "the rites for Cousin Vit." The unnamed woman in the first poem (based on a person Brooks knew well)[4] is the antithesis of Cousin Vit. Though she was a "decently wild child" and as a girl was "interested in a broach and pink powder and a curl," as a young woman she would not permit sexual contact between herself and the man with whom she had fallen in love. She continued to wait by the windows in a "gay (though white) dress," and finally decided to say "yes," though by this time it was too late because he had found a woman "who dressed in red." Though red traditionally has negative connotations where women's dress is concerned, here it is being used positively to contrast the latter woman's *joie de vivre* with the lack of it in the main character; her purity and paleness of spirit (which the white dress symbolizes) cause her to be rejected. Here Brooks has taken the conventional "scarlet woman" figure usually associated with the corrupt, sinful city and transformed her into a positive, vital force. After mourning for a long time and "wishing she were dead," the woman in white turns to religion and away from the world of the flesh.

> . . . Now she will not dance
> And she thinks not the thinnest thought of any type of
> romance
> And I can't get her to take or touch of the best cream
> Cologne (pp. 18–19)

Cousin Vit, on the other hand, has lived an exciting, full life and even in death refuses to be confined.

> . . . it can't hold her,
> That stuff and satin aiming to enfold her . . .
> Even now, surmise,
> She rises in the sunshine. There she goes,
> Back to the bars she knew and the repose
> In love rooms and the things in people's eyes.
> Too vital and too squeaking . . . (p. 109)

She has tasted much of life's pleasures and sorrows. Disappointments have not caused her to withdraw from life and miss out on its more pleasant aspects.

> Even now she does the snake-hips with a kiss,
> Slops the bad wine across her shantung, talks
> Of pregnancy, guitars and bridgework, walks
> In parks or alleys, comes haply on the verge
> Of happiness . . . (p. 109)

She has taken chances in order to find joy. Ironically, she seems more alive in death than the living woman in the previous poem. One critic has commented on her and other women in Brooks's poems who are to be admired for attempting to get the most out of their basically narrow and drab lives.

> Whatever her shortcomings, Cousin Vit has asserted her pagan self without asking questions or whining. It may be that she, Sadie, and others like them, girls who "scraped life / with a fine-tooth comb," girls who seize their love in hallways and alleys and other unconventional places—it may be that these carefree souls have a deeper understanding of the modern scene than any of their sedate sisters and friends. Perhaps they are the only ones who do understand.[5]

"Sadie and Maud" (alluded to in the previous quote) deals with two sisters whose contrasting approaches to life are somewhat analogous to the women discussed in the two previous poems. Sadie, like Cousin Vit, has gotten out of life all it has to offer, despite her limited resources.

> Sadie scraped life
> With a fine-tooth comb.

Photo: Judy Mutunhu

Nikki Grimes

Gloria I. Joseph

She didn't leave a tangle in.
Her comb found every strand.
Sadie was one of the livingest chits
In all the land. (p. 16)

Though she bore two illegitimate daughters and shamed her family, she has left her offspring a rich heritage–her fine-tooth comb —so that they will presumably also squeeze as much joy out of life as possible. She does not have wealth to leave them but she leaves them something perhaps equally valuable. Maud, on the other hand, who followed the more conventional path and went to college, is, at the end of the poem, alone and like a "thin brown mouse." Like the unnamed woman in "obituary for a living lady," she has followed society's rules, but her life has lacked the vitality and fullness which makes one's existence meaningful.

Brooks also explores the impact of poverty on the lives of her women characters. "The mother" deals with a poor woman who has had a number of abortions and who experiences anxiety and anguish as a result of these decisions. In the appendix of her autobiography Brooks refers to her as "hardly your crowned and praised and customary Mother; but a Mother not unfamiliar, who decides that *she* rather than her World, will kill her children."[6] Accepting full responsibility for her "crime," she nevertheless remains ambivalent about her actions and exactly what she has done. Though she realizes that she has shielded her unborn babies from the harsh realities of the life they were sure to lead, she also admits having stolen from them whatever joys they might have been able to experience. She wonders if she had that right.

. . . if I sinned, if I seized
Your luck
And your lives from your unfinished reach,
If I stole your births and your names,
Your straight baby tears and your games,
Your stilted or lovely loves, your tumults, your marriages, aches,
  and your deaths,
If I poisoned the beginnings of your breaths,
Believe that even in my deliberateness I was not deliberate. (p. 5)

Throughout the poem, one has the feeling that if circumstances had been different, if she had been able to provide adequately for them, they would have been allowed to live. Ironically, it was her deep concern for them as well as her own situation, which caused her to have the abortions.

> Believe me, I loved you all
> Believe me, I knew you, though faintly, and I
> loved, I loved you
> All. (p. 6)

She knew perfectly well what their fate would have been.

> You will never neglect or beat
> Them, or silence or buy with a sweet.
> You will never wind up the sucking-thumb
> Or scuttle off ghosts that come.
> You will never leave them, controlling your luscious
> sigh
> Return for a snack of them, with gobbling mother-eye. (p. 5)

Though George Kent criticizes the poem for failing "to convey the attitude of the author toward her subject—the several abortions of the mother,"[7] there is no question in my mind nor probably in the minds of women who have had abortions for similar or even other reasons where Brooks's sympathies lie.

"When Mrs. Martin's Booker T." contains a contrasting portrait of a mother and provides another view of the black urban resident. The code of behavior to which she adheres is more conventional. Mrs. Martin is disgraced by her son Booker T., who "ruins" Rosa Brown when he impregnates her before marriage. She is embarrassed to the point that she cannot face her community, so she moves to the other side of town and renounces her son. The intensity of her feelings is revealed in the simile "He wrung my heart like a chicken neck." The only cure for her damaged pride would be for her son to marry Rosa—"But tell me if'n he take that gal / And get her decent wed." Her strong sense of honor and decency will not permit her to condone behavior which reflects badly on the family. "Good" people marry when babies are on the way. It may also be that Mrs. Martin insists on marriage because she does not want Rosa and her illegitimate child to experience the hardships which usually befall those in their situation.

We also get glimpses into the lives of female ghetto dwellers in other poems from *A Street in Bronzeville* and *The Bean Eaters.* Though their world is drab and ordinary, and sometimes even fraught with danger, they go about their daily lives accepting their plight and somehow managing to survive. In "the battle" the persona (probably Hattie Scott, since this poem belongs to that series) would like to believe that she would have behaved differently from Moe Belle Jackson, who, after being beaten by her husband the night before because of a domestic quarrel, probably arose the next morning and continued with business as usual.

I like to think
Of how I'd of took a knife
And slashed all of the quickenin'
Out of his lowly life.

But if I know Moe Belle,
Most like, she shed a tear,
And this mornin' it was probably,
"More grits, dear?" (p. 39)

In "when I die" (from the same series) there is a similar acceptance of the realities of life, no matter how unpleasant. An unnamed female, again presumably Hattie, imagines that when she dies, there will be no fanfare but simply "one lone little short man / Dressed all shabbily." Her husband or boyfriend will bring his cheap flowers—"He'll have his buck-a-dozen"—but immediately after the funeral he'll shed his mourning clothes and wipe away his tears. She also has no illusions about what will happen next—"And the girls, they will be waitin' / there's nothin' more to say." She does not romanticize him or their relationship. In "the murder"[8] a mother must face the tragic death of her barely one-year-old son which was caused by his brother, who "with a grin / Burned him up for fun." She may also have to live with a guilty conscience for the rest of her life because it might not have happened had she been there.

No doubt, poor Percy looked around
And wondered at the heat,
Was worried, wanted Mother,
Who gossiped down the street. (p. 22)

There is no explanation for Brucie's behavior, which is even more terrifying.

> No doubt, poor shrieking Percy died
> Loving Brucie still,
> Who could, with clean and open eye,
> Thoughtfully kill. (p.22)

Despite their frustrations and limitations, however, happiness does penetrate the lives of the Bronzeville women, though it has to be found in small things. The woman in "patent leather" is thrilled at having a man whose hair is so slick, black, and straight that it looks like patent leather. Though the other men "don't think he's such / A much" because of his shrill voice and "pitiful" muscles (unmasculine traits as far as they are concerned), she "strokes the patent-leather hair / That makes him man enough for her" (p. 13). Similarly, the woman in "when you have forgotten Sunday: the love story" experiences extreme pleasure on Sundays when she is able to stay in bed late with her mate and forget about the cares of the week. She remembers ordinary matters such as how he reacted to interruptions during their love-making sessions, how long they stayed in bed, and what they finally had for dinner. Though their apartment is tiny and unappealing and they don't eat exotic meals, they are still able to enjoy each other on this one day of the week when their usual problems don't intrude.

> . . . we finally went in to Sunday dinner,
> That is to say, went across the front room
> floor to the ink-spotted table in
> the southwest corner
> To Sunday dinner, which was always chicken
> and noodles
> Or chicken and rice
> And salad and rye bread and tea
> And chocolate chip cookies. (p. 20)

Though this seems to be all she has to look forward to, she's happy.

> Or me sitting on the front-room radiator in
> the limping afternoon

Looking off down the long street
To nowhere,
Hugged by my plain old wrapper of no-expectation
And nothing-I-have-to-do and I'm-happy-why?
And if-Monday-never-had-to-come— (p. 20)

Although life in Bronzeville is seldom without frustrations, its inhabitants do experience moments, however temporary, when they are glad to be alive.

Other urban poems reveal the plight of the dark-skinned or kinky-haired girl because of the color prejudice within the black community. Since this problem (discussed in detail in an article mentioned below) is shared by black women no matter where they live, it will not be dealt with in detail here, though a discussion of Brooks's images of women generally would include a thorough analysis of such poems as "the ballad of chocolate Mabbie," "Ballad of Pearl May Lee," "Jessie Mitchell's Mother," and selected poems from *Annie Allen.* Beauty parlors are a crucial part of Bronzeville world as they are in other black environments, and a critic explains their significance.

> The worship of "good" hair naturally suggests the importance of beauty parlors in Bronzeville. They tend to become miracle-working shrines to which the dark girl goes in search of beauty. . . . They know that it is tough to be "cut from chocolate" and to have "boisterous hair" in a land where "white is right." To be black is to be rejected. . . .[9]

"At the hairdresser's" contains a portrait of a black girl who is almost ecstatic over the passing from the vogue of long hair. Her short hair, which Madam Walker's and Poro Grower could not help, is no longer a problem now that the "upsweep" is in style. She no longer has to feel inferior to the girls with long hair.

Gimme an upsweep, Minnie,
With humpteen baby curls.
'Bout time I got some glamour.
I'll show them girls. (p. 37)

Brooks's urban world is also inhabited by older women who have a different kind of struggle. The persona in "A Sunset of the

City" can be seen as a victim of a modern, urbanized environment, not necessarily Bronzeville, where close family ties have broken. She is resentful as she approaches middle age because of the way she is now treated by her children, husband, and lovers.

> Already I'm no longer looked at with lechery or love,
> My daughters and sons have put me away with
>   marbles and dolls,
> Are gone from the house.
> My husband and lovers are pleasant or somewhat polite
> And night is night. (p. 337)

"Night is night" rather than a time for fun and adventure as it was when she was younger. Not only is it "summer-gone" where the seasons are concerned, but she is also approaching the winter of her own life. She is like the flowers and grass which are personified.

> The sweet flowers in drying and dying down,
> The grasses forgetting their blaze and consenting to
>   brown. (p. 337)

She sees herself as a hopeless woman whose needs are no longer satisfied in her cold, empty house.

> There is no warm house
> That is filled with my need.
> I am cold in this cold house this house
> Whose washed echoes are tremulous down lost halls. (p. 338)

Like old furniture, she is "dusty," and now "hurries through her prayers," since they seem useless. She contemplates suicide as an alternative to a numb existence where she would do nothing, feel nothing, and desire nothing. This death-in-life quality has been seen before in one of Brooks's women. The poem ends on a pessimistic note with her concluding that Fate has played a cruel joke on her. One critic sees this poem as "another indication of the spiritual bankruptcy of our times," of "the meaninglessness of modern living," and "our loss of faith."[10] While the poem can be seen as having a universal theme, its central purpose should not be overlooked—the revelation of the inner turmoil of a woman as she faces a critical point in her life. The nature of the frustration she feels is in many ways different from what a man growing old would experience, yet similar.

Often Brooks's older women are seen in their relationships with their husbands, though these portraits tend to be less sharply focused then the ones which include a female figure only. In "the old marrieds" she explores, among other things, the negative impact of cramped ghetto quarters on a couple's relationship. Although the possibilities for romantic love have been perfect on this day, they are unable to communicate with each other because of circumstances beyond their control.

> And he had seen the lovers in the little side-streets.
> And she had heard the morning stories clogged with
>   sweets.
> It was quite a time for loving. It was midnight. It
>   was May.
> But in the crowding darkness not a word did they say. (p. 3)

One would surmise that though it is dark, they still do not have the privacy desired for intimate contact. So, they remain silent. One might also conclude that the passage of time has caused their relationship to deteriorate to the point where it is impossible to express love.

In "The Bean Eaters," which also deals with an older married couple, Brooks explores the effect of poverty on their lives. They, like others in Bronzeville, attempt to make the most of their economic deprivation.

> They eat beans mostly, this old yellow pair.
> Dinner is a casual affair.
> Plain chipware on a plain and creaking wood,
> Tin flatware. (p. 314)

Though they go about their daily lives in an almost mechanical manner, they refuse to give up.

> Two who are Mostly Good.
> Two who have lived their day,

But keep on putting on their clothes
And putting things away. (p. 314)

Their memories, some of which are unpleasant, keep their lives from being totally meaningless.

Remembering, with twinklings and twinges,
As they lean over the beans in their rented back room
that is full of beads and receipts and dolls
and clothes,
tobacco crumbs, vases and fringes. (p. 314)

Though the couples in these two poems do have companionship, life seems to be just something to be endured, though the latter poem gives a more positive portrayal of the mates having endured together.

Without the perspective of the black woman writer, certain aspects of life in the urban black ghetto would possibly remain hidden. Brooks explores not only what it is like to be poor and black and male but also what it is like to be poor and black and female. She treats the relationships between males and females and the joys and frustrations which women experience in a way that is different from her male counterparts. The female images she creates reflect her personal experiences with black women, her observations of them in the community, and her general knowledge of their history in this country. These images are as varied as the human types present in any community.

Her poems present a more realistic view of the diversity and complexity of black women than the stereotypes (matriarch, whore, bitch, for example) which have persisted in other literary works by black and white artists alike. The lack of uniformity in her portraits of black women would contradict the notion that there is a monolithic black woman. There are females in her poems who commit adultery ("the vacant lot") and are sexually inhibited ("Obituary for a living lady"); they are aggressive ("Mrs. Martin's Booker T.") and passive (Maud of "Sadie and Maud"); they are extraordinary (Madam Walker of "Southeast Corner") and ordinary ("Mrs. Small"); they are exploited (unnamed women in "The Sundays of Satin-Legs Smith") and protected (young girl in "a song in the front yard"). They dream in the midst of adversity ("Callie Ford" and "hunch-back girl: she thinks of heaven") and they wallow in despair ("A Sunset of the City"). Though they share a common environment and heritage, they are still presented as individuals with different priorities and values, different levels of tolerance for misery, and different ways of dealing with problems. The major portion of Gwendolyn Brooks's work does indeed reflect, among other things, an intense awareness of our identity as black women and an unusual insight into the problems we face.

NOTES

1. Blyden Jackson and Louis D. Rubin, *Black Poetry in America: Two Essays in Historical Interpretation* (Baton Rouge: Louisiana State University Press, 1974), p. 82.
2. In a 1967 interview with Illinois historian Paul Angle, which appears in Brooks's autobiography, *Report from Part One,* pp. 160–61, she says that Bronzeville was not her own title but was "invented" many years ago by the Chicago *Defender,* a black newspaper, to refer to the black community.
3. *The World of Gwendolyn Brooks* (New York: Harper & Row, 1971), p. 18. Further references to individual poems are from this edition.
4. Gwendolyn Brooks, *Report from Part One* (Detroit: Broadside Press, 1972), p. 154.
5. Arthur P. Davis, "Gwendolyn Brooks: Poet of the Unheroic," *CLA Journal,* 7 (December 1963), 118.
6. Brooks, *Report from Part One,* p. 184.
7. George Kent, "The Poetry of Gwendolyn Brooks," Part II, *Black World,* October 1971, p. 38.
8. Brooks says in *Report from Part One* that this poem was also based on a real-life situation except that the mother was really working instead of gossiping down the street. She adds, "I guess I did her an injustice there" (p. 154).
9. Arthur Davis, "The Black-and-Tan Motif in the Poetry of Gwendolyn Brooks," *CLA Journal,* 6 (December 1962), 95–97.
10. Davis, "Gwendolyn Brooks: Poet of the Unheroic," p. 117.

BIBLIOGRAPHY

Brooks, Gwendolyn. *Report from Part One.* Detroit: Broadside Press, 1972.

Davis, Arthur P. "The Black-and-Tan Motif in the Poetry of Gwendolyn Brooks." *CLA Journal,* 6 (December 1962), 90–97.

———. "Gwendolyn Brooks: Poet of the Unheroic." *CLA Journal,* 7 (December 1963), 114–25.

Jackson, Blyden, and Rubin, Louis D. *Black Poetry in America: Two Essays in Historical Interpretation.* Baton Rouge: Louisiana State University Press, 1974.

Kent, George. "The Poetry of Gwendolyn Brooks." Part I. *Black World,* September 1971, pp. 36–71.

———. "The Poetry of Gwendolyn Brooks." Part II. *Black World,* October 1971, pp. 36–71.

Miller, Jeanne-Marie. "Gwendolyn Brooks—Poet Laureate of Bronzeville, U.S.A." *Freedomways,* 10 (1970), 63–75.

Parker, John. "Saga of the Bronzeville Community." *CLA Journal,* 4 (September 1960), 59–61.

The World of Gwendolyn Brooks. New York: Harper & Row, 1971.

Zora Neale Hurston retains the honor of being the most productive Afro-American female writer, though she died in 1960 at an early fifty-seven. Her seven book-length works are an exciting combination of her acute interests in orthodox religion, folklore, anthropology, and fiction. Her short fiction and articles featured in publications as diverse as *The Crisis* (the NAACP organ edited by Du Bois), *Opportunity* (the National Urban League magazine, edited by Charles S. Johnson), and *The Saturday Evening Post* are often as enigmatic and provocative as the woman herself.

Zora Hurston was born in the all-Black town of Eatonville, Florida, where she remained enduring the hardships of an unwanted waif until her mid-teens when she traveled north. Baltimore, Washington, and New York are locations which figure in her naissance, and Alain Locke, Charles S. Johnson, Lorenzo D. Turner, Franz Boas, and Fannie Hurst can be listed among her tutelary spirits.

The combination of science (anthropology) and art (literature) in Hurston's work is a result of her folklore-filled childhood and her impressionistic and curious early adulthood. Hence, Ellease Southerland's treatise is an important and appropriate one. Just how appropriate can only be determined after the consideration of several recommended critical and primary works. Larry Neale's introduction to *Their Eyes Were Watching God* (1971) is excellent; Robert Hemenway's new (1977) full-length biographical work is important, especially for folklorists; and Hurston's *Mules and Men* (1935), *Tell My Horse* (1938), and *Moses, Man of the Mountain* (1939) are all essential. The profound impact that Haiti, Honduras, Jamaica, New Orleans, and her native Florida had on Hurston's spiritual sensitivities is clearly evident in the last three works.

For additional material on Zora Neale Hurston, we suggest the introductory "Hurston" discussion in *Black Writers of America,* Hurston's autobiography, *Dust Tracks on a Road* (1942) which employs, at times, the stroke of the fiction writer, and the African-American bibliography in this text.

The Influence of Voodoo on the Fiction of Zora Neale Hurston

by ELLEASE SOUTHERLAND

Zora Neale Hurston watched a live black cat boiled to death. And then she was given the cat bone needed for conjuring. In other ceremonies, Zora drank the warm blood of a pig, heard the sound of breaking bones as chicken necks were wrung. She saw a client asking a two-headed doctor to kill an enemy. She watched this doctor burn nine black candles, sleep in a coffin for ninety days. After the ninety days, the enemy of the client died. Zora watched and learned many formulas for killing by remote control. She also saw the people of Haiti decorate the trees in elaborate preparation for voodoo ceremonies. And she was at the Saut d'Eau where men and women, young and old, stripped naked and, in the brilliance of the moon, washed ceremoniously in a religious ceremony during which many became possessed. Able to understand and to speak patois, Zora learned the songs of the gods and goddesses, their sacrifices—all learned over a long period of time and learned at the great expense of energy, physical and emotional. It was not easy for the daughter of a minister to strip herself naked and to lie down on a couch in an unfamiliar place. She did this for three days, having only water for sustenance. It was not easy, but she did this in order to qualify as a student of a two-headed doctor. Among the emotional consequences, and experience of visions, Zora traveled across the sky with thunder and lightning at her feet. It took her several months to realize that the visions were just that: visions. During her research in Haiti, Zora's progress brought her within one step of becoming one of the highest members of the voodoo religion, able to resist fire. Zora's studies demanded years of personal participation. And one would expect her knowledge of this art to find expression in her fiction. And it does.

The voodoo influences are visible on many levels. One of its first expressions is in a system of numerology given full play in *Their Eyes Were Watching God*. This novel is certainly readable without knowledge of numbers, but the more comprehensive reading comes with this knowledge. Here the numbers have character, psychic qualities. Numbers are related to other elements of the earth; the sun has one number, the moon, another. As this novel opens, we learn that Janie Stark, the central character, has $900 in the bank. Automatically, we understand that she is financially secure. In the same work we watch Tea Cake, Janie's third husband, take nine hairs from the crown of Janie's head to ensure his gambling success. Nine is mentioned again on the occasion when Tea Cake leaves Janie, leaving her in the ninth darkness, the darkest part of hell. The number nine is expressed in both positive and negative magnitudes.

The root character of the number nine can be traced directly to its voodoo origins. In addition to the nine black candles already mentioned in the ceremony for killing by remote control, the formula requires a beef brain, beef tongue, beef heart. The enemy's name was written nine times. The beef brain was placed on his plate with nine white peppers. And in other formulas:

To Harm and Kill

> Get bad vinegar, beef gall, filet gumbo with red pepper, and put names written across each other in bottles. Shake the bottle for nine mornings and talk and tell it what you want it to do. To kill the victim, turn it upside down and bury it breast deep, and he will die.

Another: the formula to make a man come home:

> Take nine deep red or pink candles.
> Write his name on each candle, etc.

Again: to make people love you:

> Take nine lumps of sugar, nine lumps of starch, nine teaspoons of steel dust. Wet it all with Jockey Club Cologne. Take nine pieces of ribbon, blue, red, or yellow. . . . Make nine bags and place them under a rug, behind an armoire, under a step or over a door.

And to break up a love affair:

> Take nine needles, break each needle in three pieces, etc.

This recurrence of the number nine is deliberate. One client told to come at nine o'clock came at ten and was told to wait until twelve o'clock, since ten was a "bad hour." And it was said that Marie Leveau, famous voodoo woman of New Orleans, was never seen nine days before or nine days after a ceremony.

In voodoo, then, nine is a number of highest power. And in this novel it is associated with the highest forms of life, the sun, the tree, power. It is certainly to Zora's credit that she limited her use of this number so that it would not develop distracting porportions.

The limited use of this number was possible in part because the powers represented by the number nine were reinforced by other nine-symbols, the sun and the tree. This novel is packed with suns and trees, packed with the power for living. One reads of the tragedies and yet experiences the joys of life; Zora has worked her power-symbols effectively.

Their Eyes Were Watching God has what could be described as a "six-scene," where we find the number six representing elements opposite those represented by the number nine. At age sixteen, Janie marries an older man, Logan Killicks, who possessed sixty acres of land. The narrator states that after "three moons" Janie visits her grandmother to complain of her husband as having unbearable body odors and of looking like an old skull-head from the graveyard. In addition to the six in Janie's age and the six in the number of acres Killicks possesses, the six is also expressed in Logan's last name, kill-icks, and in Janie's description of his head as a skull-head. Even as the nine represented power and life, so the six represents weakness and death. The final death of this relationship comes when Killicks threatens Janie with an ax. What might have been an idle expression of anger on some other occasion was effective in bringing an end to this relationship.

Again, the effect of this number is based on its infrequent use. It does come into play at the time of the flood when Janie and Tea Cake are running to save their lives. Tea Cake heads for the six-mile bridge, wondering if they will find safety there. No. The bridge is occupied by white people, and there is no room for Tea Cake and Janie. And in the final scenes of the book, when Janie discovers a gun beneath Tea Cake's pillow, it is, of course, a six-shooter. One could, of course, comment that the number six is associated with death in the American culture, where a man is buried six feet under. But with the death comes also the symbol of the moon, the fuller expression indicating voodoo influence.

One other number deserving special attention is the number three, used in this novel to signal the conclusion of the things, the final stage of things. This number is most forceful in the scene where Janie is forced to kill her rabid husband. Before the shooting, Janie discovers the gun under Tea Cake's pillow, loaded, of course, with three bullets. Removing the gun, she reasons, will possibly excite Tea Cake's disordered mind. So she leaves the gun, but prepares another for herself, thinking that she might be able to scare him off, should things reach a crisis. There is a crisis, and when Tea Cake aims the gun at her, fires and shoots, it is not until a split second after he has actually fired the final, third shot that Janie's own shot kills him.

Before the third shot, there were other threes: the doctor saying that Tea Cake's illness was incurable because it had gone past the third week. Janie's first marriage was celebrated with three cakes, simultaneously symbolizing the final stage of her childhood and the first stage of womanhood. This first marriage ends after three moons have passed. Also, in her search for spiritual fulfillment, Janie is not content until she experiences a fullness of life with Tea Cake, her third husband. Although her life with Tea Cake was brief, merely two years, compared with twenty years of unhappy marriage to Mayor Starks, Janie feels that her life is complete, and on this happy note, the novel ends. Many traditions give special importance to the number three. But in Zora's fiction, a full consciousness of numbers is at least activated by a knowledge of voodoo.

There are other numbers used in the novel, twos and an occasional ten. But they mark time and occasions without showing any striking qualities. It would seem, then, that Zora did not press numbers into service at unnatural moments, but rather let the more natural creative process develop an intriguing system of numerology.

In voodoo, colors, like numbers, provide dynamic force. Color is crucial to ceremony. Damballa, the supreme voodoo god, is offered a pair of white chickens, a hen and a rooster. For another god, the chickens sacrificed are red. For another, black. In many of the formal voodoo ceremonies, the participants wear white. Color has life and vitality in the voodoo ceremony. And color echoes life and vitality in Zora's fiction.

Looking at *Their Eyes Were Watching God,* we see an emphasis placed on two colors, yellow and blue. The color blue originates with a series of visions Zora experienced at age seven. In these twelve visions, many of them predicting sadness, one vision of a blue dress signaled a happy period in Zora's life. And so the blue dress symbolizes happiness. In this novel, blue is the color preferred by Tea Cake. He comes to his wedding dressed in blue. He lets Janie know that blue is his favorite color, and when they start out to build a life together, Janie is wearing blue. This color takes on ceremonial importance when we see that Tea Cake is associated with the sun, called the "son of evening sun." The man is the sun with his woman as his bright and happy sky. This adds a spiritual and cosmic note to the relationship.

The second color, the yellow or gold, is first made conspicuous in the symbol of the yellow mule. The mule here symbolizes the plight of black men in America. The color gives a memorable brilliance to his form and also comments on a gold-oriented society, willing to exchange the integrity of an entire people for economic well-being. So often black writers reduce their works to two colors: black and white. Or a dulled gray. Or in its most brilliant moment, the shock of things blood-red. This restriction on color echoing the absence of color in the lives of black people is a justified one. But somehow, Zora manages to reflect brilliant color, even in a theme which restates the racial abuses blacks suffer.

Zora's concept of life in its many forms found expansion through her knowledge of voodoo. The rocks and shells, the tree and the sun, all hold life. The mule, the moon, the black cat, and the river have spirits. There is a relationship between all things, men and rocks, water and trees. And the forms of life are reversible or exchangeable. Then mules can become men, and men can become mules. And knowing this, we see a stronger tie between the yellow mule and black men. Then in addition to the brilliance, the emphasis on mulatto is suggested by the striking color of a beast who is underfed and overworked.

Mules and Men, Zora's first collection of folklore, takes its title from the knowledge that men can become mules. And this idea is more subtly stated in *Their Eyes Were Watching God.* A description of neighbors who sat on their porches and watched Janie return after a two-year absence:

> These sitters had been tongueless, earless, eyeless conveniences all day. Mules and other brutes had occupied their skins. But now the sun and the bossman were gone, so the skins felt powerful and human. They became lords of sounds and lesser things.

There is, then, a direct connection between the dehumanized conditions of the workers and the overbearing nature of the bossman.

The phrase "tongueless, earless, eyeless conveniences" recalls the description of zombies given in *Tell My Horse.* The prospective victims all died in a similar way, following a two-day sickness. The victims have all the symptoms of death; all the vital signs are arrested. But following burial, the "dead" person is removed from the grave and given an antidote which restores the vital signs, but leaves the speech center and the memory totally destroyed. The zombie, then, has eyes that stare without recognition, is tongueless, and is used as a work horse. The comment on mules and brutes is not by any means a mild social comment. Men behave like brute beasts when their minds and bodies are occupied by alien bodies, occupied by alien spirits.

The appearance of the yellow mule, then, takes on added dimension. Like the black man, he is overworked, abused. And like the black man, he is freed. And the legends sprang up about him. After his freedom, he began to act differently. He broke up a prayer meeting where the preacher was boring the congregation He went to the Pearsons' house, stuck his head through the window, and Mrs. Pearson, thinking that it was Rev. Pearson, gave him a plate of supper. And when he dies, the yellow mule is given a funeral because it is said that he died "like a natural man."

The moment of the funeral demonstrates another dimension of

irreversible life-forms. The buzzards are described as having "stooped forms" that "people" the trees. And from all appearances, the buzzards are occupied by some very human spirits. The lesser buzzards are impatient, anxious to begin, but realize that they may not start until the "parson," the leader, is present. And the leader is a most serious bird, white-headed, ponderous, and dignified. Upon reaching the carcass of the yellow mule, he first bows, giving the departed beast full ceremony. Then he asks the question "What killed this man?" The laughter this scene demands comes partially because the reader is so caught up in the believability of the moment where humor and terrible reality meet. The buzzards are about to pick the eyes from the beast, then clean his flesh down to the bones. This is the moment which shows the oneness of laughter and death.

This same unity comes to light on another occasion when life expresses itself in another form, this time through one of the basic elements: water. At the time of the flood, the people in panic and fear call the warning, "the lake is coming." This is, of course, a serious hurricane in the Florida Everglades. Zora in her own life had seen the results of a flood and had witnessed the horror of human bodies bloated and beyond recognition, their eyes "thrown open in judgement." So there is no lack of knowledge which allows for a moment of humor. It is rather a more complete knowledge of the earth and its spirits which dictates the humor. And in this tragic scene where Zora describes the water as "walking the earth with a heavy heel" men seem so small as they flee the waters, running for their lives calling, "the lake is coming." And the water, sensing the smallness of man, answers back, "Yes, I'm coming." The mood of the water is a humorous one, giving a fuller perspective to life. It would seem that what is for us so personally tragic, in the total scheme of things, is a minor comedy.

In *Tell My Horse,* Zora states that science has much to learn from the black religion. She points out that "goofer dust," dirt taken from the graveyards, and given to one's enemy, has been discovered to be rich in many potent germs. And what may have been dismissed as ignorant superstition has been discovered to be applied science. But in other instances where the ceremony and its particulars seemed unrelated to the results, Zora states that the onlooker lacks knowledge of symbols. Then the preoccupation with snake skins or with egg shells or with sprinkled dust leaves the curious onlooker uninformed of the real powers developed during the ceremony. While symbols do not have an exclusive importance, they are an indispensible part of ceremony. Among the indispensible symbols, the tree, which, together with the sun, is the symbol found throughout Zora's fiction and folklore.

Long before her folklore studies, Zora had a special fascination for trees. In *Dust Tracks on a Road* she describes a favorite but treacherous tree, which she named "The Loving Pine." She stated that this tree would take a moment at night when she was the only one watching, and move. Just a little. And whenever Zora tried to get her sister or brothers to notice, the tree would, of course, remain perfectly still. Also, Zora loved to climb trees. It was the tree that gave her the height needed to see the horizon, to get a better view of the world. And perhaps we could add that as a minister's daughter, she heard sermons of the Tree of Knowledge of Good and Evil, and of the Tree of Life. But voodoo holds its own influence in the great symbol of the tree which is rooted in the total works of Zora Neale Hurston. And in studying voodoo, she was to find the tree which is also central to that religion.

In voodoo, the tree is the symbol of the god Legba, the god who provides a way. The tree is the connection between heaven and earth; it is a medium for spirits. Haitian families have sacred trees which house the spirits of ancestors. And newborns are ceremoniously introduced to these family trees. And before ceremonies, the trees are laboriously and festively decorated, so that they become part of the brilliance that characterizes the moment.

Their Eyes Were Watching God begins in the brilliance of a pear tree in full bloom. Janie, sixteen years old, is lying on her back in a sensual position, drenched in feelings of excitement for life. Her feelings are sexual as she contemplates the sweet sting of the bee and thinks of the soft blossoms arching to meet the sting. The tree has an unearthly control of her feelings. And as she rises, Janie, like the tree, shines with new excitement of life. Moments later, when a young admiring neighbor pauses near her fence, for the first time in her life, Janie consents to kiss a young man. The tree, then, becomes the symbol of love and life. The man who will bring spiritual fulfillment to Janie must have the qualities of the tree. He must be a spiritual medium. Like Legba, he must provide a way for her, give her life new possibilties, the fullest possibilities. The men Janie marries can be described in terms of their resemblance or lack of resemblance to the tree. The first man, Logan Killicks, has worldly possessions and is able to provide an economic way. But Janie is seeking connections with things spiritual. The second husband, Mayor Jody Starks, has ambition which Janie says stands for far horizons. Ambition forces the mayor into a constant state of calculation where there is no room for the blossoms of trees. Tea Cake (Vergible Woods) had neither money nor ambition. But he had knowledge of natural things, knowledge of the sun, the water, the streets. His joy came through music and dance. Laughter. He was the man able to take the soul from the mud of the earth or the laughter of the sky. His last name, Woods, reinforces his direct relationship to the tree. And after his death, when Janie chooses something to remember him by, it is the seeds he wanted to plant. Throughout this work and others, there is the recurring symbol of the tree with an importance strongly suggesting its voodoo origins.

When Zora's *Moses, Man of the Mountain* rolled off the press, reviewers could not control their astonishment: Moses a voodoo man! Paper after paper ran sensational reviews with titles expressing awe for such a daring portrayal of the ancient religious leader. But if we remember that Zora did not publish *Moses, Man of the Mountain* before her publication of both *Mules and Men* and *Tell My Horse,* perhaps it will seem less sensational and more natural. Among the many memorable powers of the Moses as described in the first five books of the Bible are his ability to heal, and instructing the children of Israel to look up to the snake.

The snake, in voodoo, is the signature of the supreme god, Damballa. And Zora, sensing a relationship between Moses and this supreme god, set out to rewrite the story of Moses, this time showing him to be of Egyptian birth, and giving him the full description of a voodoo man. Moses has the cat bone to reinforce his power and to give his people the strength to win battles. When Moses comes before pharaoh to demand freedom for his people, he comes on a Wednesday, Damballa's day. And before he addresses pharaoh, like any well-versed voodoo man, he first salutes the cardinal points. One could say that *Moses, Man of the Mountain* was a fictional attempt to give full and complete expression to the voodoo religion. But somehow the strength of that expression was deflected by a too accurate recall of the story as related in the Bible. In its moments of pure black folklore, the story vibrates life.

No other work of Zora's fiction is written so completely within the form of the voodoo religion as *Moses, Man of the Mountain.* But there are some other scenes worth noting which take their life from the world of voodoo. In a short story, "Spunk," a strong man kills another after first taking the man's wife. The killer is a man without fear. But he does fear the powers of voodoo and meets his own death, slashed by the blade of a saw, convinced that the dead man's haunt is responsible for what appears to be an accidental death. The dramatic tension of this story is built on the implication that the powers of the dead are real. There are more "rational" explanations possible. But it would seem more accurate to conclude that when a man is so strong that no power on earth can bring fear to his heart, there are other powers which will occupy his being and give him the appearance of having destroyed himself.

In *Jonah's Gourd Vine,* we find a young minister involved in a marriage which he does not understand. And of course conjure is at the root of this marriage. Discovering that he does not love the woman and hard pressed to recall the details leading to their marriage, he wonders aloud, "Just how did I marry this woman anyway?" Seeking answers, Jonah goes to a conjure woman, who informs him that he has been conjured. And on returning home, Jonah first digs up the ground near the gatepost, then digs up the dirt under the front step, and finally tears open the mattress, discovering all the items buried to keep the conjure potent. When the wife returns home and notices the freshly dug earth, she understands that there will be serious consequences to pay. And when Jonah, in full rage, beats her unmercifully, no neighbor interferes; her crime was a serious one.

There is a similar scene in *Their Eyes Were Watching God* where Janie's second husband, Mayor Starks, sick and dying, denies his wife entrance to his sickroom. He accuses her of hating him so much that she had him conjured. In his weakened state, the mayor seeks the aid of a two-headed doctor, hoping that he will counterwork the conjure. Janie realizes the seriousness of the charge, and more than hurt, redoubles her efforts to regain her husband's confidence so that he will not die with false and ill opinion of her. This and similar scenes showed that voodoo in a quieter form is a reality for many blacks.

Perhaps the culmination of Zora's folklore is the form it gave her religious thought. There were those who wondered just how much Zora "believed" the things she studied. And in her autobiography, in the chapter entitled "Religion," Zora states that the form of worship is valid inasmuch as it is valuable to the worshiper: a rather diplomatic answer. But if one were to trace her religious thinking in her fiction, there would be discovered a new dimension of religious thought where concepts are made visible through the use of symbols traceable to voodoo ceremonies. In *Their Eyes Were Watching God,* in describing Mrs. Turner's love for Janie, a love which was more simple worship, Hurston writes:

> She felt honored by Janie's acquaintance and she quickly forgave and forgot snubs in order to keep it. Anyone who looked more white folkish than herself was better than she was in her criteria, therefore it was right that they should be cruel to her at times, just as she was cruel to those more Negroid than herself in direct ratio to their Negroness. . . . Once having set up her idols and built altars to them it was inevitable that she should accept any inconsistency and cruelty from her deity as all good worshippers do from theirs. All gods who receive homage are cruel. All gods dispense suffering without reason. Otherwise, they would not be worshipped. Through indiscriminate suffering men know fear and fear is the most divine emotion. It is the stones for altars and the beginning of wisdom. Half gods are worshipped in wine and flowers. Real gods require blood.

The wine, flowers, altar stones, and blood, all taken directly from voodoo ceremonies where certain gods are in fact worshiped with wine and flowers, others with blood. The concretes of the voodoo ceremony have been translated into a philosophy which defines the importance of fear in the lives of men. And there is here awareness that man takes a direct hand in fashioning the gods he will worship, feeling that if he has built the altar, then he is compelled to worship at that altar. Gods are cruel, and the cruelty a necessity. And although theologians preach the contrary, there is no rationale behind the suffering, except that suffering inspires fear and fear for Zora is the most divine emotion.

In the chapters devoted to a discussion of Zora's folklore collections, *Mules and Men* and *Tell My Horse,* we will see other symbols of ceremony, and recall the voodoo gods in greater detail with attention to their attributes and the particulars of their celebrations. But even then we will be impressed by the resemblance beween Zora's folklore and fiction. It simply was not possible for Zora to learn conjuring, to dance in voodoo ceremonies, and to sing the songs of the gods and not express these experiences in her fiction.

When *Sturdy Black Bridges* became something more than an idea, Jerry Ward was one of the first writers who encouraged the editors to follow through on the project. Southern, Dr. Ward was passionately cognizant of the literature available on Black folk, and he eagerly welcomed a project which would fill the void—the one encompassing truthful, realistic considerations of Black women in fiction—Black women in Africa, the Americas, and the Caribbean.

Jerry Ward's decision to write "Bridges and Deep Water," then, is less than monumental, since his beliefs about the need for Black women to write about themselves are recorded in a number of places, but his conclusions are always significant and they are usually auguries for change in the dispositions of Black American literature from year to year.

Bridges and Deep Water

by JERRY D. WARD

In the final stanza of Carolyn M. Rodgers' "It Is Deep (Don't never forget the bridge that you crossed over on)," one finds these mascon lines:

> My mother, religious-negro, proud of
> having waded through a storm, is very obviously,
> a sturdy Black bridge that I crossed over, on.

Like its companion piece, "Jesus Was Crucified, or It Must Be Deep (an epic poem)," the poem is a matrix of significant feelings in significant form: a positive image of the Black woman's correct incorrectness. Irony and paradox. The Black woman's situation in the history of African and Euro-American cultures is loaded with paradox and irony, and the reasons are in our histories. There is a constant dialectic between observed, experienced history and created history. As far as the image of The Black Woman is concerned, we mediate between real knowledge of the Black woman and fictions/images of Black women expressed and projected in various media. Stop. Check yourself. Think of all the Black women you know. How many of your images are abstractions from real persons, how many only impositions of residual "images" from newspapers, magazines, literature, movies and TV, economic and political propaganda, the graphic and plastic arts, from the ubiquitous pancake mix box? Just as there is tension in the juxtaposition of real and unreal, of the literal and the metaphorical, there is functional uptightness in dealing with the idea/image of the Black woman. A sturdy Black bridge does get you over deep water, and it is very obviously useful. When you cross over on the bridge, you cannot avoid stepping or rolling on it.

A literal reading of the four lines from Rodgers' poem plunges us into the deep water of what happens in language. Not what happens on the surface where the message is carried but what happens underground, in the preverbal, chthonic depths where the action *is*. The plunge gets us into all kinds of heady matters about innate predisposition, competence, the grasping of signs (concepts plus sound-images), the shuffling about of signs to create propositions that match given language codes. There are an infinite number of subtle operations involved in getting from concept to sign, some of them primal (simply properties of language) and some of them culturally determined (linguistic options for concretizing a welter of signals). The really important point is how culture permits one to manifest preverbal impulses and signals, and how strong is the will to resist and transcend dysfunctional "rules" in moving from the preverbal to locution and perlocution. In the underground of language, *woman* like *man* is universal, and then only perhaps for very young children and the uncivilized. All God's children got culture, but only the damned of the earth have civilization (all that pollutes mind and environment). Check the alpha points for the human species and language, the creation myths.

The nature of language and its use in social contexts give us some clues about why the image of the Black woman is, and will remain for many decades, a crucial problem. No matter how many Black men stand gazing across what Eldridge Cleaver aptly named "the naked abyss of negated masculinity," saying to the Black women on the other side, "My Queen, Soul Sister, Eternal Love,

Black Beauty, Best-Thing-God-Ever-Created, Sugar Mama," the images just hang there in the middle distance. Well, they do create some good feelings, authentic love in some cases. But are the images coming from the preverbal depths? Are they more than appropriations from culturally bound, predigested English? Are they derived from a knowing beyond language? Is the Black male in the civilization of the United States so conditioned that his imaging will always be locked into types and stereotypes? And the same questions apply to the Black female who must behold the world through the perspective of imposed femininity.

Building a bridge across the abyss of negated masculinity/neglected femininity has got to be a joint effort: Haki Madhubutis, George Barlows, and Lance Jefferses of the African-American world coming to a consensus with the Toni Cade Bambaras, the Alice Walkers, and the Mari Evanses. That will be the African-American community formulating the language in which healthy, nonescapist images can be embodied. In the sixties, we did begin changing the images, the lexical aspects of the images. But the whole process has to do with changing the grammar, the deep structures. It's a long, thankless job. And it requires the transformation of pure language into language-action, into behaviors.

Behaviors, ideologies, mind-sets. And knowing the vagaries of Black, or more precisely, African-American mind-set in the middle of the twentieth century. Doing the hard work of coming to that knowledge and not running any games on ourselves about how difficult getting back to primal image-making and positive-image using is going to be. But we start, or start again, with the notion of imaging the Black woman in language (a fascinating index of fragmented ethos). Distinguishing vision and image.

A vision of the Black woman in literature is not identical with the idea of the Black woman character, for example. We treat them differently. The first has to do with icon, a visual and basically undifferentiated image; the second, with representation of human image and action in time. Certainly, the reader can't grasp character without image. The bare bones of a narrative text must be fleshed in the imagination. However, the images used in the realization of character involve a sense of time, of history, a fourth dimension that need not concern us when we look at a vision or a portrait. This is a fine but necessary distinction. When we speak of portrait in literature, we have already transferred the language of painting, sculpture, or photography into the language of literary criticism. We have engaged in metaphoric thinking, because we hold that a specific literary text or segment of the text *is* a portrait. The modern mind tends not to demand rigid discrimination between the critical discourse appropriate to one kind of art and the terms of discourse applied to another. Thus, it is wholly permissible, and even fruitful, to exploit the metaphoric operations of language in order to make new discoveries. We do precisely that when we concern ourselves with portraiture in literature.

Examining the "icons" of the Black woman in literature, we depend on metaphor as method of learning how verbal relations function in different social contexts. The icons of the Black woman got from specific images in Iceberg Slim's *Mama Black Widow* are vastly different from those in Baldwin's *Go Tell It on the Mountain* or Sarah E. Wright's *This Child's Gonna Live.* Aside from such matters as implicit genre and authorial intention, these novels draw in images of the Black woman from the context of American society. In each there is a special kind of *seeing-the-Black-woman-as*. The ideological and cultural imperative hidden in the language of *seeing-as* (so buried that the writer may not be conscious of them) and the influence that language has on our thinking about the Black woman is at issue. The "icons" of the Black woman that metamorphize so easily from figures of speech into figures of thought are vital to our thinking about how we apprehend and reshape the phenomenological world in language. The study of visions of the Black woman in literature is quite properly a part of the larger study of language in human behavior.

Focusing on so vitriolic a subject is one way of resisting what is dysfunctional in traditional thought. It is a way, much needed at present, of pointing to new directions that must be taken if critical inquiry about literature and life is to be vital. The whole enterprise requires an awareness of method and how method determines results. It requires a radical assessment of how language and literature operate in history, of who controls or is controlled by them, of how they serve first to create and then support or undermine our most deeply rooted cultural assumptions. Racism and sexism, the politics of the penis and the vagina, and the interrelations of their expression in the world of "fictions" and in the habitable world are central in dealing with visions of women and men in the literature of the United States, of Western civilization. The Black woman has been the triple victim in the adventure of Western culture. Given that language cannot escape history, and that the Black woman is a composite of individual Black women, has it ever been or will it ever be possible to project a real image?

The answer is at once yes and no. Simple answers would only compound difficult questions. The metaphor in Rodgers' "It Is Deep"—mother is a sturdy Black bridge—fuses the strength and utility of a bridge with positive qualities of Black mothers, but there are levels of sensual association at which the positive fusion of woman and bridge are nullified. Visions of Black women in literature can be given to us only through the medium of words, and the semantic and semiotic values of words shift according to one's vantage just as a portrait seems to change as one views it from different angles. Whether visions of Black women in literature are positive or negative, true or distorted, good or bad, real or surreal, satisfying or inadequate is relative. Evaluation of the vision depends in part on some understanding of the cultural imperatives that governed its creation and in part on whether those imperatives (linguistic, social, psychological, etc.) are consonant or dissonant with our own. Metaphor, the powerful intellectual device of analogy, is both contained within these visions and should be our instrument for coming to terms with what the visions mean, for indepth probing of experience.

Why in critical discussions of the problems of the Black writers is there so little mention of the problems of the Black woman writer? Does Al Young's *Who Is Angelina?* deal more reliably with the Black woman than Carlene Hatcher Polite's *Sister X and the Victims of Foul Play?* Is the psychology of the Black woman more faithfully reproduced in Gayl Jones's *Corregidora* and Allison Mills's *Francisco* than in Ernest J. Gaines's *The Autobiography of Miss Jane Pittman?* Is there any relation between the androgynous vision and visions of Black women in literature? What do the poems of Julia Fields, Audre Lorde, Pinkie Gordon Lane, Gwendolyn Brooks, Rikki Lights, and June Jordan do to us? What are Black women saying to Black men across the shrinking abyss?

At this point in our history, literature and otherwise, the confluence of two great movements encourages us to be increasingly sensitive to how we interpret language. There is the continuing revolutionary struggle of Black people against insidious forms of oppression. In the seventies, the feminist movement, which has always been indebted to the Black struggle, heightens awareness of the rights and rites of personhood. The thinking that informs both movements is related, in a vital way, to how visions of the Black woman are structured and then explained. Should the interpreter begin with what Erik Erikson calls the "woman's productive inner space," thus raising psychoanalytic questions about specific forms of representation in language; or, given the need to fight the projection of negative identity (especially as it has been used in criticism), must the interpreter start with Black construction of reality as a concrete human event? The point of departure in interpretation is determined by vested interests, because a value-free interpretation is not possible. From the very beginning, it is clear that an unqualified connecting of the plight of women with the plight of ethnic groups in this country will terminate rather than expand dialogue and understanding.

Let me give a brief illustration. At a meeting of the Coordinating Council of Literary Magazines in 1975, a Black male writer argued that white American writers had never dealt sufficiently with race in literature: "They don't want to be Black!" A white female writer retorted: "You don't want to be a woman, either." Further rational discussion was impossible. The gut issues of racism, even within the boundaries of literature, do not share a common ground with questions of sexism. Institutionalized racism, whether or not it is masked as art, is motivated by concepts of economic and power distribution. The relevance of these concepts to inequalities determined by gender is tangential. As is all too frequently the case, the white female writer conveniently forgot she belongs to an ethnic group. And forgot the Native American woman has no public image.

No amount of sisterhooding and interethnic posturing can change basic facts. In life, as in literature, the Black woman has at various times been a queen, a slave, the burden-bearer of the race, mammy, whore, bitch, mother, lover, wife, the mule of the world, warrior, freedom fighter, the biological and spiritual bridge of racial continuity. She has been seen as all these things and many more, but have the labels been rightly assigned? Where did they originate? Have we ever had judicious visions?

The possibility of discussing how and why we *see* the Black woman in the phenomenological world as we do must always be open. Necessary topics beget necessary questions. As yet, we can only respond to the questions implicit in our seeing the Black woman in a certain way and recording that vision in media. It certainly must be corrected by the Black woman's envisioning of her self. Our prejudices, conditioned reflexes, and the flux of reality itself pull us back from attempts to leap into the abyss.

Over fifty years ago, W. E. B. Du Bois made a profound assertion:

> No other women on earth could have emerged from the hell of force and temptation which once engulfed and still surrounds black women in America with half the modesty and womanliness that they retain.

When we again touch the meaning of this truth, the bridge will have got us over deep, troubled water. Together.

Part Two The Conversational Vision

Introduction:

THE CONVERSATIONAL VISION

by ROSEANN P. BELL

In the very recent past, during one of our several nationalistic and reactionary times, we were called upon to be definitive in explaining our differences from "the other." To legitimize ourselves, our heritage, our being a Black and organic whole, we responded—we reacted—with predictable behavior, and provided ourselves and "the other" with slogans, marketable rhetoric, Afro wigs, and a revival of not-so-safe heroes. Thus, books like *Black Thunder* were exhumed, and for the first time, some young "revolutionaries" heard of Gabriel Prosser and Arna Bontemps along with Denmark Vesey and Paul Cuffe. Some even read William Styron's *Nat Turner* (and liked it), but fell short of discovering *Ten Black Writers Respond,* a commendable iconoclastic effort in deconstructing "the other's" concept of Black American history. Some read Stephen Henderson's seminal introduction to *Understanding the New Black Poetry* and picked up on words like "saturation" and "mascon," but they did not read or feel the poetry in the book—the "massive concentration of Black experiential energy." Finally, some found only the sections in *Black Fire* which applied to them—the parts which armed them with the audacity to call themselves "radicals" and to call Black women "queens" or "beautiful Black sistuhs."

We've got some time now, not to agonize over what we thought should have happened, but didn't; not to assassinate the characters of the men and women to whom we assigned the august titles of leaders, but who, very often, turned out to be just ordinary people capable of making mistakes and who were too often too eager to be bought off: That's what happens when Blackness is a commodity. We've got work to do.

Sometimes we think that the American experience has produced too few long-distance runners, but whether this determination is right or wrong, we must admit that we have been guilty, too many times, of trying to worship the gods that we have created for immediate purposes. So at times it is necessary to look beyond the particularities of an individualized Western ethos and see how we can benefit most from our sustaining conduits of culture, wherever they may be.

These avenues or bridges, to be topical, are not always found in books. Indeed, from the perspective of a people who do not read (we are told), but who watch television, listen to the beat, and remember the attending message of a song, and who would rather have our direction *told* to us, we have a fantastic reservoir of nonliterary learning resources and opportunities. However, discretion and analysis are where we most frequently fall short.

The last experience, listening to the word, is what "Conversational Vision" is all about. The late Janheinz Jahn, in *Muntu* (1961), described "Nommo"—the magic power of the word—as follows:

> . . . NOMMO is water and the glow of fire and seed and word in one. Nommo, the life force, is the fluid as such, a unity of spiritual-physical fluidity, giving life to everything, penetrating everything, causing everything.

And Aimé Césaire, Francophone poet par excellance, says of words:

> Words out of fresh blood,
> words that are spring-tides
> and swine-fevers and swamp fevers
> and lavas and bush fires and
> flames of flesh and flames of villages

But there can be no words which function in the capacities outlined by Jahn and Césaire without a concrete and material comprehension of the concepts which generate the words. People who utter memorable words have an obligation to remember where they came from, where they presently are in relation to other historical moments, and where they wish to go, based on real, tangible conditions.

When taken as a whole, the vision which surfaces in this segment produces a composite picture of past, present, and future Black motion, given life through the spoken word. From the voices of the very young, speaking about the creative energy poured into their art, to the older, seasoned sages attesting to the ever-changing mystery of life, we see a creative and critical continuum. The middle group, exceedingly vital because they are in tune with the simplicity of youth as well as the strength of age, are also bridges over which we may cross.

Many who read this section may never have had the smoothly southern or elegantly African experience of "sitting at the conf'rence table" or "sitting on the mourners' bench"—delicate and collective times which are responsible for a number of us "getting ovah." The spiritual fabric almost inherent in talking with people whom we respect (and who respect and are proud of us, too) cannot be denied because that fabric, when it is well woven, allows us to be less insular, less telescopic, more holistic. It sometimes makes us more communistic and more involved with all our people do, for we are affected by it all.

What we learn from these interviews is that our women—Black women—are intricately responsible for helping to create the holistic view among us who have not succumbed to the crass, banal, individualistic morass which is often the result of being in a money- (not people-) oriented society; we learn that there are several dimensions to every picture. We learn that the *real* heroes and heroines are not just the figures who have been provided with the momentous opportunity to stand before huge Black throngs, arms outstretched to deliver canons for temporal living. Most of our special people—those able to rise above tragedy because they understand its opposites—are jus' reg'lar folk. They are the people sitting on Clark's wide storefront porch, telling tales to each other and instructively entertaining the children in some of Zora Hurston's work. They are the thousands of women carrying large quantities of produced goods on their heads (with babies on their backs) to and from the socializing centers called markets in Africa and the Caribbean. They are young sisters at Cornell, Spelman, and Tougaloo colleges, trying to find order in what appears to be the vastness of nothingness. They are women whose last names are forgotten in places where young folks wind their way to a door which is unreluctantly opened by a "Miz Ethel" or a "Miss Louvenia"; the youngsters (who may be five, fifteen, or thirty-five) reach out for sustenance and support, and it is given unselfishly.

There are levels of meaning and apprehensions of time which are rarely captured in media other than the conversational one. One has only to read Amos Tutuola's *Palm-wine Drinkard* or *My Life in the Bush of Ghosts* to grasp my meaning. But in the absence of being privy to a Tutuolan manipulation of time and space, we can turn to the pieces in this book and expect them to provide us with a fuller comprehension of this African puzzle, recounted by Alexis Kagame in *La Philosophie Bantu Rwandaise de l'Être* (Bruxelles, 1951), and explained in *Muntu:*

> Ask about a child: "Does that child have intelligence?" And hear the reply: "He has the intelligence of books, but he does not have intelligence." The person answering means by this that although the child understands readily what he learns in school, he is wanting in the wisdom of life, in the knowledge of relationships, of situations in life in which he is placed by the play of actual circumstance. In other words, the child has a lively intelligence, but no wisdom; he cannot apply his theoretical knowledge to the practical situations of life.

The conversations which follow combine intelligence with the narrative fluidity of actual situations in life, a feat rarely accomplished except through the spoken realm of Nommo—the magic power of the word.

Ann Petry became well known after the success of her first novel, *The Street* (1946), which is an impressive naturalistic novel. *The Street* was followed by *Country Place* (1947) *The Narrows* (1953), and a novella, "Miss Muriel" (1963). In addition to the longer works, Miss Petry's numerous short stories and essays appear in various issues of *The Crisis, Phylon, Opportunity, The New Yorker, Holiday, Amsterdam News,* and *People's Voice*. She has also written three children's books: *The Drugstore Cat* (1949), *Harriet Tubman, Conductor on the Underground Railroad* (1955), and *Tituba of Salem Village* (1964). Ann Petry lives in the Connecticut village of Old Saybrook.

Ann Petry Talks About First Novel

by JAMES W. IVY

One day in October 1943, I was going through a batch of manuscripts when I picked out one with a teasing title: "On Saturday the Siren Sounds at Noon." It turned out upon examination to be a short story by Ann Petry. I had not known the name before, but a glance at the first paragraph told me that the woman was a writer. I went to my editor with enthusiastic praise for the story and we both agreed that it was "good stuff" and should be printed. We scheduled the story for our December 1943 issue. This was the first published story of a young writer of remarkable talent. Further interest was aroused in the story when one of the editors of the publishing house of Houghton Mifflin asked for copies of the December issue.

This was my first introduction to the writings of Mrs. Petry. But I never met Mrs. Petry until the winter of 1946, almost three years later. In the meantime, she had submitted for publication a long short story on the Harlem riot of August 1943. Though a brilliant psychological analysis of the frustrations, the pent-up emotions, and the tensions which provoked the outbreak, the story was too long for *The Crisis* and we had regretfully to suggest that it be offered elsewhere. In May 1945, however, we carried her study in affection, "Olaf and his Girl Friend." And in November we published "Like a Winding Sheet."

Mrs. Petry thus joins that company of brilliant young writers, Langston Hughes, et al., who first received publication in the pages of *The Crisis*.

After one of the Mifflin editors had read "On Saturday the Siren Sounds at Noon," he asked Mrs. Petry if she was working on a novel. She was and the following year she submitted the first five chapters and a complete synopsis of *The Street*. She was then awarded the $2,400 Houghton Mifflin Literary Fellowship for 1945. This enabled her to devote the next ten months to finishing the novel.

The Street was published in January and its appearance gave me an opportunity to meet Mrs. Petry. My appointment was for 11:30 in the offices of Richard Condon on East Fifty-Seventh Street, just off Fifth Avenue. Mrs. Petry met me cordially and was eager to record that her first published story in *The Crisis* had given her reputation.

In person Mrs. Petry is of medium height, pleasant manners and intercourse, and possessed of a sense of companionable good humor. She has a creamy-brown complexion, alert, smiling eyes, and a soft cultivated voice. We entered at once into the intimacy of talk and the first thing I wanted to know was how she had come to write her first published story.

"Did you have any particular message in that story? What were you trying to show?" I queried.

"Nothing in particular. I wrote it simply as a story. But it came to be written in this way. One Saturday I was standing on the 125th Street platform of the IRT subway when a siren suddenly went off. The screaming blast seemed to vibrate inside people. For the siren seemed to be just above the station. I immediately noticed the reactions of the people on the platform. They were ineresting, especially the frantic knitting of a woman seated on a nearby bench.

"I began wondering," continued Mrs. Petry, "how this unearthly howl would affect a criminal, a man hunted by the police. That was the first incident. The second was a tragedy I covered for my paper. There was a fire in Harlem in which two children had been burnt to death. Their parents were at work and the children were alone. I imagined their reactions when they returned home that night. I knew also that many Harlem parents, like Lilly Belle in the story, often left their children home alone while at work. Imaginatively combined, the two incidents gave me my story."

I then asked her where she got her knowledge of the West Indian background for "Olaf and His Girl Friend." Many of her friends and acquaintances are West Indians, and they often tell her stories about the islands and discuss West Indian customs.

"I wrote that story to show that there can be true affection among Negroes. That Negroes can love as deeply as anyone else. So many people impute to Negroes an unhampered sensuality that I felt it time to tell the truth. Now, the idea of Olaf's [the chief character in the story] seeking Belle Rose through the sailor's grapevine, I got from a friend.

"What writers have influenced you?" I asked.

"Really," replied Mrs. Petry, smiling, "I have read so many authors and so many books that I don't know. I have been an omnivorous reader since childhood. I was born and reared in a small town, and in a small town, you know, there is really nothing much to do except read."

I then asked her about her recently published novel, *The Street*.

"In *The Street* my aim is to show how simply and easily the environment can change the course of a person's life. For this purpose, I have made Lutie Johnson an intelligent, ambitious, attractive woman with a fair degree of education. She lives in the squalor of 116th Street, but she retains her self-respect and fights to bring up her little son decently.

"I try to show why the Negro has a high crime rate, a high death rate, and little or no chance of keeping his family unit intact in northern cities. There are no statistics in the book though they are present in the background, not as columns of figures, but in terms of what life is like for people who live in overcrowded tenements.

"I tried to write a story that moves swiftly so that it would hold the attention of people who might ordinarily shy away from a so-called problem novel. And I hope that I have created characters who are real, believable, alive. For I am of the opinion that most Americans regard Negroes as types—not quite human—who fit into a special category and I wanted to show them as people with the same capacity for love and hate, for tears and laughter, and the same instincts for survival possessed by all men."

Mrs. Ann Petry was born in Old Saybrook, Connecticut, and comes from a New England family that has specialized in some branch of chemistry for three generations. Her grandfather was a chemist; her father, an aunt, and an uncle are druggists. Mrs. Petry is herself a registered pharmacist in the drugstores owned by her family in Old Saybrook and Old Lyme when she began writing her first short stories.

If she had not married and gone to New York City to live, she would undoubtedly have continued her career as a pharmacist. Instead she sought and found jobs in New York that would give her an opportunity to write. She sold advertising space and wrote advertising copy for a Harlem weekly. She also edited the woman's page for a rival weekly, and covered general news stories.

While interviewing celebrities, covering political rallies and three-alarm fires, and reporting on murders and all other forms of sudden death, she acquired an intimate and disturbing knowledge of Harlem and its ancient evil, housing; its tragic, broken families; its high death rate.

She spent nine months working on an experiment in education that was being conducted in one of the city's elementary schools and thus observed at first hand the toll that segregated areas like Harlem exact in the twisting and warping of children's lives.

In addition to working on newspapers she has taught salesmanship, written children's plays, acted with an amateur theatrical group. She is a former member of the now famous American Negro Theatre. She has studied painting, and plays the piano for her own amusement, claiming to be the least promising pupil of a well-known composer and pianist. At present she is executive secretary of Negro Women Incorporated, a civic-minded organization which keeps a watchful eye on local and national legislation.

Arthenia Bates Millican was born in Sumter, South Carolina. She attended Morris College in Sumter, received an M.A. degree in English from Atlanta University, where she was stimulated by Langston Hughes to become a creative writer, and she received a Ph.D. from Louisiana University in 1972. She is featured in *Who's Who in American Women, Who's Who in America,* and *Outstanding Educators of America.*

Dr. Bates published one novel, *The Deity Nodded,* in 1973 (Harlo Press), which deals with a young woman's search for truth as she struggles between Islam and Christianity. Prior to this she published a book of short stories, *Seeds Beneath the Snow* (Greenwich Publishers, 1969). Other poetry, articles, and fiction can be found in *College Language Association Journal, Black World,* and *National Poetry Anthology.*

Reflections: Arthenia Bates Millican

by BETTYE J. PARKER

The Deity Nodded, a first and only novel by Arthenia Bates, involves a conflict between Islam and Christianity. The above statement, made by Jerry Ward, not only describes the focus of the novel but also reflects the searching and pulsating soul of the novelist. Dr. Bates was born in the South—Sumter, South Carolina—and the setting of most of her fiction is painted against the backdrop of southern folk life and culture that she knows so well. Her collection of short stories, *Seeds Beneath the Snow,* published by Greenwich Book Publishers, reflects her sensitivity to the simple and searching way of Black life. The following interview discloses Arthenia Bates's reflections on a number of literary-related subjects. When I approached her about an interview, she responded enthusiastically. Sensitive to the problems of time and money associated with conducting research, she agreed to a correspondence interview. She expressed that the kind of effort involved in molding this book will "enlighten writers and scholars in terms of the role that each must play."

QUESTION: Please comment on the status of Black women in literature. Why do you suppose that Black women have virtually gone unnoticed in the literary world?

Reflection 1

If the Black woman is accepted as human being and woman, she will be accepted as a writer. But do you realize what a woman is despite all the furor about liberation? She is still a creature of mood doing all sorts of little curious things to keep herself busy or to keep herself from going crazy until she has a husband and family to make her a woman in many quarters. You would think that the so-called weaker sex is certain to have a weaker head. And if that head is wooly, Lord help us. You know her chores—and writing is not one of them. Actually, we will have to go to the truth of sexism and racism for the answer though the Black women writers are beginning to come slowly into the limelight.

QUESTION: Is there a particular Black woman writer or group of writers whom you feel have had an important impact on the depth and growth of Black literature? And do you see any specific theme threaded through their work?

Reflection 2

Nella Larsen, a novelist of the Harlem Renaissance, is one of the first novelists to command my attention, especially in *Quicksand*. Even though she dealt with a woman of the middle class, and a light-brown complexion, she indicates how easy it is for the Black woman of talent to fall into the clutches of a mate who only delights in her body and the babies she can "churn out" in his image.

Margaret Walker impressed me with her volume of poetry, *For My People,* because of the deep "racial consciousness and social protest" as well as its idiomatic, flavorable language. *Jubilee,* her prize-winning novel, gave not only a picture of slavery but the trials and insults of Vyry, who embodies the then and now battle of the Black female in America.

Ann Petry is a writer who introduced me to the inner life of Harlem and its death-house quality for poor, struggling Blacks in its wake as depicted in *The Street*. Again the protagonist is a woman, Lutie, who is trapped as well as is her son.

Zora Neale Hurston introduces a woman who gained selfhood despite all of the old hindrances of family, friends, husbands, and gossip in *Their Eyes Were Watching God*. Her exceptional gifts as a folklorist have won a lasting place for her in the world.

Gwendolyn Brooks is impressive because of her dynamic personality and her ability to write "intellectual" poetry—yet bringing the facts down home to everyone who has the ability to listen.

Alice Walker is a young woman who is talented as a poet, critic, short story writer, and novelist. Her novel *The Third Life of Grange Copeland* is a vivid commentary on the Black male's antagonism toward the Black woman of quality. Her insight into the life and work of Zora Neale Hurston, which dramatizes what happened to a major Black woman novelist, deserves the special attention of every Black woman writer.

There are many other women writers who are "good," though I do not know them or their works. Some of the others who are "good" follow: Pinkie Gordon Lane, Carolyn Rodgers, Toni Morrison, Sarah Wright, Gayl Jones, Mari Evans, Sonia Sanchez, Lucille Clifton, Paule Marshall, Nikki Giovanni, and Maya Angelou.

QUESTION: Those of us who study and teach Black literature have begun to use a comparative approach. That is, we have finally begun to look at similarities between the Afro-American writer and other writers throughout Africa and the diaspora. Do you see related themes and functions in the works of Afro-Caribbean, African, and Afro-American Black female writers?

Reflection 3

Yes, I see apt comparisons (in terms of themes) between the African women writers and the Afro-American writers. My reading in African and Caribbean literature is negligible (not by choice), but all Black women seem to fight a common cause.

I will, nevertheless, mention themes from Efua Theodora Sutherland and Mabel Dave-Danquah of Ghana, Adelaide Casely-Hayeford of Sierra Leone, and Marion Morel of South Africa in comparing themes used by Afro-American women.

The theme of a search for the abundant life through freedom of choice for women is treated by Sutherland and Hurston. Sutherland's Foruwa and Hurston's Janie exercise and enjoy their freedom, though the first is of royal lineage and the second a nameless child. This note also appears in Pinkie Gordon Lane's poetry.

The theme of disavowal of the traditional role of the female is portrayed by Mabel Danquah and Toni Morrison. Efua and Sula seem to be a type described by Danquah as "a new type of hard-headed modern woman" who settles for the single life if marriage fails to bring the perfect lover, suitable income, and other attributes she deems necessary.

The theme of self-pride and comfort with native traditions voiced in Casely-Hayeford can be seen in the poems by Carolyn Rodgers, Mari Evans, Sonia Sanchez, and Nikki Giovanni.

Morel's theme of color caste and racial conflict stressed because of apartheid divisions among themselves [Blacks] in South Africa is also very prevalent in Afro-American novels by women. Among them are *The Street,* by Ann Petry; *Quicksand,* by Nella Larson; *Jubilee,* by Margaret Walker; *Their Eyes Were Watching God,* by Zora Neale Hurston; and *I Know Why the Caged Bird Sings,* by Maya Angelou, among others.

QUESTION: In your own fiction, how important a role has the Black past played in determining the time element and focus of your work?

Reflection 4

The Black past has played a significant role in the selection of my literary themes. The themes of pride, protest, courage, rejection, humiliation, conflict, awareness, desire, and many others are dramatized by the very life-actions of our forebears. I must deal with their life-actions in order to ground my life views of our time. I do not know who I am until I search backward as I move forward to hasten my reconstitution of the Black ethos.

Our Black historical past has been often distorted and sometimes obliterated. As a writer, it is my responsibility to assist in retelling the history of Black people (Using Carter G. Woodson's idea) by relating and interpreting their life-actions more accurately than the producer.

QUESTION: I have noted that the major setting of your fiction is in the South. Other than the fact that you were born in South Carolina and are familiar with the general southern Black motif, is there any reason why you have specifically concentrated on the South? Do you feel that Black cultural survivals are more intact in the South?

Reflection 5

I automatically selected the southern setting for *The Deity Nodded* because I have always lived mostly in the Deep South where I was born. I was so busy trying to get my idea across about the influence of "southern" dogmatic Christianity on a sensitive soul until I made no conscious effort to deal with cultural survivals per se. There is a story in my short story collection, *Seeds Beneath the Snow* ["Runetta"], which is built on folk values as well as an appreciable number of unpublished materials in the making; but I do not know if they are African cultural survivals.

QUESTION: In *The Deity Nodded,* it seems to me that you use the theme of religion as a search for truth. Am I correct? If so, what were you trying to achieve in highlighting the conflict between Christianity and Islam?

Reflection 6

The major theme of *The Deity Nodded* is the need for each person to search for a "religion" that will serve as a total guide for life in this world as he travels to the unknown.

My basic intent was to show the inadequacy of dogmatic theology which is rehearsed as the only doctrine for man's survival in a hostile universe. Harping on the Immaculate Conception, the Resurrection, and other mysteries of faith that seem impossible to understand may lead more people to accept blindness as their due because they have no way to prove or to verify similar happenings in life.

The rehearsing of the lives of persons so famous in biblical theology also lead to a kind of blind faith. So often I heard my grandmother singing "My Lord Delivered Daniel, Why Can't He Deliver Me?" She was such a noble woman, such a beautiful woman, and such a wise woman that it hurt me to see her suffering from brutal isolation, half-hunger, and blindness, waiting for the chariot to carry her home. Maybe it was good for her to believe in all the joys of heaven, but I felt that she had worked too hard, had loved too dearly, and had prayed too constantly to live so many years of suffering in this life.

My youngest sister must have been born with questions in her eyes. I was her big sister-guardian, so, no doubt, I listened more attentively to her questions than anyone else and began to realize that nobody had answers to some of them. One question started my wondering about the need or the good of religion when a lady who showed more piety than anyone else in our church pushed my sister from the water fountain so that she could drink. I began to watch the cruel deeds of adults after that, especially the so-called Christians. There was no understanding on my part about the ways of Christians. I took them for face value at their best; my younger sister concentrated on the discrepancy between what they professed to be and were not. She became a chemist; I became a teacher of literature and a free-lance writer. She became a Black Muslim because she found a rational dispensation in her discipline, and I became a Catholic trying to find some sanity in the mystery of faith. She found a happiness in the nation of Islam while I found happiness in Catholicism.

QUESTION: It seems to me that you were making a specific statement about Islam. Other than the experiences you have had with your sister, who is in the Nation, what additional aspects of the Muslim way of life have you experienced, if any?

Reflection 7

Something happened in 1965 which disillusioned me about Christianity for a brief spell. I had worked very hard in church, and while I was more in need of Holy Communion than at any other time because I was recovering from major surgery, the priest did not come until the end of the second month of my illness, when I was about ready to go to work.

During that time, The Honorable Elijah Muhammad wrote a letter giving me permission to use passages from his book *A Message to the Black Man.* When he said, "Dear Sister," I could understand why my sister found sanction in his leadership. At that moment, *The Deity Nodded* became a different book from the original plan to treat the Black Muslim faith as a hate religion. I began to see why persons visiting a Mosque for the first time joined the Nation of Islam without hesitation. I realized, then, that for us who are Christians, we need to return to the doctrines of peace and love through a channel other than the kind presented in the slave's catechism.

My knowledge of the truth about the sudden decision of many Blacks to rush to the altar is pointed up to me now as the weakest part of the novel. One critic said that I had given Tisha too strong a will to allow her to swallow the Faith without going through the same ups and downs that she experienced in Christianity and in Christian Science. I agree.

QUESTION: It seems to me that a number of unique characteristics come through in the character of Tisha. But I am also aware of a combination of factors that is visible in other female characters in the book. Were you consciously depicting specific molds of Black women?

Reflection 8

I wanted to introduce various types of Black women in order to show that even the ones who are supposedly "out of it" have some warmth and some desire to give love when and where it is needed. In examining the righteous, the riotous, and the gracious individuals, the riotous ones often came out ahead in terms of humane acts for another.

Lastly, I wanted to depict a young woman who was interested in finding her identity in terms of parenthood, religion, and social standing. But most of all, I wanted to depict a character who was interested in finding self. I wanted the character to be a young Black woman who would survive despite her problem. I wanted a girl who could envision a developing self in years to come because of her own knowledge, her own desire, and her own ingenuity.

Often it seems that critical questions wear themselves thin because of the absence of vatic vision and courage on the part of the critics. Among other reasons, a vision is required to "predigest" some works so their applicability and relevance to a time can be evaluated. Courage is necessary to depart from the vapid staleness, prejudice, and listlessness which too often assails the adjudication of Black *belles-lettres*.

In the late sixties, Addison Gayle, Jr., emerged as one among several Black writers, teachers, and critics who had the vision and courage to assault American literary assumptions about Black life and its artistic representations. Gayle was the architect of "the Black Aesthetic" in much the same way as Alain Locke was the philosophical mentor of "the New Negro Movement" (the Harlem Renaissance of the twenties).

The basic premises upon which the Black Aesthetic rests are probably best explained in Ron Karenga's article "Black Cultural Nationalism," which appears in Gayle's edited text, *The Black Aesthetic* (1971). Karenga notes that all Black art "must respond positively to the reality of revolution"; all African-based (Black) art is "functional, collective and committing or committed"; and Black art must "expose the enemy, praise the people and support the revolution."

In the same text, Gayle himself says in another theoretical piece, "Cultural Strangulation: Black Literature and the White Aesthetic,"

> The irony of the trap in which the Black artist has found himself throughout history is apparent. Those symbols which govern his life and art are proscriptive ones, set down by minds as diseased as Hinton Helper's. In other words, beauty has been in the eyes of an earthly beholder who has stipulated that beauty conforms to such and such a definition.

Gayle has conscientiously sought to alert Black people to the need for iconoclasm—the tearing down of old definitions and standards of judgment in the consideration of Black art, and replacing them with more practical and relevant ones. These aims are at the matrix of the theory discussed in the interview which follows.

Addison Gayle's work includes scores of articles on the Black Aesthetic applied to all genres of literature, and the books *The Black Situation; Black Expression; Bondage, Freedom and Beyond*: *The Prose of Black Americans; The Way of the New World: The Black Novel in America; The Black Aesthetic;* and *Wayward Child,* an autobiography. Gayle is an associate professor of English at CCNY's Bernard Baruch College.

Judgment: Addison Gayle

by ROSEANN P. BELL

A crisp New York morning on the East Side. A modern high-rise suited up in the accoutrements of "success": a uniformed doorman speaking a broken English with an exotic accent; the "spy" monitors; the intercom. An unusual place to find an architect of social change.

The apartment, removed from the grit of New York streets, is an alcove in a separate reality. Africa is there, but so is the Caribbean and the sweet flypaper of Black American life—drums, drawings, photographs, books, and two typewriters. This impressive place is where Addison Gayle lives, but I had not come to be impressed by things. I was more interested in how and why the man lives—what network of things is responsible for his energetic and astute mind being able to express itself in a proliferation of critical statements about Black American life: more than fifty articles in respected literary and popular magazines, and the books listed in the headnote.

There was an earlier time, however, when his books were not being published (or written), and when the living was not easy.

"I was born in Virginia, my family was very poor. My father was a poor secretary of the Virginia Communist party. My mother is a Christian . . . they separated, I guess, when I was about six years old and I grew up in Newport News, Virginia. I came to New York in '51 and started college when I was twenty-eight and finished. Started in the evening, got a B.A., and then went out to UCLA intending to enroll in a doctoral program, but felt the whole stupid thing was nonsense. Came back to New York with an M.A. and started teaching and writing. I don't know what else . . . married and separated, if that's important."

Addison Gayle's remembrance of things past is as precise as the diatribes he levels against incompetent teachers and administrators in Black Studies programs, or against the historical and contemporary evil ways of white folks. The issues he feels strongly about receive a dual blessing: He takes the reader (or listener) through an acute syllogistic process, dealing rapidly and clearly with the major premise, the minor premise, and the logical conclusion. Then he directs examples to remove all doubt about why he feels and says what he does (often to the chagrin of theorists whose reasoning facilities are less shrewd or less committed than his own), and he is always consistent, always balanced.

I wanted to know some special things about this controversial author, and women—the women who people Black literature and therefore sometimes find themselves the subject of a speech, an article, or a lucidly constructed paragraph by Addison Gayle, teacher, critic, Renaissance man. Who were the three-dimensional characters he could identify? Who were the classic authors, deserving that title because they had handled so beautifully and so well the artistic time and space that Black women and men spent together? He wasn't ready to talk about women yet; a declaration on the academic image of Black people had to come first.

"The problem is, first of all, the academicians have always accepted images. Most of the time, throughout history, they did not accept those images from Black people, and they're not now about to accept any images from Black people. Both Black and white academicians have not, by and large, accepted images about Black people from Black people. That goes for the Howard Universities, the Atlantas, and on down. That, historically, has always been so and it's not going to change. I think what one can do, and what people were trying to do in the sixties with the Black aesthetic movement is to go outside of the established academicians to speak directly to students and Black people and to say, 'There are other images—Faulkner is not the portrayer of images of Black people in this country.' I think that is what one could do, but as long as there is a white America, unfortunately, white people are always, whether they are in the academies or not—they're always going to accept images first, if they can get them from their own image makers, and from those Blacks who in some sort of way have images which correlate theirs."

All of that's well and good, I thought, but there are broader issues which need addressing. For instance, how do you go about communicating the truth of a statement like "white people are always going to accept their own images first . . ." to the folk, to our folk who are not in the racist educational institutions of this country—to our folk, whose analysis of the Black situation comes from a gut level? On the heels of this concern came, strobelike, visions of Black films by the score, replacing one damaging image with another. And there is another basic economic reality: We don't control the images because we don't control the forces which produce those images. We have almost no voice in television programming and production, and the newspapers, even Black ones, do not address the psychological or material needs of our people. For these enigmas Mr. Gayle's thesis seemed less than adequate. He sensed my discomfort as a "How do we do what needs to be done?" began shaping itself in my mouth.

"You don't do it! Let's be very honest, right? You don't do it because first of all we don't control the institutions. Second, we don't have people who have guts enough and independence enough to do the kinds of things that are necessary. For example, a Gordon Parks is an abomination. Any Blacks who perform in those films, who help write them for those television programs . . . are abominations. Now, unfortunately, we don't have the kinds of forces in the Black community to make people do what they ought to do anyway. Until we either get institutions run by people who have sense enough to realize that because they are Black, whether they like it or not, they, too, are involved, and unless we have those kinds of people running institutions or unless we have some force—a guerrilla force or whatever you want to call it—to make people do the things that should be done, we're not going to get it done."

We agreed that the efforts to "get it done" have been minimal. Street theaters, poetry readings in bars, avant-garde magazines, and modern visionaries like Haki Madhubuti, Mari Evans, Carolyn Rodgers, and Hoyt Fuller have not and will not be enough.

". . . I'm not very optimistic. There are people who are doing the kinds of things that you're talking about. Haki, for example, and the whole idea of Third World Press, the magazine and the Institute [of Positive Education]. Gwen Brooks is doing . . . people in Chicago . . . and then there are a couple of people in Detroit. Scattered throughout, there are a couple of people, and I would suppose that the people who are consciously doing these things will always be minimal, for a very simple reason . . . some mornings I wake up after one of those bad nights and I conclude that Black folks and white folks in this country probably deserve each other (that's before I'm fully awake). . . ."

It seemed more than a little incongruent that this man who, more than almost anyone within the last fifty years, had breathed new life into the process of interpreting Black life and culture, could be so pessimistic in a conversation about change, yet so optimistic in the wealth of words between the covers of his last critical text, *The Way of the New World.* I told him it was difficult for me to accept his admission, because people who have no optimism generally do nothing. He responded, "What you do, you do in the hope that, well, you're not going to inculcate or influence fifty million people. If you reach one person, you've done something."

There was a creative tension in the small living room; the dialogue was energized by a mutual concern for Black literary art and for Black life; after all, there really is no separation. Encouraged by this apparent mood, I felt that the time had come again to broach the subject of Black women writers and characters, and I was not in error.

"There's a very good book which [Harper & Row] released by Brenda Wilkinson called *Luddell.* It's very good. I would think that in Paule Marshall or Louise Merriweather, Black women come off pretty well. But if you're talking about modern writers like Gayl Jones and Toni Morrison, the women come off very badly because the novels are directed viciously against Black men, and somehow, the writers haven't realized that you can't very well do a hatchet job on Black men without also doing a hatchet job on Black women. Therefore, if you read *Sula,* and if you read *Corregidora,* the images of both the men and the women are equally nauseating."

His valuation of Alice Walker's work was equally caustic, the adjudication resting primarily on Walker's fictional treatment of Black history and her "inability to create complex male characters."

"If we look at her work in history, particularly if there is any great deal of historical accuracy in her portrayal of Black men, then we're in more trouble than I thought we were, and I thought we were okay. I readily admit that Black male writers have been unbelievable as far as Black women are concerned. A result is that usually when Black women writers write about Black males, they're either brutes à la *Corregidora,* or they're the old white folks' Toms, the stereotypes. I don't know one woman writer, not one single one, who moves outside of that. I think Paule [Marshall] comes close, Louise Merriweather comes close, but there is not a single one who comes all the way. And if Alice Walker is writing a good historical novel, then we're in trouble."

I wondered about his dismissal of Walker as a viable talent, given the excitement generated by the twenty-five women whom she has created in her short fiction and one novel.

"You know the problem with that," he countered.

"I know, you can't separate them—women from men."

"Right. This is the trap that Black males, Black male writers, have always fallen into. You know, it's crazy. Nothing that happens to Black men in this country does not happen to Black women, only indirectly. There's another tremendous problem, too. Black men have grown up in this country being very afraid of Black women, and a hell of a lot of Black women have grown up in this country, in too many cases, looking at Black men the way white folks looked at Black men. At that point, there are tremendous kinds of conflicts because we have not realized that the enemy is not each other. The enemy is this country. The enemy is not Black men, not Black women, it's this country . . . white folks have managed to have us believe that the enemy is poor Black folks on welfare as opposed to middle-class Black folks who want to be decent; light-skinned Black folks as opposed to dark-skinned Black folks; and Black men as opposed to Black women."

A river of words flowed, pushed out by a timeless energy consumed in an animated and familiar verbal posture.

"White folks have too much to say about how ideas are made and how things go on, but since white folks . . . since this is their country, they can afford nonsense and we can't. *We can't afford nonsense.* Somebody asked me at a lecture what I thought about Black men marrying white women; it always comes up. Really, I don't care who people marry. I think some Black guys ought to marry white women, because if they believe that Black women are what they say they are, then they ought to marry white ones, just as I think there are some Black women who I think ought to marry white men, and if some of these Black women writers . . . if Gayl Jones believes that Black men are what she says they are, she ought to get a white man. If Lorraine Hansberry and Alice Walker really believed that Black men are what they say they are, good . . . they have done the best thing. I see nothing wrong with that. If I believed that Black women were bitches, dominating bitches, castrating bitches, out to run over me and to hold me back, then I'd marry a white woman—if I believed that. Why fool yourself in a psychologically debilitating situation? I have no quarrel with that. The enemy is not the Black woman that I know; it's this country."

I should have expected that rejoinder. Maybe I did, because when I registered no surprise, did not change the expression on my face, he closed the subject of women writers, women characters, women as citizens in a country run by whites, women as victims as well as exploiters, etc.

I gathered my tools and prepared to go. He had been smoking rather consistently throughout our meeting, alternating between a rich tobacco blend in his pipe and a pack of long cigarettes. Now he tapped out the charred leavings in the bowl of the pipe and made no gesture toward refilling and lighting it or a cigarette again. I had to leave and find a synthesis from what the previous hour and a half had presented. After several weeks' labor, I did.

Addison Gayle comes out of a tradition where male critics, when they deal with women writers or characters at all, write very condescendingly about them. That's a historical reality, since anyone who takes a literature course in this country, and who concentrates on literary criticism, is deluged with the eighteenth-century English literature critical formulas. But an exciting certainty is that Gayle has *come out* of that sterile and binding intimidation.

Our conversation was to center on Black women. Instead, we moved, very naturally, into several foci—all of which *included* women because it was natural for them to be there. In effect, my effort to separate Black women writers from Black male writers, Black women writers and characters from Black *people* who don't write and would not make fully developed characters, was not tolerated.

Ultimately, I appreciated his tenacity and his unlimited view of Black life and literature. This apprehension also provided me with a fuller understanding of the "how" and the "why" he lives and produces as he does: Addison Gayle and the figures whom he respects—fictional or real—are "outsiders."[1]

NOTES

1. ". . . before men can move outside of the traditions and mores which seek to enslave them anew, they must become outsiders in the true sense of the term. Salvation for black people can come, therefore, only when they have taken the existential plunge outside canons which affront man's sense of decency and justice: To be an outsider is to be removed from the paradigms of the past and to be one with men, from ancient times to the present day, whose history and culture have been distinguished by a hatred of injustice and oppression and who have fought, long and hard, against man's tyranny, physically or mentally, against man." Addison Gayle, *The Way of the New World* (Garden City, N.Y.: Doubleday & Company, 1973), p. 148.

Similar to Addison Gayle's insistence on honesty and commitment in evaluating Black literature, George Kent's wisdom, passion, and objective experience play a major role in his critical decisions. He is the author of a major volume, *Blackness and the Adventure of Western Culture,* and many significant articles on various aspects of Black and American literature. The articles appear in scholarly journals such as *Phylon, Black World, College Language Association Journal,* and *Black Books Bulletin,* among others.

Dr. Kent has given more than passing attention to a few Black female authors, most notably Nella Larsen and Gwendolyn Brooks, on whom he is preparing a full-length study. His verbal and written style are laconic and precise, and his conclusions are shared only after disciplined reflections have been consulted. He lives in Chicago and teaches at the University of Chicago.

Substance: George Kent

by ROSEANN P. BELL

If we are lucky, at some point in our lives we meet people who make the merger between ontology and epistemology comprehensible; they make the continuous rigor and the mysterious joy of living passionately real. George Kent is such a man. If we call him a critic, we do him a partial disservice, since that designation carries with it some elements of negativism: We expect critics to be acerbic and haughty rather than iconoclastic and visionary. The good ones, like Kent, are rarely celebrated because their commodity, common sense, is neither championed nor materially encouraged to the degree it should be. Such is to be expected where propaganda sells well but logic and a communal understanding of humanity do not.

His hometown is light years away from the place where he now spends much of his time engaging the minuscule details of the conundrum called Black literature—in a cluttered, productive-looking office on the University of Chicago campus. But the Columbus, Georgia, spirit, and the high school that replaced a swamp and was "the one big contribution to progress" in Columbus, are still liquid marrow in the bones of George Kent.

A prolific author of major work in Black literary studies (more than twenty-five seminal critical articles, two books, and innumerable speeches), the seasoned gentleman is a profound voice in the camp of serious Black scholarship.

Our six-hour conversation (I prefer to call it a communion) firmly re-established my prior judgments about him; a part of that opulent, almost eucharistic experience follows.

BELL: What is a critic?

KENT: (*Laughs*) I guess I'd have to answer that in a way which might be different from what somebody else would say. I see a critic as being a kind of intelligent (hopefully) reader mediating between the writer and the audience, with very strong obligations to both. Obligations to the writer in trying as hard as you can to know what he's doing, and obligations to the audience in trying to stimulate some kind of focus or framework or to try to speak stimulatingly enough about the work so that the audience will understand the particular customs and conventions of the work and of the writers in general, and how it [the work] relates (if it's Black literature) something very tangibly to its own tradition. Now, for that, I'm always interested in saying something about folk forms because I think they contain the most tangible vocabulary.

There are strong kinds of traditions, whether they are adequate or not. The kind of blues tradition, the spirituals tradition, and then there's a kind of middle-class, in-between position. Some of them contain more order and more possibility than others. While I admire a good deal of the blues tradition, it seems to me to contain a good deal of instability and disorder. On the other hand, the spirituals tradition, while including a lot of escapism, also turned out many of the people who were able to give a sense of substantial order. To be concrete, I'm thinking of, say, Aunt Hagar in Langston Hughes's *Not Without Laughter,* who the people have to keep looking to for order, whether or not we admire her attitude toward the whites or not. Or even in so recent a work as Maya Angelou's *I Know*

Why the Caged Bird Sings, moreso than in the subsequent autobiographies. There's something repelling at times about the grandmother, but they [the characters] get their biggest sense of order out of her. They get a lot of spontaneous love out of what I call the "blues people" like the mother. The mother, as I pointed out in an article, is not, in giving all she gives, able to protect [the protagonist] from being raped. It's very unstable, the kind of blues thing where people get so absorbed in their own lives. The individual blues people—they can be very spontaneously generous, but not consistently caretaking.

BELL: The other night I talked with Gayl Jones on the phone.

KENT: Oh, you did?

BELL: . . . author of *Corregidora* [and since this interview was completed, *Eva's Man, Almeyda,* and *White Rat*].

KENT: Yes, a fascinating book.

BELL: . . . and she expressed her wish that if anybody does not get anything else out of *Corregidora,* that they will understand that she has written a metaphor for the blues. The whole process between Ursa and Mutt is a blues sequence. Right before I talked with Jones, I had just completed reading the article by Stephen Henderson in *New Directions* on Sterling Brown [October 1975]. Now, you mention the establishment of order, and it seems to me that critics, especially Black critics, and some writers are trying to establish a sense of order among all that has appeared to be relatively chaotic. But I don't know if I can quite come to grips with your suggestion that on the one hand, spirituals "do" it and on the other hand, the blues does not. It may be that what I'm thinking is that blues does it for a larger segment of our community, and it may do it in a more temporary fashion than spirituals do, but the important thing to me is that it gets done. Henderson speaks about how the blues helps us to be affirmative about depression and sadness. How do I handle that within the framework you give?

KENT: Well, you see, the blues and spirituals are mixed up together, if you want to get more complicated. I'm talking about the blues *life* when I'm talking about instability. Finally, as much as I admire this book by Gayl Jones, when the woman finally seems about to become reconciled with this man, she is about forty-six or seven years old, and that's pretty wild. . . .

BELL: Gayl Jones explained to me that the ending is a redemption on Ursa's part—she realizes that she does not have to be reconciled with Mutt or with anybody. She finds an internal source of spirituality that she has not previously had. The pattern of the book is very interesting, I think, especially since she wrote it in only three months.

KENT: She wrote that book in three months?

BELL: Yes, that's what she said. I don't know how long it took her to do her research, but she said the actual writing only took three months.

KENT: It's a remarkable book.

BELL: She's written some very good poetry, too, in which she uses a blues ethic to accompany her dialogue. She says she's very much influenced by older blues singers and jazz singers. There's a lovely poem of hers called "Scat"—about Ella Fitzgerald. Have you seen it?

KENT: I don't think I've seen it.

BELL: It's nice. I'll send you a copy of it.

KENT: I know I was very much impressed by her, but I have a reservation on the use of all our traditions. Realistically, you get to an ending point. The blues thing in some sort of way might enable people to deal with formlessness, but it contains a whole lot of precariousness, I've observed, actually. I can even remember people who could be better to you than your own parents could, but they wouldn't be able to deal with you consistently . . . the next day they're out after their own thing; they're dealing with the self once more, on their own basis. I'm afraid of romanticizing the blues. I don't think I go as much with it as Henderson does, and I don't want to romanticize spirituals, either, because their limitations are marked in practically every work. That's the kind of thing I notice even in Maya Angelou's work. The grandmother's there, but the mother might have to ship these kids across the country with "to whom they concern" on them. And she can give them a beautiful party on one night because she's got all those total feelings in her. But she can't consistently deal with them. I don't mean every blues life is like that, but there's a threat, it seems, to be always in the blues area. You've got to learn to get out and pay your dues real early and real quick and to a lot of people, maybe too quick.

BELL: Maybe this is a kind of inappropriate extension to make, but would you then say that blues is more individualistic and the spirituals are more collective?

KENT: Yes, I think that's good.

BELL: And people make an emotional choice between the two (or more) apprehensions because they are trying to make sense (achieve order) out of the world?

KENT: Yes, I think that there's a certain way you can apply that. It does represent a very collective, tangible, almost too tangible body of behavior patterns. Those people [the spirituals people] think they know what you're supposed to do every minute, but this can be very damned annoying.

BELL: Is the attraction with the spirituals that we know what those limitations are, but with the blues we never know what the ending is going to be, and so the mystery of life can continue?

KENT: That's correct. I think you're quite right about that.

BELL: Yes, maybe that's why I like the blues.

KENT: Yeah, I like the blues, too, but when I sit down to a solid evaluation, I try to keep certain things in mind so that I don't romanticize the blues. The blues singer has some pattern for all of us to follow: "It sure hurts me, the way my brother is suffering, but I can't get to him."

We talked more about musical and literary art forms, about the direction of Black studies on the nation's campuses, about the lessons we can learn on the Black aesthetic from Africa and the Caribbean, and about writers—Black women writers and their creations.

BELL: In *Blackness and the Adventure of Western Culture,* when you are discussing the works of Nella Larsen and Jessie Fauset, it seems that you approach their works more so than their images of women, and I was glad to see that. But it appears also that you only choose their works on the basis of their being a reflection of the cosmopolitan Harlem Renaissance writer. Now, is that an unfair criticism, even though I know your position on Nella Larsen, particularly in terms of the psychological possibilities suggested in her works? Is there, for example, any reason why the kind of attention you give to McKay and Wright, no woman has received?

KENT: What about Gwendolyn Brooks?

BELL: Well, Brooks is always an exception, and I was thinking about novelists.

KENT: I've written my longest article on her [Brooks], you know. . . . I'll tell you what I had wanted to do—something on Zora Neale Hurston. This may sound almost like chauvinism, but I do have a feeling that it would be helpful if some thoroughgoing woman would do it first. The reason that I say this is because there are certain things about Zora Hurston that turn me off fast. And then I come back and say to myself, how would this look if you thought about it in terms of a woman at that time trying to assert her existence with an almost complete autonomy and without any kind of support, and to really begin to judge her as if she had the little sanction that was given to Black men. And at that point I usually stop, but I think that Nella Larsen has done some nice things and it might be that I was following images, I'm not sure. I was particularly impressed with her use of contrast, the themes, the actual folk positions . . . things like that. I don't know if I was getting images or not. Who has said that and gotten those images?

BELL: Alice Walker says it indirectly in the interview with John O'Brien. Her position is that the personality of the writer often gets in the way of the [male] critic's ability to evaluate the work of the author.

KENT: You mean the personality of the novelist?

BELL: Yes, the female author. The personality of the female author gets in the way of serious criticism being done on the work. A parallel would be something you've mentioned before—critics traditionally looking at a historical set piece and then trying to throw in examples, as opposed to picking out people and then doing a good analysis of the work. Now that there's the current vogue in Black female writers, we will probably be inundated (as we have been) with a lot of statements about a certain kind of work rather than a thorough analysis of given works.

I have read a good deal of criticism on Black women writers and I partially agree with Walker. Her statement is akin to the situation we had when "liberal" white critics were evaluating all [Blacks] instead of *just Another Country* or *just Go Tell It on the Mountain*. They were elevating Baldwin to the status of *the* spokesman for all Black people. In a way, I thought this was what Walker meant.

KENT: I don't think my response tends in that direction. I could see that I could be drawn in to some degree by Zora, but my over-all feeling about her has to do with my suspicion that she felt that simple people really were simple, which is really a comment about her works. By that I mean I admire her work, but I think that she is overly self-congratulatory about her ability as a graduate of Barnard to come back to these simple people . . .

BELL: She's patronizing?

KENT: I think that's behind it, well, in the novels. I don't feel that in some of the works that people are as complex as they usually appear to be in life. For example, in *Jonah's Gourd Vine,* I don't find the minister really that complex.

BELL: She didn't really find her father [the model for the minister] that complex, though, did she?

KENT: No, she did not, and I wonder if she overcame that educational gap [responsible for that attitude]. She wasn't too easy with the idea that she would ever overcome it. Or, when I go to *Mules and Men* there seems to me, I think, the self-congratulatory parts which stand out.

BELL: Are you familiar with the work that Bob Hemenway has done on Hurston?

KENT: I just knew that he was doing a book on her. Did he ever get it finished?

BELL: Yes, he's waiting on a suitable arrangement with a publisher, but the work is finished. Hemenway and some other people who are working on Hurston think that her training at Barnard and the influence of Boaz got in the way of her being able to come to grips with her patronage of "simple folks."

KENT: I would certainly agree, because she was obviously a very complex person herself and it just doesn't seem to me that she gave her creations enough dimensionality. But I guess that statement would have to be modified somewhat if we look at Janie Starks [in *Their Eyes Were Watching God*].

BELL: I was going to ask you about her, next.

KENT: What strikes me always is that she poses two issues in the book. One is included in the image of the pear tree—how can a woman flower reach her natural rhythmical maturity, so to speak. The other is, what happens when an older woman deals with a young man? I thought that if she'd really pursued that, she might have created a very great novel, but she killed the man off. Tea Cake. I mean, everybody's been celebrating this love affair between them . . .

BELL: And they forget about that.

KENT: Yes, they forget about that, but it was definitely raised as an issue in the novel. "Can Tea Cake really love me, and continue to do this. . . ." I think she's about eleven or twelve years older than he is, a fairly good distance. Of course, they have all kinds of exciting times for a period, I think it's a year, then he gets killed, so you don't really deal with that other issue at all.

That's a thing that bothers me, but nobody seems to care. I have another problem with McKay that also doesn't seem to bother many people, and that's McKay's Bita Plant; he really doesn't resolve that situation at all. Here is a woman returning to her culture, but there are obvious difficulties. If you ask, will a highly educated woman make it that easily with a peasant, you're raising a traitorous issue for Black unity.

BELL: We talked earlier about the Euro-American need to be moralistic and to always set up models for the rest of the world to look at, and there is always combined the nature of economics and a sense of clear consciousness. There's very little that Hurston could have done, given her training and background; there's very little that McKay could have done, given the British impact on his own life.

With Hurston, you've answered a question posed to me by Hemenway. He wondered if Zora, who, on the one hand comes out of the oral tradition, almost the storytelling custom of the griot, was limited by the prescriptions of a capitalist Western world. From what you've just described, it seems that she was limited because she never resolved that tension, that confusion between what the two life-styles demand—the two moral orders demand.

KENT: I don't know whether I thought of this quite that way, but I think it finally comes down to that. Another economic-related area concerns me about those writers—especially the Harlem group. Despite all this breakthrough publicity on the Harlem Renaissance, I wonder how much those people stayed stranded for money, and whether they had time to polish and work their novels. I know she [Hurston] was good at getting patrons and that sort of thing, but I still wonder whether those involvements really gave her time to *write*. . . . Sometimes, I wonder very much about those things. I know that McKay, of course, splurged whenever he did get anything, and then some of them died young, some of them defected; I would like to have a real knowledge of what went on with those publishers.

BELL: In the chapter on the Harlem Renaissance in *Blackness and the Adventure of Western Culture,* you almost ignore Zora. Is a reason for that that her most productive period, as far as novels are concerned, came after 1929, the date you used as a cutoff for the period? What about her stories in *The Crisis* and *Opportunity?*

KENT: Hmmm. I think that the novel belongs in there because my concept of the Harlem Renaissance is that it is marked, more or less, by the attempt of the writers to emphasize race, and in the 1930's, you get a tension between race and class. But her novel is a Renaissance novel. I would not have mentioned her short stories anyway, because I don't think that much of them, frankly. There, she gets into a certain simple-mindedness. I remember one called "Spunk" that seemed to have some of the sentimentalism of Bret Hart, and there's another one in which the man throws money in the door ["Gilded Six-Bits"]. That one suggests that really simple people could suddenly resolve all problems by suddenly forgiving each other very easily. I haven't read it in quite a while, but I just recall that incident being very tediously resolved. I don't recall a really imposing short story by her, but I would have had to mention that novel if something had not been blocking my consciousness. It might be that male thing you were talking about.

BELL: Do you consider Zora a marginal character, in the sense of marginality that was popularized around here [at the University of Chicago]—the Robert Parkes definition of the "Marginal Man" or the "Marginal Woman"?

KENT: You mean caught between two cultures?

BELL: Yes, and if so, would that marginality be an extension of your assessment about Hurston's inability to resolve a folkloristic, simple outlook and the professionalism of a Boaz in the study of anthropology?

KENT: I'm not sure how I would put that because it seems to be more complex and to have sources in her own personality. I remember reading her autobiography and I guess that maybe you could extend that concept there, but it just seems to me that she either, well, either she didn't feel enough at times not to be the simple entertainer and to say silly things or to make silly evaluations, or to appear to polish the apple just when it goes, from a point of logic, against all common sense. I'm referring to things like when she went to Morgan and some of the upper-class Black girls would let her wear their dresses—she just got carried away with that. Or, she could run right over a problem like Should a Black barber exclude Blacks in the shop? I don't mean necessarily that he could help it, but it seems to me that she could get over problems like that too easily. She could just sing all kinds of songs for people; I don't know whether that was a personality thing or not. And it's hard to get it out of anybody who knew her. I remember this man, Huggins, just said flatly that she lost sight of the fact that she was acting a role. I'm not sure of that. I mean, I'm just in limbo. I wonder could a woman that intelligent and that sharp, say in a book like hers on folklore in Haiti [*Tell My Horse*], really completely lose sight of herself. In that book she makes some very interesting distinctions.

BELL: That disturbed me, too, in Huggins, and also in *In a Minor Chord*.

KENT: Turner's book.

BELL: Right . . . his judgment of her. But the greatest source of my own puzzlement comes from my having read her letters to Van Vechten. Now, I realize we are infringing on the patronage and personal thing, but some of those letters are so sensitive and, as you say, so intelligent and profound, that one does wonder how much of what she did in audiences that were primarily composed of white people was done for the sake of acting, and how much she did not realize she was doing—off on a trip or something.

KENT: That's why it's so hard for me to answer that question that you're asking. And Langston Hughes doesn't help us a bit —calls her just a delightful child—and you can't really tell if they had a romance or not. I have a vague feeling that there was something in that odyssey—in her having to make it on her own, and where some personality elements flowered, other personality elements might have gotten confused.

BELL: That surely adds credence to your judgment that she was so complex and probably a lot more intelligent than even she thought she was. Maybe she was a little frightened at being that way. I find her an extremely fascinating person.

KENT: Somebody should do a very thorough job on her. I remember I was out somewhere and someone thought it was very amusing to describe the way she was when she taught in South Carolina . . . some college there. She couldn't make it in any kind of way with the administration. She had to fulfill obligations in an almost elementary way, and they, they were after her, I think, about the boys—the football boys. The woman who was describing her thought it was all very amusing, and I guess, under a cocktail situation, maybe it is. But I sense a tragic element is there, and it may relate to that marginal area and to something very complicated about a woman trying to get out there and make it, and not having very much that she can count on behind her except her wit and her resourcefulness.

Yes, that's one I think a woman should do, first. I don't know how that sounds . . . I think I would be invited into some kind of generalization which wouldn't encompass the privacy of that kind of woman's experience. Whatever it sounds like, that's where I am. I won't say I won't try it, I may try very hard.

We turned from Zora to the general portraiture of Black women, and the assumed predilections of Black women writers.

KENT: I think that the failure [in works by some Black female writers] is often to explore real depth. I think there is something in what Mary Helen Washington says in her discussions on images of power. Often, the problem is that you don't get a deep enough definition of all the things that the woman encounters which are her responses to power.

Among the male writers, the strongest one I've seen has been Ernest Gaines's first book, not the one that everybody likes, but *Blood Line,* in which the woman is trying to transform the man into the boy, and the boy-husband into a man. I get strong, young images there. I really do think it is a matter of depth and that probably it has to be what Paule Marshall called "working through our history." It's something that makes the works of people like Paule Marshall, Toni Morrison, and Alice Walker important. Not that they have completely gotten to the point which we would like, the point that would help us the most, but it seems like we have gotten to some deep levels in the examination of their responses and problems—but how these women look at the world in their situations—I miss a lot of that. I think the absence of that quality makes us object to the images of Black women we find in literature. They are just not explored to their fullest potential depth.

Alice Walker's definition of what women confronted on the plantations seems worth profound treatment, and we get overtones of it in certain short stories by Jean Wheeler Smith . . . "That She Would Dance No More"; it appears in *Black Fire.* There are two or three stories like that where I feel that we're getting a deep suggestion about what people were up against and what they were responding to. Gaines does a good deal of that with his people, but he also does other things which are not so good and for which he is now receiving blanket praise.

In *Of Love and Dust* the only Black woman that one could even think of getting close to would be the older woman, the very old woman who is about to die with the plantation. The male rebel in that story is regaining a new innocence through this rather fluffy picture of a white woman, and on the other hand, she is gaining a new innocence through him. And then there is the portrait of the "hip" Black woman, a Cajun, and she goes out to exploit him and then gets new innocence through having to understand him. He is being pulled into innocence. And so, we are left with a highly generalized humanism finally, although it has to be because of the history of the plantation in there. That's why *Blood Line* attracts me more.

Gaines has one section in *The Autobiography of Miss Jane Pittman,* between the woman and the animal tamer. I thought the book brought the tensions to the surface better than the picture did; there is a fairly deep struggle between a man and a woman going on in there. That's what I mean by depth, and when you get finished, you feel you have something rather compelling to reflect upon.

In *Blood Line* I thought that Gaines did create two or three women and carry on a very lively, vital sort of love affair. On the other hand, I would say that Black women writers that I've read don't seem to get much into subtle possibilities. I'm thinking again of Alice—Alice in her short stories. Where is there a moment in which a man and woman seem to occupy the same space together? It seems she is always conscious, always, of exploitation; I don't see much possibility, and I'm not sure that there is always depth.

In 1974 Toni Cade Bambara moved to Atlanta, Georgia, and began to organize Black communities around humanistic philosophies. The media for her activities were lectures at the Atlanta University Center and other institutions in the area, classes at various community centers, and her home.

Prior to the Atlanta experience, Toni Cade Bambara became respected during the sixties when, in the North (mostly New York and New Jersey), she made a significant impact with her poetry and dramatic scripts which were produced on educational television networks. *The Black Woman,* her sociopolitical and literary production, was the first major volume of its kind, and it was especially praised because of its relevance to Black Americans' interdisciplinary concerns in the early seventies. *Tales and Short Stories for Black Folk* and *Gorilla, My Love* followed.

Toni Cade Bambara's most recent work is a collection of short stories: *The Sea Birds Are Still Alive* (New York: Random House, 1977), and she is presently at work on a novel and a revision of *The Black Woman.*

Commitment: Toni Cade Bambara Speaks

by BEVERLY GUY-SHEFTALL

Toni Cade Bambara was one of the first persons Roseann and I consulted nearly six years ago when we began talking about the need for an anthology of readings dealing with images of black women in literature. Toni had recently moved to Atlanta and her anthology *The Black Woman* had been in print for three years. She encouraged us to pursue this task and offered valuable suggestions concerning the procedure to follow, having been involved in such an undertaking herself. It seems, therefore, appropriate to return to Toni, not simply to remind her of the inspiration she provided, but because her particular vision—as a teacher, writer, mother, world traveler, social critic, community worker, and humanist—can provide alternative ways, perhaps, of viewing certain aspects of our culture. Here, Toni speaks on a variety of subjects—at times eloquently and passionately, sometimes with gentleness and humor, but always with candor and conviction. As the conversation unfolds, Toni reveals herself to be a pragmatist and a realist, a keen observer of her environment, and a skillful user of language. It is also clear that her perceptive grasp of the complexity of black female experiences is paralleled by her firm grip on the most essential aspects of the black condition generally.

This interview, which took place on two afternoons at Toni's home, makes it possible for a larger audience to share the thoughts, observations, frustrations, and dreams of an extraordinarily talented black woman whose view of the world, though critical, is always tinged by the knowledge that with human beings there is always the potential, even the inevitability, of change.

SHEFTALL: Would you describe your early life and what caused you to start writing?

BAMBARA: I can't remember a time when I was not writing. The original motive was to try to do things that we were not encouraged to do in the language arts programs in the schools, namely, to use writing as a tool to get in touch with the self. In the schools, for example, writing, one of the few crafts we're taught, seems to be for the purpose of teaching people how to plagiarize from the dictionary or the encyclopedia and how to create as much distance from your own voice as possible. That was called education. I'd call it alienation. You had to sift out a lot, distort a lot, and lie a lot in order to jam the stuff of your emotional, linguistic, cultural experience into that form called the English composition.

The original motive for writing at home was to give a play to those notions that wouldn't fit the English composition mold, to try and do justice to a point of view, to a sense of self. Later on, I discovered that there was a certain amount of applause that could be gotten if you turned up with the Frederick Douglass play for Negro History Week or the George Washington Carver play for the assembly program. That talent for bailing the English teachers out created stardom, and that became another motive.

As I got older, I began to appreciate the kinds of things you could tap and release and learn about self if you had a chance to get cozy with pencil and paper. And I discovered too that paper is very patient. It will wait on you to come up with whatever it is, as opposed to sitting in class and having to raise your hand immediately in response to someone else's questions, someone else's concerns.

I don't know that I began getting really serious about writing until maybe five years ago. Prior to that, in spite of all good sense, I always thought writing was rather frivolous, that it was something you did because you didn't feel like doing any work. But in the last five or six years I've come to appreciate that it is a perfectly legitimate way to participate in struggle. That writing, sharing insights, keeping a vision alive, is of value and that is pretty much the motive for writing now. Although I can't really say I have a motive for writing now. I'm compelled. I don't think I could stop if I wanted to.

SHEFTALL: Do you remember the very first story you wrote and the circumstances surrounding it?

BAMBARA: No, no. I was really little. I'm talking about kindergarten. Sometimes even now, a line will come out that will take me back to some utterance made in a story or poem I wrote or tried to write when I was in pink pajamas and bunny slippers. It's weird. I've been in training, you might say, for quite a while. Still am.

SHEFTALL: Were you conditioned by your family members to assume a traditional female role? I'm asking this because of the number of black female children in your fiction who do not conform to American society's notion of what is "proper" female behavior.

BAMBARA: I think within my household not a great deal of distinction was made between pink and blue. We were expected to be self-sufficient, to be competent, and to be rather nonchalant about expertise in a number of areas. Within the various neighborhoods I've lived in, there was such a variety of expectations regarding womanhood or manhood that it was rather wide-open. In every neighborhood I lived in, for example, there were always big-mouthed women, there were always competent women, there were always beautiful women, independent women as well as dependent women, so that there was

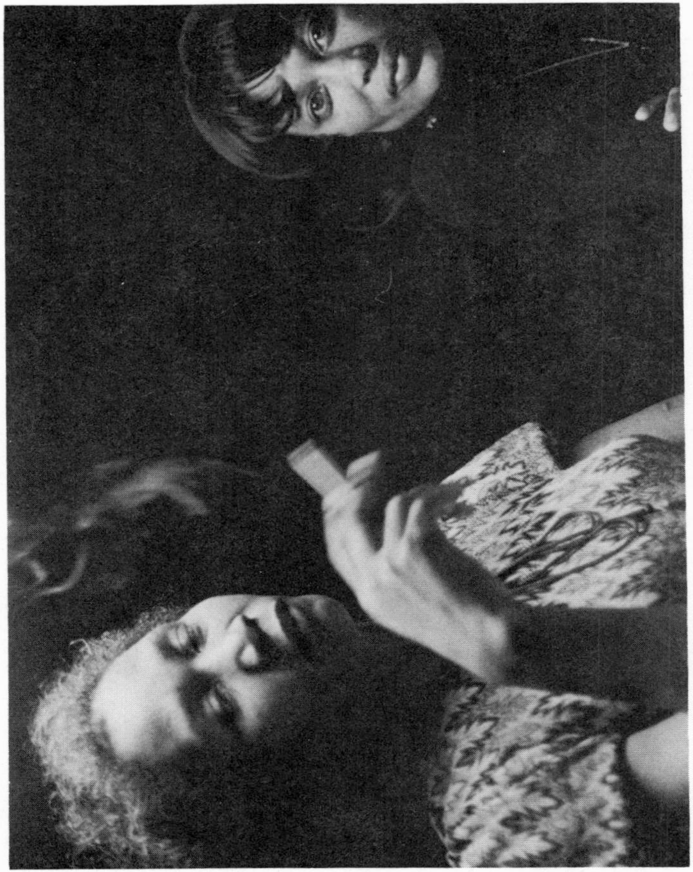

Photo: Judy Mutunhu

Dawoud Bey/First Image

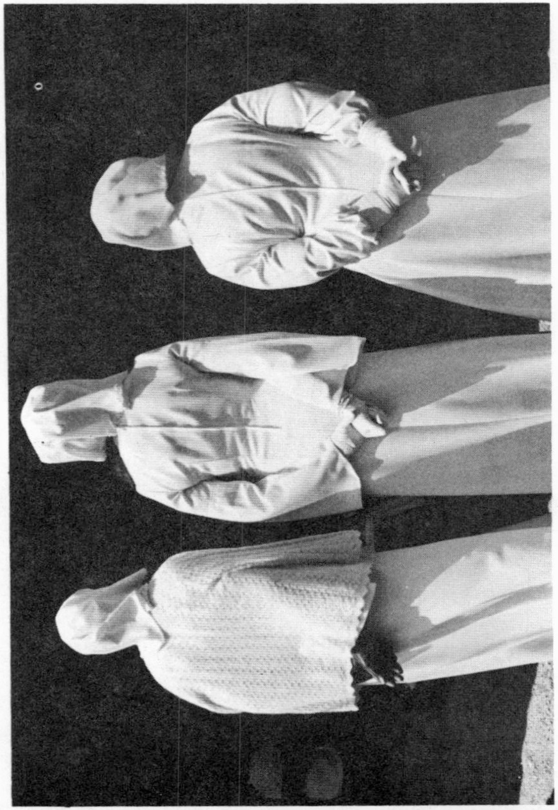

Gloria I. Joseph

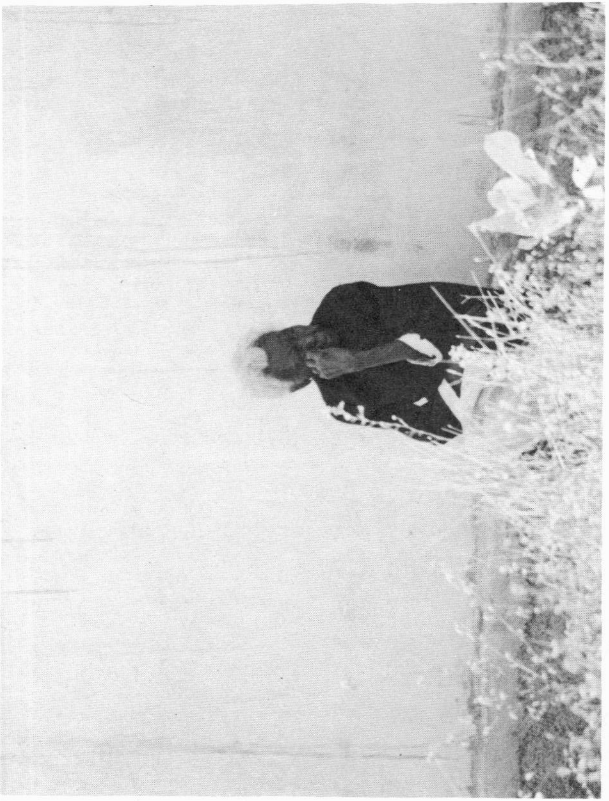

Gloria I. Joseph

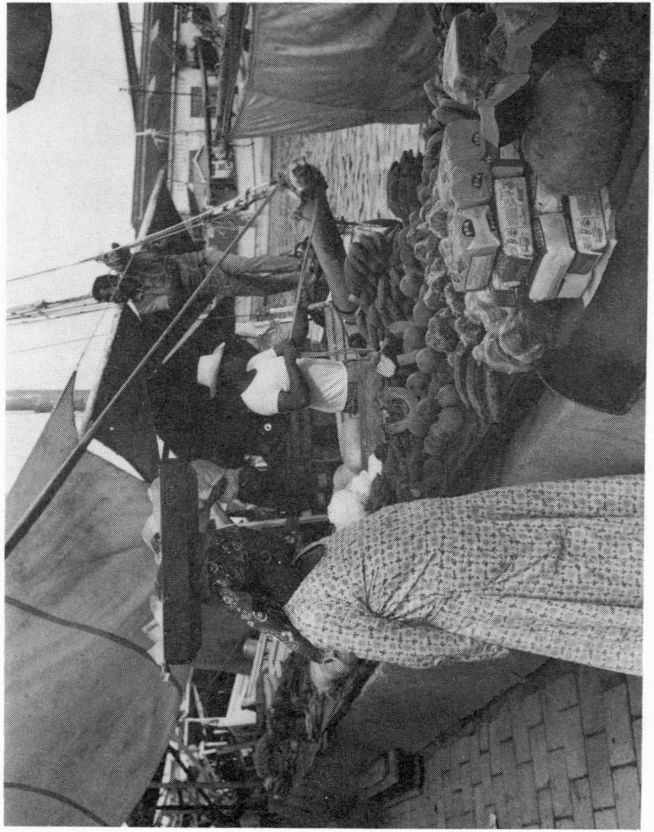

Gloria I. Joseph

Gloria I. Joseph

Gail A. Hansberry

a large repertoire from which to select. And it wasn't until I got older, I would say maybe in college, that I began to collide with the concepts and dynamics of "role-appropriate behavior" and so forth. I had no particular notion about being groomed along one particular route as opposed to another as a girl-child. My self-definitions were strongly internal and improvisational.

SHEFTALL: Take the little girl in "Gorilla, My Love," a favorite story of mine. Would you say that she was like little girls you grew up with? Does she come out of your personal experience?

BAMBARA: I would say that she's a highly selective fiction. There are certain kinds of spirits that I'm *very* appreciative of, people who are very tough, but very compassionate. You put me in any neighborhood, in any city, and I will tend to gravitate toward that type. The kid in "Gorilla" (the story as well as in that collection) is a kind of person who will survive, and she's triumphant in her survival. Mainly because she's so very human, she cares, her caring is not careless. She certainly is not autobiographical except that there are naturally aspects of my own personality that I very much like that are similar to hers. She's very much like people I like. However, I would be hard pressed to point out her source in real life.

SHEFTALL: Have women writers influenced you as much as male writers?

BAMBARA: I have no clear ideas about literary influence. I would say that my mother was a great influence, since mother is usually the first map maker in life. She encouraged me to explore and express. And, too, the fact that people of my household were big on privacy helped. And I would say that people that I ran into helped, and I ran into a great many people because we moved a lot and I was always a nosey kid running up and down the street, getting into everything. Particular kinds of women influenced the work. For example, in every neighborhood I lived in there were always two types of women that somehow pulled me and sort of got their wagons in a circle around me. I call them Miss Naomi and Miss Gladys, although I'm sure they came under various names. The Miss Naomi types were usually barmaids or life-women, nighttime people with lots of clothes in the closet and a very particular philosophy of life, who would give me advice like, "When you meet a man, have a birthday, demand a present that's hockable, and be careful." Stuff like that. Had no idea what they were talking about. Just as well. The Miss Naomis usually gave me a great deal of advice about beautification, how to take care of your health and not get too fat. The Miss Gladyses were usually the type that hung out the window in Apartment 1-A leaning on the pillow giving single-action advice on numbers or giving you advice about how to get your homework done or telling you to stay away from those cruising cars that moved through the neighborhood patrolling little girls. I would say that those two types of women, as well as the women who hung out in the beauty parlors (and the beauty parlors in those days were perhaps the only womanhood institutes we had—it was there in the beauty parlors that young girls came of age and developed some sense of sexual standards and some sense of what it means to be a woman growing up)—it was those women who had the most influence on the writing.

I think that most of my work tends to come off the street rather than from other books. Which is not to say I haven't learned a lot as an avid reader. I devour pulp and print. And of course I'm part of the tradition. That is to say, it is quite apparent to the reader that I appreciate Langston Hughes, Zora Hurston, and am a product of the sixties spirit. But I'd be hard pressed to discuss literary influences in any kind of intelligent way.

SHEFTALL: Did you grow up in New York primarily?

BAMBARA: Primarily.

SHEFTALL: Let's move to some of your reactions to the literary scene. What would you consider to be some contemporary or past positive images of black women in literature, either by male or female or black or white writers?

BAMBARA: I would define "positive" as usable, characters who can teach us valuable lessons of life, characters who are rounded and who give dimension to the type or stereotype that they are closest to. For example, Sula in the Morrison novel is interesting. She's a champion. She's an adventurer, and she gives us another dimension of the bitch stereotype. She makes us aware of how many people are locked up in that particular cage. Eva, who very much resembles the stereotypic matriarch, is more than that and she too helps to break open that old stereotype and force us to look for qualities, lessons, eclipsed by the stereotypic label. I regard them as positive, for they touch deep. In the contemporary poetry—that is, the poetry that came out of the Neo-Black Arts Movement—there are female personae who are assertive and rounded and they also break open the bitch stereotype for us, so that we find under that label locked-up vibrancy—activities, combatants, the Harriet Tubman heirs, people who come from that championship tradition. That's what I would call positive and in fact there are very few works that are available to us now, say in the last decade, that are not like that. We have very little deadwood in the works that have come out of the sixties and are currently being produced. Very few flat, stupid, useless, and careless portraits.

SHEFTALL: Is there a particular black woman writer of fiction who you think best illuminates the black female experience, specifically the double oppression of race and sex?

BAMBARA: No, and I think that's okay. I think if we were designing a course that attempted to project the profile of the contemporary black woman, particularly in respect to double or triple oppression, to someone who did not understand it, it would be necessary to pull out a lot of people because there are a lot of experiences. There is no *the* woman or *the* experience or *the* profile. I would assemble the works of writers like Zora Hurston, Toni Morrison, Carolyn Rodgers, Lucille Clifton, Eloise Lofton, and a good many others and particularly young writers who are coming out of the workshops, in the Southeast particularly, and out of the Berkeley group.

SHEFTALL: Do you think the black woman writer has been treated fairly by the critical community, both black and white?

BAMBARA: I have no idea. It's not something I have any comments on because it's not something I generally think about, that is to say, the black woman writer. We know for sure that any cultural product of black people has not been treated intelligently and usefully by white critics. That's one kind of answer. The fact that a good many black women writers do not get into anthologies that are put together by black men is another kind of answer. The fact that black women critics sometimes approach black women's writing as though they were highly particular and had no connection to the group traditions, that's another kind of issue.

I'm not so much concerned with whether black women writers are dealt with fairly but rather with what they're dealing with. And I think the great accomplishment of particularly the poets of the Neo-Black Arts Movement (sister poets) and perhaps to a lesser degree the dramatists, novelists, short story writers, have contributed a great deal toward not only commenting on, correcting, and countering the stereotypic images, but in blasting open a new road, if you will, for younger writers who are coming along now: dealing with women who have not been dealt with before, raising issues that have not been tackled before, grabbing hold of a vision that we have let slip and maybe never have laid out in print before. The production itself I find far more interesting than critical response.

SHEFTALL: Near the end of her introduction to *Black-eyed Susans,* a collection of short stories by and about black women, Mary Helen Washington asserts with respect to the black woman writer that "there still remains something of a sacred-cow attitude in regard to black women that prevents exploration of many aspects of their lives." "There has been a desire," she goes on to say, "to protect and revere the black woman's image." She argues then that we need books about black women who have nervous breakdowns, who are "overwhelmed by sex," who are not faithful, who abuse and neglect their children, and so forth. That is, we also need stories about "real black women," stories which "interpret the entire range and spectrum of the experiences of black women." Would you agree with her assessment of the black woman writer with respect to these issues?

BAMBARA: I don't approach literature from quite that direction. I think I understand what she's saying, but writing for me is still an act of language first and foremost. I don't know that I need to read a book about a nervous breakdown in order to understand nervous breakdowns or to protect my health. As an act of language, literature is a spirit informer—an energizer. A lot of energy is exchanged in the reading and writing of books and that gets into the debate of whether it is more important to offer a usable truth or to try to document the many truths or realisms that make up the black woman's experience.

I think I see her point and it's all very lovely but it doesn't concern me, and I'm not altogether sure it's valid or true. It is true that we're so defensive about our detractors, which I think is what one of her points is, that we are not approaching the complexity of ourselves in a fearless way. That is true, but I don't know that the nervous breakdown is what I would argue for. I would argue rather that there is an aspect of black spirit, of inherent black nature, that we have not addressed: the tension, the power that is still latent, still colonized, still frozen and untapped, in some 27 million black people. We do not know how to unleash, we do not even know how to speak of it in a courageous manner, *yet*. I think that is because we have been so long on the defensive and have invested a great deal of time and energy posturing and trying to prove that indeed we are as clean as they are. Since the sixties, however, a great many of us have been released from that posturing through having dialogues with each other which is a very radical and new dimension to the dialogue of cultural worker and community. It is in relation to potential that I might argue Mary Helen's same general point. Namely, that we are not terribly fearless and courageous and thoroughgoing in dealing with the complexity of the black experience, the black spirit. As a matter of fact, music is probably the only mode we have used to speak of that complexity. But I would argue the point in relation to other aspects of self rather than to nervous breakdowns and the kinds of things that Mary Helen is talking about, which is not to say that it has no usefulness, but it doesn't strike me as a priority at all.

SHEFTALL: Do you think that the black woman has an advantage or special perspective that may enable her to reveal those aspects of the black experience or black spirit to which you refer?

BAMBARA: No, I wouldn't say that black women or children or elders or men or any other sector of the community are any more in command of it or in touch with it than any other. I find it interesting in this period, the seventies, that we have begun to embrace within our community (and we can see parallels in the national as well as international community) an interest in holistic healing systems: astrology, voodoo, TM, etc. No, I don't think that any group within the community has any monopoly on that kind of wisdom, a grasp on that new way to prepare for the future.

SHEFTALL: Speaking of parallels, have your travels revealed to you how American black and other Third World women can link up in their struggles to liberate themselves from the various kinds of oppression they face as a result of their sexual identity?

BAMBARA: Yes, I would say that two particular places I visited yielded up a lot of lessons along those lines. I was in Cuba in 1973 and had the occasion not only to meet with the Federation of Cuban Women but sisters in the factories, on the land, in the street, in the parks, in lines, or whatever, and the fact that they were able to resolve a great many class conflicts as well as color conflicts and organize a mass organization says a great deal about the possibilities here. I was in Vietnam in the summer of 1975 as a guest of the Women's Union and again was very much struck by the women's ability to break through traditional roles, traditional expectations, reactionary agenda for women, and come together again in a mass organization that is programmatic and takes on a great deal of responsibility for the running of the nation.

We missed a moment in the early sixties. We missed two things. One, at a time when we were beginning to lay the foundations for a national black women's union and for a national strategy for organizing, we did not have enough heart nor a solid enough analysis that would equip us to respond in a positive and constructive way to the fear in the community from black men as well as others who said that women organizing as women is divisive. We did not respond to that in a courageous and principled way. We fell back. The other moment that we missed was that we had an opportunity to hook up with Puerto Rican women and Chicano women who shared not only a common condition but also I think a common vision about the future and we missed that moment because of the language trap. When people talked about multicultural or multiethnic organizing, a lot of us translated that to mean white folks and backed off. I think that was an error. We should have known what was meant by multicultural. Namely, people of color. Afro-American, Afro-Hispanic, Indo-Hispanic, Asian-Hispanic, and so forth. Not that those errors necessarily doom us. Errors may result in lessons learned. I think we have the opportunity again in this last quarter of the twentieth century to begin forging those critical ties with other communities. It will be done. That is a certainty.

SHEFTALL: Do you consider it a dilemma for the black woman today who considers herself both a feminist and a warrior in the race struggle?

BAMBARA: A dilemma? Personally, no. I'm not aware of what the problem is for people who do feel that's a dilemma. I don't know what they're thinking because it's not as if you're a black *or* a woman. I don't find any basic contradiction or any tension between being a feminist, being a pan-Africanist, being a black nationalist, being an internationalist, being a socialist, and being a woman in North America. I'm not sensitive enough to people caught in the "contradiction" to be able to unravel the dilemma and adequately speak to the question at this particular point in time. My head is somewhere else.

SHEFTALL: Turning to your own writings, you said in your preface to *The Black Woman,* an anthology of readings by contemporary black women published in 1970, that among other evils this country "regards its women as its monsters." Have you seen over the past seven years or so any changes in this country's attitude toward women, especially the black ones?

BAMBARA: The country at large, no. You look at "That's My Mama" and I think it's clear that television program really centers around the son and the activities in the barbershop. That's the most dynamic aspect of that drama. But because the mammy looms so large in the American mentality, is such a durable, persistent psychosexual obsession on the part of white people, male and female, that need demands the presence of the mama figure: on the one hand, a gracious, giving, enduring mammy, but also a Hattie McDaniel sass. Sass as a comic-menace element. The menace element is a white fiction that is meshed into our women, that has to do with their whole "momism" pathology. So they get their thing off in three ways through her: She's useful to keep the "boy" thing going; she's the mother's milk nurturer; plus the "hate mom" white thing can be projected onto her.

I don't know that I have seen any change, by and large, in white America. In terms of black America, there are authors still—I'm thinking of John A. Williams in particular, as well as many other writers who don't come to mind at the moment—who are still a little scary in terms of the assertive black woman, still look at Sapphire as a threat, and who do not come to grips with how that myth functions in American society. The bitch helps to justify, for example, hustlers and other collaborators. The presence of the bitch myth also helps those societal restraints that operate on black women, as well as the rest of the community. No, I haven't noticed a lot of change among black male writers either. Ron Milner's women are a change, though.

SHEFTALL: If you were to do another anthology of readings by contemporary black women today, what kind of pieces would you include?

BAMBARA: The papers that I was most concerned with at that time never got into the book, and those were position papers from the Women's Caucus of SNCC, of the Panthers, of a number of other organizations that eventually did produce papers for publication through Third World Women's Alliance. I was particularly concerned with the evolution of women's groups that had begun as consumer education or single-issue action groups, began studying together and engaging in community organizing and are now, some ten years later, the core network of what will soon become, we hope, a national black women's union. I would include in a new collection writings from the campus forces, the prison forces, tenant's groups, and most especially southern rural women's works, particularly from the migrant workers and sharecroppers of the Deep South.

SHEFTALL: How did you go about selecting the pieces that were included in the collection you edited entitled *Tales and Stories for Black Folks,* which was published in 1972?

BAMBARA: The first half of the book consists of stories I wished I had read growing up, stories by Alice Walker, Pearl Crayton, and particularly Langston Hughes. The stories in the second half of the book were documents that came out of a course that I was teaching (a freshman composition course, which has always been my favorite). The students had begun working with kids in an independent community school and I asked them to produce term paper projects that were usable to someone. So a great many of them took traditional European tales and changed them so as to promote critical thinking, critical reading for the young people they were working with outside of the class. And out of that group of term papers came a number of really remarkable, thoughtful pieces, such as "The True Story of Chicken Licken," which raises questions about the nature of truth or the nature of responsible journalism. The story pivoted on the idea that perhaps it was not a piece of sky that fell on Chicken Licken's head after all but maybe she got caught up in a community action and got hit on the head by the cops and then they put out a press release that she had been attacked by a piece of cloud. All of the stories in the second half of the book came out of the materials that had been submitted to me by students that year.

SHEFTALL: You are one of the few black literary artists who could be considered a short story writer primarily. Is this a deliberate choice on your part or coincidental?

BAMBARA: It's deliberate, coincidental, accidental, and regretful! Regretful, commercially. That is to say, it is financially stupid to be a short story writer and to spend two years putting together eight or ten stories and receiving maybe half the amount of money you would had you taken one of those short stories and produced a novel. The publishing companies, reviewers, critics, are all geared to promoting and pushing the novel rather than any other form.

I prefer the short story genre because it's quick, it makes a modest appeal for attention, it can creep up on you on your blind side. The reader comes to the short story with a mind-set different than that with which he approaches the big book, and a different set of controls operating, which is why I think the short story is far more effective in terms of teaching us lessons.

Temperamentally, I move toward the short story because I'm a sprinter rather than a long-distance runner. I cannot sustain characters over a long period of time. Walking around, frying eggs, being a mother, shopping—I cannot have those characters living in my house with me for more than a couple of weeks. In terms of craft, I don't have the kinds of skills *yet* that it takes to stay with a large panorama of folks and issues and landscapes and moods. That requires a set of skills that I don't know anything about yet, but I'm learning.

I prefer the short story as a reader, as well, because it does what it does in a hurry. For the writer and the reader make instructive demands in terms of language precision. It deals with economy, gets it said, and gets out of the way. As a teacher, I also prefer the short story for all the reasons given. And yes, I consider myself primarily a short story writer.

SHEFTALL: You are attempting a novel, though, for the first time?

BAMBARA: No, not for the first time. Like every other writer, I have fifteen thousand unfinished novels brewing under the bed. But having come to grips with the nature of publishing, I understand that it is shrewd and in my interest to produce a novel before I come out with another collection of short stories, so I'm doing both.

SHEFTALL: Will the novel be anything like your short stories?

BAMBARA: Surely, it's the same mind working, after all. They're the same in the sense that the vision hasn't changed. My affinity for certain kind of people is the same.

SHEFTALL: Is the setting North or South?

BAMBARA: It seems to be South. It seems to be everywhere. I've got a sixty-page chunk of it and there are several thousand characters running around and it seems to be vaguely Louisiana and there's also a character who's obviously from New York and there's somebody else who's obviously from the Coast and I have a couple of West Indian folk and I have an Arapaho in there as well as an Aleutian and two people from the Philippines. So I'm not sure what the setting of the novel is. But it's driving me crazy.

SHEFTALL: That leads me into the next question which is about the process involved in your writing a story. Do you have the whole idea of it before sitting down to write, or does it unfold as you're writing?

BAMBARA: It depends on how much time you have. There are periods in my life when I know that I will not be able to get to the desk until summer, until months later, in which case I walk around composing while washing dishes and may jot down little definitive notes on pieces of paper which I stick under the phone, in the mirror, and all over the house. At other times, a story mobilizes itself around a single line you've heard that resonates. There's a truth there, something usable. Sometimes a story revolves around a character that I'm interested in. For example, "The Organizer's Wife" in the new collection. I've always been very curious about silent people because most people I know are like myself—very big-mouthed, verbally energetic, and generally clear as to what they're about because their *mouth* is always announcing what they're doing. That story came out of a curiosity. What do I know about people like that? Could I delve into her? The story took shape around that effort.

There are other times when a story is absolutely clear in the head. All of it may not be clear—who's going to say what and where it's taking place or what year it is—but the story frequently comes together at one moment in the head. At other times, stories, like any other kind of writing, and certainly anybody who's writing anything—freshman compositions, press releases, or whatever—has experienced this, that frequently writing is an act of discovery. Writing is very much like dreaming, in that sense. When you dream, you dialogue with aspects of yourself that normally are not with you in the daytime and you discover that you know a great deal more than you thought you did. So there are various kinds of ways that writing comes.

Then, too, there is a kind of—some people call it automatic writing—I call it inspiration. There are times when you have to put aside what you intended to write, what got you to the desk in the first place, and just go with the story that is coming out of you, which may or may not have anything to do with what you planned at all. In fact, a lot of stories (I haven't published any of these because I'm not sure they are mine) and poems have come out on the page that I know do not belong to me. They do not have my sense of vision, my sense of language, my sense of reality, but they're complete. Each of us has experienced this in various ways, in church, or fasting, or in some other kind of state, times when we are available to intelligences that we are not particularly prone to acknowledge, given our Western scientific training, which have filled us with so much fear that we cannot make ourselves available to other channels of information. I think most of us have experienced, though we don't talk about it very much, an inspiration, that is to say, an in-breathing that then becomes "enthusiasm," a possession, a living-with, an informing spirit. So some stories come off like that.

SHEFTALL: Do you make many revisions before the story is finished and ready for publication?

BAMBARA: Oh yes. I edit mercilessly. Generally, my editing takes the form of cutting. Very frequently, a story will try to get away from me and become a novel. I don't have the staying power for a novel, so when I find it getting to be about thirty or forty pages I immediately start cutting back to six. To my mind, the six-page short story is the gem. If it takes more than six pages to say it, something is the matter. So I'm not too pleased in that respect with the new collection, *The Sea Birds Are Still Alive*. Most of those stories are too sprawling and hairy for my taste, although I'm very pleased, feel perfectly fine about them as pieces. But as stories, they're too damn long and dense.

SHEFTALL: Let's move to a specific discussion of *The Sea Birds,* your most recently published collection of short stories, which I thoroughly enjoyed. Barbara Mahone, in her review which appears in the May/June 1977 issue of *First World,* asserts that your handling of black male-female relationships is different from at least two other black female writers, Alice Walker and Ntozake Shange, because they leave, she says, "this bitter residue of bad feelings between men and women," whereas in your stories, "the net social effect" is more positive. Do you agree with her?

BAMBARA: One might just as easily argue that the difference is that they're telling the truth and I'm not. Or one could just as easily argue that they're getting into the more painful side of the relationship and I am not. Temperamentally, I'm much more concerned with the caring that lies beneath the antagonisms between black men and black women. There is a great deal of static that informs our relationships, above and beyond the political wedge that has been jammed between us by myth makers of the oppressor class. Whereas other writers, other women, other people, are more concerned with the hurt of it all, the hurt doesn't teach me anything and I'm concerned primarily with usable lessons. The caring does teach me something and I think I can offer a usable something for someone else.

It is very facile to talk about male-female antagonisms in the Western world or in the United States in a pat fashion that enables you to sound as though you're talking about all people. It's easy to talk about *the* War Between the Sexes which is characteristic of the United States as it is no other place. When foreigners watch Hollywood movies and see Clark Gable drop Claudette Colbert in the mud, the response is a gasp. That is something peculiarly American, that belligerency, that warfare. A great many folk are in the process of speaking about women/men relationships in our community in that kind of generalized way of trying to make it "universal." That's very dangerous and kind of sloppy and not very valid because what distinguishes relationships between men and women in our community is the level of caring that informs the tension.

If a white woman attacks a white man in general or in particular about being a chauvinist pig, underneath that is the legacy of Europe, is the notion of a God complex with the woman as martyr who will forgive everything and manipulate shrewdly under the table with cunning and craft, but mostly she will be a martyr on the cross and that gives her moral superiority to condemn all or forgive all—to play God. Black women, on the other hand, do not deal with themselves as God, nor do they remove Him from the human frame of reference. We start with the premise "I am not God" and therefore have a right to call you on that play. That's a very different mind-set and a very different frame of reference, a very different moral code. I hope we can get to the point where we recognize, again, that if we love each other, we are concerned with development. And that means being mutually responsible to each other—criticism, hardheaded demands.

Getting back to Barbara Mahone's comment, it's not terribly useful for *me* to make comparisons. One could take her contrast to prove any number of things. I am simply more interested in the caring network that exists between men and women, men and men, women and women, children and elders. One of the reasons those links are links of vulernerability at one moment has to do with the level of caring and the degree to which that caring can push against the synthetic conflicts that white society orchestrates in its interests, not ours.

SHEFTALL: Of the reviews I've read of *The Sea Birds,* none has mentioned "The Girl's Story," a fascinating though possibly perplexing piece. Why has her family mistaken her first menstrual period for an abortion?

BAMBARA: Well, this is a family where not much touching goes on, as is played on throughout the story. There are great distances, even though the people live close-quartered. For example, the girl hears a certain quality in her brother's voice only once in a while. She can embrace her grandmother or her grandmother can embrace her only in a very particular kind of way and it's not closeness. It's not touching. In a household like that, it stands to reason that a lot of secretiveness and isolation travel under the guise of privacy. So it's not unlikely at all that they would not know she's begun her menses.

In almost every household that I can think of when I was growing up, the onset of the menstrual period was mysterious and frightening and totally without information and totally without support from the immediate household. Most frequently, young girls could find a sympathetic godmother or maybe some older girl in the neighborhood who understood and recognized it right away and got the wagons in a circle. I know very few households when I was growing up where it would have been dealt with in any other way than it is depicted in the story—which is why the title is general, "A Girl's Story."

SHEFTALL: Yes, that was an aspect of the story that I suspect many women of past generations can relate to. It is true that many aspects of the menstrual period were and possibly still are shrouded in mystery. What's interesting, however, is that when I have used fiction that mentions this issue with students in my college classes (such as *Browngirl, Brownstones, The Bluest Eye*), many of them have not been very responsive. They tend to think that dealing with circumstances surrounding the first menstrual period in a work of literature is unnecessary and you find yourself saying to them that for some women the experience was traumatic. Some students even found it difficult to remember what it was like.

BAMBARA: It might be true that the particular traumas and dangers of womanhood are not valued as a crucial part of our culture. As a matter of fact, that is why the cult of the Amazon, the cult of strength, the bear-up-under-everything woman figure came into play because we did not admit, were not allowed to, could not afford to *admit* pain and suffering and hardship. You're not supposed to do that if you're a black woman. In line with that, anyone who's ever visited the neighborhood chiropractor's office or who has ever watched healing services in our own community is probably well aware that black women have tremendous problems with their backs. And I wonder if part of that isn't the unnecessary burden of taking on that cult of strength, that Amazon figure, and internalizing that whole madness.

For students in the generation behind us not to be able to identify with the trauma of the first menses is open to a number of interpretations. I would like to think that their nonchalance or impatient response means that it was all very breezy and pleasant.

The initiation or rites of passage of the young girl is not one of the darlings of American literature. The coming of age for the young boy is certainly much more the classic case. I wonder if it all means that we don't put a value on our process of womanhood.

SHEFTALL: Have you been generally pleased with the reviews of *Sea Birds?*

BAMBARA: All of the reviews have been very favorable. Some have been quite cogent and favorable. Some have been stupid and favorable. I found the *First World* review that was in the Chicago *Tribune* by Bruce Allen critically constructive. It focused on the flaws and the faults of the book and I found it very helpful. The piece that Ruby Dee wrote (I'm not sure where it will appear; I imagine in the *Amsterdam News*) I found the most *moving* in the sense that she makes highly particular the public and personal values. It just had me in tears. It helped me to answer some of the questions one always has in one's mind while writing: whether it works, what doesn't work, to what degree is it overdone, to what degree is it too understated, questions of that sort. The Ruby Dee piece was somp'n, honey.

SHEFTALL: One of the characteristics of your fiction which is apparent in *Gorilla, My Love,* an older collection of short stories, as well as in *The Sea Birds* is the extent to which—though one knows you're there—you can remove yourself from the narrative voice. You don't intrude. Is that deliberate?

BAMBARA: Well, I'm frequently there. You see, one of the reasons that it seems that the author is not there has to do with language. It has to do with the whole tradition of dialect. In the old days, writers might have their characters talking dialect or slang but the narrator, that is to say, the author, maintained a distance and a "superiority" by speaking a more premiumed language. I tend to speak on the same level as my characters, so it seems as though I am not there, because, possibly, you're looking for another voice.

SHEFTALL: I rarely get the impression that your fiction comes directly out of your personal experience, even though it's obvious that what you have written about has been filtered through your consciousness. I don't have the impression that these particular characters or that particular incident are very close to what you may have actually experienced. Is that correct?

BAMBARA: Yes, that's correct. I think it's very rude to write autobiographically, unless you label it autobiography. And I think it's very rude to use friends and relatives as though they were occasions for getting your whole thing off. It's not making your mama a still life. And it's very abusive to your developing craft, to your own growth, not to convert and transform what has come to you in one way into another way. The more you convert the more you grow, it seems to me. Through conversion we recognize again the basic oneness, the connections, or as some blood coined it: "Everything is Everything." So, it's kind of *lazy* (I think that's the better word) to simply record. Also, it's terribly boring to the reader frequently, and, too, it's dodgy. You can't tell to what extent things are fascinating to you because they're yours and to what extent they're useful, unless you do some conversion.

SHEFTALL: What can we expect from you in the future?

BAMBARA: I'm working on several things—some children's books, a new collection of short stories, a novel, some film scripts.

"Children of Struggle" is a series I've been working on that dramatizes the role children and youth have played in the struggle for liberation—children of the Underground Railroad, children of Frelimo, children of the Long March, of Granma, of El Grito de Lares, The Trail of Tears, and so forth.

The major question that corners me at the moment is what constitutes development for the systematically underdeveloped. I've tackled the question in several forms. I'm thinking now of putting together a critique of pedagogical perspectives, examining the premises of Freud, Montessori, Piaget, learning theories, educational models, to reveal how the training of children is being approached as a management problem rather than a *development* question; two, that there really are few sound development theories at all. First, we're children to the Freudians, then we're neurotic. No model of adulthood or maturity there. Or, we're innocent babes to be protected from controversy, problems, disturbances; then we're responsible adults, somehow; then we're senile, useless crones. Fanon and of course Friere (*Pedagogy of the Oppressed*) offer another view of the process. But they are too incomplete.

I'm doing a film script about a particular group of combatants in the 1850s (Tubman, Douglass, John Brown, etc.) with the focus on the much neglected figure of Mammy Pleasant, who bankrolled so many of the Kansas actions and set up an intelligence network on the Coast. Fascinating woman!

The new collection begins where *Sea Birds* leaves us, stories that dramatize the international operation of colonialism and celebrates too the international nature of liberation struggles. One is set in Ponce and Mayagüez, Puerto Rico, another in the New Hebrides, another in Laos, another in the Kenyan countryside. I hope to get to Brazil this year and back to Africa as well.

As for the novel—it's still a mystery to me. I started out with a simple story of a carnival society that decides to stage an old slave insurrection as their contribution to the pageant. It's developed into—well, you can imagine. Hard work, writing. A continual act of discovery!

Toni Morrison has received literary acclaim as both a novelist and an editor for a major publishing house. As a senior editor at Random House, she has published a number of works by prolific and important young writers such as Gayl Jones, John McClusky, and Henry Dumas. She also edited *The Black Book,* a documented history of Black culture, in 1971.

An artist in her own right, she published her first novel, *The Bluest Eye,* in 1970. Her second novel, *Sula,* was published in 1974 (Alfred A. Knopf). *Song of Solomon,* her third novel, was published by Knopf in 1977 and is being applauded nationally as a superb fictional account of a Black family's experience.

Ms. Morrison was born in Lorain, Ohio, and attended Howard and Cornell universities. Before going to Random House, she taught English at Howard and Texas Southern University. Currently, she lives in New York.

Toni Morrison's women. Who are they? Sula, Nell, Pecola, Eva, Claudia, Hagar, and the bewitching and bootlegging Aunt Pilate. These and others are the female characters in Morrison's three novels. *The Bluest Eye* is a haunting, stylistically impressive novel about many things, among which is a racist society-taught Black self-hatred. *Sula* is a powerful tale which explores, attacks, and reconstructs myths surrounding the stereotypes of the dutiful Black daughter and the self-effacing mother. The view of many Black critics sensitive to feminist, racial, and economic situations is that *Sula* is Morrison's best work. *Song of Solomon* was hailed by the literary power brokers as an extraordinary and credible complement to Alex Haley's phenomenal *Roots* because of *Solomon's* intricate and poignant statements on Black family life only a few years removed from slavery.

The interview that follows is an early one—pre-*Solomon*—and thus provides current Morrison readers with even more critical perspectives. Morrison is a candid and effective writer, and a divorced mother of two sons. She is also a meticulous craftsperson who is able to distill her life experiences into finely honed pieces of art.

Complexity: Toni Morrison's Women— An Interview Essay

by BETTYE J. PARKER

". . . Anything I have ever learned of any consequence, I have learned from Black people. I have never been bored by *any* Black person, ever. . . ."

I noticed that the sun had forced its way over the East River through the smog and was trying desperately to energize the early morning persons rushing about on New York's fashionable East Side. A beam of light slipped through a drapery panel, in the room where I sat, and shone directly on a photograph of Muhammad Ali. Although I was partially blinded by the insistent sun, I kept staring at the eyes in the photograph which dominated the other objects on the wall. The voice that spoke to me diverted my attention from the photograph.

". . . you see, my juices come from a certain place. I am like a painter who is preoccupied with painting violins, and may never do moods or paint a tree. . . ."

Toni Morrison was testifying. Her soul was breathing. As senior editor at a major publishing house, she has for some time been deliberately encouraging and cultivating a certain kind of Black work. And, even as a personal preoccupation, she has concentrated on a specific folk element in her own fiction. Without a doubt, her office reflects her trade. Books. Some folks decorate their offices with exotic plants, ashtrays, and an ornamental book here and there. In Toni Morrison's office, books are everywhere. It reminds one, at a quick glance, of an overstuffed dinner table. Copies of *The Black Book,* a documented history of Black culture, edited by her in 1971, occupied most of the coffee table. Several copies of Henry Dumas' *Ark of Bones* and *Play Ebony Play Ivory* along with John McClusky's *Look What They Done to My Song* were neatly lined on a center bookshelf. These represented some of the fruits of her labor. Resting on the left corner of her desk was a copy of *Corregidora,* a novel by Gayl Jones and one of Mrs. Morrison's earliest projects. Directly behind her desk was a colossal painting of Africa dipped in red between a faint black outline. The distance between Lorain, Ohio, and Random House publishing company could only be a stone's throw away for a woman who knew how to get where she had to go. During this interview she seemed radiant and at peace with herself as she talked to me about the parallels between living and loving in and out of fiction.

The testimony that she was giving about her strengths and virtues explained the presence of simple settings and full Black characterization as well as the absence of white characters in her fiction. I asked her to explain the motive behind writing *The Bluest Eye.*

"I wrote about a victim who is a child, and adults don't write about children. The novel is about a passive kind of person and the people around her who create the kind of situation that she is in. I did not think that it would be widely distributed because it was about things that probably nobody was interested in except me. I was interested in reading a kind of book that I had never read before. I didn't know if such a book existed, but I had just never read it in 1964 when I started writing *The Bluest Eye.*"

An element of mysticism envelops Toni Morrison's fiction. It comes through both of her major fiction pieces like plaited hair with different color ribbons woven in. Each color knows exactly when to surface. One first notices this mystic thread in *The Bluest Eye.* For example, a strong kinship exists between Pecola's stunted growth and the growth of the marigolds. It is sewn throughout her second novel, *Sula,* which is steered by blackbirds and birthmarks and fire and water. I asked her outright if she was superstitious. First, she laughed in much the same way that I would expect the seven voodoo sisters in Algiers, Louisiana, to laugh at such an untactful question. Secondly, she picked up her pipe and began to refill it. She never smoked it during the interview. She just kept stuffing it. I was mesmerized by her serious response.

"I am very superstitious. And that is a word that is in disrepute, but whatever it is that I am has something to do with my relationship to things other than human beings. In *Sula* the people are like the people I have always known who may or may not be superstitious but they look at the world differently. Their cosmology is a little bit different. Their relationship to evil is what preoccupied me most throughout the book. How they see it. What they do with it. Black people in general don't annihilate evil. We are not well known for erecting stoning centers or destroying people when they have disagreements. We believe that evil has a natural place in the universe. We try to avoid it or defend ourselves against it but we are not surprised at its existence or horrified or outraged. We may, in fact, live right next door to it, not only in the form of something metaphysical, but also in terms of people."

Now her voice had staccato movements. I asked her to reflect on the women in *Sula.* They are such a disturbing bunch. And they seem motivated by a force other than Toni Morrison. Sula seems to be a mixture of Hannah, Eva, and Nel. Or are these three women fragments of Sula? I questioned. She nodded her head in understanding my concern.

"In *Sula* I tried to posit a situation where there was a so-called good and a so-called evil people. Nel and Sula are symbolic of this condition. And of course, you can't always tell which is which. Nel is the kind of person I like because I like people who 'do it.' No matter what happens, they do what they have to do. She will take care of the children and do the work but will never have the fire and the glory or the glamour. But the bread will be there. Nobody ever thinks about these people. So they just sit on buses and carry the weight of the world forever. Nel has limitations and she doesn't have the imagination that Sula has.

"On the other hand, I also like people like Sula. They are exciting, and they are willing to trust their instincts completely which is what Sula does. She has absolutely no plans for any series of moments. Yet she and Nel are very much alike. They complement each other. They support each other. I suppose the two of them together could have made a wonderful single human being. But, you see, they are like a Janus' head."

Mrs. Morrison's telephone rang and I took the opportunity to reverse the tape in my recorder. I refocused my mind on Sula and Nel. Sula was much more complex than Nel. Her relationship with Ajax simply compounded her internal disorder. The way she acted during the course of their relationship seemed somewhat out of tune with her general behavior. After the brief telephone conversation, Mrs. Morrison talked more about Sula.

"When creating Sula, I had in mind a woman of force. In a way she is distilled. She doesn't stop existing even after she dies. In fact, what she left behind is more powerful after she is dead than when she was alive. But back to Ajax. Sula behaves like Nel while she is going with Ajax. She does a little number with the dishes and cleans up her house and puts a ribbon in her hair. Her attempt to be domestic is the thing that makes him leave because he liked her for what she was."

This analysis of Sula and Ajax was especially impressive. Despite the fact that Sula "didn't care bout nobody," she did break down and put a ribbon in her hair for Ajax. However, this need on the part of Sula to be "different" with Ajax than with other men is possibly the great flaw in the web that she has woven for herself. And, on a more general plane, all the women in the book have healthy attitudes toward the men with whom they come in contact. Mrs. Morrison played around with her pipe and continued to comment on these women.

"Sula's mother, Hannah, is sexually selfish. But she is not a selfish person. There is also nothing sinister about her, although she is lazy. She doesn't want an affair, a relationship, or a meaningful anything. She is not about the possession of other people. She has a streak of kindness about her. Sula didn't have that. Hannah is uncomplicated and really and truly knows nothing about jealousy or hostility. And when you take that kind of innocence and put it in an adult, it has reverberations. The people in the town all gossip about her but they miss her when she is gone. And they take care of her when she burns and weep for her when she dies."

The women in the community who cared for Hannah and cried for her were certainly aware of her relationship with their men. Often she made love to their men in her pantry in the afternoon and later helped the wives cook dinner and gossiped with them. Why, then, did they mourn her so? Without so much as a pause, Mrs. Morrison explained.

"Hannah makes a statement of lust about their husbands. Even though they may not want their men to be sleeping with her, it was a compliment to know that somebody else wanted them. It was this quality that made her a perfectly charming person. Of course, she couldn't keep a friend for long because they, being like most of us, have conflicts about love and marriage and who owns and who goes with and all of that. She does not flaunt or boast or go around trying to look cute. She does nothing."

A puzzling woman, in another sense, is Eva. Whether or not she actually had her leg cut off by the train to collect insurance money may or may not be accurate or important. Nonetheless, she handled the men in her life with a special flavor. The checkers games she played with them in her quarters were spirited and non-competitional. But when her son, Plum, the one man whom she actually gave life, tried to re-enter her womb, she set his body aflame. Was this, I questioned, an act of mother's love?

"Eva is a triumphant figure, one-legged or not. She is playing God. She maims people. But she says all of the important things. She tells Nel, for example, that there is no difference between her and Sula. She tells her, 'I just saw it. I didn't watch it.' Now, 'watch' is something different from 'saw.' You have to be participating in something that you are watching. If you just saw it, you just happened to be there. But she is there at the end and she knows that they are putting something in her orange juice. So she just eats oranges. She is old and senile and Sula has put her in the old folks' home! This is the act that is so unbelievable about Sula. You know like I know that *we* don't put old people in old folks' homes. We take care of them like they took care of us. Anyway, the older you get the more prestige you have. There is nothing prestigious about being young. When old women walk into a room, people stand up and act like they have some sense."

With all the current uproar about and among Black women, the concerns about choices and the preoccupation with roles, I asked Toni Morrison if her women were prototypic of present Black women. Or, I quizzed, were they antithetical to the current confusion?

"There is something inside us that makes us different from other people. It is not like men and it is not like white women. We talked earlier about the relationship between my women and the men in their lives. When they sing the blues it is one of those 'somebody is gone' kind of thing but there is never any bitterness.

Personally, I have always felt this way and I have recognized it in other women. They are sorry that the man is gone at the moment and may sit around on porches and cry but there is no bitterness and there is no whining, either. You see, I don't have to make choices about whether to be a mother or whether to work. I do them both because they both exist and I don't feel put out about it. I don't dwell on the idea that I am a full human being. I know that. But, speaking of choices, a woman can either choose to have a child or not to have a child, for example. Well, it also has to be the other way around. If she chooses to have it, the man can choose to ignore it. And that is a double-edged sword. If she doesn't have to be the mother and manufacture it, then obviously he doesn't have to be the father. And this is a liberty that Black men have always taken. They have always made that choice. Now, they have been cursed out for years for doing it, but nevertheless, they have always done it and there is no way to stop them. And I think that is called abandonment of the family or something. On the other hand, Ulysses abandoned his child for twenty years and he didn't go anywhere since he was just hanging out over there with the Sicilians. But he is considered a hero! His wife stayed home and did little wifely things. He knew that there was a child there and never once said that he had to go home to his son. He said he had to go home to his property. But, you see, he is a classic!"

The morning was growing into noon. By now the ray of sunlight that had stolen its way into the room had doubled in size. I thought of Zora Neale Hurston, Nella Larsen, Ann Petry. In their way and their time they had plowed the furrows of Black life through the medium of literature. Yet, even now they are only shadows in the literary world. I asked Toni Morrison why she felt that Black women writers had never been taken seriously.

"Because no women writers were taken seriously for a long time, unless they were cultivated by someone. In earlier years, Black women were not compelled to write. If they wanted to do something creative, they would generally not write. You see, if Sula had any sense she'd go somewhere and sing or get into show business. Writing is a formidable thing to break into for anybody. For most Black women in the past there was no time to write. I have never yet figured out how they found time to do all the things they did. Those who went to school and presumably had leisure had few choices. They became teachers and things of that sort. Things are not that much different now."

Mrs. Morrison noticed that I was again looking at the eyes in the photograph that hung on the wall. She leaned back in her chair, her head almost touching the map that framed her. This time she lit a cigarette and pushed the pipe out of the ashtray.

"That picture would have been good on the cover of Ali's autobiography. It is different from anything I have seen of him. I have just finished editing his autobiography. And it is beautiful. It is also massive. It was almost like editing the Bible and every comma became a thesis. Now that it is complete, I can get back to my own work."

I asked her if she was working on another novel.

"I think I am almost finished with my third novel [*Song of Solomon*]. I must get it to my editor. There is so little time to do what we have to do. But it should be available soon."

I gathered my things and rose to leave. Toni Morrison is a legend in her time. She has certainly moved one step beyond her literary mothers. They made that possible for her just as she will continue to pave the way for others. Margaret Walker said once that literature is like a chain. Toni Morrison is easing her link into that chain in much the same way that the sun eased its way into her office.

Cyril Lionel Robert James was born in Trinidad in 1901 and was educated among a group of intellectuals who were later to become major spokesmen for West Indian culture and politics. Two of this number were Alfred Mendes, author, and Albert Gomez, editor of *The Beacon,* a fine and brilliantly organized magazine which established the Beacon Group as a significant force in the serious literary awakenings of the Caribbean during the late twenties and early thirties.

When he was thirty-one, C. L. R. James went to England to establish himself as a literary artist: Markets and conduits were scarce in the Caribbean, and a writer writes to be read. *Minty Alley* (1936) is James's only novel, but his short stories and essays expand upon the verve, energy, and imagination initiated in that novel.

James is perhaps best known for his various treatises on the politics and history of the Caribbean. His works include *The Black Jacobins; History of Pan African Revolt; Beyond a Boundary; Facing Reality; Party Politics in the West Indies; Mariners, Renegades and Castaways; World Revolution;* and scholarly and popular articles. Dr. James lectures widely and teaches at Howard University's African Studies Center in Washington, D.C.

Wisdom: An Interview with C. L. R. James

by L. ANTHONY-WELCH

DR. WELCH: You stated in a recent television program that Alice Walker and Toni Morrison are the two most important contemporary writers of the black experience. Would you elaborate on that statement?

DR. JAMES: Today, I agree that they are two of the writers whom I find most interesting and most important, but I wouldn't say they are *the* most important.

DR. WELCH: Then why are they important?

DR. JAMES: They are important because our conversation revolves around black women as artists, and there haven't been many. Margaret Walker has written poetry, but what is happening to Toni Morrison and particularly to Alice Walker is that they are black women writing [fiction] about black women today. They are writing not about how black women are being persecuted and being spat upon by white imperialism, they are talking about black women and their dealings with women and black men. They aren't seeking to impress white people at all. They are not seeking to show how black people are moving on. They are taking the black people for what they are. Now, in Toni Morrison's book *Song of Solomon,* I felt that here was a woman who was part of the American literary world, sophisticated, well educated, etc., but who was still writing about black people but looking at them from the point of view of sophisticated literary writing in the United States. There are intimate friends of mine who say I am mistaken about Toni Morrison. I said maybe.

A young woman gave me a book called *Sula,* and there I saw, particularly in the second half of the book, that Toni Morrison had written about a black woman with the eyes and the feelings of a writer who was interested in the black woman. I mean *Sula* had nothing to do with what white people thought or what Westerners thought—she [Morrison] said, "I have my own standards in the life I have lived." But in *Song of Solomon,* Morrison doesn't really get down to it as she does in *Sula.*

There is no question about Alice Walker's being interested in anything else but what the black people are doing. I find that in everything I have read by Alice Walker there is that sentiment of seeing black people for what they are and judging them according to their own standards and doing more than that. Alice Walker has been there, and at times she's showing that black people, using their own standards, their own history, their own experience, will be able to take part in any big movement that is going to take place for the reconstitution of the American civilization. She says the black people, living among other black people, their habits and their religion, will enable them to take part. That is in the book *Meridian.*

Alice Walker is writing about a part of America that the others have not written about yet. But she is using the techniques that artists have always used: minute observation, creative ability, structural ability from what she sees, and she draws general conclusions from immediate practices and so forth. She's writing about black people and she's writing about them in the way that they work and think. But that is not a black aesthetic. She is following an aesthetic that is a basic literary aesthetic that has been followed for many generations.

That is how I feel about those two [Morrison and Walker]. Now, there is something else that I want to talk about. You know that one who wrote *Colored Girls . . . ?*

DR. WELCH: Ntozake Shange is the playwright, and the title of the play is *For Colored Girls Who Have Considered Suicide When the Rainbow is Enuf.*

DR. JAMES: Yes. Now that I have heard the play criticized by a very sophisticated young black man, and an anti-black, and a reactionary, I have to disagree with them. But it is an opinion that has to be considered because this is a very serious criticism by people who are familiar with black literature on a sophisticated level. I was at a man's house the other day and he told me that Alice Walker and Ntozake Shange and some others have cut a line through the black community. There are two sides where some people say that Alice Walker and Shange are writing the way the American imperialist establishment wants and others who say they're not. Do you know more of what the Black community feels about Shange's play?

DR. WELCH: There was so much intense feeling in Chicago that people became physically involved with each other. They became that angry about it. I don't hear people addressing the work, the literary work, or the play. I hear them addressing Shange's personal life. I heard only one comment on the work, and that comment was that she made the black woman so very negative in *Colored Girls* on the stage and in her poetry. That was number one. Two, yes. There were some other things, such as that she was historically inaccurate in places. The part about Toussaint L'Ouverture. That was inaccurate.

DR. JAMES: No, but there is no sense in saying that was inaccurate. She knows that it was, and that that is the kind of mentality that the black people have who have picked up her book. But they haven't discussed that issue of historical accuracy because they don't know it well. But when some reality, a real young man, came in the play, the female character went with him. To me that was very good. I am quite satisfied.

DR. WELCH: Some people are saying that the play is a composite of what black women are generally, and some are resenting that composite. They're saying we are not monolithic, and that there are differentials, variables, that we have to also look at such things as the fact that there are soft, kind, happy black women.

DR. JAMES: Yes, but at the same time, the majority of black women are having a hard time just as the women in that play are. We had portrayals of that before, regularly.

DR. WELCH: Yes, I know.

DR. JAMES: In the Caribbean they say white do this, white do that, but they have seen hardship is real. This is the basis. Without this you get nowhere.

There is another woman writer who used to be a Black Muslim?

DR. WELCH: Yes, Sonia Sanchez.

DR. JAMES: Her book is a bit strange, but I have read it over and over again. She has a great reputation. I find in her work some genuine poetic element, undoubtedly. But her brilliance is not as plain and she is absolutely antagonistic to seeing the black people striving to be like whites. Those people have nothing to do with her work and I like it for that and the writing as well.

DR. WELCH: Can you recommend any Caribbean women who are doing exceptionally good work, especially in literature?

DR. JAMES: I know one woman, who, in my opinion, has got an intellect that is surpassed by nobody in the Caribbean. Her name is Sylvia Wynter, and she is in charge of the Afro-American Department at Stanford. I know that some people are critical of her, but I say, quite freely, that I don't know of anyone in the Caribbean or among the Caribbean people who has an intellect that is any way superior in dealing with social and literary matters like Sylvia Wynter. That woman is highly qualified in every respect.

DR. WELCH: Do you think there are similarities in the works of Walker, Morrison, Shange, and other Caribbean writers?

DR. JAMES: Yes. There are writers like Wynter, Lovelace, and

Anthony who have a view of society which is based on what the common and ordinary people are doing, which, I can assure you, is something quite new. That's why the black society is so torn with Alice Walker and Toni Morrison and Shange. A famous Englishman once said, never—you cannot ignore reality. And reality begins with the common people. These people—these black women—were not writing ten years ago. This is something new. They're the product of the sixties in a way.

DR. WELCH: Have you addressed anything on the black woman in any of your work?

DR. JAMES: Not particularly, but I have written about black people in general. I have written about black people and have taken society as a whole. But I have been struck, since I came here in 1969. It is the first time the entry of the black woman into political and social activity has hit me as never before in my life. Before, they were just a part of the general struggle, and I saw them in Trinidad taking part and doing good work but the way they've come to the front is exciting and nothing is going to take place without them.

DR. WELCH: Do you think that the emerging women's movement will have a decided effect on black art?

DR. JAMES: I don't know, but Alice Walker, Toni Morrison, and Shange—they're not worried about any women's movement. No, they're writing about a certain section of American society. There's some thirty million blacks and twenty million of them are ordinary people. These people are adding a new dimension to American literature and American social thought.

Edited by
Roseann P. Bell

The truths that ultimately find their way into myth are laden with details and examples which amplify the causes célèbres of Black southern mothers, the most vivid of which is the raising of "strong" Black children. The measure of strength has been, for so many years in the United States, the children's ability to withstand, overcome, or even "conquer" situations reflective of racial, political, sexual, and economic oppression. Beyond their survival instructions to the young, there were and are, of course, survival lessons that Black southern mothers have had a number of opportunities to share with others even before the "Roots" phenomenon in the 1970s. Then, and many times during the WPA forties, the integrationist fifties, and the Black Power sixties, anthropologists and sometimes unscrupulous individuals who sought to capitalize on the exoticism of Blackness carried tape recorders and cameras into the Deep South (North and South Carolina, Georgia, Alabama, and Mississippi are thought to be the places where "authentic" Black Americans live).

Often, the questions they asked were loaded, as were their expensive pieces of equipment which also recorded personally subjective as well as collective biases. Frequently, there were insensitive conversations held which, over the years, led to the fomenting of stereotypic slots like "Black Eve or Black Madonna" (see Daryl Dance's article, p. 123, especially in literature written by Black American authors. That result is to be expected, however, when the subjects of study do not control the manner or means by which their lives are popularized.

The conversations Bettye Parker had with five Black southern women of venerable ages and wisdoms took place over a period of two years. That is not phenomenal if an author intends to do credible "research." However, what is especially significant is the fact that these Mississippi mothers were Dr. Parker's neighbors who did, indeed, participate in her growth. The publication of what used to be just ordinary conversations is only one attempt these women and Bettye Parker have made to oversee their images—to be able to recognize themselves and to be proud that the truths they inherited and promulgated have not been tampered with. Future incremental successes will follow as more serious, sedulous, sensitive, and creative authors and others (and particularly Black women in both these categories) *conduct their own research among their own families and friends.*

Mississippi Mothers: Roots

Lillie V. McKenzie
Seventy-two years old (approximately)

BETTYE: How old are you, Mrs. Lillie V.?

MRS. LILLIE V.: I'm not sure, honey.

BETTYE: Do you remember what year you were born?

MRS. LILLIE V.: Around 1904.

BETTYE: Do you remember anything about your grandmother?

MRS. LILLIE V.: Not very much. I was too young when she died.

BETTYE: Let's just talk about your life and what it was like growing up here in Mississippi. Have you lived around here all your life?

MRS. LILLIE V.: All my life, yes. I was born out there around St. Peter way.

BETTYE: What year did you get married?

MRS. LILLIE V.: Oh, around 1929.

BETTYE: How long were you married?

MRS. LILLIE V.: About five years. I had three children and raised them all by myself. I stayed married about five years before he got killed in '32.

BETTYE: How did your husband get killed?

MRS. LILLIE V.: Down at the ice plant. His bossman killed him—shot him to death.

BETTYE: Why was he shot? Do you know?

MRS. LILLIE V.: No. I wasn't able to ever find out. They tell me that he and the white man who was over the ice plant got into it over the work down there and he just shot him. I sued the ice company but the lawyer got all the money.

BETTYE: Do you know how much money was involved?

MRS. LILLIE V.: No. He was to take his fee out but never gave the rest to me. I don't reckon I got but ten or fifteen dollars out of it. He kept the rest.

BETTYE: How far did you go in school?

MRS. LILLIE V.: To the eighth grade. I started at Red Bone School and then went to Summer Hill and Parrish High.

BETTYE: Describe the Red Bone School.

MRS. LILLIE V.: Well, it was one room and had one teacher. Everybody sat in the same room and we were divided into sections according to classes. We studied reading, writing, spelling, arithmetic, geography, and health.

BETTYE: Why did you stop going to school?

MRS. LILLIE V.: I needed to go to work. See, my mother had too many children to raise by herself. So she couldn't keep us together like I did with my children. So she just gave us away. Some folks took me in and raised me. They weren't related to me by blood.

BETTYE: Tell me how you trained your own daughters. How did you teach them to cook?

MRS. LILLIE V.: My mother taught them because I worked out.

BETTYE: What do you mean by working out?

MRS. LILLIE V.: I worked at private homes and the box factory. When I first started I made a dollar and a half a week.

BETTYE: It must have been difficult to raise three children on a dollar and a half a week.

MRS. LILLIE V.: Oh yes. This was during the Depression, too. I made it with the help of the Lord.

BETTYE: Tell me about the Depression.

MRS. LILLIE V.: Goodness gracious. We had to stand in line with food stamps to get food and shoes. It was not enough to really live on. It's been a long time ago. It may be like that again soon. The way things are going, you can't never tell.

Annie Amiker (Aunt Sis), 1900–77
Johnnie Ruth Pearl Ellis (Aunt Saint), born 1904

BETTYE: Do you remember any specific lynchings?

AUNT SIS: I heard of a man who was hung. He was chained to a tree right up by the bank. He was chained to an old oak tree and they poured oil on him and set him afire. That was back there before I was born.

BETTYE: What year were you born Aunt Saint?

AUNT SAINT: 1904.

BETTYE: So this happened before the First World War?

AUNT SIS: Yes, it was before the First World War.

BETTYE: What do you remember about the lynching? Did they put tar on him too, and burn him to death?

AUNT SAINT: They chained him to that tree and they poured oil on him. I don't know if it was gas or not but they poured oil on him and burned him alive.

BETTYE: Were there a lot of people standing around to see it?

AUNT SAINT: It wouldn't be no Negroes around in crowds like that.

BETTYE: They would be too scared, and they might get hung themselves.

AUNT SAINT: Do you want me to tell you what he was hung about?

BETTYE: Yes.

AUNT SAINT: There was a white man who raped his stepdaughter and killed her and laid it on this colored fellow. And that's what they hung him about. And later on, this white man took sick and he told the true story before he died.

AUNT SIS: Is that the same colored man who they picked up because he was coming from rabbit hunting and he had rabbit blood on him and they saw that rabbit blood and they thought he was the one that killed the girl?

AUNT SAINT: Yes. Yes.

AUNT SIS: Did they ever put the colored man in jail?

AUNT SAINT: No, they took him and just hung him up.

AUNT SIS: I didn't know much about it but did they put that white man in jail? I thought they say he died in jail when he told it.

AUNT SAINT: No, he took sick at home and told it. He didn't tell it until he got down sick and before he died he told it. See, his conscience was working on him, that's the reason he told it. He knew he had done wrong.

BETTYE: Do you remember any cases where Black people killed white people down here anywhere?

AUNT SAINT: No.

BETTYE: You ever remember hearing any stories from your great-grandmothers or grandmother or grandfather or anybody about slavery—about what took place during this time. You ever hear them talk about it?

AUNT SAINT: I heard Grandpa talking about it.

BETTYE: Do you remember any of the stories he told you about it?

AUNT SAINT: Well, he said his white master whipped him until the blood ran down to his feet—whipped him with one of these plaited whips. When he got up he took an ax—see, he was cleaning the new ground—you know folks in slavery time cleaned off the grounds for work—he looked and saw the blood and drew it back at his master and told him that if he ever did that again he would split him wide open. I don't think the man ever did that any more. You see, grandpa was a half-white man.

BETTYE: Do you ever remember anybody talking about how to cure sicknesses?

AUNT SAINT: You know, one time I had a complaint of sleeping sickness. And I slept seven years unaware. When that illness was on me I'd sleep anywhere. I could lay down in the rain and sleep. The way my mama did was she went and got some polk salad and she got the roots of that polk salad and she washed it real good and she boiled it and she made a big jar of tea. And she put one or two tablespoonfuls of saltpeter in there. You know saltpeter will clean your blood too. Well, I was supposed to take a tablespoon of that in the morning time and a tablespoon at noon. And that's the way I took it. You know I don't know what had me sleeping, but whatever it was, it ran that humor out of my blood. And it come out through my back. My back just got raw with big sores and they would just itch and I would scratch and the blood would run down and I'd still scratch. But when I scratched it didn't hurt, it just itched. After I took up the medicine that she fixed for me, all that went off my back. I woke up. So my skin got smooth and I ain't had it since.

BETTYE: How old were you about that time?

AUNT SAINT: I was grown. But that healed that. Then I'll tell you another thing people used to use back there. It's a weed . . . we called it, I've forgotten it now, but it's used for constipation. I tell ya, some of that medicine that they used back there would work on you quicker than some of this they have now.

BETTYE: We were healthier, too.

AUNT SIS: Let me tell you this, Aunt Betty's baby boy took sick with the pneumonia. The doctor gave him three days to live. Aunt Betty sent for Mama. Mama took me over there with her and we spent the night. They sent me and the children out in the woods, we got the same stuff she named. Mama cooked that stuff and set up all night teaing that baby. That baby had his eyes set and wasn't doing nothing. So Mama teaed that baby all night long. The next morning when Aunt Betty passed the bed he cast his eyes on Aunt Betty. Aunt Betty hollered! That boy is living in Hazelhearst right now. The old-time remedies are all right.

BETTYE: What about when you were teen-agers and used to court—could you have more than one boyfriend?

AUNT SAINT: Well, I tell you I didn't do very much courting.

AUNT SIS: We didn't do much courting. I imagine we married the first thing we got to.

AUNT SAINT: A lot more was like us; they didn't court in those days. We just married off.

BETTYE: Were there any parents who let their daughters court that you might have known about?

AUNT SIS: I'd see them walking in the moonlight going to church. I could see the girl and boy walking in front of the girl's parents. When they got to that church they better sit in there until it's time to go home.

BETTYE: Were there a lot of girls who had babies out of wedlock during that time?

AUNT SIS: Well, there was some but not many—not many because when you run upon a girl who had a child the other girls wouldn't have nothing to do with her. Your parents wouldn't let you go around that girl, she was counted as a grown person, so she wasn't counted among the young people.

BETTYE: When it happened, did the girl's mother help her take care of the baby, or was she alone. How did that go?

AUNT SIS: They didn't put them out, but they taught them how to get out in that field and work for that baby. They were treated like they were grown.

BETTYE: What about when you did get married, were there big weddings? Did they take place in the house or church?

AUNT SIS: Well, some of them married at home and some married at church, but I never went to a church wedding in them days. That depended on whether or not the parents were able. Some would just give a big wedding at home.

BETTYE: When you had them at the house did people come from miles around to the wedding—was the whole community invited to the wedding?

AUNT SIS: Yes.

BETTYE: What about when babies were born since you couldn't go to the doctors—they had a lot of midwives?

AUNT SIS: Yes, right.

BETTYE: Did either of you ever have that experience?

AUNT SAINT: Yes, I did. I delivered Walter, my nephew, with a midwife. Down in the country we couldn't get a doctor and most of the time the midwife didn't live too far. They could do more for you than the doctors. 'Cause the doctor came in the door and delivered the baby and left, but the midwife would wash things for you and bathe the baby. And then she would come back an see to you until you got able to get up. There was one lady named Aunt Charlotte who waited on Sis. We enjoyed her. Afterwards, she would sit down and talk to us about slavery time.

BETTYE: Do you remember anything she said?

AUNT SAINT: Yes, she was a little girl during slavery. She said she ran off from her marster and he had dogs behind her trying to catch her and she ran and ran all she could—and she ran over a log and she could hear the dogs and the horses coming and when she ran over the log she laid right down by it and the dogs and the horses jumped over the log too. Then she got up and went the other way and ran until she got to the Mississippi River. I think she went over that on a log or something.

BETTYE: Do you remember anything else she told you about that time.

AUNT SAINT: She would tell us about how she would work hard. Well, another woman, Aunt Minnie, said they would dress her up and put her high up on a high thing. See, they would auction them off and just like somebody wanted to buy a slave, they might say, "I want that girl." Aunt Minnie talked until she died about how they would bid on her during slavery time.

BETTYE: You ever hear anybody talk about voodoo or hoodoo practices?

AUNT SIS: I hear them talk about it, but I ain't never seen none.

AUNT SAINT: I heard talk of it, too—the grown folks would talk about it, but if they caught us listening, they would put us out of there.

BETTYE: What about a rolling store, did you ever see one of those?

AUNT SIS: Oh yes, they came through when we were picking cotton.

AUNT SAINT: We'd buy food off it and would stay in the field all day.

BETTYE: Did they come by people's houses, too?

AUNT SAINT: Yes.

BETTYE: Do you remember any other stories? I remember my grandmother on my father's side would comb her hair and burn all that came out in the comb. She said birds would make a nest out of it—did you ever hear of anything like that?

AUNT SAINT: Well, I've heard that, too. We used to straighten our hair with a fork.

BETTYE: What was a hack?

AUNT SIS: A hack was something like a float but it had a top over it. It was pulled by horses. During funerals, family folk would ride in surreys and hacks. A surrey is a double-seated buggy; a buggy was single-seated. All the close relatives rode in those. The surries and buggies and even the horses were jet black. It really looked more like funerals during them days.

BETTYE: So black was symbolic of death?

AUNT SIS: That's right. Mostly everybody wore black to the funeral.

BETTYE: Did they generally have wakes at the house before the funeral?

AUNT SAINT: Yes, they would have them in the house. There wasn't much embalming then. . . .

BETTYE: Did people sit up all night at the house?

AUNT SIS: Yes. Now, these days people bring food to wakes, but didn't nobody eat at no wake during those days. They would sing and pray. At church people just sang—everybody did. They didn't have choirs. The spirit would be there. They would sing hymns like "Amazing Grace."

BETTYE: During the wakes did they keep the body uncovered in the house?

AUNT SAINT: Yes.

BETTYE: Who would generally dress the body? Close relatives or friends?

AUNT SIS: It would mostly be friends who would come.

BETTYE: So you didn't really have time for people to come long distances because you had to go on and bury the relative, right?

AUNT SIS: It was only a few people who would be far off. Most people didn't hardly go anywhere.

BETTYE: You said you didn't go to school much. Was it because you had something else to do?

AUNT SIS: My mother didn't have a boy in the house to do her heavy work. So Saint and I had to stay home to do it plenty of times. The younger ones went to school. I would have to plow. I worked like a man. I have done any kind of work a man has done. I thank the Lord for being here, even though I didn't get to go to school much. I was able to learn to read the Bible. I didn't mind helping my mother since she didn't have anybody to help her.

BETTYE: Where was your father?

AUNT SIS: He left for work and never came back. I was 'bout three years old. Others say they saw him later, but I never did.

BETTYE: What kind of house did you live in?

AUNT SIS: The house had two rooms. I called it a shack. It wasn't a warm house, but living in the country, we could get pine and other trees to make a fire that lasted all night.

BETTYE: When did your mother die?

AUNT SIS: In 1940. She was sixty-three when she died.

Mrs. Lena (Gorgeous) Smith
Eighty-eight years old

BETTYE: Do you remember anything that your mother or grandmother might have told you about slavery?

GORGEOUS: I don't remember much about my gorgeous grandmother. Child, I been through so much—been knocked and baffled around so until I don't know now what I remember. I know they said you couldn't go to no church or nothing 'cause we didn't have time. And if they sung a song or something they had to turn the washpot down to catch the sound so ol' marster wouldn't hear it.

BETTYE: What would he do if he heard?

GORGEOUS: Whop your back, that's what! Lord, I ain't thought about all that in so long! Most of it probably's done gone out of my head. But I heard plenty things about what they said they done in slavery time. You know that the other race ain't never done right about us no way. And now they all about to die off 'cause push has done come to shove and they can't do like they use to do no more. The Black folks is coming to some senses—they seem to have more sense now than they use to have. Of course, we use to didn't have nothing to lay on. But these young folks are different. They don't take no mess. You see me sitting around here now. This is just as same as slavery. I just have to sit around and all, but I worked a many day.

BETTYE: What kind of work did you do?

GORGEOUS: I worked in the field—farming. I never went to school. We didn't have but three months' school in Madison County and I never went a whole term in my life. The only way I could go to school, it would be raining and freezing. We use to have icicles as big as my wrist hanging around the trees and breaking the limbs down and Mama would be telling us we better be careful and watch so them tree limbs wouldn't fall on us and knock us in the head. That's the only way I could go to school and I'd be so glad when it'd freeze. We don't have icicles like that down here no more.

BETTYE: What did they teach you in school?

GORGEOUS: Reading, writing, and 'rithmetic, what little time I went. I can read and write, good enough, but I ain't never had no chance to go to school like people go to school. You know what I mean. And the next thing about it is, I learned at home from my sisters' and brothers' books. They were going to school. See, I am the baby. I am the last child—the sixteenth child of my mother. Course a whole lot of the others died when they were little infants.

BETTYE: Do you recall anything you may have seen or heard about lynchings or lynch mobs here in Mississippi?

GORGEOUS: Yeigh! What do you mean, do I remember! I was a grown woman when they hung ol' Red Milbrew up yonder in Madison County on George Johnson's place.

BETTYE: What did they hang him for?

GORGEOUS: What did they hang him for?! They hung him because they wanted to do just like they always do with us. Some folks claim that the old white man who hung him was going with Red's wife. Now, that's what they claim. But, you know, I wasn't there and I don't know for sure. Red's ol' wife was named Polly. Anyway, George Johnson said Madison County would feel it as long as they live. They hung him on his place.

BETTYE: Did you see him hanging up there?

GORGEOUS: No! No, I didn't see him. But I was living up there and I know that they made a road through them woods looking for Red. You see, a fellow had taken Red across the river in a car but good as he felt, he came back. Red wasn't too real bright. When the fellow got back here, he looked and saw Red stepping back up there in Madison County. And they got him and hung him and castrated him and made him eat it. Now, I wasn't there and didn't see it, but that's what they say was done.

BETTYE: Tell me about your life when you were a girl. Did you court a lot?

GORGEOUS: No! I never did believe in a whole ocean of folks.

BETTYE: How many boyfriends did you have at one time?

GORGEOUS: One!! Never did believe in but one. And I still got that method. You know what I tell the young women today? I tell them—and not many old folks will say this—I tell them that I been young, I ain't always been old, and you can't always keep up with no man. But some old women say, "Chile, I wouldn't let him get by me. He's going with so-and-so and you get you another man." I don't tell them that. I tell them now look, you can't court with no man because a man is a man. I tell them to hold themselves up and he will be done run out soon and you will be just in your prime.

BETTYE: What do you mean prime?

GORGEOUS: What?! Being just like a . . . being a . . . Oh, you know, you know what I mean. Better get away from me—better get out of my face!! I'm old, but I ain't crazy. All right, our men run around—some women do too, and I have to be fair about this—they don't know who they want. Some women will lose time with any man that comes along. It don't matter who he is or what he looks like or nothing. Some men are the same way. And all the Black people marrying white men and women can help themselves, but I wouldn't want one. Humph! I'm sitting up here like this now but I could have had plenty gorgeous white boyfriends if I had wanted—if I had been that type. I had a schoolmate, Hattie Lee Poindexter, good-looking little round-faced girl, but her little hair was just about that long [makes snapping finger gesture]. She was a good-looking little thing. And she got tied up with ol' Carl, a white man, who had a store up there in Glustadt. And they always tell me that whenever a colored woman gets tied up with a white man, she can't get rid of him. He'll kill her before he'll let her go. So that's one reason I never would have one. Lord, Hattie Lee outdone me so bad. That cracker was the death of her. She was killed down there in Louisiana. They'll kill you and call you! But some of our women so foolish and get hooked up with them 'cause they better to them than our men are sometimes. They treat you better, take care of them, and see about them, they say. I know another woman up in Canton who went with a white man for years and had a grown son that's his. He bought her a home and everything and took care of her. Well, you know our men, some of them ain't going to do right by nobody. But regardless, I don't care, I went along with it all my life when they didn't do nothing right and I sho ain't about to change now.

BETTYE: Were you ever married?

GORGEOUS: Yeigh! I had two of them things they call husbands.

BETTYE: Did you court them a long time before you married them?

GORGEOUS: No. Ain't no sense in that. I didn't court no way. They the ones that did the courting to me, anyhow.

BETTYE: Have you ever seen a coachwhip snake?

GORGEOUS: No. But I have heard about them so much until it seems like I have seen them. They got tails like a whip and can wrap around you and lay you out. I also heard of stinging snakes but I ain't seen them either.

BETTYE: You have lived here in Jackson most of your life, haven't you?

GORGEOUS: No! I lived in Madison County most of my life. I just came to Jackson in 1933.

BETTYE: Do you remember a man in the 1920s by the name of Marcus Garvey?

GORGEOUS: No. I don't seem to get that to my mind.

BETTYE: What about the Great Migration? Do you remember when Black people left the South in large numbers going North during World War I?

GORGEOUS: Yes. I know about that. But I didn't think about going. I ain't never wanted to go all over the creation.

BETTYE: Do you remember church meetings in the South called track-de-meeting?

GORGEOUS: Do I remember?! You know we always had track-de-meetings! Now we call them revivals. But they were meetings where we sang and prayed and all the sinners—the unborn—came up to be prayed for and joined the church. Sometimes they'd open with a big dinner spread out on the ground. Different preachers were invited and they all preached. They still do it at some places.

BETTYE: Do you know anything about voodoo and hoodoo?

GORGEOUS: Yes. I heard a whole lot of folks say a whole lot a things folks do and can do and did do.

BETTYE: I understand Black women have often used this method to get their men back if they left home. Is this true?

GORGEOUS: Yeigh, that's what they say. But if that's the way I had to get one back he could stay gone. I wouldn't walk from here to the porch steps to get one back. David said in one of his writings, "I was young, now I am old. But I have never seen the righteous forsaken nor his seed begging bread." I wouldn't go nowhere looking for no man. If I had a husband and he was living and he left and didn't come back, I wouldn't go looking for him because he knows where he left me.

BETTYE: You think you may get married again?

GORGEOUS: What?

BETTYE: You heard me.

GORGEOUS: What am I going to marry? I could have been married again but most of these gorgeous slew-footed, knock-kneed, bowlegged, pigeon-toed men want folks to wait on them.

You see some of these women give the men they gorgeous money and they just ruint the men! They so common until men don't appreciate women no more like they use to.

BETTYE: Why do you think the women ruined the men like that?

GORGEOUS: Because they didn't have no sense!! Humph!!

BETTYE: Did you ever hear your parents talk about Africa?

GORGEOUS: Sho. And you know these white folks been wanting to send us back there. That ol' devil horse, the one that was worse than Eastland—Bilbo—he wanted to send all niggers down here back to Africa. A ol' bowlegged scoundrel! But he's dead now. Humph!

BETTYE: Do you know anything about the uses of herbs and plants for medicine?

GORGEOUS: I ain't never been sick. I ain't never had the flu, pneumonia, or none of that [knocks on the wooden arms of her rocking chair.] I think they used things though. I just ain't never needed anything. [Continues to knock on wood.]

BETTYE: Are you superstitious?

GORGEOUS: No! But they say that when you talk about something you ain't never had it's best to knock on wood and it will ward off what you ain't had.

BETTYE: Is there anything else you want to talk about?

GORGEOUS: No. But if you had caught me in a good mood, I could have told you some things that would have made you remember me for the rest of your life.

BETTYE: I'll remember you anyway.

GORGEOUS: Humph! Let me tell you one last thing. It's just a shame the way these young women raising their children these days. All they doing is feeding them these high-priced groceries and letting them grow up. They done took God out of everything and put all this doggy-woggy mess and TV mess in its place. They break their necks spending every penny they can rake and scrape sending these children to college and they ain't thinking about nothing. They ain't got no respect for their mother and nobody else. We all the cause of this and it is a shame on the race. Humph!

Malinda Wango, born 1896 (and sisters Katy and Emma)

BETTYE: Your sister, Mrs. Malinda, has been talking to me about your lives as you have lived them here in rural Mississippi. If you don't mind, I'd appreciate it if you would join in the conversation.

KATY: I don't reckon we mind. What is it you want to know about?

BETTYE: Well, I have been interested in a number of folk stories about nature and people and she was telling me about the coachwhip snake. I was wondering if you have ever seen one.

KATY: Of course. One time we found a big one in one of the mule's collars. It had crawled up in the collar when we put it on the ground.

BETTYE: Is that the only one you have seen?

KATY: No, I have seen a many of them. They have long plaited tails and are sometimes eighteen to twenty feet long. They could jump the length of themselves and wrap around you and squeeze you to death.

BETTYE: Do either of you know anything about the uses of plants and herbs for medicines?

EMMA: Chile, you done come a little late. I don't remember all of that this evening.

MALINDA: Lord, my mama use to could go out there and get things to cure anything, didn't matter what the complaint was.

KATY: Mama could even cure cancer.

BETTYE: It's too bad she is not here today. Tell me, do you remember hearing stories about slavery? About the way we were treated during that time?

MALINDA: Yeah, I remember hearing the old folks talk plenty about what went on and what a time they had. My grandmother lived back in slavery time. She used to talk about how they would go to the field and get greens and bring them home and wash them and cook them in a washpot.

KATY: She sure did say that. I remember that as if she told it yesterday.

MALINDA: And she said that when they were cooked they would put them in troughs, like hog troughs, and they would cook bread outside with a lid over it. . . .

EMMA: Sho did, Malinda. Sho did! Tell it!

MALINDA: . . . and they would go to the woods and pick up wood and chips and bark and make a fire on top of the lid of the skillet. . . .

KATY: They would put bark on their head and put the skillet on top and go on to work in the fields. . . .

EMMA: She said the bread would be cooking on their heads. . . .

MALINDA: . . . Sho did.

BETTYE: We must be a strong people to have endured that. Do you think we have that kind of strength now?

MALINDA: No, baby. The Bible said that we grow weaker and wiser and we couldn't go through the hardship that them older people went through. We couldn't do it. We went through things you couldn't go through.

EMMA: Yeah, I don't think they could either. I can remember taking a buck saw and sawing two whole truck loads of wood at one time. I have cut logs and paper wood with a power saw and everything when I was working by the day. Yeah, I have outworked a many men when I worked with a crosscut saw.

BETTYE: You are right. I don't think I could do that given the way I have been trained.

MALINDA: I read a story not too long ago in the newspaper about a 133-year-old slave from Florida who talked about what life was like then. Seems like he was born over in Africa around 1842. He was sold in New Orleans when he was about twelve years old to somebody out in Texas.

KATY: Grandpa was born around the same time as that man you talking about. He worked around the Civil War. Seems like he was about fifteen years old.

EMMA: He don't know how old he was. They didn't tell them things like that.

MALINDA: Sure didn't. I remember he said he was over there in Vicksburg when that war was going on. He slipped off and went back home.

EMMA: Grandma used to tell us about a lot of things. I remember some things that she told us about dead people. She said that if a person dies in a room with a mirror and the mirror is not covered up or turned around, big spots would form on the mirror.

BETTYE: Do you know the reason for this?

EMMA: No. I sure don't, honey. But that head must go out the door first and the body has to be buried in an east-west position. The head must face the east so that when they rise they face the sun.

BETTYE: Do you remember any details of hangings in the South?

MALINDA: Sure. Sims Edwards was hung down there around that lake. They tied him to a tree and put brushes and poured tar all over him and set him afire. They also cut off his privates and kept them for souvenirs.

KATY: Yeah, I remember that well. Seems he had been rabbit hunting and had blood from the rabbits all over him. An ol' white man had raped and killed his own stepdaughter and when they saw Sims they caught him and accused him of the murder. Years later when the old white man was sick and dying he confessed to the crime. But it was too late.

MALINDA: Once Mama told us about a colored man who was hung for stealing. Before they cut the rope he asked for his mama. When she got there he asked if he could kiss her and instead he reached down and bit one of her ears off.

BETTYE: Why did he do that?

MALINDA: He told her that if she had chastised him when he first stole something, he would not be hanging that day. He blamed her for his predicament.

EMMA: Emmit Till was the saddest thing I ever knowed about.

BETTYE: I was still living in Mississippi at that time. Do you remember how Black people reacted to that?

EMMA: Yeah, they were bitter. But the boy's grandparents were scared. They had to be. Now, I have one boy and he got children and if one came to live with me, and somebody tried to get in my house to get him, don't you know they would not get out alive.

MALINDA: The newspapers gave all the details. They had pictures of him after they picked him up right after dark on a pickup truck. They showed a picture where they went by a gin and picked up a big wheel and took him and cut his little privates out and made him swallow them. They took him to the river and put the wheel around his neck and throwed him in. And they don't know if he was living or dead when they throwed him in. They said that when they got through with him, he would never whistle at another white woman. Me and Emma talked with a woman off that plantation, didn't we, Emma?

EMMA: Sure did. His mama let them do an autopsy and they found all he had swallowed.

MALINDA: I can tell you about plenty cases like this. There was Medgar Evers and Sharp Eye Shooter. In 1961 or '62, Sharp Eye killed about sixteen or eighteen white people up there in the Delta. They burned his house down and he had lots of sweet potatoes in the house. He would slip through the lines of police cars and Ku Klux Klans and go to the house and eat the cooked potatoes. He stayed down with his whiskey still and they tried to catch him with the nigger dogs. His daddy was a white man and they finally took him to the insane institution instead of killing him outright. It all started in the first place because some white men were trying to make a pass at his wife. So he just killed until he got tired.

BETTYE: Let me change the subject somewhat and talk about your personal lives. How many boyfriends did you have at one time when you were courting?

EMMA: Only one at the time. Papa and Mama sat around the fireplace with us and nobody had to tell nobody when to leave. The big clock on the mantle was always put where everybody could see. When the clock struck nine, it was time for everybody to go.

BETTYE: Were you able to steal a little kiss every now and then?

MALINDA: Steal what?! You must be out of your mind. We couldn't even go to the door. Those old folks didn't let you get away with nothing.

BETTYE: Did any courting take place in church at track-demeeting time?

KATY: No way.

BETTYE: How did women get along with each other, especially when it came to sharing men. Or did they share their men?

EMMA: Honey, it was a do-it-yourself thing then and it's the same way now. Some cared about each other then and some care now.

KATY: Our grandpa had two families—one on one end and the other way down on the opposite end of the country. Grandma didn't know that other woman. At Grandpa's funeral, children came from everywhere and none knew each other.

MALINDA: Grandpa didn't let his right hand know what his left hand was doing. He felt that whatever God gave you, you ought to use it like you want to.

BETTYE: Things haven't changed much then, have they?

MALINDA: They ain't changed too much.

EMMA: No. I wouldn't say that.

KATY: Well, it's hard to tell.

Gayl Jones is the product of a vibrant and historically rich Lexington, Kentucky, background. Her professional training includes doctoral work in creative writing at Brown University under the tutelage of the poet Michael Harper.

Jones's style is exceptional. It is terse, stark, and full-bodied, resonating with a formidable quality which has established itself as phenomenal. Equally outstanding are her achievements in the naissance of her career: four full-length novels; numerous short stories, plays, and poems published in respected magazines and scholarly journals in the United States and abroad. (See African-American bibliography in this text and "Gayl Jones: A Voice in the Whirlwind," by Roseann P. Bell, in *Studio Africana* (Spring 1977, University of Cincinnati.)

Gayl Jones is twenty-nine, writes and teaches at the University of Michigan in Ann Arbor. The focus of this interview is her first novel, *Corregidora.*

Gayl Jones Takes a Look at "Corregidora"—An Interview

by ROSEANN P. BELL

Two things were evident to me as I read *Corregidora* for the first time: The book is infused with an awesome sense of history, and the author evinces a sensual respect for Black urban folklore. Gayl Jones was only twenty-six when this, her first novel, was published. In the work, she exhibits a kind of literary maturity that is very rare.

When I called the author about an interview, she responded immediately and positively. Since the time the interview was conducted, she has published a second novel, *Eva's Man,* and a third, *Almeyda,* as well as a collection of short stories called *White Rat.* The following interview, however, which is extracted from a lengthy telephone conversation, focuses on *Corregidora.*

BELL: I first heard the name Gayl Jones from Michael Harper, a well-known poet and one of your former teachers. I attended one of his readings and he read some of your work. How much of an influence has Harper's style and his handling of the past had on you?

JONES: A major influence has been the connection his poetry makes between the past and one's personal life, and how the two are connected. I don't think that that kind of connection would have surfaced in *Corregidora* had I not had the contact with him and his work. The connection between the past and the contemporary part of Ursa's life possibly would not have been there had it not been for Michael's influence.

BELL: Is there a particular volume of Michael's poetry or a specific poem that has the strain of the past that you feel has been more influential than others? What about "Song I Want a Witness" or "History Is Your Own Heartbeat?"

JONES: I think I see connections in practically everything he has written. Particularly, the past runs rampant through "History Is Your Own Heartbeat" and "Nightmare Begins Responsibility."

BELL: What other writers have been significant sources of encouragement to you?

JONES: I have been influenced by a number of writers. I especially like Carlos Fuentes and Alice Walker.

BELL: Why did you write *Corregidora?*

JONES: It is difficult for me to say why I write certain things. In a way *Corregidora* grew out of things I tried to do in my earlier writings. This book probably brings them all together. My earlier writings have been concerned with the relationship between men and women. Most of them are written in first person from a woman's point of view and the setting is usually Lexington, Kentucky, even though I don't specify a place. And most of the women are more independent than Ursa is.

BELL: How long did it take you to complete the entire novel?

JONES: About three months.

BELL: That was short. I was extremely impressed with your fusion of history with Black urban folklore. Which one of these elements required the most attention from you as a craftsman, in your efforts to fictionalize them?

JONES: The language, the linguistic patterns that run throughout, have been with me all along. The history, the past, not so much in terms of personal past but a collective past, is something that was relatively recent. At the time I was writing, I was doing a lot of reading in slave history in South America—Brazil—and I guess my mind was trying to make connections between the differences there and here in North America. It's really difficult to say which was the most demanding.

BELL: If your knowledge of Brazilian history was used to document that particular aspect of the past, did you have to do any primary research concerning folklore in this country—on specific Kentucky folklore or ethnomusicology?

JONES: Not really. It was just a matter of living in a certain place and listening to certain people. Knowledge of Ursa's past, going back to 1948, was extracted from conversations that my parents often engaged in.

BELL: The way you have used Ursa and other characters in *Corregidora* suggests that there is a wealth of information that we can get from using oral history whether we gather it from talking with our parents or through more formalized methods such as those Zora Neale Hurston used. Even in many Black colleges where there are our own potential writers, there are no courses in oral history. There is no emphasis placed on gathering folk material. What ways do you suggest that aspiring creative writers could develop themselves in terms of culling out an oral tradition?

JONES: I hesitate to approach it on a formal level. When I think of Zora Neale Hurston, I am more inclined to think of her anthropological training, and for me that seems to get in the way of her creative writing. For creative writers, I think the best thing is to be a good listener. I think formal gathering of material is important in terms of documentation, but I think an anthropologist would document material differently from a creative writer. I really think that in a lot of ways, when the two are brought together in one person, certain kinds of conflicts can develop.

BELL: Stephen Henderson has an interesting article in *New Directions,* a Howard University periodical, in which he discusses the blues tradition, and the way Sterling Brown has used it so beautifully in *Southern Road,* published in 1935. I consider *Corregidora* a part of this blues tradition, first because the major figure is a blues singer, and two, because you are able to create an affirmation of life out of the harshness, cruelty, bitterness, despair, and degradation that has been so much a part of our Black reality. Are there writers who used the blues tradition who inspired this element in your work other than Michael?

JONES: I have always been interested in blues singers. I would point more to singers than writers in this case. I like blues singers all the way back to Ma Rainey. I also like a lot of early jazz singers.

BELL: I notice that in your poetry, such as the piece called "Deep Song: For B.H.," you rely on the blues ethic, too. Is this the direction you plan to pursue in your future writing?

JONES: I don't know. Some of the relationships that I am dealing with now are similar to those found in *Corregidora.* Some people have questioned the relationship that exists between Ursa and Mutt. They particularly refer to the tensions. I explain that I was dealing with a blues relationship. Toward the end of the book, there is a sense of pointing toward a kind of redemption. I think that some of my other work is dealing with similar relationships and I think I may want to move out of that and deal more with what happens toward the end of *Corregidora.* Perhaps I may concentrate on redemption being within rather than pointing toward.

BELL: Since we are discussing tradition, are there other traditions in Black life or writing you consciously tried to exploit in *Corregidora?* For example, certain elements of African culture which have remained intact?

JONES: One of the things that I was consciously concerned with was the technique from the oral storytelling tradition that could be used in writing. A story is told to someone in the same way when Ursa sings. She picks someone out to sing to. The book has layers of storytelling. Perceptions of time are important in the oral storytelling tradition in the sense that you can make rapid transitions between one period and the next, sort of direct transitions.

BELL: It comes off very well. Would you talk a little about two prevailing images in the book: seeds and coffee beans or coffee grounds, including the bruised seeds as well as the healthy ones?

JONES: In the beginning of the story, the use of the coffee beans is simple. That was the kind of plantation that they had. In terms of an image, the color of the beans, roasted beans anyway, could tie in with the color of the woman. They are related to the whole theme of regeneration.

BELL: At one point, Ursa says that she will ground coffee beans into her uterus and a baby will come forth. The image comes at you over and over again, and of course now you speak of coffee being related to the woman and color and life. When I was reading some of your poetry, the same imagery came through. In either "Deep Song" or "Scat" you talk about the color of the man and I think that when you refer to Ella Fitzgerald you make some comment about her color being close to coffee beans or something like that. You seem fascinated with this particular kind of imagery.

JONES: Perhaps you are right. I remember a short story where the same imagery is used. I can't really add anything significant except that it is a recurring pattern and that it relates to the story that Ursa's great-grandmother told her. In dreams, you sort of revisualize things and in memory things can take on different forms.

BELL: Students have made political interpretations about the recurring statement that Ursa "cannot make generations." Did you have any political intent? She is upset because her womanhood and her ability to produce generations are gone.

JONES: I don't think I had any special meaning in mind.

BELL: Who among Black women writers, past and present, do you feel have made the most progressive statements about creating positive, realistic, and productive generations which will improve the material conditions of Black life?

JONES: I admire Sherley Williams a great deal, especially *The Peacock Poems.*

BELL: I know that you also have a great deal of respect for Ann DuCille and Brother Kambon Obayani.

JONES: . . . and Melvin Dixon is very good.

BELL: Back to *Corregidora,* . . . what does that novel and the process of creative writing teach us?

JONES: It is difficult to say what it should teach. I don't start off thinking of the writing itself as being instructive, not in the sense of message. It may teach in the sense that we learn from life processes and a story does create a kind of life/living.

I think the book [*Corregidora*] may ask questions. But they are questions that have been there all along. I don't see the book as any kind of final statement. It is something that you add on to.

Part Three The Creative Vision

Introduction:

THE CREATIVE VISION

by BEVERLY GUY-SHEFTALL

As the title of this section implies, all of the selections here fall in the category of imaginative literature and contain images of Black women. The initial motive for this anthology was to provide those interested in seeing more positive images of Black women with alternatives to those one-dimensional and often distorted images which are a part of the required reading for students and which fill the pages of what is available for the general reader. In the place of the Black female types—matriarch, whore, bitch, tragic mulatto, to name a few—which permeate the writings of numerous male and female authors alike, we wanted to offer Black women who are multidimensional, nonstereotypical, and who bear some resemblance to their counterparts in the real world. Though we object to the notion that "*the* Black woman" can be portrayed in a definitive manner by any group of image makers—novelists, poets, playwrights, filmmakers, television producers—we do believe it is possible to provide readers with some sense of what it means to be Black and female in various cultures by turning to selected literary works which have attempted to capture something of the experience of Black women.

Images which perpetuate the old stereotypes of Black women were deliberately excluded because they reinforce myths about us which are damaging, degrading, and useless. Material which was easily available elsewhere and generally familiar to most readers interested in the subject matter was also avoided.

The selections range from the writings of relatively well known authors to that of unknown ones whose works are largely unpublished. Though this latter category is represented in greater numbers than the former, aesthetic merit was considered as a means of selection. The selections also include those genres suitable for an anthology of this type—poetry, short stories, and plays. In only a few instances are excerpts from larger works included. In addition, Afro-American and to a lesser extent, African and Caribbean writers, both male and female, are represented. The rationale here was to present a variety of settings in which Black women appear so that cross-cultural comparisons might be made.

Several criteria were used for the various pieces which follow. First, they were chosen for their ability to reflect some of the realities of Black women's lives in America, Africa, and the Caribbean. Secondly, specific writers were singled out for their sensitivity to and knowledge of the culture from which their work emerged. Finally, it was important to include a variety of images and perspectives of Black women so that readers would be left with a sense of their diversity as well as their common heritage.

Poetry is the dominant art form represented here for a number of reasons. It seems to be a better gauge for measuring the subtleties and nuances of what it means to be Black and woman. The poems included provide insights into the often unspoken, hidden, and unanalyzed aspects of the psyche of Black women. They lay bare those preoccupations and yearnings which are too much overlooked in works which focus primarily on the external reality of Black women.

Women writers are in the majority here (though we don't pretend they have a monopoly on truth), because the primary definitions of a group must come from the "inside." Since Black women have been defined traditionally by others—by white males and females and Black males–it is entirely fitting and long overdue that we hear from Black women themselves, especially those from Africa and the Caribbean, where women writers are still a rarity. While this anthology makes only a small attempt in this direction, such an approach must become more commonplace in the future.

It is hoped that the stories, poems, and plays in Part Three will not be approached in a vacuum but rather from a perspective which includes insights gained from Parts One and Two. A further hope is that readers will be better able to analyze images of Black women wherever they appear as a result of having experienced this book. Equally important should be the realization that women writers can provide perspectives which are as crucial to our understanding of the Black experience in America, Africa, or the Caribbean as the perspective of the slave himself or herself would be in our understanding of the plantation system of the South.

When alternative images of Black women like those included in this section, become more accessible and widespread, then it will be impossible to continue to see the Black woman as she has been viewed traditionally.

The Collector of Treasures

by BESSIE HEAD

The long-term central state prison in the south was a whole day's journey away from the villages of the northern part of the country. They had left the village of Puleng at about nine that morning and all day long the police truck droned as it sped southward on the wide, dusty cross-country track road. The everyday world of plowed fields, grazing cattle, and vast expanses of bush and forest seemed indifferent to the hungry eyes of the prisoner who gazed out at them through the wire-mesh grating at the back of the police truck. At some point during the journey, the prisoner seemed to strike at some ultimate source of pain and loneliness within her being and, overcome by it, she slowly crumpled forward in a perishing heap, oblivious to everything but her pain. Sunset swept by, then dusk, then dark, and still the truck droned on.

At first, faintly on the horizon, the orange glow of the city lights of the new independence town of Gaborone appeared like an astonishing phantom in the overwhelming darkness of the bush, until the truck struck tarred roads, neon lights, shops, and cinemas and made the bush a phantom amidst a blaze of light. All this passed untimed, unwatched by the crumpled prisoner; she did not stir as the truck finally droned to a halt outside the prison gates. The torchlight struck the side of her face like an agonizing blow. Thinking she was asleep, the policeman called out briskly:

"You must awaken now. We have arrived."

He struggled with the lock in the dark and pulled open the grating. She crawled painfully forward, in silence.

Together, they walked up a short flight of stairs and waited awhile as the man tapped lightly, several times, on the heavy iron prison door. The night-duty attendant opened the door a little wider for them to enter. He quietly and casually led the way to a small office, looked at his colleague, and asked: "What do we have here?"

"It's the husband murder case from Puleng village," the other replied, handing over a file.

The attendant took the file and sat down at a table on which lay open a large record book. In a big, bold scrawl he recorded the details: Dikeledi Mokopi. Charge: Manslaughter. Sentence: Life. A night-duty attendant appeared and led the prisoner away to a side cubicle, where she was asked to undress.

"Have you any money on you?" the attendant queried, handing her a plain green cotton dress, which was the prison uniform. The prisoner silently shook her head.

"So, you have killed your husband, have you?" the attendant remarked, with a flicker of humor. "You'll be in good company. We have four other women here for the same crime. It's becoming the fashion these days. Come with me," and she led the way along a corridor, turned left, and stopped at an iron gate which she opened with a key, waited for the prisoner to walk in ahead of her, and then locked it with the key again. They entered a small, immensely high-walled courtyard. On one side were toilets, showers, and a cupboard. On the other, an empty concrete quadrangle. The attendant walked to the cupboard, unlocked it, and took out a thick roll of clean-smelling blankets which she handed to the prisoner. At the lower end of the walled courtyard was a heavy iron door which led to the cell. The attendant walked up to this door, banged on it loudly, and called out: "I say, will you women in there light your candle?"

A voice within called out, "All right," and they could hear the scratch-scratch of a match. Then the attendant again inserted a key, opened the door, and watched for a while as the prisoner spread out her blankets on the floor. The four women prisoners already confined in the cell sat up briefly and stared silently at their new companion. Then, when the door was locked, they all greeted her quietly and one of the women asked: "Where do you come from?"

"Puleng," the newcomer replied, and the women were seemingly satisfied with that, the light was blown out, and they lay down to continue their interrupted sleep. And as though she had reached the end of her destination, the new prisoner too fell into a deep sleep as soon as she had pulled her blankets about her.

The breakfast gong sounded at six the next morning. The women stirred themselves for their daily routine. They stood up, shook out their blankets, and rolled them up into neat bundles.

The day-duty attendant rattled the key in the lock and let them out into the small concrete courtyard so that they could perform their morning toilet. Then, with a loud clatter of pails and plates, two male prisoners appeared at the gate with breakfast. They handed each woman a plate of porridge and a mug of black tea and the women settled themselves on the concrete floor to eat. They turned and looked at their new companion, and one of the women, a spokesperson for the group, said kindly:

"You should take care. The tea has no sugar in it. What we usually do is scoop the sugar off the porridge and put it into the tea."

The woman, Dikeledi, looked up and smiled. She had experienced such terror during the awaiting-trial period that she looked more like a skeleton than a human being. The other woman smiled, but after her own fashion. Her face permanently wore a look of cynical, whimsical humor. She had a full, plump figure. She introduced herself and her companions: "My name is Kebonye. Then that's Otsetswe, Galeboe, and Monwana. What may your name be?"

"Dikeledi Mokopi."

"How is it that you have such a tragic name," Kebonye observed. "Why did your parents have to name you *tears?*"

"My father passed away at that time, and it is my mother's tears that I am named after," Dikeledi said, then added: "She herself passed away six years later and I was brought up by my uncle."

Kebonye shook her head sympathetically, slowly raising a spoonful of porridge to her mouth. That swallowed, she next asked:

"And what may your crime be?"

"I have killed my husband."

"We are all here for the same crime," Kebonye said, then with her cynical smile asked: "Do you feel any sorrow about the crime?"

"Not really," the other woman replied.

"How did you kill him?"

"I cut off his special parts with a knife," Dikeledi said.

"I did it with a razor," Kebonye said. Then she sighed and added: "I have had a troubled life."

A little silence followed while they all busied themselves with their food, then Kebonye continued, musingly:

"Our men do not think that we need tenderness and care. You know, my husband used to kick me between the legs when he wanted that. I once aborted with a child, due to this treatment. I could see that there was no way to appeal to him if I felt ill, so I once said to him that if he liked he could keep some other woman as well because I couldn't manage to satisfy all his needs. Well, he was an education officer and each year he used to suspend about seventeen male teachers for making school girls pregnant, but he used to do the same. The last time it happened the parents of the girl were very angry and came to report the matter to me. I told them: 'You leave it to me. I have seen enough.' And so I killed him."

They sat in silence and completed their meal, then they took their plates and cups to rinse them in the washroom. Then the attendant produced some pails and a broom. Their sleeping quarters had to be flushed out with water; there was not a speck of dirt anywhere, but that was prison routine. Then all that was left was inspection by the director of the prison. Here again Kebonye turned to the newcomer and warned:

"You must be careful when the chief comes to inspect. He is mad about one thing—attention! stand up straight! hands at your sides! If this is not done you should see how he stands here and curses. He does not mind anything but that. He is mad about that."

Inspection over, the women were taken through a number of gates to an open sunny yard, fenced in by high barbed wire, where they did their daily work. The prison was a rehabilitation center where the prisoners produced goods which were sold in the prison store: the women produced woolen and garments of cloth; the men did carpentry, shoemaking, brickmaking, and vegetable production.

Dikeledi had a number of skills—she could knit, sew, and weave baskets. All the women at present were busy knitting woolen garments; some were learners and did their work slowly and painstakingly. They looked at Dikeledi with interest as she took a ball of wool and a pair of knitting needles and rapidly cast on stitches. She had soft, caressing, almost boneless hands of a strange power—work of a beautiful design grew out of those hands. By midmorning she had completed the front part of a jersey, and they all stopped to admire the pattern she had invented in her own head.

"You are a gifted person," Kebonye remarked admiringly.

"All my friends said so," Dikeledi replied, smiling. "You know, I was the woman whose thatch does not leak. Whenever my friends wanted to thatch their huts, I was there. They would never do it without me. I was always employed because it was with these hands that I fed and reared my children. My husband left me after four years of marriage, but I managed well enough to feed those mouths. If people did not pay me with money for my work, they paid me with gifts of food."

"It's not so bad here," Kebonye said. "We get a little of the money saved for us out of the sale of our work and if you work like that you will still produce money for your children. How many children do you have?"

"I have three sons."

"Are they in good care?"

"Yes."

"I like lunch," Kebonye said, oddly turning the conversation. "It is the best meal of the day. We get samp and meat and vegetables."

So the day passed pleasantly enough with chatter and work and at sunset the women were once more taken back to the cell for lockup time. They unrolled their blankets and prepared their beds, and with the candle lit, continued to talk awhile longer. Just as they were about to retire for the night, Dikeledi nodded to her newfound friend, Kebonye.

"Thank you for all your kindness to me," she said softly.

"We must help each other," Kebonye replied, with her amused, cynical smile. "This is a terrible world. There is only misery here."

And so the woman Dikeledi began phase three of a life that had been ashen in its loneliness and unhappiness. And yet she had always found gold amidst the ash, deep loves that had joined her heart to the hearts of others. She smiled tenderly at Kebonye because she knew already that she had found another such love. She was the collector of such treasures.

There were really only two kinds of men in the society. The one kind created such misery and chaos that he could be broadly damned as evil. If one watched the village dogs chasing a bitch in heat, one saw that they usually moved around in packs of four or five. As the mating progressed one dog would attempt to gain dominance over the festivities and oust all the others from the bitch's vulva. The rest of the hapless dogs would stand around yapping and snapping at its face while the top dog indulged in a continuous spurt of orgasms, day and night until he was exhausted. No doubt, during that herculean feat, the dog imagined his was the only penis in the world and that there had to be a scramble for it. That kind of man lived near the animal level and behaved just the same. Like the dogs and bulls and donkeys, he also accepted no responsibility for the young he procreated, and like the dogs and bulls and donkeys, he also made females abort.

Since that kind of man was in the majority in the society, he needed a little analyzing as he was responsible for the complete breakdown of family life. He could be analyzed over three time spans. In the old days, before the colonial invasion of Africa, he was a man who lived by the traditions and taboos outlined for all the people by the forefathers of the tribe. He had little individual freedom to assess whether these traditions were compassionate or not—they demanded that he comply and obey the rules, without thought. But when the laws of the ancestors are examined, they appear on the whole to have been vast external disciplines for the good of the society as a whole, with little attention given to individual preferences and needs.

The ancestors made so many errors, and one of the most bitter was that they relegated to men a superior position in the tribe, while women were regarded, in a congenial sense, as being an inferior form of human life. The colonial era and the period of migratory mining labor to South Africa was a further affliction visited on this man. It broke the hold of the ancestors. It broke the old traditional form of family life, and for long periods a man was separated from his wife and children while he worked for a pittance in another land in order to raise the money to pay his British colonial poll tax. British colonialism had scarcely enriched his life. He had then become "the boy" of the white man and a machine tool of the South African mines. African independence seemed merely one more affliction on all the afflictions that had visited this man's life.

Independence suddenly and dramatically changed the pattern of colonial subservience. More jobs became available under the new government's localization program, and salaries skyrocketed at the same time. It provided the first occasion for a family life of a new order, above the childlike discipline of custom, the degradation of colonialism. Men and women, in order to survive, had to turn inward to their own resources. It was the man who arrived at this turning point a broken wreck with no inner resources at all. It was as though he was hideous to himself, and in an effort to flee his own inner emptiness, he spun away from himself in a dizzy kind of death dance of wild destruction and dissipation.

One such man was Garesego Mokopi, the husband of Dikeledi. For four years prior to independence, he had worked as a clerk, in the district administration service, at a salary of fifty rand a month. Soon after independence his salary shot up to two hundred rand per month. Even during his lean days he had had a taste for womanizing and drink; now he had the resources for a real spree. He just was not seen at home again and lived and slept around the village, from woman to woman. He left his wife and three sons—Banabothe, the eldest, aged four; Inalame, aged three; and the youngest, Motsomi, aged one—to their own resources. Perhaps he did so because she was the boring, semiliterate traditional sort, and there were a lot of exciting new women around. Independence produced marvels indeed.

There was another kind of man in the society with the power to create himself anew. He turned all his resources, both emotional and material, to his family life and he went on and on with his own quiet rhythm, like a river. He was a poem of tenderness.

One such man was Paul Thebolo, and he and his wife, Kenalepe, and their three children came to live in the village of Puleng in 1966, the year of independence. Paul Thebolo had been offered the principalship of a primary school in the village. His family was allocated an empty field beside the yard of Dikeledi Mokopi, for a new home.

Dikeledi Mokopi kept an interested eye on the yard of her new neighbors. At first, only the man appeared with some workmen to erect the fence, which was set up with incredible speed and efficiency. The man impressed her immediately when she went around to introduce herself and find out a little about the newcomers. He was tall, large-boned, slow-moving. He was so peaceful as a person that the sunlight and shadow played all kinds of tricks with his eyes, making it difficult to determine their exact color. When he stood still and looked reflective, the sunlight liked to creep into his eyes and nestle there; so sometimes his eyes were the color of shade and sometimes light brown.

He turned and smiled at her in a friendly way when she introduced herself and explained that he and his wife were on transfer from the village of Bobonong. His wife and children were living with relatives in the village until the yard was prepared. He was in a hurry to settle down, as the school term would start in a month's time. They were, he said, going to erect two mud huts first and later he intended setting up a small house of bricks. His wife would be coming around in a few days with some women to erect the mud walls of the huts.

"I would like to offer my help, too," Dikeledi said. "If work always starts early in the morning and there are about six of us, we can get both walls erected in a week. If you want one of the huts done in woman's thatch, all my friends know that I am the woman whose thatch does not leak."

The man smilingly replied that he would impart all this information to his wife, then he added charmingly that he thought she would like his wife when they met. His wife was a very friendly person; everyone liked her.

Dikeledi walked back to her own yard with a high heart. She had few callers. None of her relatives called for fear that since her husband had left her she would become dependent on them for many things. The people who called did business with her; they wanted her to make dresses for their children or knit jerseys for the wintertime, and at times when she had no orders at all, she made baskets, which she sold. In these ways she supported herself and the three children, but she was lonely for true friends.

All turned out as the husband had said—he had a lovely wife. She was fairly tall and thin with a bright, vivacious manner. She made no effort to conceal that normally, and every day, she was a very happy person. And all turned out as Dikeledi had said. The work party of six women erected the mud walls of the huts in one week; two weeks later, the thatch was complete. The Thebolo family moved into their new abode, and Dikeledi Mokopi moved into one of the most prosperous and happy periods of her life. Her life took a big, wide upward curve. Her relationship with the Thebolo family was more than the usual friendly exchange of neighbors. It was rich and creative.

It was not long before the two women had going one of those deep, affectionate, sharing-everything kinds of friendships that only women know how to have. It seemed that Kenalepe wanted endless amounts of dresses made for herself and her three little girls. Since Dikeledi would not accept cash for these services—she protested about the many benefits she received from her good neighbors—Paul Thebolo arranged that she be paid in household goods so that for some years Dikeledi was always assured of her basic household needs: the full bag of corn, sugar, tea, powdered milk, and cooking oil. Kenalepe was also the kind of woman who made the whole world spin around her; her attractive personality brought a whole range of women to her yard and also a whole range of customers for her dressmaking friend, Dikeledi. Eventually, Dikeledi became swamped with work, was forced to buy a second sewing machine and to employ a helper. The two women did everything together—they were forever together at weddings, funerals, and parties in the village. In their leisure hours they freely discussed all their intimate affairs with each other, so each knew thoroughly the details of the other's life.

"You are a lucky someone," Dikeledi remarked one day wistfully. "Not everyone has the gift of a husband like Paul."

"Oh yes," Kenalepe said happily. "He is an honest somebody." She knew Dikeledi's list of woes and queried: "But why did you marry a man like Garesego? I looked carefully at him when you pointed him out to me near the shops the other day and I could see at one glance that he is a butterfly."

"I think I mostly wanted to get out of my uncle's yard," Dikeledi replied. "I never liked my uncle. Rich as he was, he was a hard man and very selfish. I was only a servant there and pushed about. I went there when I was six years old, when my mother died, and it was not a happy life. All his children despised me because I was their servant. Uncle paid for my education for six years, then he said I must leave school. I longed for more because, as you know, education opens up the world for one. Garesego was a friend of my uncle's and he was the only man who proposed for me. They discussed it between themselves and then my uncle said: 'You'd better marry Garesego because you're just hanging around here like a chain on my neck.' I agreed, just to get away from that terrible man. Garesego said at that time that he'd rather be married to my sort than the educated kind because those women were stubborn and wanted to lay down the rules for men. Really, I did not ever protest when he started running about. You know what the other women do. They chase after the man from one hut to another and beat up the girl friends. The man just runs into another hut, that's all. So you don't really win. I wasn't going to do anything like that. I am satisfied I have children. They are a blessing to me."

"Oh, it isn't enough," her friend said, shaking her head in deep sympathy. "I am amazed at how life imparts its gifts. Some people get too much. Others get nothing at all. I have always been lucky in life. One day my parents will visit—they live in the south—and you'll see the fuss they make over me. Paul is just the same. He takes care of everything so that I never have a day of worry. . . ."

The man Paul attracted as wide a range of male friends as his wife did female friends. They had guests every evening: illiterate men who wanted him to fill in tax forms or write letters for them; his own colleagues who wanted to debate the political issues of the day—there was always something new happening every day now that the country had independence. The two women sat on the edge of these debates with wise, earnest expressions.

"Men's minds travel widely and boldly," Kenalepe would comment. "It makes me shiver the way they freely criticize our new government. Did you hear what Petros said last night: He said he knew all those bastards and they were just a lot of crooks who would pull a lot of dirty tricks. Oh, dear! I shivered so much when he said that. The way they talk about the government makes you feel in your bones that this is not a safe world to be in, not like the old days when we didn't have governments. And Lentswe said that ten per cent of the population in England really control all the wealth of the country, while the rest live at starvation level. And he said communism would sort all this out. I gathered from the way they discussed this matter that our government is not in favor of communism. I trembled so much when this became clear to me . . ." She paused and laughed proudly. "I've heard Paul say that several times: 'The British only ruled us for eighty years.' I wonder why Paul is so fond of saying that."

And so a completely new world opened up for Dikeledi. It was so impossibly rich and happy that as the days went by she immersed herself more deeply and quite overlooked the barrenness of her own life. But it hung there like a nagging ache in the mind of her friend, Kenalepe.

"You ought to find another man," she urged one day, when they had one of their personal discussions. "It's not good for a woman to live alone."

"And who would that be?" Dikeledi asked, disillusioned. "I'd only be bringing trouble into my life, whereas now it is all in order. I have my eldest son at school and I can manage to pay the school fees. That's all I really care about."

"I mean," said Kenalepe, "we are also here to make love and enjoy it."

"Oh, I never really cared for it," the other replied. "When you experience the worst of it, it just puts you off altogether."

"What do you mean by that?" Kenalepe asked, wide-eyed.

"I mean it was just jump on and jump off and I used to wonder what it was all about. I developed a dislike for it."

"You mean Garesego was like that!" Kenalepe said, flabbergasted. "Why, that's just like a cock hopping from hen to hen. I wonder what he is doing with all those women. I'm sure they are just after his money and so they flatter him . . ." She paused and then added earnestly: "That's really all the more reason you should find another man. Oh, if you knew what it was really like, you would long for it, I can tell you! I sometimes think I enjoy that side of life far too much. Paul knows a lot about all that. And he always has some new trick with which to surprise me. He has a certain way of smiling when he has thought up something new and I shiver a little and say to myself: 'Ha, what is Paul going to do tonight!' "

Kenalepe paused and smiled at her friend slyly.

"I can loan Paul to you if you like," she said, then raised one hand to block the protest on her friend's face. "I would do it because I have never had a friend like you in my life before whom I trust so much. Paul had other girls, you know, before he married me, so it's not such an uncommon thing to him. Besides, we used to make love long before we got married, and I never got pregnant. He takes care of that side, too. I wouldn't mind loaning him because I am expecting another child and I don't feel so well these days. . . ."

Dikeledi stared at the ground for a long moment, then she looked up at her friend with tears in her eyes.

"I cannot accept such a gift from you," she said, deeply moved. "But if you are ill, I will wash for you and cook for you."

Not put off by her friend's refusal of her generous offer, Kenalepe mentioned the discussion to her husband that very night. He was so taken off guard by the unexpectedness of the subject that he at first looked slightly astonished, then burst out into loud laughter and for such a lengthy time that he seemed unable to stop.

"Why are you laughing like that?" Kenalepe asked, surprised.

He laughed a bit more, then suddenly turned very serious and thoughtful and was lost in his own thoughts for some time. When she asked him what he was thinking, he merely replied: "I don't want to tell you everything. I want to keep some of my secrets to myself."

The next day Kenalepe reported this to her friend.

"Now, whatever does he mean by that? I want to keep some of my secrets to myself?"

"I think," Dikeledi said, smiling, "I think he has a conceit about being a good man. Also, when someone loves someone too much, it hurts them to say so. They'd rather keep silent."

Shortly after this Kenalepe had a miscarriage and had to be admitted to hospital for a minor operation. Kideledi kept her promise "to wash and cook" for her friend. She ran both their homes, fed the children, and kept everything in order. Also, since people had complained about the poorness of the hospital diet, she scoured the village for eggs and chickens, cooked them, and took them to Kenalepe at the lunch hour.

One evening Dikeledi ran into a snag with her routine. She had just dished up supper for the Thebolo children when a customer came around with an urgent request for an alteration on a wedding dress. The wedding was to take place the next day. She left the children seated around the fire eating and returned to her own home. An hour later, her own children asleep and settled, she thought she would check the Thebolo yard to see if all was well there. She entered the children's hut and noted that they had put themselves to bed and were fast asleep. Their supper plates lay scattered and unwashed around the fire. The hut which Paul and Kenalepe shared was in darkness. It meant that Paul had not yet returned from his usual evening visit to his wife. Dikeledi collected the plates and washed them, then poured the dirty dishwater on the still-glowing embers of the outdoor fire. She piled the plates one on top of the other and carried them to the third additional hut that was used as a kitchen. Just then Paul Thebolo entered the yard, noted the lamp and movement in the kitchen hut, and walked over to it. He paused at the open door.

"What are you doing now, Mma-Banabothe?" he asked, addressing her affectionately in the customary way by the name of her eldest son, Banabothe.

"I know quite well what I am doing," Dikeledi replied happily. She turned around to say that it was not a good thing to leave dirty dishes standing overnight, but her mouth flew open with surprise. Two soft pools of cool liquid light were in his eyes, and something infinitely sweet passed between them; it was too beautiful to be love.

"You are a very good woman, Mma-Banabothe," he said softly.

It was the truth and the gift was offered like a nugget of gold. Only men like Paul Thebolo could offer such gifts. She took it and stored another treasure in her heart. She bowed her knee in the traditional curtsy and walked quietly away to her own home.

Eight years went by for Dikeledi in a quiet rhythm of work and friendship with the Thebolos. Then the crisis came with the eldest son, Banabothe. He had to take his primary school leaving examination at the end of the year. This serious event sobered him up considerably as, like all boys, he was very fond of playtime. He brought his books home and told his mother that he would like to study in the evenings. He would like to pass with a Grade A to please her. With a flushed and proud face Dikeledi mentioned this to her friend, Kenalepe.

"Banabothe is studying every night now," she said. "He never really cared for studies. I am so pleased about this that I bought him a spare lamp and removed him from the children's hut to my own hut, where things will be peaceful for him."

She also opened a savings account at the post office in order to have some stand-by money to pay the fees for his secondary education. They were rather high—eighty-five rand. But in spite of all her hoarding of odd cents, toward the end of the year she was short by twenty rand to cover the fees. Midway during the Christmas school holidays the results were announced. Banabothe passed with a Grade A. His mother was almost hysterical in her joy at this achievement. But what to do? The two younger sons had already started primary school, and she would never manage to cover all their fees with her resources. She decided to remind Garesego Mokopi that he was the father of the children. She had not seen him in eight years except as a passer-by in the village. Sometimes he waved, but he had never talked to her or inquired about her life or that of the children. It did not matter. She was a lower form of human life. Then this unpleasant something turned up at his office one day, just as he was about to leave for lunch.

Dikeledi had heard, from village gossip, that Garesego had eventually settled down with a married woman who had a brood of children of her own. He had ousted her husband, in one of the typical village sensations of brawls, curses, and abuse. Most probably the husband did not care because there were always arms outstretched toward a man, as long as he just looked like a man. The attraction of this particular woman for Garesego Mokopi, so her former lovers said, with a snicker, was that she went in for heady forms of love-making like biting and scratching.

Garesego Mokopi walked out of his office and looked irritably at the ghost from his past, his wife. She obviously wanted to talk to him, and he walked toward her, looking at his watch all the while. Like all the new "success men," he had developed a paunch. His eyes were bloodshot, his face bloated, and the odor of the beer and sex of the previous night clung faintly around him. He indicated with his eyes that they should move around to the back part of the office block where they could talk in privacy.

"You must hurry with whatever you want to say," he said impatiently. "The lunch hour is very short, and I have to be back at the office by two."

Not to him could she talk of the pride she felt in Banabothe's achievement, so she said simply and quietly: "Garesego, I beg you to help me pay Banabothe's fees for secondary school. He has passed with a Grade A, and, as you know, the school fees must be produced on the first day of school or else he will be turned away. I have struggled to save money the whole year but I am short by twenty rand."

She handed him her post office savings book, which he took, glanced at, and handed back to her.

"Why don't you ask Paul Thebolo for the money?" he said. "Everyone knows he's keeping two home and that you are his spare. Everyone knows about that full bag of corn he delivers to your home every six months—so why can't he pay the school fees as well?"

She neither denied this nor confirmed it. The blow glanced off her face, which she raised slightly, in pride. Then she walked away.

As was their habit, the two women got together that afternoon and Dikeledi reported this conversation with her husband to Kenalepe, who tossed back her head in anger and said fiercely: "The filthy pig himself! He thinks every man is like him, does he? I shall report this matter to Paul, then he'll see something."

And indeed Garesego did see something, but it was just up his alley. He was a female prostitute in his innermost being and like all professional prostitutes, he enjoyed publicity and sensation—it promoted his cause. He smiled genially and expansively when an angry Paul Thebolo came up to the door of the house where he lived with *his* concubine. Garesego had been through a lot of these dramas over those eight years and he almost knew by rote the dialogue that would follow.

"You bastard!" Paul Thebolo spat out. "Your wife isn't my concubine, do you hear?"

"Then why are you keeping her in food?" Garesego drawled. "Men only do that for women they fuck! They never do it for nothing."

Paul Thebolo rested one hand against the wall, half-dizzy with anger, then he said tensely: "You defile life, Garesego Mokopi. There's nothing else in your world but defilement. Mma-Banabothe makes clothes for my wife and children and she will never accept money from me, so how else must I pay her?"

"It only proves the story both ways," the other replied vilely. "Women do that for men who fuck them."

Paul Thebolo shot out the other hand, punched him soundly in one grinning eye, and walked away. Who could hide a livid, swollen eye? To every surprised inquiry, he replied with an injured air:

"It was done by my wife's lover, Paul Thebolo."

It certainly brought the attention of the whole village toward him, which was all he really wanted. Those kinds of men were the bottom rung of government. They secretly hungered to be the president with all eyes on them. He worked up the sensation a little further. He announced that he would pay the school fees of the child of his concubine, who was also to enter secondary school, but not the school fees of his own child, Banabothe. People half-liked the smear on Paul Thebolo; he was too good to be true. They delighted in making him a part of the general dirt of the village, so they turned on Garesego and scolded: "Your wife might be getting things from Paul Thebolo, but it's beyond the purse of any man to pay the school fees of his own children as well as the school fees of another man's children. Banabothe wouldn't be there had you not procreated him, Garesego, so it is your duty to care for him. Besides, it's your fault if your wife takes another man. You left her alone all these years."

So that story was lived with for two weeks mostly because people wanted to say that Paul Thebolo was a part of life too and as uncertain of his morals as they were. Then the story took such a dramatic turn that it made all the men shudder with horror. It was some weeks before they could find the courage to go to bed with women; they preferred to do something else.

Garesego's obscene thought processes were his own undoing. He really believed that another man had a stake in his hen-pen and, like any cock, his hair was up about it. He thought he'd walk in and re-establish his own claim to it and so, after two weeks, once the swelling in his eye had died down, he espied Banabothe in the village and asked him to take a note to his mother. He said the child should bring a reply. The note read, incredibly: "Dear Mother, I am coming home again so that we may settle our differences. Will you prepare a meal for me and some hot water that I might take a bath. Gare."

Dikeledi took the note, read it, and shook with rage. All its overtones were clear to her. He was coming home for some sex. They had had no differences. They had not even talked to each other.

"Banabothe," she said, "will you play nearby? I want to think a bit, then I will send you to your father with the reply."

Her thought processes were not very clear to her. There was something she could not immediately touch upon. Her life had become holy to her over all those years she had struggled to maintain herself and the children. She had filled her life with treasures of kindness and love she had gathered from others and it was all this that she wanted to protect from defilement by an evil man. Her first panic-stricken thought was to gather up the children and flee the village. But where to go? Garesego did not want a divorce; she had left him to approach her about the matter; she had desisted from taking any other man. She turned her thoughts this way and that and could find no way out except to face him. If she wrote back, "Don't you dare put foot in the yard, I don't want to see you," he would ignore it. Black women didn't have that kind of power. Then a thoughtful, brooding look fell upon her face. At last, at peace with herself, she went into her hut and wrote a reply: "Sir, I shall prepare everything as you have said. Dikeledi."

It was about midday when Banabothe sped back with the reply to his father. All afternoon Dikeledi busied herself making preparations for the appearance of her husband at sunset. At one point Kenalepe approached the yard and looked around in amazement at the massive preparations, the large iron pot full of water with a fire burning under it, the extra cooking pots on the fire. Only later did Kenalepe bring the knife into focus. Then it was a vague blur, a large kitchen knife used to cut meat. Dikeledi knelt at a grinding stone and sharpened it slowly and methodically. What was in focus then was the final and tragic expression on the upturned face of her friend. It threw her into confusion and blocked their usual free-and-easy feminine chatter. When Dikeledi said, "I am making some preparations for Garesego; he is coming home tonight," Kenalepe beat a hasty retreat to her own home, terrified. Kenalepe and Paul knew that they were involved because when she mentioned this to Paul he was distracted and uneasy for the rest of the day. He kept on doing upside-down sorts of things, not replying to questions, absent-mindedly leaving a cup of tea until it got quite cold, and every now and then, he stood up and paced about, lost in his own thoughts. So deep was their sense of disturbance that toward evening they no longer made a pretense of talking. They just sat in silence in their hut. Then, at about nine o'clock, they heard those wild and agonized bellows. They both rushed out together to the yard of Dikeledi Mokopi.

He came home at sunset and found everything ready for him as he had requested and he settled himself down to enjoy a man's life. He had brought a pack of beer along and sat outdoors slowly savoring it while every now and then his eye swept over the Thebolo yard. Only the woman and children moved about the yard. The man was out of sight. Garesego smiled to himself, pleased that he could crow as loud as he liked with no answering challenge.

A basin of warm water was placed before him to wash his hands in, and then Dikeledi served him his meal. At a separate distance she also served the children and then instructed them to wash and prepare for bed. She noted that Garesego displayed no interest in the children whatsoever. He was entirely wrapped up in himself and thought only of himself and his own comfort. Had he offered the children any tenderness, it might have broken her and swerved her mind away from the deed she had carefully planned all that afternoon. She was also beneath his regard and notice, for when she eventually brought her own plate of food and sat near him, he never once glanced at her face. He drank his beer and cast his glance every now and then at the Thebolo yard. Not once did the man of the yard appear until it became too dark to distinguish anything any more. He was completely satisfied with that. He could repeat the performance every day until he broke the mettle of the other cock again and forced him into angry abuse. He just liked that.

"Garesego, do you think you could help me with Banabothe's school fees?" Dikeledi asked at one point.

"Oh, I'll think about it," he replied casually.

She stood up and carried buckets of water into the hut. This she poured into a large tin bath that he might bathe himself; then while he took his bath, she busied herself tidying up and completing the last of the household chores. Then she entered the children's hut. They played hard during the day and they had already fallen asleep from exhaustion. She knelt down near their sleeping mats and stared at them for a long while, with an extremely tender expression. Then she blew out their lamp and walked to her own hut.

Garesego lay sprawled across the bed in a manner that indicated that he only thought of himself and did not intend sharing that bed with anyone else. Satiated with food and drink, he had fallen into a deep, heavy sleep the moment his head touched the pillow. His concubine had no doubt taught him that the correct way for a man to go to bed was naked. So he lay, unguarded and defenseless, sprawled across the bed on his back.

The bath made a loud clatter as Dikeledi removed it from the room, but still he slept on, lost to the world. She re-entered the hut and closed the door. Then she bent down under the bed and reached for the knife, which she had merely concealed with a cloth. With the precision and skill of her hard-working hands, she grasped hold of his genitals and cut them off with one stroke. In doing so, she slit the main artery which ran on the inside of the groin. A massive spurt of blood arched its way across the bed. And Garesego bellowed. He bellowed his anguish. Then all was silent. She stood and watched his death anguish with an intent and brooding look, missing not one detail of it. A knock on the door stirred her out of her reverie. It was the boy, Banabothe. She opened the door and stared at him, speechless. He was trembling violently.

"Mother," he said in a terrified whisper. "Didn't I hear Father cry?"

"I have killed him," she said, waving her hand in the air with a gesture that said—well, that's that. Then she added sharply: "Banabothe, go and call the police."

He turned and fled into the night. A second pair of footsteps followed hard on his heels. It was Kenalepe running back to her own yard, half out of her mind with fear. Out of the dark Paul Thebolo stepped toward the hut and entered it. He too took in every detail and then he turned and looked at Dikeledi with such a tortured expression that for a time words failed him. At last he said: "You don't have to worry about the children, Mma-Banabothe. I'll take them as my own and give them all a secondary school education."

An African Tribute

by SAMUEL OTOO

Do you remember
when I first smiled in your lap
when out of pain and suffering
you brought me into the world
and nurtured me
when together we wept
into the earth to soften it
when we could not break
the hard ground for food

I remember you
a mother in a land by
the great sea
weaving the mat of
my life on your knees

Do you hear me!
My heart is filled
with longing for you
I pine for you, Mother.

Return of the Native

by PAULE MARSHALL

"Leesy."
"Who the body is?"
"Bull."
"The Lord."

He dropped the other small stone he was about to lob like a cricket ball against the side of the house and it seemed to fall a long way before it struck ground as though the darkness which was without height was also without depth, depthless, so that he and the house he could scarcely discern in front of him as well as the hills over which he had just traveled by car, by lorry, by donkey cart, and by foot finally were not fixed on solid ground but suspended, weightless, in the vast warm womb of the tropic night.

He waited, hesitant as a stranger, on the low embankment between the house and the road. It would be some time before she opened the door, he knew. She would have to dress. As carefully as if it were morning, she would put on the innumerable slips and petticoats over the flannel undershirt and long drawers she wore even in bed (her vest and trousers she called them) and finally the dress, attaching weights to the weightless husk of her body lest the wind take her. Then slowly and as though it caused her unimaginable pain she would wind a white cloth around her head: a shield against the night air.

The sheep stirred anxiously under the house and Bull saw the thin yellow lines of light between the loose boards of the wall facing him—like lines drawn with a fine quill across the darkness—as she turned up the kerosene lamp she kept burning all night. He jumped lightly down into the yard.

The house had been built with one blank windowless side to the road to frustrate the curious and the front facing a small cluttered yard half hidden from the road by a huge mango and clammer cherry tree at its edge, the trees hung with the night now as with some dark heavy fruit. Beyond them a fence of frayed rusted galvanize separated Leesy from the neighbor to whom she hadn't spoken in twenty years because of an argument over a sheep. And on the other two sides of the house the sugar cane pressed up against the walls, begrudging the house its space.

Stepping over a root of the mango tree which arched up out of the ground, remembering where it was despite the three years he had been away cutting canes in Florida, Bull watched the light bloom fully behind the panels of flowered glass in the narrow front door. The panels were new. And suddenly it was as if they had been put there for him, to celebrate his return. He smiled at the thought and the smile together with the rush of light as Leesy opened the door drove back the darkness.

"Oh, he's laughing, the vagabond," she cried severely and as severely embraced and drew him in. "Come pelting rock-stone at the old house, come calling out my name in the night like some duppy or the other, and he's laughing. How did he find his way back here anyway? And where did he get that fancy hat and suit and those long-toe shoes? Oh, God, look how this boy has fallen away in his skin."

He stood smiling broadly, pleased, in the center of the small room, truly the boy as he posed a little for her in his loose, wide-shouldered, one-button lounge suit of powder-blue sharkskin and the hat, a shaggy velour of the same blue with an oversized brim and an outrageously high crown which he had seen advertised in *Ebony* magazine and ordered through the mail and the long sharp-toed shoes which distorted his foot.

But Leesy hardly seemed to notice him after that first scrutinizing glance. Instead, with a few deft motions, she set about putting their life in order again. Moving among the shadows which claimed the room despite the lamplight, she laid the table with the remainder of her supper which she would have eaten in the morning: rice and green bananas with a thin gravy of salt fish over it. And all the while her voice sounded the welcome that was like one long reproof.

". . . and don't think I didn't know you was to come. I had the sign." And she gave a little knowing snap of her head which was like a tic. "Two months ago your mother-self that died in baby-bed having you came to me as I was out in the ground hoeing. Just so. Standing there in front of me as good as you are now. She was dressed all in scarlet. The hat and all was scarlet. And she said, 'Dear-aunt, I not resting easy these days. I studying Bull too bad. I beg you go down to the Labor Office and ask them if they know when he's due back.' And quick so I bathe my skin, put on clothes, and I gone. The morning bus had left so I start walking. The sun warm but I walking. And every week God send I went and ask them for you. Today and all. Yes, Bo, I knew you was coming. If not today, tomorrow; if not tomorrow, the day after. Come," she said, suddenly shy as she held a chair for him. It was a new Bentwood with the skittish legs of a foal and a nosegay of flowers printed on the back rest. "Come and sit or the clothes too pretty to sit in?"

"No . . ." he said, as shy suddenly. "It's just that everything is kinda changed up." And he did not just mean the new chair and the panels in the door, but the subtle alteration that had taken place in the familiar objects as well. The small dark cubicle of a room which looked as if it had been swept by a flash fire, then a flood, and finally a horde of wood ants and had gone down in defeat before them all seemed to crowd and sag more than ever around him. More of the color had drained from the blond laughing woman on the Coca-Cola ad and from the already faded Christ on the calendar which read May 1940, as it had ever since he could remember, the month and year Leesy's husband had died. The newspaper pictures of Pearl Bailey and the Queen pasted to the bare wall were almost completely absorbed now by the wood, and the faces of their relatives who had left the island had withdrawn deeper into the brown obscurity of their photographs. Only the silver plaques which bore the names of the family dead and which Leesy appropriated from the coffins at the graveside and hung in a neat row on the wall and polished every week were the same. And the smell: a damp distillation of wood rot and mold and the smoke of dead fires, of all the salt fish that had ever been cooked there and the lump of camphor she wore in a sack pinned to her undershirt.

"Everything changed up," he repeated, awed, and sat down.

"What you think, things must always stay the same?" she said.

She took a seat some distance away and watched him closely as he scooped up the first forkful of rice, her eyes like shards from some dark rock within the yellowed whites.

"Ah," he said, swallowing. "Too sweet to my mouth."

She gave the little nod at his smile and with her arms folded high on her flat chest said, "So tell me, how did you find it down there? Some the fellas that came back before you said they smelled hell."

He shrugged. "No, it wasn't so nice, I don't guess. For one, they put us to live in a barracks all the way out in some backwoods like we was criminals. Nothing but bush when you look out the window and all kind of alligator and big snake about the place. And we had to eat a lot of rough food. And the weather wasn't so nice neither. Plenty of warm sun during the day and then cold cold 'pon a night. Some the fellas got sick enough from it."

"And how you found the work?"

He laughed, proud and superior now, "How you mean? The work hard, man. Canes! You think you see canes here?" He sucked his teeth. "In Florida, man, it's like the whole world's planted in canes. And they plant different to us, you know. Instead of cane holes they do theirs in rows, so when they spring thick and . . ."

Slowly, pausing to eat, he explained the differences and Leesy pressed forward in her chair, her breathing stopped, it seemed.

". . . Another thing they burn their fields just before cutting 'cause of snakes I was telling you about. And the soil so rich it holds the heat for days sometimes. But the boss would want us to go in and start cutting all the same. Before the ground even cool down good. Some the fellas wouldn't go, but I always went. Some got disgusted and broke the contract and came on back home. Some of them ran away to New York and they ain't find them yet."

"That's where I thought you was when I stopped hearing from you."

"I tried," he said—and suddenly his face closed and his voice went dead. "But I didn't meet with a success."

For a long time he said nothing more, but simply ate, his expressionless face bent to meet the fork and the hard muscle moving beneath his dark jaw as he chewed the food. Then, finally putting down the fork, he spoke, his voice flat, matter-of-fact, uninvolved with what he was saying. He told her that once when he had been sent to work on a truck farm in New Jersey he had run away and found his way to a relative of theirs in Brooklyn.

"So I asked Uncle Seon a question: if he would let me stay," he said. "But he said it would be too big a risk to have me there illegal. He promised he would try to get me in legal though. He was to talk to his lawyer. And he treat me very nice the two days I was there. He had a big house and a big car, a Chrysler, and I met all the family except for the boy my age that was away studying medicine. . . ."

"You making joke."

". . . Uncle Seon even give me the money to buy this suit. He was to write and let me know what the lawyer said, but I haven't heard. He wrote you?" And he could not hide the small hope in his eyes which sought her face.

"Me? Seon does write me any more? Do any of them write—except maybe to send a five dollars at Christmas?" And then as quickly, she added, "But I know. They're busy. That's all it 'tis." She gave the nod. "You can't take the time to be writing and foolishness in those busy places."

He started to tell her otherwise, but realizing perhaps the futility of it, simply took up his fork and said, "Well, when I lost the chance to stay, my mind turned from America. I made out I was sick and couldn't do the work so they put me on a place and I come on back where I had to come."

He resumed eating, his legs spread, the slightly pegged pants ballooning a little around his calves, his face closed, immuned. And it had remained closed, immuned, you sensed, through all that had happened to him. The three years in that distant place, in those alien fields, which had scarred and swollen his hands so that they were like those of an old man and hardened his muscles prematurely, which had refused him asylum and turned him out with the parting gift of the jitterbug suit and hat and shoes had not been able to shake the crude innocence and seeming unconcern of that face. Flat, the broad features almost flush with each other, the face appeared unfinished, like a piece of sculpture upon which only the boasting had been done. Only the cheekbones were defined—and they overwhelmed the face. You knew looking at them that as he aged and his flesh thinned, that broad bone slanted high under his eyes would stretch the black skin taut and the slight hollows underneath would deepen and fill with shadows, until the time he was forty-five or fifty, an old man playing dominoes in the rum shop and tossing down the small glass of white rum, his lips trembling a little, those dark hollows would have become the repository of his dead dreams.

For a long time there was only the sound of his fork against the plate and the wind breaking in a warm wave over the roof. With each gust the lamp flickered and almost failed and the shadows made little joyous incursions into the area of light around the table.

Finally Leesy asked very gently, "But tell me, where you was all this time, Bull, and the plane from America got in at noon today."

"About in town."

"About in town! doing what?"

"Just looking."

"Looking for what? Where?"

"Whitehall Lane. Mayfair Alley. About in there," he said, but without looking up from his plate.

"Whitehall Lane! Mayfair Alley! Where all the sailor clubs are?"

And then she knew. "Oh the Lord, you mean to say the first thing you did as you got off the plane was to go looking for that girl? What you want with her still? She's gone. Didn't I write and tell you that over a year now? She's gone and the money's gone and the child's dead and there's nothing you can . . ."

The face he turned to her was as expressionless as ever but a hard intent had shrunk the pupils of his eyes and edged his voice now as he spoke. "I wish to ask her a question, that's all."

"You wish to put yourself in trouble, you mean. But what it 'tis with you a-tall?"—and her voice which time had worn to a single, hopelessly raveled thread almost broke with her bewilderment. "Why you so bullheaded . . . ? But what to do?"—and her voice collapsed. "You was always that way. Take this business of going to Florida. You wasn't even of age. But once you got it in your head to go, there wasn't no stopping you. You put up your age and you went. Playing the man. That's all it was.

"And the same when you start with that girl. What right you, a seventeen-year-old boy, had with somebody like that? She wasn't no quality or class for you. Those red people from up Canterbury Hill are all crossbreed and worthless. And she had a dirty style from small. Could curse nasty! And loved clothes. She would sell her soul for clothes. I saw her in town the other day styling in more hobble skirt and wrist watch. A real sports. But she could afford to be a sports now she take the money and kill the good child it was sent for. Yes, killed it," she cried. "Bare bare murder. And a nice boy-child, everything like you. But I know it didn't live a full six months. Every morning God send she had it in a hot bath, stewing it, and she would leave it alone in the house with not little tea for the day. And as soon as it dead she pick up and went to live in town with the other free-bees like herself. But let her stand. She can't see good."

She waited for some word from him, but he gave her only a remote little smile that made him seem suddenly older and wiser than her.

"The crop start yet?" he asked.

"You ain't heard what I said about the girl?"

"I heard," he said easily.

"But I heard it before. You wrote and told me all that in a letter."

"Yes, and you stopped writing after that," she cried, aggrieved. "Only sending the few dollars once in a while but never a word after that, like you was vex with me instead of the girl."

"I ask if the crop start."

"It start," she almost shouted, giving way. "But I might not finish."

"How you mean?"

She swung aside her face angrily, refusing to answer for a moment, but then taking a deep breath, straining the ancient lungs, she gathered together the frail wreckage of her body to speak. The face she turned back to him was drawn, and as reamed and burned as inside the bowl of a pipe, the features lost amid the scrabbled lines, negligible, mere apertures through which she breathed and spoke and kept her eyes close scrutiny. Her expression now was the one which appeared whenever she spoke of the land: a single-mindedness which reduced all else to insignificance; an arrogance and authority which declared she knew everything there was to growing canes; a pertinacity which said that she had set her life upon the narrow track which wound among the two acres of cane in back of the house and she would not be moved; a vast durable love which asked nothing in return.

"Well, Bo," she said.

"They're talking about closing down the sugar factory at Cane Vale."

He sucked his teeth and again he seemed older and more knowing. "They been saying that for years."

"Yes, but a mind tells me they mean it this time. Things getting too critical. The machines keep breaking down. They say they're losing money keeping it open because the canes so slight they don't bring much of a yield. And it's true 'bout the canes. All the fertilizer you put to them still doesn't help. The rain's not even falling when it should. And worse, there's scarce anybody to cut them any more. The young fellas your age that years ago would be glad for the work scorning it now. They rather spend the day in Delbert's rum shop playing a juke box he got there from America. Their hands soft as the Queen's. Their talk: bare cars, bare clothes. Good thieves, all of them.

"I tell you if you hadn't come back I didn't know what I would do this crop season. I worried till I got a beating in the head and had to 'tend the doctor. He told me to stop confusing myself with the piece of ground and either sell or rent it. But how I could do that? And then when the others come back what? . . ." She was talking to herself now; Bull forgotten. "When the work in England or America gets slight or they fall sick or get old and must come home, what? No. Bo, I must care it for them so when they come or their children come (and even Seon will be back, never mind the big house and the car he got now) if nothing else they'll be able to work the ground and get little money to buy rice. . . ."

It was a familiar recital, the belief around which she had ordered her life and which alone sustained her, as old for him as his own memory. Hearing it again after the three years' absence—the words unchanged and spoken in the same stark, sparing style of a plain song—he felt the old life close around him. He might not have been away even. And this feeling along with the rice and green banana weighing his stomach and the exhaustion of the long day slowly bore his head down in sleep. Leesy looked at the dark head drooping like a huge wilted boutonniere on the oversized lapel of his suit and said, rising, "His belly full and he's sleeping."

Again with a few brisk turns she prepared his old bed in the shed adjoining the house and when he was in bed and the blue suit and hat put away, she said, turning down the lamp, "Tomorrow, please God, we'll see to the few canes."

The Word Is Love

by LORNA V. WILLIAMS

"You know what is true, Girlie," my granny say to me, "I don't like how you and that knotty-head boy got your head into one another mouth so much. I know young people supposed to talk and laugh and enjoy themself together. But somehow, my spirit don't take to that Freddie, who you got a-come over at my yard at evening time."

Me, now, couldn't see what Granny did a-go on with. For is she, same one, did a-stick out 'bout how she want me to try and put myself into a position to buy my own cake. Not a man must be able to look on me and tell me to take off the drawers what he take his good good money and buy give me. No, sir. Leave that to all those let-go beast around Gimme-me-bit, who not under any proper rule and care, and who begin box around from pillar to post from their eye at their knee. Decent somebody like me supposed to got my mind on better things, so that when the time come, me will be ready. For good things come to those who wait.

All like how me could neither seven nor eleven with the General Science it, me was so glad when Freddie offer to come help me with the experiment them what Teacher show we in class at daytime. For Freddie him did got good brain. Sometime when he stay there a-get away into the pistil and stamen, my mind would be there a-run on what Granny did a-cook for dinner. Miss Varry drop by the yard one evening, and catch we a-sit down on the veranda with the *Murchie's Science Reader* spread out between the two of we. So hear her now:

"You smart. Oonoo do well to form like say is schoolwork you out here a-do, when everybody done know long time what young people give. If Miss Tamah know what I know, she better mind how she allow you to stay out late at evening time, say she a-make you take any private class, Miss Girlie. For they got too much bush on the road between here and Free Town School."

Me never have a chance to answer her, for she move off same time to go look for Granny. All the better. For from the look on Freddie face, he did just a-get ready to tell her two fat bad word.

That night, Granny take down with pain worse than ever. From I born, I never hear her groan so much. Me had was to wake up in the middle of the night and make up fire, so as to get her the hot water so that she could rub down good with the Sloan's Liniment. Still for all, she was no better. Next morning, she couldn't even get up out of the bed, the way she take down with pain and bad feeling.

By this time, Emancipation Day was around the corner, and Teacher did a-plan to carry we on outing go to Discovery Bay. All the pickny them in private class did got their mind set on go. Sake of so, all the talk what you would hear at evening time was about what they going wear from what they not going wear. Me, now, did just a-dead to go too. So me beg my friend, Tiny, mother to go ask Granny if she would make me go this time. Granny she come talk 'bout how she can't send me, for like how she never stop me from school, not even when I got sore foot, she a-depend on me this one day to help her out with the washing and ironing.

"I getting old and tired, Miss Minna, and I soon can't manage. So you, Miss Girlie, had better begin catch your practice from now with the looking after yourself."

"True, Miss Tamah," Miss Minna put in. "I quite understand. But I think Girlie could do with the little sea breeze after all these years of keeping her head in the book."

"I know you not going agree with me," Granny turn to me and say. "But I doing this for your own good. You are young bird. You don't know hurricane. All day long you pick up paper, read 'bout how pickny drown at sea. Not a thing more than they take their hard-ears and won't listen to the big people who know more than them. They know they can't swim. But still for all, they will pick up themself and go out into deep water, just to be own-way."

You can imagine how me did grudge all those pickny when me look out and see them a-climb into Maas' Ran truck! And when they begin sing "Flow gently, sweet Afton." Lord! My heart just leave to burst. That whole day, Granny she could not be nicer. Like how she know me love fry dumpling from morning, she get up soon soon and fry up a whole heap, give me for breakfast. Later on now, she cook up one big pot of stew peas. You want to see the amount of pig's tail she did got in there! Still for all, when she see me a-pick pick on the food, hear her now:

"Wait. Me did think say you love stew peas?"

"Yes, Ma. But somehow, my mind don't give me for it today."

"Oh. You just hear what I have to tell you, Miss Girlie. As long as you living under my roof, you going eat up whatsoever I provide so till you can buy your own silken food."

Me did think that everybody who was anybody in Gimme-me-bit did gone to Discovery Bay that day. But lo and behold, when me did a-sit down on veranda, a-crochet one doily, who should step through the gate but Freddie. He come make me know say they a-keep up dance at Burr Common. If me don't want to go?

"You mad, yaa, boy!" me say to him. "If Granny never want send me go to Discovery Bay, is dance she going make me go to?"

"She don't have to know," Freddie him say.

"How you mean? . . . Mm, mm. And like how all these people here so chat-chat, what a bangarang when Granny find out!"

"Cho, man!" Freddie give out. "That is small matters. After all, you can't make your granny keep you here under lock and key like nun forever. You got to break out and start spree your blouse sometime. After all, you only live once. Is holiday. Come on, man. Make we go spread some joy."

You should see me a-fling my foot when the band strike up with "May May!" So hear Freddie him now:

"Stop. Me did think you say you couldn't dance?" But me just laugh and go on move my body in time to the music. That whole night, not a soul never get a chance to come near me, for Freddie make certain that we never miss a tune. But when the crowd start thin out now, me begin get frighten, especially when Freddie start hold me close so that me could hardly breathe. You can imagine the fretration me was under when we did a-walk go back home! With all the try Freddie did a-try to get me to look on the moon, what look like a peeled banana, me, now, couldn't see a thing except my granny a-walk into my room and find out say that the old cloth them what stuff up into the bed was not me. Sure enough, as me take my time creep into the house, who should my eye them make four with, but Granny!

"Yes, Miss Girlie," she give out. "So you a-turn woman on me, eh?! Well, let me tell you. Whether you know it or not, two bull cannot rule into the same pen." With that, she wheel go inside with the lamp, and leave the two of we a-stand up into the dark in the hall. Me did think she gone to her bed. But few minutes' time, she was back on the scene, and begin throw down my clothes them one one. My heart leap same time. Me begin beg and beseech, and tell Granny that we won't do it again. But Granny never have no cool down to cool down, it favor. For she begin beat up her gum 'bout how she try her best. Lord know, she try her best. But is what she do to deserve a crosses like this? It look like some people just born flat-minded. Is she wrong to stay there a-try force the issue, say she a-make something out of me, when all the while, me did a-plan to bring her gray hairs down to the grave. Nowadays pickny stay different, it favor. Don't know what in their best interest. There it is, with all the try she try show me the light, me take my carry-down self and take up man put on my head before time, like say when me get big, me won't got all the time in the world to sport. But if is man me want, me can go on. She wash her hands off me. For God see and know that she try her best.

All this time, Freddie was speechless. But when he see me a-carry on, a-grab on to Granny, and that Granny wasn't out to budge, he bend down and start pick up my clothes them piece by piece. So hear him now:

"Come on, yaa, Girlie. After all, we don't have to stay here listen to this." So that is how me end up a-live with him down at his Aunt Gerzel. The first few years weren't bad. Freddie get a good job as sugar boiler up at Monymusk Estate, and he take care of we as good as ever. After Nicey born though, he start stay out late. Say he can't bear to hear how she just a-bawl bawl like goat. One night now, he never even bother come home at all. Tiny tell me that me mustn't trouble myself too much, for is so man stay. That sooner or later, Freddie will realize that good woman hard to find, and he will soon start behave himself again. So said, so done. The next evening, Mr. Freddie was back on spot with a big bag of bun and cheese for Aunt Gerzel, and a nice dress-length for me and Nicey. All the same, you could stay slap into the kitchen and smell the white rum on his breath.

Since he look as if he was out to turn over a new leaf, me never want to say anything to Mr. Freddie 'bout he and his rum drinking, for fear he stop come home at nighttime again. But the Friday evening when he come in and puke up the place from end to end, me couldn't do better. Especially when me notice say that next morning, he wasn't out to shape up himself. Long after milk truck pass, he still a-laze off into bed.

"Wait," me say to him. "You not going to work today?"

"Just rest me, yaa, woman! Just rest me!" he bellow after me. Aunt Gerzel come in to come find out what happen, when she notice that the tea, what she draw from soon soon, a-get cold on the table. But it look like say Freddie did a-get off his head that morning. For before we know what did a-happen good, he pick up some old shoes and fling them after we. Little 'most he lick out one of Nicey eye.

'Bout midday or so, when the hungry must be bite him, he get up and come out of the room. As he sit down there a-wait for Aunt Gerzel to bring him the roast breadfruit and fry pork, he make me know that he lost the job up at Monymusk. That they had was to lay him off, for the factory a-lose money. You can imagine my distress! Then now, when Aunt Gerzel she come in and see that Freddie face make up like when rain set, she say to him:

"Wait. Maasa, is who eat your white fowl today?" So me make her know what happen.

"Jesus Savior, pilot me!" she let out. "Is how we going manage, eh?"

Same time, Nicey she start bawl for hungry.

"Missis, hush up your mouth!" Aunt Gerzel snap after her.

Me never like how she bawl after my pickny, so me take her to task 'bout it. So she turn on me now, and begin make me know how me is an old Jezebel, who only know how to lead people good good pickny astray. If Freddie did only listen to her all along, he wouldn't be in this pickle today. By now, he would be a big big man, with his own property and all. But no. He take his careless, and gone mix up with a dirty-foot girl, who only know how to drag him down into the gutter with her. Is the same thing she did a-say to Freddie all along. Don't walk 'bout, eat eat at people place. For you never know what they set into their victual for you. Is that old witch me got for a granny, who put me up to catch the one decent boy-pickny in the whole of Gimme-me-bit. And there it is, me blight his prospects by giving him baby. Who to tell, the baby is not even for Freddie. For who knows what me did up to at daytime when me say me did a-go down to Miss Minna to go learn to sew!

Since me wasn't out to stay there and make anybody take step with me, I find myself into the room, and gather up the few piece of things what belong to me. And then I pawn my pickny, and waltz straight through the door. Granny she never even look shocked to see me. She only murmur something to the effect that she surprised that it take me so long to come back, for she never see how the whole of we hold into that little bird-nest, what Miss Gerzel call house. But now that me come home, me won't have to worry 'bout a thing again, for everything that she own in this world belong to me and me one.

So we stay there and stay there, so till Nicey she turn big woman. Yes, sir. That's right. A-take private class and all. In fact, see her here right now, a-come through the gate. But Jesus wept! This is something to hurt anybody.

"Girl! Is where you going?! You don't see that I got bands of things in here for you to do?!"

Stay here, a-hackle up myself so that the pickny will be in a position to buy her own cake. But no. Instead of pay attention to her book, so that she can position herself when the break come, she can't find a thing better to do than a-walk on road with headman boy!

"Girl! Don't you got bands of schoolwork to do?!" But Nicey, like say she turn deaf all of a sudden. For she just run inside to come put down her book. And then she wheel her tail and gone back outside to her Sonny.

Mis' Lou

by JACQUELYN FURGUS HUNTER

Mis' Lou
Sunny as a poui
Smiling, singing
And humming
And
Limping hipshorted about
Doing her chores

She greets
The passersby
With a chirruppy
"Good Morning"
"Good Afternoon"
"Good Night."

Her gray kinky hair
Is sprinkled with
Black
All of it is neatly circled
On her small pea-shaped head
In rows of very
Little plaits.

Her apron is tied
Around her narrow waist
And a pair of white canvas shoes
Hug her little feet.
She moves about busily
Preparing for the day
And for business.

She takes the
Light green and cream covering
From the corn
Except for the husks.

Her iron coal-pot
Is filled with coals
And chips of wood
Nestle in the middle

CARTY

Rick Powell

Leo Carty

Leo Carty

Of the black charcoal
Ready for the pitch-oil
And match.

She lights up the coal pot
And fans it to a glowing
Orange and amber flame.
Mis' Lou sets
Her square steel-meshed
Strip of wire
Above the burning
Coal-pot of embers.

Then she rests the
Husked corn gently
In a neat line
On top of the wire
And she perches
On a wooden crate
With her flowered
Cotton dress and apron
Tucked between
Her thighs.
She bends toward the corns
Ready to tend them.

She turns the corns
Carefully and lovingly
As she watches them
Roast on the wire
Sending out a crackle and a pop
And small sparks of flame.
They get brown and browner
And slightly black.

The corns are roasted
And need to be shifted.
She rests them
Near the edge of
The wire netting
Away from the hot fire
So that they can be
Warm and juicy.

They are cooked
And waiting
To be bought
By the hungry strollers
Who want
To nibble
And chew
A freshly
Roasted corn.

Arah: One

by MARVIN WILLIAMS

West indian woman, antigua's pride
when you smile quiet craters form
detailed magics
on your mellow mango cheeks,

in my bowels there is a gurgling
gasp & frenzy bubbling—a tropical
shark surfacing for islands' breath;

i say introvert pores open
their doors to excited oils, vulnerably
as hibiscus yawning to come awake.

Arah: Two

diners, we met
over maubi and patteh

in june
heated like desire, ebony
eyes sang my name.

as moons
we sat through nights'
black and white moods

swaying on viney lines
like ripe soursaps
in bloom.

tonight your calypso embrace drugs
me
a patient
i'm strengthened by the politics
transfused into my blood.

Letter to the Lady #3

by MARVIN WILLIAMS

lady when i talk to you
i talk to islands &
islands of nostalgia come
blowing virgin sustenance
like trade winds
through my mind's ivy disturbance.

a fig tree grows bananas
a pear tree grows avocadoes
st. croix grows americans &
everywhere the preacher went
colonization was sure to go.

antigua lives
richly in your cane-giggles &
lends its fried-plantain scent
to our love's calypso aroma.
thinking of the island that is you
arah i can visualize
the flirtatious smile of a belly-full
papaya calculating coquettishly
on a green stem in the carib sun.

feeling at home
i blow my snotty nose
in the blue sea water
that clears my head.

Arah: Five

beneath a sea-grape tree
on magens bay
we slept at noon
with laughter as lullaby &
our bodies, pillows.

broken by calypso chatter
our sleep sulked away.
deep wrinkles &

dreams were ironed out
in rhythm
with our ha-ha cadences.
we're standing in annaly
bay's valley, a fertile field—
we feel scents
fruiting into our blood's nose—it is
holy-water:

a soursap hangs
from a straining stem,
throws its ripe weight
against the wall of air &
flexes its aromatic muscle
like an enticing bully.

cracked mespels shoot
sun-simmered sugar out,
halt working red ants'
colony for a lunch break &
gives us our name—afro
west indians.

Arah: Six

dawn wind drips dew
drops through tree-leaves
where we sit
waiting for seven-thirty.

the casanova sun
hiccups between rainclouds' pursuit—
rain, like a relief
pitcher has been warming up
all night, procrastinating
we weren't.

a young female
voice tumbles
down the hill over us,
somersaults and deposits
dana into our ears:
dana mocks marc,

worries wayne into waking &
tickles our kisses into breaking
apart with laughter.

seven-thirty ticks
in your eyes' fear—
the people will be
passing our love-bench soon.

soon as they come honey
child i want us to sit
down like glue on our love,
i want us to enjoy
their stares' heavy embarrassment.

Poem for a Rasta Daughter

by MARVIN WILLIAMS

sea bath, sun drying
soil for bed, food
is bread and butter,
peanut, bean and banana
is herb all you want
they wonder

crocus bag, dress rag-
gedy headrag, handbag
hand without lotion

no need for drug
stores live in coconut
oil for smooth healing
at no cost
the cast waits on a calypso
climber up the womb of culture

canebrake, cane sugar
carrot cake, bake
brown sugar
maybe maubi or
boiled down ginger
beer from the earth

no car, only car
tire for shoes—
you buy no want
no credit, no longer
do they give you any

since you've shed that pale
shadow calling you
lovely in a distorted tongue

you've skank out your island
reggae and smile when i call
you black

Angela Davis

by NICOLÁS GUILLÉN

I have not come to tell you you are lovely. That you are beautiful I do believe but that is not what it is all about. The matter is they wish that you were dead. They need your scalp to grace the Big Chief's collection together with the bodies of Jackson and Lumumba.

Angela, where we are concerned, we need your smile.

We're going to change for you the walls which hate has built for the transparent walls of air. Change the roof of your anguish for a sky of clouds and birds. Change the guard who hides you for an archangel with his sword.

How your hangmen are just deceiving themselves; you are made of a burning and tough substance force that can't be used up—capable of enduring through suns and rains, through winds and moons in the open air.

You belong to that class of dreams in which time has always founded its statues and written its songs. Angela, I am not using your name directly to speak to you of love like an adolescent nor to desire you as a satyr; that is not what it is all about. What I am saying is that you are strong and plastic to leap at the neck fracturing it of those who have wanted and still want, will always want to see you burn alive tied to the South of your country. Tied to a charred post. Tied to an oak without foliage. Tied to a cross burning alive, tied to the South.

The enemy is sluggish. He wants to silence your voice with his own, but we all know that your voice is the only one which sounds out, the only one which flames high in the night like a blazing column, a sustained beam of light.

An upright scorching fire, repeated stabbing light in whose glare dance again negroes with burning fingernails, peoples unprotected and full of anger.

From within the Utopia where I live, linked by the business like militia to the bitter edge of this terrible but friendly sea, seeing furious waves break themselves on the wall I cry, and make my voice travel on the shoulders of the eventful hurricane my wind, our Caribbean father.

I call your name, Angela, at the top of my voice. I put my hands together not in requests, prayers, supplications, plagiaries, that your jailers pardon you, but in the act of applause, hand on hand, hard and strong–very strong—hand on hand, so that you may know that I am yours.

The 7:25 Trolley

by MARI EVANS

ain't got time for a bite to eat
I'll have to catch my trolley at the end of the block
and if I take
my coffee
there
she looks at the cup and she looks at the clock
        (Sure hope I don't miss my car . . .

my house looks like a hurricane
if I did what I ought to do I'd stay at home today
I can't eat no
hurricane
broke as I am I need what she will pay
        (Hope I just don't miss my car . . .

wish my life was a life of ease
a main cook and butler runnin' at my beck and call
I may scrub floors
but
I don't
get on my knees . . .
and someday
I won't go at all
        (Sure hope I don't miss my car . . .

Lineage

by MARGARET WALKER

My grandmothers were strong.
They followed plows and bent to toil.
They moved through fields sowing seed.
They touched earth and grain grew.
They were full of sturdiness and singing.
My grandmothers were strong.

My grandmothers are full of memories
Smelling of soap and onions and wet clay
With veins rolling roughly over quick hands
They have many clean words to say.
My grandmothers were strong.
Why am I not as they?

The Women Gather

by NIKKI GIOVANNI

for Joe Strickland

the women gather
because it is not unusual
to seek comfort in our hours of stress
   a man must be buried
it is not unusual
that the old bury the young
   though it is an abomination
it is not strange
that the unwise and the ungentle
carry the banner of humaneness
   though it is a castration of the spirit
it no longer shatters the intellect
that those who make war
call themselves diplomats
we are no longer surprised
that the unfaithful pray loudest
every sunday in every church
and sometimes in rooms facing east
   though it is a sin and a shame
   so how do we judge a man
most of us love from our need to love not
because we find someone deserving
most of us forgive because we have trespassed not
because we are magnanimous
most of us comfort because we need comforting
our ancient rituals demand that we give
what we hope to receive
   and how do we judge a man
we learn to greet when meeting
to cry when parting
and to soften our words at times of stress
the women gather
with cloth and ointment
their busy hands bowing to laws that decree

willows shall stand swaying but unbroken
against even the determined wind of death
  we judge a man by his dreams
not alone his deeds
  we judge a man by his intent
not alone his shortcomings
  we judge a man because it is not unusual
to know him through those who love him
the women gather strangers
to each other because
they have loved a man
it is not unusual to sift
through ashes
and find an unburnt picture

10:15 A.M.—April 27, 1969

poem

by SONIA SANCHEZ

and
        every thing
                that is any
                   thing
begins again.
             stops
                   to make a left turn
at one/way/streets.
                      and the self
                                becomes reduced
in time to the nothingness of this
white/assed/universe
              and down/the/cheek/tears
flow south/ward
           to the womb
                      buryen
a wild/nigguh/woman's dreams
in
     bamboo madness.

Southlands
The Double Year

by NATHANIEL JOHNSON

She enters what most of night has left us
joining, cleaving the chrome-plated
junked-up intermission
in two. She has the sleek, closed form of a 1959 Invicta
        but her raised head, flared hips & her pliant torso
throb: an earlier Corvette
waiting to make-up time beneath
an obstinate, dim-witted red light, expressing
anxiety
        & assurance: a ballast of vapor partly docks
an essential musk, aloof like borrowed crystal,
a public dusk finally in union she uses to polarize
& select the slow, deeper night, rumbling at equipoise:
                                        "Things
of beauty, grace & speed," quoth Alfalfa,
"are usually referred to as she."
                        DIG IT,
the last intermission. before the last set.
the last night. of the class re union. dig it,
everybody's warm & ready, circulating
mates, dudes, ladies, done with circulating,
drift to warm seats
where a companion or competition sat before.
The band: All the way from Vicksburg, the REDD TOPPS:
digg itt, exhaling their liquid & gaseous deliberations
charmingly, manlily (,) go into red jackets,
strip-off little riffs from musical wads
like five-dollar bills: WE'RE GONNA GIT Y'ALL DOWN:
TONITE:
        The class griot, voted most likely to suc-
ceed, picks his way beneath a leopard-skin cap,
& with his great shilelagh: xok xok xok,
announces:
        STODDARD. Jamesetta Lucille.
of Henri & Mary. once wedded to Wally Wilkinson.

No kids. Yet. No debts. Has been the owner of
a Nova. a Skylark. a Sedan de Ville. Has, taken from the horizon,
a steel-gray Mercedes. Owner of Six Apartments in Detroit.
Possesses the eye of an old banker. Everybody now,
Rise & Dance. Rise & Dance.

Cleaning out the Closet

by MAE JACKSON

I was standing there, on the outside, with a cigarette in my hand. I had no particular reason for being there 'cept I like looking through the window at the lives of other people.

I am a writer and my job is to record what I see. I am a storyteller from way back when. This story that I am about to tell you was given to me along with the stipulation that I "pass it on."

Her name is Cindy. She is tall but not "too" tall. I can tell by the titles of the books that line her walls that once she wore an Afro.

She is sitting on the side of the bed looking the way people often look after they've made some important decision.

On the bedroom floor is a very large map of the world. I strain myself pulling closer to the window so that I might understand the sadness I see in this woman's back.

Now sitting on the floor, at the foot of the map, Cindy takes out a pencil and closing her eyes as if she doesn't want to see, she points.

"That's it . . . that's where I'll go," she says out loud as if someone else other than her pain was there in the room to hear her.

More determined than ever, she moves again. Realizing the importance of finding some place to go, she folds the map and places it on the night table. This woman is in love. I can tell by how bad she looks. It has something to do with the taking care of someone else and the neglecting of one's own self. I swear I am tempted to say something to her. Instead I remain outside of her window looking in and smoking still another cigarette.

Cindy rolls a joint. It's that good shit. I can smell it from out here. At a time like this, a time when a woman can find no conversation at "The First Baptist Church," a joint can make a world of difference.

I'd once thought about giving up smoking (cigarettes, that is), until I discovered it was all I had to hold on to. I sometimes awaken in the middle of the night needing someone to talk to.

Needing someone to hold on to. When all else fails me, I know I can reach out for a cigarette and it will be there.

The apartment that Cindy lives in knows her better than all her friends. She has lived here ten years, or more. Cindy's life has been so difficult that once even the walls couldn't take it any longer and had begun to peel and crack. And the plaster had started to fall. If those walls could talk, ain't no telling what kind of stories they would tell. All the memories, all the pain of this child's life, right here in this one place and because they cannot move away from her she must now move away from it.

Her closet is filled with the smell of moth balls and perfume. The smell of something old and something new. As Cindy approaches the closet she realizes for what must be the fifth time today, it is difficult, always, to remove anything for the very last time. The adding of something is always the easier of the tasks. Often we do so without thought of the consequences. It is the taking away—the subtraction—that causes the problems. Cindy has removed her luggage from the top shelf of the closet. Placing them on her bed, she opens one. The smell of her last trip rises to greet her as she brushes away the tears. Not because she doesn't want to cry but because this is a day of seeing. Back to the closet. Always back. Cindy pulls from the hanger a low-cut green evening dress. It had been one of her favorites. She recalls wearing it the night she had met Skeet.

Skeet had been a sailor. A tall and handsome man. A strong man who had the kind of strength that protected; perhaps this had been a part of her attraction to him.

Cindy was a dancer. She was agile and precise. She was the color of a Hershey candy bar and her breasts were no more than a mouthful. In all of that she had been good to him. So good to him that Skeet, reflecting on a night he and Cindy had spent together, had smilingly asked another sailor, "Have you ever made love to a dancer?"

His sailor friend shook his head no, he had never made love to a dancer. That had been a long, long time ago. She'd almost forgotten Skeet, or thought she had. Pain subsides but it never goes away, no matter what we might think. So today. A very sad day in the life of Cindy, she had come across all the things she had placed in the back of her heart, or had either tucked away some place in the back of her closet behind the newer clothes and trinkets. This shit was getting heavy. Cindy lit another joint. This one being just as good as the first, if only it would last longer, then this packing and stuff would be all over with.

There isn't much of a story to tell about Cindy and Skeet. He had said he loved her deeply. Cindy had said the same. Skeet had asked her to marry him and she had said yes. They became engaged. One day Skeet sailed away to a place called Vietnam. She was eighteen. He was nineteen. Neither understood.

Some seven months later she received a telegram. It was over, this young man's life. She was nineteen. He would have been twenty.

. . . and there it was. The white dress. Not the kind you see in the fashion magazines. It was a poor version of an expensive dream. She had saved herself for the man she loved, and Skeet had taken her with so much tenderness. Together they had sung life's first sweet song. It was entitled, "Every Evening When the Sun Goes Down." That white dress had cost $89. It had been the most expensive dress she owned. Cindy had wanted it to last a lifetime and sad enough it had. That green dress. That white dress—a painful ensemble. She'd thought about leaving it behind. Deciding against that, she packed it away, along with the joy and pain of having loved someone so very much that the thought of not having it near was far more than she could bear. Cindy had been tempted to ask, "Why me?" She knew that life's answer would probably be, "Why not you?" There are some things better left unasked.

At twenty-one she pushed the pain aside to join the many young men and women who filled the streets shouting, "Hell no, I won't go." It was a personal movement for her. Very personal.

For a long time I could not decide what I wanted to become. A writer or a storyteller. I selected the latter. In doing so I don't have to be bothered with periods. Or commas, or new paragraphs. All I have to do is tell the story. . . .

"A taste of white wine would be good. Something light and dry," she thought to herself as she placed a crystal wineglass to chill in the freezer compartment of her refrigerator. Cindy had grown to become the perfect picture of sophisticated lady and what was in her heart today was nobody's business. Tasting the white wine made her feel all warm inside and a bit high. Cindy had been saving this wine for a very special occasion, for the day her man would be released from prison. There was no need to preserve it any longer. He was coming home, but not to her. He didn't have to tell her this, women have a sixth sense about this kind of thing, and she knew from a feeling that had started from the pit of her stomach and had rushed to the throat, it was over. Cindy sipped the wine and leaned against the wall that had known her better than all her friends. She cried and the walls heard it all and did not move one iota of an inch. They understood.

It had been four years since Cindy had been introduced to Michael. A friend had suggested that she correspond with him and had given her this man's prison address. For four years Cindy attempted to live in two worlds. His and hers. It had been hard. Just thinking about it made her light up another joint. This was her third. Michael had said he was a revolutionary. Cindy had never known one. She was impressed. At last she had found someone committed to loving and not hurting. In time they grew close. They grew into what is commonly called love. The exchanging of letters between them was really the story of two people writing out the final chapters of their lives. Each becoming the other's critic. Most of her friends had come out and said point blank that in the end he would only hurt her. One friend had said to her, "Let me ask you one honest question. When that man gets out of jail, do you really think he's coming home to you?"

"Yes, I do," replied Cindy. Deep inside, that question had bothered her. Why do people always want to be honest at the wrong time?

Cindy's reaching out to Michael had something to do with her understanding of loneliness. In a very small and insignificant way she had tried to take a bit of her outside world into his inside world. That was not so bad, was it? No. Not if you are the storyteller. Not if you are the one listening to the story. It's bad, meaning the pain, if you happen to be one of the characters in the story.

My legs are tired. My back has started to ache. Still I am going to stand here, outside of this window, and watch this drama unfold. If I see where this is not going to end well for Cindy, I am going to step in and write her a happy ending. That's the advantage of being a writer. Even if you aren't in control of the beginnings, you can at least help write a fairly decent ending. That's the way it should be.

Then it happened just as she had anticipated it would. Michael stopped writing . . . no more letters . . . no more nothing. No one was at fault, not really. You can't blame Michael. He had never touched Cindy. He had never experienced her body movements. He had never known her to be a real person. If he had known the smell of her breath. If he had seen her suffering with her monthly cramps. If Michael had known about the time she tried to insert that damn diaphragm and how after applying all that gooey jelly the diaphragm had popped out of her hand landing on the bathroom ceiling, then maybe, just maybe things would have been different.

So this is the moment of truth. Try as she may to escape it, it was there before her eyes. Cindy and Michael's love had been a paper love, not so much for her as it had been for him. Michael would, of course, deny this but the truth of what it had meant to him had never gone any further than the boxes of letters tucked in the back of Cindy's closet.

Today. This very sad day of packing found her removing the boxes of letters. This was all she had to show, and rereading them again would not change anything. She'd thought about taking them with her, but no. It was over, so why pretend? She deposits the letters in the garbage can and sets them afire. As they burn Cindy stands there watching four years of something she cannot define go up in smoke. It was a very difficult thing for her to do. She was trying to be rational and mature about the whole matter. Her life was going to be different now that she had cleaned out her closet. In the process of burning up the letters she almost burned herself. Pots and pots of water, along with the fresh tears, puts out the fire in her life. The kitchen floor is flooded and that doesn't matter at all. For once in her life let her be the one to leave a mess for someone to clean up.

I haven't any idea what Cindy was in her previous life. I am hoping that in her reincarnation she returns as a tornado, for obvious reasons. She has told no one that she is leaving. Cindy did not need a chorus line bidding her farewell to the tune of "I Told You So." A simple fanfare of nothing would be okay.

We as human beings sometimes make our own battles hard to

fight. Cindy would try to avoid this. What happened? I don't know. I am just a storyteller. I cannot explain love's failures. If I could, then I would have done more than any of you. All that needs to be said is that she loved the man. Let Cindy drink her wine. Smoke her herb. Let her awaken in the morning with a headache instead of a heartache.

Cindy sits in a position known only to dancers. From her purse she takes out a twenty-five-dollar fountain pen. She has such good taste in things. Such poor taste in men. What the hell, it's only life. For a dancer to lose a leg is not the worst thing that could happen. It is when the dancer has lost the feeling of movement.

For a writer to lose a pen or paper is not the worst thing to happen. It is when the writer has lost the ability to see, to feel, to hear a story.

Cindy begins to compose her last letter to Michael. Let her if it'll make her feel better.

Dear Michael:

When I assumed you loved me I guess I assumed too much. I am blinded not so much by what I see but what I have chosen to see. And you are gone not because I loved you too little but because I loved you too much.

Yesterday's shoes were too tight. Today they fit. Yesterday it was a love song. Today it's the blues. Today I am here. Tomorrow I'll be gone.

When I assumed you loved me I assumed too much.

Good-bye,
Cindy

Cindy continues to sit. She is trying to put the pieces together. She asks out loud, "What is love . . . is love when your heart beats real fast?"

I tap softly on the window to reply, "No. That's a heart attack."

"Is love when you give all of yourself?"

Again I reply, "No. That's a favor."

"Well, tell me this," Cindy asks. "Is love when you find you can't live without a certain person?"

I reply, "No. That's a widow."

"Oh, I see," said Cindy, in a very childlike voice. "Love is when you think you've found the right person?"

Again I reply, "No. That's discovery."

"Am I getting warm?" she wanted to know. "Just answer this. When you wake up in the middle of the night feeling your body drenched in sweat, what is that?"

I smile before I answer, "That's dreaming."

"Is love when you want to spend the rest of your life with some-one?"

"No, Cindy," I tell her patiently. "That's called moving in."

"What the hell is love?"

I say nothing at all.

Cindy understood. It was over. Final. She completed packing her shit. Removing the fur coat her best friend, Anna, had given to her as a birthday gift. Cindy was leaving behind nothing she wanted to take. The past and all it represented would be left there in the apartment. She would no longer cry over her answered prayers. There was someone waiting for her in much the same way as she had waited seven months and then finally four years. She had cleaned out the closet of her life and now things would be different.

I am tired from standing out here watching Cindy through the window. I climb inside and lie on her bed sipping the dry wine and smoking the unfinished joint Cindy had left behind.

You see, I told you I'd write a happy ending.

Alice

by PAULETTE CHILDRESS WHITE

Alice. Drunk Alice. Alice of the streets. Of the party. Of the house of dark places. From whom without knowing I hid love all my life behind remembrances of her house where I went with Momma in the daytime to borrow things, and we found her lounging in the front yard on a dirty plastic lawn chair drinking warm beer from the can in a little brown bag. Where flies buzzed in and out of the always open door of the house as we followed her into the cool, dim, rank-smelling rooms for what it was we'd come. And I fought frowns as my feet caught on the sticky gray wooden floor but looked up to smile back at her smile as she gave the dollar or the sugar or the coffee to Momma, who never seemed to notice the floor or the smell or Alice.

Alice, tall like a man, with soft woolly hair spread out in tangles like a feathered hat and her face oily and her legs ashy, whose beauty I never quite believed because she valued it so little but was real. Real like wild flowers and uncut grass, real like the knotty sky-reach of a dead tree. Beauty of warm brown eyes in a round dark face and of teeth somehow always white and clean and of lips moist and open, out of which rolled the voice and the laughter, deep and breathless, rolling out the strong and secret beauty of her soul.

Alice of the streets. Gentle walking on long legs. Close-kneed. Careful. Stopping sometimes at our house on her way to unknown places and other people. She came wearing loose flowered dresses and she sat in our chairs rubbing the too-big knees that sometimes hurt, and we gathered, Momma, my sisters, and I, to hear the beautiful bad-woman talk and feel the rolling laughter, always sure that she left more than she came for. I accepted the tender touch of her hands on my hair or my face or my arms like favors I never returned. I clung to the sounds of her words and the light of her smiles like stolen fruit.

Alice, mother in a house of dark places. Of boys who fought each other and ran cursing through the wild back rooms where I did not go alone but sometimes with Alice when she caught them up and knuckled their heads and made them cry or hugged them close to her, saying funny things to tease them into laughter. And of the oldest son, named for his father, who sat twisted into a wheel chair by sunny windows in the front where she stayed with him for hours giving him her love, filling him with her laughter, and he sat there straining his words, which were difficult but soft and warm like the sun from the windows.

Alice of the party. When there was not one elsewhere she could make one of the evenings when her husband was not storming the dim rooms in drunken fits or lying somewhere in darkness filling the house with angry grunts and snores before the days he would go to work. He'd sit near her drinking beer with what company was there—was always sure to come—greedy for Alice and her husband, who leaned into and out of each other, talking hard and laughing loud and telling lies and being real. And there were rare and wonderously wicked times when I was caught there with Daddy, who was one of the greedy ones and could not leave until the joy-shouting, table-slapping arguments about God and Negroes, the jumping up and down, the bellowing "what about the time" talks, the boasting and reeling of people drunk with beer and laughter and the ache of each other was over and the last ones sat talking sad and low, sick with themselves and too much beer. I watched Alice growing tired and ill and thought about the boys who had eaten dinners of cake and soda pop from the corner store, and I struggled to despise her for it against the memory of how, smiling, they'd crept off to their rooms and slept in peace. And later, at home, I, too, slept strangely safe and happy, hugging the feel of that sweet fury in her house and in Alice of the party.

Alice, who grew older as I grew up but stayed the same while I grew beyond her, away from her. So far away that once, on a clear early morning in the spring, when I was eighteen and smart and clean on my way to work downtown in the high-up office of my government job, with eyes that would not see, I cut off her smile and the sound of her voice calling my name. When she surprised me on a clear spring morning, on her way somewhere or from somewhere in the streets and I could not see her beauty, only the limp flowered dress and the tangled hair and the face puffy from too much drinking and no sleep, I cut off her smile. I let my eye slide away to say without speaking that I had grown beyond her. Alice, who had no place to grow in but was deep in the soil that fed me.

It was eight years before I saw Alice again and in those eight years Alice had buried her husband and one of her boys and lost the oldest son to the county hospital where she traveled for miles to take him the sun and her smiles. And she had become a grandmother and a member of the church and cleaned out her house and closed the doors. And in those eight years I had married and become the mother of sons and did not always keep my floors clean or my hair combed or my legs oiled and I learned to like the taste of beer and how to talk bad-woman talk. In those eight years life had led me to the secret laughter.

Alice, when I saw her again, was dressed in black, after the funeral of my brother, sitting alone in an upstairs bedroom of my mother's house, her face dusted with brown powder and her gray-streaked hair brushed back into a neat ball and her wrinkled hands rubbing the tight-stockinged, tumor-filled knees and her eyes quiet and sober when she looked at me where I stood at the top of the stairs. I had run up to be away from the smell of food and the crowd of comforters come to help bury our dead when I found Alice sitting alone in black and was afraid to smile remembering how I'd cut off her smile when I thought I had grown beyond her and was afraid to speak because there was too much I wanted to say.

Then Alice smiled her same smile and spoke my name in her same voice and rising slowly from her tumored knees said, "Come on in and sit with me."

And for the very first time, I did.

Ritual

by OKOYO LOVING

Yes, she'd seen it all before
the boozed up dreams
the acid crashes
the sex diseases . . . and three abortions
the singles bar
and the beer parties in the all girls dorms.

her graduate degrees did not save her from
the dirty sheets piled up in the corners of her loveless life
or the bodies sleeping next to her, lying half-cocked
whose health she hardly trusted
and whose draining pumping motions gave her no release
as she fingered the bud that nestled aroused between her lips.

her eyes are sunless valleys as she prepares herself for morning,
wakes him before the kids are conscious
and wipes and flushes out

the cups in her sink are memories of clay

somewhere between trapped and stranded, between maintenance
 and survi-
val, unconnected, dissipated, and rupturing from acquaintances
she cleans his hair from her sink, and shakes her head
and dresses her best, neatly and puts on make-up.

let's see what tomorrow will bring and she faces the world
goes through the motions of eating brown rice and gardening
her harmless vegetables, and taking disco lessons from her
daughters . . . and faithfully does her yoga and never eats meat.
And here we go again . . . the ritual
Cause her finely sculptured body and gentle hands do not
excuse her from pain
or the hateness and hurtness from embraces unremembered
or erratic and rootless passion he calls love but is really
conquest and meaningless thrashings on meaningless mattresses
and sometimes meaningless money to take the edges away.

And this time, grateful for the come
She still nudges him awake
and showers for an hour.
And only then does she sleep.

Women's Lib

by MARGARET DANNER

Everyone knows how much I admire
beautiful women,
but I don't want to open my own doors
and certainly don't want to see
any woman change a tire
and no matter how elegant she might be
There is no woman who can light my fire

Sundown Sigh

by MELBA JOYCE BOYD

If you own
your soul
the mornings come
heavy
and the nights
become sweet
surrender.

The touch
of a goodbye kiss
smooths
our moves
seeking through
thick lies
hoping to spit us
into the sidewalk
like gum
chewed flat
and placid
to the tongue.
with weed on ice
the good humor man
passes through smoke
deciphering
sex and the virgin birth;
credit cards
and Santa Claus;
greasy ladies
beating babies; and
poor people paying
Reverend Ike on TV
praying
the streets into gold.

meanwhile . . .
the parasitic
keeps pushing

Coca-Cola in Soweto
and the water's
gone wrong.

Inside the shit
of the day
I cannot find
my smile.
but the hush
of sundown
wraps us
soundly
around
our nakedness
away from yesterday
with whispers
of a Tanzanian
twilight.

Lovesong for Rochelle

by KENNETH A. McCLANE

When always I come to ask you
  the firethorn, sweetflag and arrow-
head
  show me to the windy
ridgehaunt
  and like a landed sailor
knowing the taints
  of wind & vice
I wander
  like a covey of starlings

And downslope
  the light
burns a disk of possibility
    on the shoaly windwater
and I think of the precious providence
  (Clothos, Lachesis and harrowing (shearful)
    Atropos) that has roused me:

Oh, evensong
windfall
magnolia limbs of children
Oh small
troutlily, spineless
rock ivy
Oh
burdened wheatear
lying in the bulk
of song

And barely has the light
  become a raft—a canoe
when a man
  downs from the landing
to row us:

promising in the throat
  he says:

come before the water
muscles
and the wind
spoils
our thin rafting: come

And as the light
sinks in the juneberry
he pulls into the dark.

cracked

by GLORIA GAYLES

seven years ago
or more
we heated it in the intensity of our dreams
making it strong and shatterproof
that it would endure
against tremors
                    and quakes
                              and explosions
carefully planned

with tears from eyes
that had seen the vision
we polished it
shined it
cleared it of streaks
                    and blurs
                              and distortions
expertly drawn

and then
in jubilation
we dressed for it
we scrubbed our skin
clean of paints and creams
that run when tears fall
and circles of red that become
displaced when tight-skinned faces
wrinkle for thick-lipped smiles
and
we grew Afros for it
tilling them well
until each strand of hair
was a natural harp playing
the melody of true reflections

in seven years
or more
we are again

as before
a people of pomades and hot metal
a people whose eyes are lined in pastels
whose lips speak frosted words

even our men
sit under steel bonnets
and emerge in tight grease curls
that carry a sickening fragrance
and
our children
seeing us
hold Barbie dolls tightly
and dress them as queens
in a wardrobe of Fifth-Avenue originals
in miniature

for seven years
or more
no one asked questions about our beauty
for we were clear reflections of the answer

today
the mirror is cracked
and we will wander
through seven years
of harsh distortions

Sometimes as Women Only

by GLORIA GAYLES

we know the hard heavy pull of
weights riveted to our dreams
and yet
sometimes as women only
do we gasp in narrow spaces
and remain locked behind walls
too rough for etchings from our soul

we are new queens of ebony
celebrating ourselves in
diadems of natural beauty
feeling the swing of large gold hoops
around our tight-skinned smoothness
walking a regal dance and singing the music
of a clear struggle that names us well

but
as women
we are sometimes marked beyond adornment
for we have seen white lines run
east west north south cracking on our flesh
like earthquakes that no longer tremor
and we have felt the pressure of rigid staves
peaking breasts grown limp from the pull
of hungry mouths we alone can feed
we
are
fragile figurines
whose neurosis comes and goes
with the pull of the moon

black sturdy shoulders
we are monuments that refuse to crumble
deep-rooted oaks from which the generations
like thick-leaved branches grow and thrive
we are the strong ones
having balanced the weight of the tribe
having made our planting as deep as any man's

and yet
as women
we have known only meager harvests
we sing strong songs
and the world hums a sweet lullaby
we write rich poems
and the world offers muted applause
for a jingling rhyme

sometimes
as women only
do we weep
we are taught to whisper
when we wish to scream
assent
when we wish to defy
dance pretty
        (on tiptoe)
when we would raise circles of dust
before the charge

Parade

by GLORIA GAYLES

from the laps of women
who have known hard toil
the very young dangle
mosquito pinched legs
greased to a Sunday shine

the women talk of sun strokes
and open black umbrellas
too torn for storms
and sit on cushions of newspaper
Friday's fish frying did not use

through Woolworth lenses
they watch the dance of passion
of girls in Argo-stiff skirts
and boys in tight-creased jeans
who are not old enough to count
the mouths that must be fed

a drumroll
the first chord of a fast allegro
and the parade begins
under plastic pennants of red/white/blue
the women watch the marchers
costumed in braids of gold
and the thick-calfed queens painted in
Revlon smiles
and the easy leaders propped in moving chrome
bowing distinguished beads
now left   now right

confetti falls
eager small hands loose
pastel circles of helium to a southern sky
and the parade promenades to the viewing box
where professional potentates sit cool
awarding crepe paper crowns
now left   now right

the women watch the parade
knowing that their lives have been
slow dirges
they have never stepped high to joyous rhythms
never worn costumes of gold
or felt the gentle pressure of crowns
all their lives
it seems
they have been uniforms in white
polishing jewels for emaciated queens
and yet
each year
they pack their bag lunches
and travel ten blocks
to a concrete space on a Beale Street curb

they watch the parade
with its commercial symbols of empty success
and they dream
for their young

Turning Corners

by LYNN SURUMA

You know the problem:
Change and move
To switch the tracks
Confound the train
of events
Your killer-time must
Catch you
first.

Following behind
Necessarily
makes time a watcher
of moves.

We reject the new
For fear
we'll hate the old
pieces of our/selves
Grafted on to memory.

But, the new will be
Old, eventually.
Old/New just
Signposts and Magic people
lighting your tracking imprints
Footprints in the shaking sand.

In a Minute

by ROBERT ALVIN BELL

A black woman on a bus
no one to talk to—
5:15

Her face like a raisin
aged, kind nothing new
5:16

I speak, her face aglow
Her tongue responds
5:17

She understands—I know
Life is a mystery. Don't run
5:20

She gives me a cake. Thanks
Here is my picture–just one
5:21

She tells me to visit her
Summer words and she calls me son
5:31

I talk of my family. She tells me
of hers. Her tears meet my eyes
5:36

Through traffic my street comes
I remember—I rise
5:47

She rises also. Her legs weak
with age. I help—A horn cries
5:51

The bus departs—she sits
on a bench. Good-bye
5:53

She waits for the next bus
A Georgian dusk—Another ride
6:00

From "The Book of Life"
by HAKI R. MADHUBUTI

36
Only fools limit their women.
the full potential of a nation
cannot be realized unless the
full potential of its women
is realized.
only fools limit their women.

37
a nation cannot grow without its women
the intelligence of a nation
is reflected in its women
who bear the children for the nation
and are charged with the early education of the nation.
a nation cannot have intelligent women
unless the women are treated intelligently
and given much love.

38
The substance and mental attitude of a nation
can be seen in its women, in the way they act
and move throughout the nation being productive.
if the women have nothing to do it reflects
what the nation is not doing.
If the women have substance and are given responsible positions
the nation has substance and is responsible.

39
If a woman covers herself with paints
of blues, reds, grays and yellows
she unknowing kills her skin,
she unknowingly smothers life from the first layer covering.
to paint a flower white that is naturally red is to
close its breathing pores and interrupt its natural skin growth
the flower will soon die.
to paint black skin green, orange and other colors
is to display black skin as something that
should be hidden from the actual world
and slowly suffocated from life.

40

It is normal
for man to look at woman
but
it is abnormal to look
at woman the way we
have been taught to
look at her in the western world.

The Neighborhood
A Short Story
by BETTY DE RAMUS

I'm half-asleep, but I can hear Irene. She's in the back yard cursing Woody, letting her voice rise above the morning, making it full, so that she sounds almost like a preacher giving a belly-rousing sermon.

"Goddamn you, niggah," she screams. "You think I got ta put up wid this? Smell yo' filth and watch you waller like a hog? You cra-zee, you think *that*. I' through wid you, Woody."

It is not the first time Irene and Woody have quarreled: Old women have been peeking around curtains all summer, watching them, while small children sniggered and threw stones across the path of their anger. But there is a new tone to Irene's voice—the satisfied tone of a butcher with a new knife. Squinting sleepily through my bedroom window, I manage to bring them into focus: Irene's curly black hair snarls in the wind as though it, too, is angry; she stands with hands on the hips of baggy jeans, a defiant scarecrow. Woody is sprawled on the ground as if he has been scattered, like seed, and his face is an old crushed paper bag. The neighborhood, I think, has got to them at last.

It's a short block, our street, and was rejected even by the builders of the nearby freeway—I guess they figured it would topple soon enough on its own. Most of the apartment buildings around here *have* lost a lot of bricks, but what's really pulling the neighborhood down is the people. I don't mean just the little girls in shorts who leap into cars after sundown. Or the local theater owners who show movies like *The Maid's Night Off* and *Too Hot to Cuddle*. It's hard to say just what I mean. But the other morning, I got up early enough to catch Mrs. French in our back yard with her dog. It was peeing on the fence.

"Why you lettin' him do that?" I yelled, tears of irritation staining my face.

Mrs. French kept her face blank, and her dog kept on peeing.

"Get away wit' that ole dog!"

She stood there like someone of quality misplaced in a house of rude people until her dog was done. Then she took up his leash and hurried away. This is the kind of summer it has been.

We've only lived here since the spring, and I'm going to be attending the college on the other side of the freeway this fall: I hope to be a writer some day. (My high school dug up a scholarship for me after a teacher saw me reading *The Sun Also Rises* in the library, but that same teacher snatched my library card because she was afraid I wouldn't study for my finals.) The thing is this is one of those neighborhoods which haven't made up their minds what color they're going to be; it's not black, it's not white, and it's not gray either. People around here don't mix much; this is no melting pot but a smörgäsbord where each kind of food rests on a separate tray. When people do bump shoulders, it usually hurts. For instance, there's this English professor who lives across the street and whose books I used to borrow. We were talking about Baldwin one day when suddenly his arm wound about my waist. I was scared, but I didn't want him to know.

"Don't be stupid," I said.

"I'm trying to be *kind*. You can't learn everything from books."

"I know what you want. You wanna—*make love.*"

"Your skin is such a pretty color. White skin never gets that color, not even when it tans."

He kissed me, and in a moment, I dashed out of his apartment, dropping borrowed books in my confusion. I won't go back either. Not that he's such a bad guy, but his body is all flesh, no hint of muscle or bone, and always carries with it the odor of beer. The person I'd like for a lover is Dominic, my Puerto Rican neighbor.

Dominic croons quiet Spanish songs on his back porch, and whenever I pass, slowly spaces his mouth into a smile. Once we stayed outside very late, and a body electricity began to draw us together. We were only inches apart, staring into each other's eyes, when it must have hit us both that we could have been brother and sister—not that much difference, after all, in brown skin and black hair—and a barrier fell.

Then Dominic's mother snapped that thin thread of understanding by anxiously calling him home. He was back in a minute after assuring her, I suppose, that he was not in any trouble, but the mood of the night had changed. He had heard a voice reminding him who he was, and the voices in my heart bubbled up, too, until we had to restrain ourselves from throwing rocks, running, stretching our faces like clowns, anything to get him back to the shy sixteen-year-old he had been and myself to a somewhat more grown-up seventeen, not ready for too much pain.

What I'm trying to say is that you can never predict how things are going to turn out. Right now my mother, who has joined me at the window listening to Irene curse, says so matter-of-factly that for a moment it does not register:

"Where you reckon she get that shotgun?"

"Sho-shotgun," I stutter stupidly. "Whut shotgun?"

"Over at the garbage can. You ain' seen it?"

I do see it then, the battered piece of wood that could settle the score once and for all between these two who are rolling over and over in the dirt. I understand the new edge to Irene's voice: It is power. My mother suddenly turns from the window and heads for the kitchen. I wonder if anything touches her, this mother of mine, that cannot be sniffed, tasted, or touched within four walls. She is frying bacon in the kitchen now, and I wonder. I hear my father arising, coughing for his breath, and I wonder about him, too, my asthmatic father who has been ill so long I cannot remember his days of health. He is running water in the bathroom, still wheezing in the morning air. Then my mother is calling us to breakfast—biscuits, ham, and eggs. I haven't realized how hungry I am until I bite deep into a buttery biscuit. My father is on his second helping before he asks:

"Whut all the fussin' about?"

"Irene and Woody," my mother says.

"Fightin'?"

She nods. "She got a gun."

"Jess like niggers ta be fightin' 'fo' breakfus, ain't it?" my father says, his voice a blend of humor and disgust.

"You think she gonna shoot him?" I ask. I am trembling as I ask the question, for the answer could cast the neighborhood in a new light. It is, perhaps, not just a matter of black against white or black against black, but worn bricks and mortar, ugly reminders of decay, against us all.

"Nobody kin tell *what* a nigger might do," my father says, picking up another biscuit. "Jess be glad it ain't you."

I did not learn until later in the day that Woody had been rushed to the hospital in critical condition. Instead of shooting him, Irene had busted her shotgun over his head. If Woody's skull had not parted, it had bled. Passing their backyard, I saw that his blood had formed a crazy quilt of interlooping circles as though, in the moments after the blow, he had performed a dance. Blood was on the ground; it had stuck to the garbage can and dried in the alley. As the smell entered my nostrils—a smell of bodies, blood, and garbage—I found myself wanting to heave up my breakfast in a kind of obscene atonement. But I could not manage even that poor tribute: My stomach clung to its nourishment like a man-hungry old maid, and I could understand, suddenly, why a lot of people stayed indoors.

Solstice

by AUDRE LORDE

We forgot to water the plaintain shoots
when our houses were full of borrowed meat
and our stomachs with the gift of strangers
who laugh now as they pass us
because our land is barren
the farms are choked
with stunted rows of straw
and with our nightmares of juicy brown yams
that cannot fill us.
The roofs of our houses rot from last winter's water
but our drinking pots are broken
we have used them to mourn the death of old lovers
the next rain will wash our footprints away
and our children have married beneath them.

Our skins are empty.
They have been vacated by the spirits
who are angered by our reluctance
to feed them
in baskets of straw made from sleep grass
and the droppings of civets
they have been hidden away by our mothers
who are waiting for us at the river.

My skin is tightening
soon I shall shed it
like a monitor lizard
like remembered comfort
at the new moons rising
I will eat the last signs of my weakness
remove the scars of old childhood wars
and dare to enter the forest whistling
like a snake that had fed the chameleon
for changes
I shall be forever.

May I never remember reasons
for my spirit's safety

may I never forget
the warning of my woman's flesh
weeping at the new moon
may I never lose
that terror
which keeps me brave
may I owe nothing
that I cannot repay.

It Is Deep

by CAROLYN RODGERS

Having tried to use the
witch card
that erases the stretch of
thirty-three blocks
and tuning in the voice which
   woodenly stated that the
   talk box was "disconnected"

My mother, religiously girdled in
her god, slipped on some love, and
laid on my bell like a truck,
blew through my door warm wind from the south
concern making her gruff and tight-lipped
      and scared
that her "baby" was starving
she, having learned, that disconnection
         results from non-payment of bill(s).

She did not recognize the poster of the
grand le-roi (al) cat on the wall
had never even seen the books of
Black poems that I have written
thinks that I am under the influence of
                    ** communists **
when I talk about Black as anything
other than something ugly to kill it befo it grows
   in any impression she would not be
considered "relevant" or "Black"
                              but
there she was, standing in my room
not loudly condemning that day and
not remembering that I grew hearing her
curse the factory where she "cut uh slave"
and the cheap j-boss wouldn't allow a union,
not remember that I heard the tears when
they told her a high school diploma was not enough,
and her now, not able to understand, what she had
been forced to deny, still—

she pushed into my kitchen so
she could open my refrigerator to see
what I had to eat, and pressed fifty
bills in my hand saying "pay the talk bill and buy
some food; you got folks who care about you. . . ."

My mother, religious-negro, proud of
having waded through a storm, is very obviously,
a sturdy Black bridge that I
crossed over, on.

Bibliographies

Selected African-American Women Writers

This selected bibliography contains a partial list of general works dealing with all aspects of the Black female experience in America, but focuses primarily on the literary output of Black females and the secondary sources dealing with that output. Since other bibliographies on Afro-American women have focused on the historical and sociological material related to this subject, and since this anthology includes mostly literary material, it was felt that a bibliography which provided information on the most significant Black female literary artists would be a valuable addition to the growing number of bibliographies which focus on the Black woman. In addition, the bibliography also includes a section on other bibliographies dealing with Black women, a section on interviews with Black women, a section on the treatment of Black female characters in the writings of male authors, and a list of previously published anthologies which also focus on the Black woman.

I. GENERAL: HISTORICAL, SOCIOLOGICAL, LITERARY

Anderson, Mary Louise. "Black Matriarchy: Portrayal of Women in Three Plays." *Negro American Literature Forum*, 10 (Fall 1976), 93–95.

Aptheker, Herbert. "The Negro Woman." *Masses and Mainstream*, February 1949, pp. 10–17.

Barksdale, Richard, and Kinnamon, Kenneth, eds. *Black Writers of America: A Comprehensive Anthology*. New York: Macmillan, 1972.

Beal, Frances. "Double Jeopardy: To Be Black and Female." In *Sisterhood Is Powerful,* edited by Robin Morgan. New York: Vintage Books, 1970.

Bigsby, C. W. E., ed. *The Black American Writer.* Vol. 1: Fiction. Vol. 2: Poetry and Drama. Baltimore: Penguin Books, 1971.

Black Scholar, December 1971. Devoted to the Black woman.

Black Scholar, March–April 1973. Devoted to Black women's liberation.

Black Scholar, March 1975. Devoted to the Black woman.

Black Scholar, April 1978. Devoted to Blacks and the sexual revolution.

Bone, Robert. *Down Home: A History of Afro-American Short Fiction from Its Beginning to the End of the Harlem Renaissance.* New York: G. P. Putnam's Sons, 1975.

———. *The Negro Novel in America.* New Haven: Yale University Press, 1958.

Boulware, Marcus Hanna, ed. *The Oratory of Negro Leaders, 1900–1968.* Westport, Conn.: Negro University Press, 1969.

Brawley, Benjamin. *Early Negro American Writers: Selections with Biographical and Critical Introductions.* Chapel Hill: University of North Carolina Press, 1935.

Brown, Sterling A. *Negro Poetry and Drama and the Negro in American Fiction.* New York: Atheneum Publishers, 1969.

Bullock, Penelope. "The Mulatto in American Fiction." *Phylon,* 6 (1945), 78–82.

Butterfield, Stephen. *Black Autobiography in America.* Amherst: University of Massachusetts Press, 1974. Contains chapter on autobiographies of black women.

Cherry, Gwendolyn, et al. *Portraits in Color: The Lives of Colorful Negro Women.* Paterson, N.J.: Pageant Books, 1962.

Cook, Mercer, and Henderson, Stephen. *The Militant Black Writer in Africa and the United States.* Madison: University of Wisconsin Press, 1969.

Cooper, Anna J. *A Voice from the South by a Black Woman of the South.* Xenia, Ohio: Aldine Printing House, 1892.

Crummell, Alexander. "The Black Woman of the South—Her Neglects and Her Needs." In *Africa and America: Addresses and Discourses.* Washington, D.C.: B. S. Adams, 1883.

Culp, D. W., ed. *Twentieth Century Negro Literature.* Naperville, Ill., and Toronto: n.p., 1902. Contains section by Black women.

Dandridge, Rita. "On Novels by Black American Women: A Bibliographic Essay." *Women's Studies Newsletter,* 6 (Summer 1978), 28–30.

Daniel, Sadie Gola. *Women Builders.* Washington, D.C.: Associated Publishers, 1931.

Davis, Angela. "Reflections on the Black Woman's Role in the Community of Slaves." *Black Scholar,* 3 (December 1971), 3–15.

Davis, Arthur P. *From the Dark Tower: Afro-American Writers, 1900–1960.* Washington, D.C., Howard University Press, 1974. Discusses Zora Hurston, Margaret Walker, Gwendolyn Brooks, Lorraine Hansberry.

Davis, Elizabeth. *Lifting As They Climb: The National Association of Colored Women.* Washington, D.C.: National Association of Colored Women, 1933.

Davis, John P., ed. *The American Negro Reference Book.* Englewood Cliffs, N.J.: Prentice-Hall, 1966. Contains "The American Negro Woman," by Jeanne Noble.

Doyle, Mary Ellen. "The Heroine of Black Novels." In *Perspectives on Afro-American Women,* edited by Willa D. Johnson and Thomas Green. Washington, D.C.: ECCA Publications, 1975.

Ebony, September 1963. Devoted to Black women in American society.

Field, E. J. "The Woman's Club Movement in the United States." Master's thesis, Howard University, 1948.

Flexner, Eleanor. *Century of Struggle, The Woman's Rights Movement in the United States.* Cambridge, Mass.: Harvard University Press, 1959.

Foster, Frances S. "Changing Concepts of the Black Woman." *Journal of Black Studies,* 3 (June 1973), 433–54.

Gayle, Addison, Jr. *The Way of the New World: The Black Novel in America.* Garden City, N.Y.: Doubleday & Company, 1973. Discusses Jessie Fauset, Zora Hurston, Nella Larsen, Ann Petry, Phillis Wheatley.

Genovese, Eugene. "The Slave Family, Women—A Reassessment of Matriarchy, Emasculation, Weakness." *Southern Voices,* 1 (August/September 1974), 9–16.

Gloster, Hugh. *Negro Voices in American Fiction.* Chapel Hill: University of North Carolina Press, 1948. Discusses Pauline Hopkins, Frances Harper, Sarah Fleming, Jessie Fauset, Nella Larsen, Zora Hurston.

Harley, Sharon, and Tarborg-Penn, Rosalyn, eds. *The Afro-American Woman, Struggles and Images.* Port Washington, N.Y.: Kennikat Press, 1978.

Hemenway, Robert, ed. *The Black Novelist.* Columbus, Ohio: Charles E. Merrill Publishing Company, 1970.

Hill, James Lee. "Bibliography of the Works of Chester Himes, Ann Petry and Frank Yerby." *Black Books Bulletin,* 3 (Fall 1975), 60–72. Annotated.

Hobson, E. C., and Hopkins, C. E. *Report Concerning the Colored Women of the South.* Baltimore: Slater Fund, 1896.

Hoffman, Nancy. "White Woman, Black Women: Inventing an Adequate Pedagogy." *Women's Studies Newsletter,* 5 (Winter/Spring, 1977), 21–24.

Horton, Rod W., and Edwards, Herbert. "Black Writers: Soul and Solidarity." In *Backgrounds of American Literary Thought,* edited by R. W. Horton and H. W. Edwards. 3rd ed. Englewood Cliffs, N.J: Prentice-Hall, 1974

Huggins, Nathan. *Harlem Renaissance.* London and New York: Oxford University Press, 1971.

Hughes, Carl. *The Negro Novelist: A Discussion of the Writings of American Negro Novelists, 1940–1950.* New York: Citadel Press, 1953.

Jackson, Jacquelyne. "Black Women in a Racist Society." In *Racism and Mental Health,* edited by Charles Willie, et al. Pittsburgh: University of Pittsburgh Press, 1972.

Jivell, Karen. "An Analysis of the Visual Development of a Stereotype: The Media's Portrayal of 'Mammy' and 'Aunt Jemima' as Symbols of Black Womanhood." Ph.D. dissertation, Ohio State University, 1976.

Jones, Claudia. *An End to the Neglect of the Problems of the Negro Woman.* New York: National Women's Commission, 1930.

Journal of Afro-American Issues, Summer 1974. Devoted to Black women in America.

Journal of Afro-American Issues, 3 (Summer/Fall, 1975). Devoted to Black women in America.

Journal of Social and Behavioral Sciences, 21 (Winter 1975). Devoted to contemporary research on Black women.

Ladner, Joyce. *Tomorrow's Tomorrow, The Black Woman.* Garden City, N.Y.: Doubleday & Company, 1971.

Lerner, Gerda, ed. *Black Women in White America: A Documentary History.* New York: Random House, 1972.

———. "Letters from Negro Women, 1827–1950." *Masses and Mainstream,* February 1951, pp. 24–33.

Littlejohn, David. *Black on White: A Critical Survey of Writings by American Negroes.* New York: Grossman Publishers, 1966.

Loewenberg, Bert, and Bogin, Ruth, eds. *Black Women in Nineteenth-Century American Life.* University Park: Pennsylvania State University Press, 1972.

Major, Clarence. *The Dark and Feeling: Black American Writers and Their Works.* New York: The Third Press, 1974.

Molette, Barbara. "They Speak: Who Listens? Black Women Playwrights." *Black World,* 25 (April 1976), 28–34.

Mossell, Gertrude E. *The Work of the Afro-American Woman.* Philadelphia: C. S. Ferguson Co., 1908.

Negro American Literature Forum, Fall 1975. Devoted to Black women writers.

"The Negro Woman in American Literature." *Freedomways,* 6 (1966), 8–25. Panel discussion with Sarah Wright, Abbey Lincoln, Alice Childress, and Paule Marshall.

Potter, Velma R. "New Politics, New Mothers." *CLA Journal,* 16 (December 1972), 247–55. Discussion of Black women in drama.

Reid, Inez. *"Together" Black Women.* New York: Emerson Hall, 1971.

Rosenblatt, Roger. *Black Fiction.* Cambridge, Mass.: Harvard University Press, 1974.

Rushing, Andrea. "An Annotated Bibliography of Images of Black Women in Black Literature." *College Language Association Journal,* 21 (March 1978), 435–42.

Russell, Michele. "Black-eyed Blues Connection: Teaching Black Women." *Women's Studies Newsletter,* 4 (Fall 1976), 6–7; 5 (Winter/Spring 1977), 24–28.

Scrupp, Lawson Andrew. *Women of Distinction.* Raleigh, N.C.: The Author, 1893.

Sherman, Joan R. *Invisible Poets: Afro-Americans of the Nineteenth Century.* Urbana: University of Illinois Press, 1974.

Smith, Barbara. "Doing Research on Black American Women." *Women's Studies Newsletter,* 4 (Spring 1976), 4–7.

———. "Teaching About Black Women Writers." *Women's Studies Newsletter,* 2 (Spring 1974), 2.

———. "Toward a Black Feminist Criticism." *Conditions: Two,* 1 (October 1977), 25–44.

Sochen, June. *The Unbridgeable Gap: Blacks and Their Quest for the American Dream, 1900–1930.* Chicago: Rand McNally Publishing Co., 1972.

Staples, Robert. *The Black Woman in America: Sex, Marriage and the Family.* Chicago: Nelson-Hall Publishers, 1973.

Towns, Saundra. "The Black Woman as Whore: Genesis of the Myth." In *The Black Position,* No. 3, edited by Gwendolyn Brooks. Detroit: Broadside Press, 1974.

Ward, Jerry W. "Speculations About Contemporary Black Literature." In *The Contemporary Literary Scene,* edited by Frank N. Magill. Englewood Cliffs, N.J.: Salem Press, 1974.

Washington, Mary Helen. "Black Women Myth and Image Makers." *Black World*, 23 (August 1974), 10–18.

Washington, Mary Helen. "Teaching Black-eyed Susans: An Approach to the Study of Black Women Writers." *Black American Literature Forum*, 2 (Spring 1977), 20–24.

Williams, Kenny J. *They Also Spoke: An Essay on Negro Literature in America, 1787–1930*. Nashville: Townsend Press, 1970.

II. BIBLIOGRAPHIES

Brigano, Russell. *Black Americans in Autobiography: An Annotated Bibliography of Autobiographies and Autobiographical Books Written Since the Civil War*. Durham: Duke University Press, 1974. Also includes unannotated check list of autobiographies and autobiographical books written before 1865.

Cole, Johnetta B. "Black Women in America: An Annotated Bibliography." *Black Scholar*, 3 (December 1971), 42–54.

Davis, Lenwood G. *The Black Family: A Selected Bibliography of Annotated Books and Articles*. Westport, Conn.: Greenwood Press, 1978.

———. *The Black Woman in American Society: A Selected, Annotated Bibliography*. Boston: G. K. Hall, 1975.

———. "The Black Woman in American Autobiographical-Biographical Materials." *Northwest Journal of African and Black American Studies*, 2 (Winter 1974), 14–19.

———. *Black Women in the Cities: 1872–1972: A Bibliography of Published Works on the Life and Achievements of Black Women in the United States*. Monticello, Ill.: Council of Planning Librarians, 1972.

Gross, Seymour L., and Hardy, John E. "Bibliography: The Negro in American Literature, A Checklist of Criticism and Scholarship." In *Images of the Negro in American Literature*, edited by S. L. Gross and J. E. Hardy. Chicago: University of Chicago Press, 1966.

Jackson, Jacquelyne J. "A Partial Bibliography on or Related to Black Women." *Journal of the Study of Behavioral Sciences*, 21 (Winter 1975), pp. 90–135.

John, Janheinz. *A Bibliography of Neo-African Literature from Africa, America and the Caribbean*. London: André Deutsch, 1965.

Kaiser, Ernest. "Black Images in the Mass Media: A Bibliography." *Freedomways*, 14 (Third Quarter, 1974), 274–87.

Kaplan, Louis. *A Bibliography of American Autobiographies*. Madison: University of Wisconsin Press, 1961.

Loff, Jon N. "Gwendolyn Brooks: A Bibliography." *CLA Journal,* 17 (September 1973), 21–32.

Mahoney, Heidi. "Selected Checklist of Material by and About Gwendolyn Brooks." *Negro American Literature Forum,* 8 (Summer 1974), 210–11.

Myers, Carol Fairbanks. *Women in Literature: Criticism of the Seventies.* Metuchen, N. J.: Scarecrow Press, 1976.

Porter, Dorothy. "Early American Negro Writing: A Bibliographical Study." *The Papers of the Bibliographical Society of America,* 39 (1945), 132–268.

Williams, Ora. *American Black Women in the Arts and Sciences: A Bibliographic Survey.* Metuchen, N.J.: Scarecrow Press, 1973.

———. "A Bibliography of Works Written by American Black Women." *CLA Journal,* 15 (March 1972), 354–77.

———. "Works by and About Alice Ruth (Moore) Dunbar-Nelson: A Bibliography." *CLA Journal,* 19 (March 1976), 322–26.

Women and Literature: An Annotated Bibliography of Women Writers. Cambridge, Mass.: Sense and Sensibility Collective, 1971.

III. ANTHOLOGIES

Brown, Hallie Quinn, ed. *Homespun Heroines and Other Women of Distinction.* Xenia, Ohio: Aldine Publishing Co., 1926.

Cade, Toni, ed. *The Black Woman.* New York: Signet Books, 1970.

Carson, Josephine, ed. *Silent Voices: The Southern Negro Woman Today.* New York: Delacorte Press, 1969.

Exum, Pat Crutchfield, ed. *Keeping the Faith: Writings by Contemporary Black American Women.* Greenwich, Conn.: Fawcett Publications, 1974.

Washington, Mary Helen, ed. *Black-eyed Susans: Classic Stories by and About Black Women.* Garden City, N.Y.: Doubleday & Company, 1975.

Watkins, Mel, and David, Jay, eds. *To Be a Black Woman: Portraits in Fact and Fiction.* New York: William Morrow & Co., 1970.

IV. INTERVIEWS

Bakerman, Jane. "The Sears Can't Show: An Interview with Toni Morrison." *Black American Literature Forum,* 12 (Summer 1978), 56–60.

"Black Books Bulletin Interviews Gwendolyn Brooks." *Black Books Bulletin,* 2 (Spring 1974), 28–35.

"The Black Scholar Interviews Maya Angelou." *Black Scholar,* 8 (January–February 1977), 44–53.

A Dialogue: James Baldwin and Nikki Giovanni. Philadelphia, J. B. Lippincott Co., 1973.

Giddings, Paula, ed. *A Poetic Equation: Conversations Between Nikki Giovanni and Margaret Walker.* Washington, D.C.: Howard University Press, 1974.

Hull, Gloria, and Gallagher, Posey. "Update on *Part One:* An Interview with Gwendolyn Brooks." *CLA Journal,* 11 (September 1977), 19–40.

Jones, Gayl. "Interview with Lucille Jones," *Obsidian,* 3 (Winter 1977), 26–35.

Lewis, Ida. "Conversation: Gwendolyn Brooks and Ida Lewis." *Essence,* April 1971, pp. 27–31.

O'Brien, John. *Interviews with Black Writers.* New York: Liveright, 1973. Contains interviews with Alice Walker and Ann Petry.

Stravos, George. "An Interview with Gwendolyn Brooks." *Contemporary Literature,* 4 (Winter 1970), 1–20.

Walker, Alice. "Something to Do with Real Life." *Harvard Advocate,* Winter 1973. Interview with Eudora Welty.

"Women on Women." *American Scholar,* 41 (Fall 1972), 599–622. Contains forum with Alice Walker. See also Patricia McLaughlin, "Comment," ibid., 622–37.

Ward, Jerry. "Legitimate Resources of the Soul: An Interview with Arthenia Bates Millican." *Callaloo,* 3 (Spring 1977), 14–34.

V. DISCUSSION OF BLACK FEMALE CHARACTERS IN WORKS BY MALE AUTHORS

Alexander, Charlotte. "The 'Stink' of Reality: Mothers and Whores in James Baldwin's Fiction." *Literature and Psychology,* 18 (1968), 9–26.

Brown, Calfin S. "Dilsey: From Faulkner to Homer." In *William Faulkner: Prevailing Verities and World Literature,* edited by Wolodymyr Zyla and Wendell Aycock. Lubbock, Tex.: Texas Tech University, 1973.

Burns, Mattie Ann. "The Development of Women Characters in the Works of William Faulkner." Ph.D. dissertation, Auburn University, 1974.

Chase, Patricia. "The Women in *Cane.*" *CLA Journal,* 14 (March 1971), 259–73.

Dandridge, Rita B. "The Black Woman as a Freedom Fighter in Langston Hughes' 'Simple's Uncle Sam.'" *CLA Journal,* 18 (December 1974), 273–83.

Davis, Arthur P. "The Tragic Mulatto Theme in Six Works of Langston Hughes," *Phylon,* 16 (1955), 195–204.

Dohner, Ellen. "Stereotypes of Black Women in Novels by White Authors from 1925 to 1935." Master's thesis, Florida State University, 1971.

Geismar, Maxwell. "William Faulkner: The Negro and the Female." In his *Writers in Crisis.* Boston: Houghton Mifflin, 1942.

George, Felice. "Black Woman, Black Man." *Harvard Journal of Afro-American Affairs,* 2 (1971), 1–17. Discussion of James Baldwin.

Greer, Dorothy. "Dilsey and Lucas: Faulkner's Use of the Negro as Gauge of Moral Character." *Emporia State Research Studies,* 9 (1962), 43–61.

Hoeveler, Diane Long. "Oedipus Agonistes: Mothers and Sons in Richard Wright's Fiction." *Black American Literature Forum,* 12 (Summer 1978), 65–68.

Howe, Irving. "Faulkner and the Negroes." In *William Faulkner: A Critical Study,* edited by Irving Howe. New York: Random House, 1962.

———. "William Faulkner and the Negroes: A Vision of Lost Fraternity." *Commentary,* 12 (1951), 359–68.

Howell, Elmo. "A Note on Faulkner's Negro Characters." *Mississippi Quarterly,* 11 (1958), 201–3.

Kane, Patricia, and Wilkerson, Doris. "Survival Strategies: Black Women in *Ollie Miss* and *Cotton Comes to Harlem.*" *Critique: Studies in Modern Fiction,* 16 (1974), 101–9.

Keady, Sylvia. "Richard Wright's Women Characters and Inequality." *Black American Literature Forum,* 10 (Winter 1976), 124–28.

Kent, George. "The Black Woman in Faulkner's Works, with the Exclusion of Dilsey." *Phylon,* 35 (December 1974), 430–41; 36 (March 1975), 55–67.

Margolies, Edward. "Race and Sex: The Novels of Chester Himes." In his *Native Sons: A Critical Study of Twentieth-Century Negro American Authors.* Philadelphia: J. B. Lippincott Co., 1969.

Mathis, C. H. "The Concept of Feminine Beauty in Novels by Negroes." Master's thesis, Fisk University, 1937.

Miller, R. Baxter. "'No Crystal Stair': Unity, Archetype and Symbol in Langston Hughes's Poems on Women." *Negro American Literature Forum,* 9 (Winter 1975), 109–14.

Nilon, Charles. *Faulkner and the Negro.* New York: Citadel Press, 1965.

Page, Sally R. *Faulkner's Women: Characterization and Meaning* Deland, Fla.: Everett Edwards, 1972.

Pyne-Timothy, Helen. "Perceptions of the Black Woman in the Work of Claude McKay." *CLA Journal,* 19 (December 1975), 152–64.

Seiden, Melvin. "Faulkner's Ambiguous Negro." *Massachusetts Review,* 4 (1963), 675–90.

Sheftall, Beverly. "The Treatment of Women in Faulkner's Major Novels." Master's thesis, Atlanta University, 1969.

Smith, Barbara. "Sexual Politics in the Works of Richard Wright." Paper presented at MLA convention, New York, December 1976.

Sylander, Carolyn. "Ralph Ellison's *Invisible Man* and Female Stereotypes." *Negro American Literature Forum,* 9 (Fall 1975), 77–79.

Taylor, Brooke Battle. "You Not the Man Your Mamma Was": A Study of Women Characters in Selected Black Fiction." Master's thesis, Stephen F. Austin State University, 1971.

Waldron, Edward E. "The Search for Identity in Jean Toomer's 'Esther.'" *CLA Journal,* 14 (March 1971), 277–80.

Westeffield, Hargis. "Jean Toomer's 'Fern': A Mythical Dimension." *CLA Journal,* 14 (March 1971), 274–76.

VI. INDIVIDUAL AUTHORS

MAYA ANGELOU

Primary Sources:

Gather Together in My Name. New York: Random House, 1974.

I Know Why the Caged Bird Sings. New York: Random House, 1969.

Just Give Me a Cool Drink of Water 'for I Die. New York: Random House, 1971.

Oh Pray My Wings Are Gonna Fit Me Well. New York: Random House, 1975.

Singin' and Swingin' and Gettin' Merry Like Christmas. New York: Random House, 1976.

Secondary Sources:

Elliot, Jeffrey. "Maya Angelou: In Search of Self." *Negro History Bulletin,* 40 (May–June 1977), 694–95.

TONI CADE BAMBARA

Primary Sources:

"Black Theater." In *Black Expression,* edited by Addison Gayle. New York: Weybright & Talley, 1969.

"Black Theater of the 60's." In *Backgrounds to Black American Literature,* edited by Ruth Miller. New York: Chandler Publishing Company, 1971.

The Black Woman (ed.). New York: New American Library, 1970.

Gorilla, My Love. New York: Random House, 1972.

The Sea Birds Are Still Alive. New York: Random House, 1977.

Tales and Stories for Black Folks (ed.). Garden City, N.Y.: Doubleday & Company, 1971.

GWENDOLYN BROOKS

Primary Sources:

Aloneness. Detroit: Broadside Press, 1969.

Annie Allen. New York: Harper & Row, 1949.

The Bean Eaters. New York: Harper & Row, 1960.

Bronzeville Boys and Girls. New York; Harper & Row, 1956.

In the Mecca. New York: Harper & Row, 1953.

Maude Martha. New York: Harper & Row, 1953.

Report from Part One; An Autobiography. Detroit: Broadside Press, 1972.

Riot. Detroit: Broadside Press, 1969.

Selected Poems. New York: Harper & Row, 1963.

A Street in Bronzeville. New York: Harper & Row, 1945.

The World of Gwendolyn Brooks. New York: Harper & Row, 1971.

Secondary Sources:

Baker, Houston. "The Achievement of Gwendolyn Brooks," *CLA Journal,* 16 (September 1972), 23–31.

Barrow, W. "Five Fabulous Females." *Negro Digest,* 12 (July 1963), 78–83.

Brown, F. L. "Chicago's Great Lady of Poetry." *Negro Digest,* 11 (December 1961), 53–57.

Crockett, J. "An Essay on Gwendolyn Brooks." *Negro History Bulletin,* 19 (November 1955), 37–39.

Davis, Arthur. The Black-and-Tan Motif in the Poetry of Gwendolyn Brooks." *CLA Journal,* 6 (December 1962), 90–97.

———. "Gwendolyn Brooks: A Poet of the Unheroic." *CLA Journal,* 7 (December 1963), 114–25.

Dobbs, Jeanine. "Not Another Poetess: A Study of Female Experience in Modern American Poetry." Ph.D. dissertation, University of New Hampshire, 1973.

Emmanuel, James A. "Gwendolyn Brooks." In *Contemporary Novelists,* edited by James Vinson. New York: St. Martin's Press, 1972.

Furman, Marva Riley. "Gwendolyn Brooks: The 'Unconditioned Poet.'" *CLA Journal,* 17 (September 1973), 1–10.

Garland, P. "Gwendolyn Brooks: Poet Laureate." *Ebony,* July 1968, pp. 48–50.

Hansell, William. "Aestheticism Versus Political Militancy in Gwendolyn Brooks's 'The Chicago Picasso' and 'The Wall.' " *CLA Journal,* 17 (September 1973), 11–15.

———. "Gwendolyn Brooks's "In the Mecca": A Rebirth into Blackness." *Negro American Literature Forum,* 8 (Summer 1974), 199–207.

———. "The Role of Violence in Recent Poems of Gwendolyn Brooks." *Studies in Black Literature,* 5 (Summer 1974), 21–27.

Hudson, Clenora F. "Racial Themes in the Poetry of Gwendolyn Brooks." *CLA Journal,* 17 (September 1973), 16–20.

Hull, Gloria. "A Note on the Poetic Technique of Gwendolyn Brooks," *CLA Journal,* 19 (December 1975), 280–85.

Jackson, Blyden, and Rubin, Louis D. *Black Poetry in America: Two Essays in Historical Interpretation.* Baton Rouge: Louisiana State University Press, 1974.

Jaffee, Dan. "Gwendolyn Brooks: An Appreciation from the White Suburbs." In *The Black American Writer,* edited by C. W. E. Bigsby. Vol. 2. Baltimore: Penguin Books, 1971.

Kent, George E. *Blackness and the Adventure of Western Culture.* Chicago: Third World Press, 1972.

———. "The Poetry of Gwendolyn Brooks." *Black World,* 2 (September 1971), 30–43; 2 (October 1971), 36–48.

———. "The World of Gwendolyn Brooks." *Black Books Bulletin* 2 (Spring 1974), 28–29.

Lee, Don. "The Achievement of Gwendolyn Brooks." *Black Scholar,* 3 (Summer 1972), 36–48.

Loff, John. "To Be a Black Woman in the Poetry of Gwendolyn Brooks." Master's thesis, University of Wisconsin at Stevens Point, 1972.

McCluskey, John. "In the Mecca." *Studies in Black Literature,* 4 (Autumn 1973), 25–30.

Madhubuti, Safisha N. "Focus on Form in Gwendolyn Brooks." *Black Books Bulletin,* 2 (Spring 1974), 24–27.

Park, Sue S. "A Study in Tension: Gwendolyn Brooks's 'The Chicago Defender Sends a Man to Little Rock'." *Black American Literature Forum,* 2 (Spring 1977), 32–34.

———. "Social Themes in the Poetry of Gwendolyn Brooks." Ph.D. dissertation, University of Illinois (Champagne-Urbana), 1972.

Rollins, Charliemae. *Famous American Negro Poets.* New York: Dodd, Mead & Co., 1965.

Shands, Annette Oliver. "Gwendolyn Brooks as Novelist." *Black World,* June 1973, pp. 22–30.

Shaw, Harry. "Gwendolyn Brooks: A Critical Study." Ph.D. dissertation, University of Illinois (Champagne-Urbana).

Towns, Saundra. "Black Autobiography and the Dilemma of Western Artistic Tradition." *Black Books Bulletin,* 2 (Spring 1974), 17–23.

Walker, Cheryl Lawson. "The Women's Tradition in American Poetry." Ph.D. dissertation, Brandeis University, 1973.

JESSIE FAUSET

Primary Sources:

The Chinaberry Tree. New York: Frederick A. Stokes Co., 1931.

Comedy, American Style. New York: Frederick A. Stokes Co., 1933.

"The Gift of Laughter." In *Black Expression,* edited by Addison Gayle. New York: Weybright & Talley, 1969.

Plum Bun. New York: Frederick A. Stokes Co., 1929.

There Is Confusion. New York: Boni & Liveright, 1924.

Secondary Sources:

Braithwaite, William Stanley. "The Novels of Jessie Fauset." *Opportunity,* 12 (1934), 24–28.

Davis, Arthur P. *From the Dark Tower.* Washington, D.C.: Howard University Press, 1974.

Feeney, Joseph. "Greek Tragic Patterns in a Black Novel: Jessie Fauset's *The Chinaberry Tree.*" *CLA Journal,* 18 (December 1974), 211–15.

Gayle, Addison. *The Way of the New World: The Black Novel in America.* Garden City, N. Y.: Doubleday & Company, 1975.

Huggins, Nathan. *Harlem Renaissance.* New York: Oxford University Press, 1971.

Sato, Hiroko. "Under the Harlem Shadow: A Study of Jessie Fauset and Nella Larsen." In *The Harlem Renaissance Remembered,* edited by Arna Bontemps. New York: Dodd, Mead & Co., 1972.

Sochen, June. *The Unbridgeable Gap: Blacks and Their Quest for the American Dream, 1900–1930.* Chicago: Rand McNally, College Publishing Co., 1972.

Starkey, Marion L. "Jessie Fauset." *Southern Workman,* 61 (1932), 217–20.

Sylvander, Carolyn. "Jessie R. Fauset, Black American writer: Her Relationships, Biographical and Literary, with Black and White

Writers, 1910–1935." Ph.D. dissertation, University of Wisconsin, 1976.

NIKKI GIOVANNI

Primary Sources:

Black Feeling, Black Talk, Black Judgement. New York: William Morrow & Co., 1971.

"Black Poems, Poseurs, and Power." *Negro Digest,* 18 (June 1969), 30–34.

Gemini: An Extended Autobiographical Statement. Indianpolis: Bobbs-Merrill Co., 1971.

My House. New York: William Morrow & Co., 1972.

Night Comes Softly: Anthology of Black Female Voices, (ed.). New York: Nik-Tom Publications, 1970.

Spin a Soft Black Song: Poems for Children. New York: Hill & Wang ,1971.

The Women and the Men. New York: William Morrow & Co., 1975.

Secondary Sources:

Bailey, Peter. "Nikki Giovanni: 'I Am Black, Female, Polite.'" *Ebony,* 27 (February 1972), 48–52, 53–54, 56.

Brooks, Russell. "The Motifs of Dynamic Change in Black Revolutionary Poetry." *CLA Journal,* 15 (September 1971), 7–17.

Lee, Don. "The Poets and Their Poetry: There Is a Tradition." *Dynamite Voices: Black Poets of the 1960's.* Detroit: Broadside Press, 1971.

Palmer, R. Roderick. "The Poetry of Three Revolutionists: Don L. Lee, Sonia Sanchez, and Nikki Giovanni." *CLA Journal,* 15 (September 1971), 25–36.

LORRAINE HANSBERRY

Primary Sources:

A Raisin in the Sun. New York: Random House, 1959.

Les Blancs: The Collected Last Plays of Lorraine Hansberry. New York: Random House, 1972.

The Movement: Documentary of a Struggle for Equality. New York: Simon & Schuster, 1964.

"The Negro in American Culture." In *The Black American Writers,* edited by C. W. E. Bigsby. Vol. 1. Baltimore: Penguin Books, 1971. (Symposium).

The Sign in Sidney Brustein's Window. New York: Random House, 1965.

To Be Young, Gifted and Black: Lorraine Hansberry in Her Own Words, adapted by Robert Nemiroff. Englewood Cliffs, N.J.: Prentice-Hall, 1969.

Secondary Sources:

Abramson, Doris. *Negro Playwrights in the American Theater, 1925–1959*. New York: Columbia University Press, 1969.

Brown, Lloyd W. "Lorraine Hansberry as Ironist: A Reappraisal of *A Raisin in the Sun.*" *Journal of Black Studies,* 4 (March 1974), 237–47.

Davis, Arthur P. *From the Dark Tower: Afro-American Writers,* 1900–1960. Washington, D.C.: Howard University Press, 1974.

Davies, Ossie. "The Significance of Lorraine Hansberry," *Freedomways,* 5 (Summer 1965), 396–402.

Farrison, W. Edward. "Lorraine Hansberry's Last Dramas." *CLA Journal,* 16 (December 1972), 188–97.

Gill, Glenda. "Techniques of Teaching Lorraine Hansberry: Liberation from Boredom." *Negro American Literature Forum,* 8 (Summer 1974), 226–28.

Horton, Rod W., and Edwards, Herbert. "Black Writers: Soul and Solidarity." In *Backgrounds of American Literary Thought.* Englewood Cliffs, N. J.: Prentice-Hall, 1974.

Issacs, Harold. "Five Writers and Their African Ancestors: Part I." *Phylon,* 21 (1960), 66–70.

Lewis, Theophilus. "Social Protest in *A Raisin in the Sun.*" *Catholic World,* 190 (1959), 31–35.

Mitchell, Lofton. *Black Drama.* New York: Hawthorn Books, 1967.

Potter, Velma R. "New Politics, New Mothers." *CLA Journal,* 16 (December 1972), 247–55.

Willis, Robert J. "Anger and the Contemporary Black Theater." *Negro American Literature Forum,* 8 (Summer 1974), 213–15.

FRANCES HARPER

Primary Sources:

Atlanta Offering Poems. Philadelphia: George S. Ferguson, 1895.

"Colored Women of America." *Englishwomen's Review,* 57 (January 15, 1898), 10–15.

Forest Leaves or *Autumn Leaves.*

Idylls of the Bible. Philadelphia: n.p., 1901.

Iola Leroy or *Shadows Uplifted.* Philadelphia: Garriques Brothers. 1892.

Moses. A Story of the Nile. N.p., n.d.

Poems. Philadelphia: Merryhew & Sons, 1871.

Poems on Miscellaneous Subjects. Boston: n.p., 1854.

Sketches of Son Life. Philadelphia: Merryhew & Sons, 1872.

Sketches of Southern Life. Philadelphia: Merryhew & Sons, 1872.

The Sparrow's Fall and Other Poems. N.p., n.d.

"The Two Offers." In *International Library of Negro History from 1746 to the Present,* edited by Lindsay Patterson. New York: Publishers, Inc., 1969.

Secondary Sources:

Gloster, Hugh M. *Negro Voices in American Fiction*. Chapel Hill: University of North Carolina Press, 1948.

O'Connor, Lillian Mary. *Pioneer Women Orators*. New York: Columbia University Press, 1954.

Riggins, Linda N. "The Works of Frances E. W. Harper." *Black World,* December 1972, pp. 30–36.

Still, William. *The Underground Railroad*. Philadelphia: Porter and Coates, 1872.

PAULINE HOPKINS

The Pauline E. Hopkins Papers are located at Fisk University Library, Nashville, Tennessee.

Primary Sources:

A Primer of Facts Pertaining to the Early Greatness of the African Race. . . . Cambridge: P. E. Hopkins & Co., 1905.

Contending Forces. Boston: The Colored Cooperative Publishing Company, 1900.

Moses, Story of the Nile. Philadelphia: Merryhew, 1869.

Of One Blood or *The Hidden Self*. In *Colored American Magazine*. Began November 1902; ran for twelve months.

One Scene from the Drama of Early Days. Drama. N.p., n.d.

One Theme from the Drama of Early Days. N.p., n.d.

Poems on Miscellaneous Subjects. Boston: J. B. Yerrinton & Sons, 1854.

Slaves Escape or *The Underground Railroad*. N.p., n.d.

Winona, A Tale of Negro Life in the South and Southwest. In *Colored American Magazine*. 5 (October 1902). Serialized short novel.

Secondary Sources:

Shockley, Ann. "Pauline E. Hopkins: A Biographical Excursion into Obscurity." *Phylon* (Spring 1972), 22–26.

KRISTIN HUNTER

Primary Sources:

God Bless the Child. New York: Charles Scribner's Sons, 1964.

The Landlord. New York: Avon Books, 1969.

The Soul Brothers and Sister Lou. New York: Avon Books, 1968.

Secondary Sources:

Booth, Martha F. "Black Ghetto Life Portrayed in Novels for the Adolescent." Ph.D. dissertation, University of Iowa, 1971.

Reilly, John M. "Kristin Hunter." In *Contemporary Novelists*, edited by James Vinson. New York: St. Martin's Press, 1972.

ZORA NEALE HURSTON

Primary Sources:

"Characteristics of Negro Expression." In *Negro: An Anthology*, edited by Nancy Cunard. New York: Frederick Ungar Publishing Company; reprinted 1970.

Dust Tracks on a Road. Philadelphia: J. B. Lippincott Co., 1942.

Jonah's Gourd Vine. Philadelphia: J. B. Lippincott Co., 1934.

Moses, Man of the Mountain. Philadelphia: J. B. Lippincott Co., 1939.

Mules and Men. Philadelphia: J. B. Lippincott Co., 1935.

Seraph on the Suwanee. New York: Charles Scribner's Sons, 1948.

Tell My Horse. Philadelphia: J. B. Lippincott Co., 1938.

Their Eyes Were Watching God. Philadelphia: J. B. Lippincott Co., 1937.

Secondary Sources:

Blake, E. L. "Zora Neale Hurston: Author and Folklorist." *Negro History Bulletin*, 29 (April 1966), 149–50.

Bone, Robert. *Down Home*. New York: G. P. Putnam's Sons, 1975.

Byrd, James W. "Zora Neale Hurston: A Novel Folklorist." *Tennessee Folklore Society Bulletin*, 20 (1955), 35–41.

Davis, Arthur P. *From the Dark Tower*. Washington, D.C.: Howard University Press, 1974.

Howard, Lillie P. "Marriage: Zora Neale Hurston's System of Values." *CIA Journal*, 11 (December 1977), 256–68.

Gayle, Addison. *The Way of the New World: The Black Novel in America*. Garden City, N.Y.: Doubleday & Company, 1975.

Giles, James. "The Significance of Time in Zora Neale Hurston's *Their Eyes Were Watching God*." *Negro American Literature Forum*, 6 (Spring 1972), 52–54.

Hemenway, Robert. *Zora Neale Hurston, a Literary Biography*. Urbana, Ill.: University of Illinois Press, 1977.

———. "Folklore Field Notes from Zora Neale Hurston." *Black Scholar,* 7 (April 1976), 39–46.

Hunter, Charlotte. "Zora Neale Hurston: A Critical Biography." Ph.D. dissertation. Florida State University, forthcoming.

Hurst, Fannie. "Zora Hurston: A Personality Sketch." *Yale University Library Gazette,* 35 (1961), 17–22.

Jackson, Blyden. "Some Negroes in the Land of Goshen." *Tennessee Folklore Society Bulletin,* 19 (1939), 103–7.

Jordan, June. "On Richard Wright and Zora Neale Hurston: Notes Toward a Balancing of Love and Hatred." *Black World,* 23 (August 1974), 4–8.

Kent, George. *Blackness and the Adventure of Western Culture.* Chicago: Third World Press, 1972.

Kilson, Marian. "The Transformation of Eatonville's Ethnographer." *Phylon,* 33 (Summer 1972), 112–19.

Lomax, Alan. "Zora Neale Hurston—a Life of Negro Folklore." *Sing Out!,* 10 (October–November 1960), 12–13.

Murray, Marian. *Jump at the Sun: The Story of Zora Neale Hurston.* New York: Third World Press, 1975.

Neal, Larry. "Eatonville's Zora Neale Hurston: A Profile." *Black Review,* No. 2, edited by Mel Watkins. New York: William Morrow & Co., 1972.

Pratt, Theodore. "A Memoir: Zora Neale Hurston, Florida's First Distinguished Author." *Negro Digest,* 11 (February 1962), 52–56.

———. "Zora Neale Hurston." *Florida Historical Quarterly,* 40 (July 1961), 37–41.

Rayson, Ann L. "*Dust Tracks on the Road:* Zora Neale Hurston and the Form of Black Autobiography." *Negro American Literature Forum,* 7 (1973), 39–45.

———. "The Novels of Zora Neale Hurston." *Studies in Black Literature,* 5 (Winter 1974), 1–10.

Rosenblatt, Roger. *Black Fiction.* Cambridge, Mass.: Harvard University Press, 1974.

Sato, Kiroko. "Under the Harlem Shadow: A Study of Jessie Fauset and Nella Larsen." In *The Harlem Renaissance Remembered,* edited by Arna Bontemps. New York: Dodd, Mead & Co., 1972.

Southerland, Ellease. "Zora Neale Hurston: The Novelist-Anthropologist's Life/Works." *Black World,* 23 (August 1974), 20–30.

Turner, Darwin. "The Negro Novelist and the South." *Southern Humanities Review,* 1 (1967), 21–29.

———. "Zora Neale Hurston: The Wandering Minstrel." In his *A Minor Chord: Three Afro-American Writers and Their Search for Identity.* Carbondale: Southern Illinois University Press, 1971.

Walker, Alice. "In Search of Zora Neale Hurston." *Ms.,* 3 (March 1975), 74–79, 85–89.

Walker, S. Jay. "Zora Neale Hurston's *Their Eyes Were Watching God:* Black Novel of Sexism." *Modern Fiction Studies,* 20 (Winter 1974–75), 519–27.

Washington, Mary Helen. "The Black Woman's Search for Identity: Zora Neale Hurston's Work." *Black World,* 21 (August 1972), 68–75.

Young, James O. *Black Writers of the Thirties.* Baton Rouge: Louisiana State University Press, 1973.

JUNE JORDAN

Primary Sources:

Dry Victories. New York: Avon Books, 1975.

Fannie Lou Hamer. New York: Thomas Y. Crowell Co., 1972.

"For Beautiful Mary Brown." *Freedomways,* 11 (Second Quarter, 1971), 191. Short story.

His Own Where. New York: Dell Publishers, 1971.

New Days: Poems of Exile and Return. New York: Emerson Hall Pubs., 1973.

New Life: New Room. New York: Thomas Y. Crowell Co., 1975.

"Second Thoughts of a Black Feminist." *Ms.,* 5 (February 1977), 113–15.

Some Changes. New York: E. P. Dutton & Co., 1971.

Soulscript: Afro-American Poetry (ed.), Garden City, N.Y.: Doubleday & Company, 1970.

Things That I Do in the Dark: Selected Poems. New York: Random House, 1977.

The Voice of the Children. New York: Holt, Rinehart and Winston, 1970 (with Torri Bush).

Who Look at Me. New York: Thomas Y. Crowell Co., 1969.

NELLA LARSEN

Primary Sources:

Passing. New York: Alfred A. Knopf, 1929.

Quicksand. New York: Alfred A. Knopf, 1928.

Secondary Sources:

Davis, Arthur P. *From the Dark Tower.* Washington, D.C.: Howard University Press, 1974.

Gayle, Addison. *The Way of the New World: The Black Novel in America.* Garden City, N.Y.: Doubleday & Company, 1975.

Kent, George. *Blackness and the Adventure of Western Culture.* Chicago: Third World Press, 1972.

Ramsay, Priscilla. "A Study of Black Identity in 'Passing' Novels of the 19th and Early 20th Century." *Studies in Black Literature,* 7 (Winter 1976), 1–7.

Sato, Hiroko. "Under the Harlem Shadow: A Study of Jessie Fauset and Nella Larsen." In *The Harlem Renaissance Remembered,* edited by Arna Bontemps. New York: Dodd, Mead & Co., 1972.

Thornton, Hortense, "Sexism as Quagmire: Nella Larsen's *Quicksand.*" *CLA Journal,* 16 (March 1973), 285–401.

Whitlow, Roger. *Black American Literature.* Chicago: Nelson-Hall Publishers, 1973.

Youman, Mary. "Nella Larsen's *Passing: A Study in Irony.*" *CLA Journal,* 18 (December 1974), 235–41.

AUDRE LORDE

Primary Sources:

Between Ourselves. Point Reyes, Calif.: Eidolon Editions, 1976.

Cables to Rage. London: Paul Breman, 1970.

Coal. New York: W. W. Norton & Co., 1968.

The First Cities. New York: Poets Press, 1968.

From a Land Where Other People Live. Detroit: Broadside Press, 1973.

The New York Head Shop and Museum. Detroit: Broadside Press, 1974.

PAULE MARSHALL

Primary Sources:

Brown Girl, Brownstones. New York: Random House, 1959.

The Chosen Place, the Timeless People. New York: Harcourt, Brace & World, 1969.

"The Negro Woman in American Literature." *Freedomways,* 6 (Winter 1966), 20–25.

"Reena." In *American Negro Short Stories,* edited by John H. Clark. New York: Hill & Wang, 1966.

"Shaping the World of My Art." *New Letters,* 40 (October 1973), 97–112.

"Some Get Wasted." In *Harlem U.S.A.,* edited by John Henrik Clarke. Berlin: Seven Seas, 1974.

Soul Clap Hands and Sing. New York: Atheneum Publishers, 1961.

"To Da-duh, in Memoriam." In *Black Voices,* edited by Abraham

Chapman. New York: New American Library, Mentor Books, 1968.

Secondary Sources:

Benston, Kimberly. "Architectural Imagery and Unity in Paule Marshall's *Brown Girl, Brownstones.*" *Negro American Literature Forum,* 9 (Fall 1975), 67–70.

Bond, Jean Corey. "Allegorical Novel by Talented Storyteller." *Freedomways,* First Quarter, 1970, pp. 76–78.

Braithwaite, Edward. "Rehabilitation." *Critical Quarterly,* 13 (Summer 1971), 175–83.

———. "West Indian History and Society in the Art of Paule Marshall's Novel." *Journal of Black Studies,* 1 (December 1970), 225–38.

Brown, Lloyd W. "The Rhythms of Power in Paule Marshall's Fiction." *Novel,* 7 (Winter 1974), 159–67.

Butcher, Philip. "The Younger Novelists and the Urban Negro." *CLA Journal,* 4 (March 1961), 196–203.

Kapai, Seela. "Dominant Themes and Techniques in Paule Marshall's Fiction." *CLA Journal,* 16 (September 1972), 49–59.

Keizs, Marcia. "Themes and Style in the Works of Paule Marshall." *Negro American Literature Forum,* 9 (Fall 1975), 67–76.

Nazaruh, Peter. "Paule Marshall's Timeless People." *New Letters,* 40 (Autumn 1973), 116–31.

Stoelting, Winifred. "Time Past and Time Present: The Search for Viable Links in *The Chosen Place, the Timeless People.*" *CLA Journal,* 16 (September 1972), 60–71.

Washington, Mary Helen. "Black Women Image Makers." *Black World,* 23 (August 1974), 10–18.

Whitlow, Roger. *Black American Literature: A Critical History.* Chicago: Nelson-Hall Publishers, 1973.

LOUISE MERIWETHER

Primary Sources:

Daddy Was a Number Runner. Englewood Cliffs, N.J.: Prentice-Hall, 1970.

Don't Take the Bus on Monday: The Rosa Parks Story. Englewood Cliffs, N.J.: Prentice-Hall, 1973. Children's book.

The Freedom Ship of Robert Smalls. Englewood Cliffs, N.J.: Prentice-Hall, 1971. Children's book.

The Heart Man: Dr. Daniel Hale Williams. Englewood Cliffs, N.J.: Prentice-Hall, 1972. Children's book.

"That Girl from Creektown." In *Black Review,* No. 2, edited by Mel Watkins. New York: William Morrow & Co., 1972.

"The Thick End Is for Whipping." *Negro Digest,* 18 (November 1968), pp. 55–62.

TONI MORRISON

Primary Sources:

"Behind the Making of *The Black Book.*" *Black World,* 23 (February 1974), 86–90.

The Bluest Eye. New York: Holt, Rinehart & Winston, 1920.

"Rediscovering Black History." *The New York Times Magazine,* August 11, 1974.

Song of Solomon. New York: Alfred A. Knopf, 1977.

Sula. New York: Alfred A. Knopf, 1974.

"What the Black Woman Thinks About Women's Lib." *The New York Times Magazine,* August 22, 1971.

Secondary Sources:

Bischoff, Joan. "The Novels of Toni Morrison: Studies in Thwarted Sensitivity." *Studies in Black Literature,* 6 (Fall 1975), 21–23.

PAULI MURRAY

Primary Sources:

Dark Testament. Comstock, Ill.: Silvermine Publishers, 1970.

"The Negro Woman in the Quest for Equality." Address delivered to Leadership Conference of the National Council of Negro Women, Washington, D.C., November 14, 1963.

Proud Shoes: The Story of an American Family. New York: Harper & Brothers, 1956.

ANN PETRY

Primary Sources:

Country Place. Boston: Houghton Mifflin Co., 1947.

Harriet Tubman: Conductor of the Underground Railway. New York: Thomas Y. Crowell Co., 1955.

Legends of the Saints. New York: Thomas Y. Crowell Co., 1964.

"Miss Muriel" and Other Stories. Boston: Houghton Mifflin Co., 1971.

The Narrows. Boston: Houghton Mifflin Co., 1953.

"The Novel as Social Criticism." In *The Writers Book,* edited by Helen Hull. New York: Harper's, 1950.

The Street. Boston: Houghton Mifflin Co., 1946.

Tituba of Salem Village. New York: Thomas Y. Crowell Co., 1964.

Secondary Sources:

Adams, George R. "Riot as Ritual: Ann Petry's 'In Darkness and Confusion.'" *Negro American Literature Forum,* 6 (Summer 1968), 54–57, 60.

Bone, Robert. *The Negro Novel in America.* New Haven: Yale University Press, 1968.

Dempsey, Davis. "Uncle Tom's Ghost and the Literary Abolitionist." *Antioch Review,* 6 (1946), 442–48.

Emmanuel, James. "Ann Petry." In *Contemporary Novelists,* edited by James Vinson. New York: St. Martin's Press, 1972.

Gayle, Addison. *The Way of the New World.* Garden City, N.Y.: Doubleday & Company, 1975.

Green, Marjorie. "Ann Petry Planned to Write." *Opportunity,* 24 (1946), 78–79.

Ivy, James. "Ann Petry Talks About Her First Novel." *Crisis,* 53 (1946), 48–49.

———. "Mrs. Petry's Harlem." *Crisis,* 53 (1946), 43–46.

Littlejohn, David. *Black on White: A Critical Survey of Writing by American Negroes.* New York: Viking Press, 1966.

Maund, Alfred. "The Negro Novelist and the Contemporary American Scene." *Chicago Jewish Forum,* 12 (1954), 28–34.

Rosenblatt, Roger. *Black Fiction.* Cambridge: Harvard University Press, 1974.

Shinn, Thelma. "Women in the Novels of Ann Petry." *Critique,* 16, No. 1, 110–20.

CAROLYN RODGERS

Primary Sources:

"Black Poetry—Where It's At." *Negro Digest,* September 1969, pp. 7–16.

The Heart as Ever Green. Garden City, N.Y.: Doubleday/Anchor, 1978.

How I Got Ovah. Garden City, N.Y.: Doubleday/Anchor, 1975.

"The Literature of Black." *Black World,* June 1970, pp. 5–11.

Love Raps. Chicago: Third World Press, 1969.

Paper Soul. Chicago: Third World Press, 1961.

Songs of a Black Bird. Chicago: Third World Press, 1969.

SONIA SANCHEZ

Primary Sources:

A Blue Book for Blue Black Magical Women. Detroit: Broadside Press, 1974.

Homecoming. Detroit: Broadside Press, 1968.

It's a New Day. Detroit: Broadside Press, 1971. Children's book.

"Sister Son/Ji." In *New Plays from the Black Theater,* edited by Ed Bullins. New York: Bantam Books, 1969.

We a BaddDDD People. Detroit: Broadside Press, 1970.

Secondary Sources:

Brooks, A. Russell. "The Motif of Dynamic Change in Black Revolutionary Poetry." *CLA Journal,* 15 (September 1971), 25–36.

Clarke, Sebastian. "Sonia Sanchez and Her Work." *Black World,* 20 (June 1971), 45–48, 96–98.

Lee, Donald L. "The Poets and Their Poetry." In *Dynamite Voices 1: Black Poets of the 1960's,* edited by Don Lee. Detroit: Broadside Press, 1971.

MARY E. VROMAN

Primary Sources:

Esther. New York: Bantam Books, 1963.

Harlem Summer. New York: Berkeley Publishing Corporation, 1968.

ALICE WALKER

Primary Sources:

"The Black Writer and the Southern Experience." *New South,* 25 (Fall 1970), 23–26.

"But Yet and Still, the Cotton Gin Kept on Working." *Black Scholar,* 1 (January/February 1970), 17–21.

"Eudora Welty: An Interview." *Harvard Advocate,* 106 (Winter 1973), 68–72.

In Love and Trouble: Stories of Black Women. New York: Harcourt Brace Jovanovich, 1973.

"In Search of Our Mothers' Gardens," *Ms.,* 2 (May 1974), 64–70, 105.

"In Search of Zora Neale Hurston." *Ms.,* 3 (March 1975), 74–79, 85–89.

Langston Hughes. New York: Thomas Y. Crowell Co., 1974.

"Lulls." *Black Scholar,* 7 (May 1976), 3–12.

Meridian. New York: Harcourt Brace Jovanovich, 1976.

Once. New York: Harcourt, Brace & World, 1968.

Revolutionary Petunias. New York: Harcourt Brace Jovanovich, 1973.

The Third Life of Grange Copeland. New York: Harcourt Brace Jovanovich, 1970.

"The Unglamorous but Worthwhile Duties of the Black Revolutionary Artist, or of the Black Writer Who Simply Works and Writes." *The Black Collegian,* October 1971.

Secondary Sources:

Callahan, John. "The Higher Ground of Alice Walker." *The New Republic,* September 14, 1974, pp. 21–22.

Coles, Robert. "To Try Men's Souls," *The New Yorker,* February 27, 1971, pp. 104–6.

Collier, Betty. "Review of *In Love and Trouble." Journal of Social and Behavioral Sciences,* 21 (Winter 1975), 136–42.

Fowler, Carolyn. "Solid at the Core." *Freedomways,* 14 (First Quarter, 1974), 59–62.

Greil, Marcus. Review of *Meridian. The New Yorker,* June 7, 1976, pp. 133–36.

Hairston, Loyle. "Work of Rare Beauty and Power." *Freedomways,* 2 (Second Quarter, 1971), 170–77.

Harris, Trudier. "Folklore in the Fiction of Alice Walker: A Perpetuation of Historical and Literary Traditions." *Black American Literature Forum,* 2 (Spring 1977), 3–8.

———. "Violence in *The Third Life of Grange Copeland." CLA Journal,* 19 (December 1975), 238–47.

Schorer, Mark. "Novels and Nothingness," *American Scholar,* Winter 1970–71, pp. 169–70.

Smith, Barbara. "The Souls of Black Women." *Ms.,* 2 (February 1974), 42–43, 78.

Washington, Mary Helen. "Black Women Myth and Image Makers." *Black World,* 23 (August 1974), 10–18.

MARGARET WALKER

Primary Sources:

For My People. New Haven: Yale University Press, 1942.

How I Wrote "Jubilee." Chicago: Third World Press, 1972.

Jubilee. Boston: Houghton Mifflin Co., 1966.

"New Poets." In *Black Expression,* edited by Addison Gayle, Jr. New York: Weybright & Talley, 1969.

Prophets for a New Day. Detroit: Broadside Press, 1970.

"Some Aspects of the Black Aesthetic." *Freedomways,* 16 (Second Quarter, 1976), 95–103.

Secondary Sources:

Emmanuel, James A. "Margaret Walker." In *Contemporary Novelists,* edited by James Vinson. New York: St. Martin's Press, 1972.

Giddings, Paula. "A Shoulder Hunched Against a Sharp Concern: Some Themes in the Poetry of Margaret Walker." *Black World,* 21 (December 1971), 20–25.

Klotman, Phyllis Rauch. "Oh Freedom—Women and History in Margaret Walker's *Jubilee." Black American Literature Forum,* 2 (Winter 1977), 139–45.

Littlejohn, David. *Black on White: A Critical Survey of Writing by American Negroes.* New York: Viking Press, 1966.

Powell, Bertie. "The Black Experience in Margaret Walker's *Jubilee* and Lorraine Hansberry's *The Drinking Gourd*." *CLA Journal,* 11 (December 1977), 304–11.

Randall, Dudley. "The Black Aesthetics in the Thirties, Forties, and Fifties." In *The Black Aesthetic,* edited by Addison Gayle. Garden City, N.Y.: Doubleday & Company, 1971.

Rollins, Charlemae. *Famous American Negro Poets*. New York: Dodd, Mead & Co.. 1965.

PHILLIS WHEATLEY

Primary Sources:

Memoir and Poems of Phillis Wheatley, A Native African and a Slave. Boston: Issac Knapp, 1938.

The Poems of Phillis Wheatley. Chapel Hill: Julian D. Mason, 1966.

Poems on Various Subjects, Religious and Moral. London: Bell, 1773.

Secondary Sources:

Applegate, Anne. "Phillis Wheatley: Her Critics and Her Contributions." *Negro American Literature Forum,* 9 (Winter 1975), 123–26.

Brewster, Dorothy. "From Phillis Wheatley to Richard Wright." *The Negro Quarterly,* 1 (1945), 80–83.

Collins, Terence. "Phillis Wheatley, the Dark Side of the Poetry." *Phylon,* 36 (March 1975), 75–88.

Gregory, Montgomery. "The Spirit of Phillis Wheatley." *Opportunity,* 1 (1923), 374–75.

Holmes, Wilfred. "Phyllis Wheatley." *Negro History Bulletin,* 6 (1943), 117–18.

Hull, Gloria. "Black Women Poets from Wheatley to Walker." *Negro American Literature Forum,* 9 (Winter 1975), 91–96.

Jamison, Angelene. "Analysis of Selected Poetry of Phillis Wheatley." *Journal of Negro Education,* 43 (Summer 1974), 408–16.

Malson, R. Lynn. "Phillis Wheatley—Soul Sister?" *Phylon,* 23 (Fall 1972), 222–30.

Renfro, Hebert G. *Life and Works of Phillis Wheatley*. Washington, D.C.: Robert L. Pendleton, 1916.

Richmond, Merle A. *Bid the Vassal Soar: Interpretive Essays on the Life and Poetry of Phillis Wheatley and George Moses Horton*. Washington, D.C.: Howard University Press, 1974.

Rigsby, Gregory. "Form and Content in Phillis Wheatley's Elegies." *CLA Journal,* 19 (December 1975), 248–57.

Robinson, William H. *Phillis Wheatley in the Black American Beginnings.* Detroit: Broadside Press, 1975.

Silverman, Kenneth. "Four New Letters by Phillis Wheatley." *Early American Literature,* 8 (Winter 1974), 257–71.

Slattery, J. R. "Phillis Wheatley, the Negro Poetess." *Catholic World,* 39 (1884), 484–98.

Smith, Eleanor. "Phillis Wheatley: A Black Perspective." *Journal of Negro Education,* 43 (Summer 1974), 401–7.

Selected African Women Writers

Ademola, Frances (Ghana), ed. *Reflections: Nigerian Prose and Verse.* Lagos: African Universities Press, 1962, 1965.

Aidoo, Ama Ata (Ghana). *Dilemma of a Ghost* (play), London: Longmans, Green & Co., 1969: Garden City, N.Y.: Doubleday & Company, 1970. *No Sweetness Here* (short stories), London: Longmans, Green & Co., 1970. "The Message," in *African Writing Today,* London: Penguin Books, 1967. "A Gift from Somewhere," in *New African Literature and the Arts,* Vol. 1, edited by Joseph Okpaku. *Anowa,* London: Longmans, Green & Co., 1970. Stories in *Présence Africaine, Negro World, Black Orpheus, Okyeame.*

Casely-Hayford, Gladys May (Ghana). *Take 'um So,* Freetown: New Era Press, 1948. Poetry in *Poems from Black Africa,* edited by Langston Hughes; *West African Verse,* edited by Donatus Ibe Nwoga; Philadelphia *Tribune,* October 14, 1937.

Danquah, Mabel (Ghana). "Anticipation," "Payment," and "The Torn Veil," in *African New Writing,* edited by T. Cullen Young. Stories in *An African Treasury,* edited by Langston Hughes; *The African Assertion,* edited by A. J. Shelton; *A Selection of African Prose: 2 Written Prose,* edited by W. H. Whiteley.

Dube, Violet. *Wonzanazo izindaba zika Phoshozwayo* (Tell Us the Stories of Phoshozwayo). London: Oxford University Press, 1935.

Emecheta, Buchi (Nigeria). *The Bride Price.* New York: George Braziller, 1976.

———. *In the Ditch.* London: Barrie & Jenkins, 1972.

———. *Second-class Citizen.* New York: George Braziller, 1975.

Espirito Santo, Alda de (St. Thomas). *Poetas de S Tomé e Príncipe; Antologia.* Prefacio de Alfredo Margarido. Lisboa: Casa dos Estu dantes do Império, 1963.

———. in *Cadorno de poesia negra de espressão portuguesa,* 1953.

———. in *Modern Poetry from Africa,* 1968.

———. in *New Sum of Poetry from the Negro World,* Vol. 57. Paris: Présence Africaine, 1966.

Futshane, Zora T. (South Africa), *Ujujuju no mhla ngenqaba* (Mhla in Trouble). Lovedale, South Africa: Lovedale Press, 1960.

Head, Bessie. (Pietermaritzburg, South Africa). *Maru*. London: Victor Gollancz, 1971: London: William Heinemann, 1972.

———. *When Rain Clouds Gather*. New York: Simon & Shuster, 1968.

———. *A Question of Power*. London: William Heinemann, 1974.

———. Stories in *Black World, Ms.*, and numerous other journals and magazines.

Henries, A. Doris Banks (Liberia). *A Biography of President William V. S. Tubman*. London: Macmillan, 1967.

———. *Heroes and Heroines of Liberia*. New York: Macmillan, 1962.

———. *Liberian Folklore*. New York: Macmillan, 1966.

———. ed. *Poems of Liberia (1836–1961)*. London: Macmillan, 1966.

Itayemi, Phebean (Nigeria). "Nothing So Sweet." In *African New Writing*, edited by T. Cullen Young. London: Lutterworth Press, 1947.

Jabavu, Noni Helen Nontando (Cape Province, South Africa). *Drawn in Color, African Contrasts*. London: John Murray, 1960.

———. *The Ochre People: Scenes from a South African Life*. London: John Murray, 1963; New York: St. Martin's Press, 1963.

Kakoza, Lillith (South Africa). *Intyatyambo yomzi* (The Flower in the Home). Cape Town: Methodist Book Room, 1913.

———. *Utandiwe Wakawa Gcaleka* (Tandiwe, a Damsel of Gaikaland). Cape Town: Methodist Book Room, 1914.

Khaketla, Carolone Ntseliseng 'Masechele Ramolahloane (Lesotho). "Mahlopha-a-senya" (Both Good and Bad at the Same Moment) (a play). Unpublished manuscript, 1954.

———. *'mantsopa* (poetry). Cape Town: Oxford University Press, 1963.

———. *Mosali eo u 'neileng eena* (The Woman You Gave Me) (a play). Morija: Morija Sesuto Book Depot, 1956.

Kimenye, Barbara, (Uganda). *Kalasanda*. London: Oxford University Press, 1965.

———. *Kalasanda Revisited*. London: Oxford University Press, 1966.

———. *The Smugglers*. London: Thomas Nelson & Sons, 1966, 1968.

———. "The Winner." In *Pan African Short Stories*, 1965.

Macauley, Jeanette (Freetown, Sierra Leone). "The Idea of Assimilation." In *Protest and Conflict in African Literature*, 1969.

Margarido, Maria Manuela (St. Thomas). *Alto como o silêncio.* Lisbon: Publicaçoes Europa-América, 1957.

———. *Antologia da poesia São Tomé e Príncipe,* Lisbon, 1963.

———. *Poetas e contistas africanos de expressão portuguesa.* São Paulo: Editora Brasiliense, 1963.

———. Poetry in *New Sum of Poetry from the Negro World,* Vol. 57. Paris: Présence Africaine, 1966.

M'Baya, Annette (Senegal). *Poèmes Africains* Paris and Toulouse: Centre d'Art National Français, 1965.

———. Poetry in *New Sum of Poetry from the Negro World,* Vol. 57. Paris: Présence Africaine, 1966.

Morel, Marion (South Africa). "Girls About Town." In *An African Treasury,* edited by Langston Hughes. New York: Crown Publishers, 1960; London: Victor Gollancz, 1961.

Njau, Rebecca (Kenya). "The Scar" and "The Round Chain." In *Transition,* No. 8 (March 1963).

———. "Alone with the Fig Tree." Unpublished manuscript.

Ntantala, Phillis P. (South Africa). "The Widows of the Reserve." In *Africa South,* n.d.

Nwapa, Flora (Nigeria). *Efuru.* London: William Heinemann, 1966.

———. *Idu.* London: William Heinemann, 1970.

———. *This Is Lagos and Other Stories.* London: William Heinemann, 1971.

Nxumalo, Natalie Victoria (Natal, South Africa). *Ubu Abuphangwa* (It's Not So Easy to Get to the Top). Pietermaritzburg: Shuter & Shooter, 1936.

Ogot, Grace Akinye (Kenya). *Land Without Thunder.* Nairobi: East African Publishing House, 1968.

———. *The Promised Land.* Nairobi: East African Publishing House, 1968.

———. Stories in *Pan African Short Stories,* 1965; stories in various issues of *Black Orpheus* magazine.

Segun, Mabel Joloaso, *My Father's Daughter* (a novelette). Lagos: African Universities Press, 1965.

———. "The Unfinished House." In *Reflections: Nigerian Prose and Verse,* edited by Frances Ademola. Lagos: African Universities Press, 1962, 1965.

Sutherland, Efua Theodora (Ghana). "Anansegora." In *Présence Africaine,* 22 (Summer 1964). English language ed.

———. *Edufa* (a play). London: Longmans, Green & Co., 1967, 1969.

———. *Foriwa.* (a play). Accra: State Publishing Corporation, 1967.

———. "Little Wild Flowers," "Mumunde my Mumunde," "It Happened." In *Pan African Short Stories,* 1966.

———. *Vulture! Vulture! Two Rhythm Plays.* Accra: Ghana Publishing House, 1968.

———. Stories in *Modern African Prose,* edited by Richard Rive, 1964; and in many other anthologies.

Swaartbooi, Victoria (Nqamakwe District, South Africa). *U-Mandisa.* Lovedale, South Africa: Lovedale Press, 1933.

Ulasi, Adaora Lily (Nigeria). *Many Things You No Understand.* London: Michael Joseph, 1970.

Wheatley, Phillis (Senegal). See bibliographies of Afro-American writing.

A Selected Bibliography

OF CARIBBEAN WOMEN WRITERS AND GENERAL CARIBBEAN LITERATURE

INCLUDING CRITICISM, FICTION, DRAMA, AND POETRY

Criticism

Blackman, Peter. "Some Thoughts on West Indian Writing." *Présence Africaine,* June–September 1957, pp. 296–300.

Bostock, H. F. "A Study of Contemporary Haitian Literature." *Phylon,* Third Quarter, 1956, pp. 250–56.

Braithwaite, E. "The African Presence in Caribbean Literature." In *Slavery, Colonialism, and Racism,* edited by Sidney Mintz. New York: W. W. Norton & Co., 1975.

———. "West Indian Prose Fiction in the Sixties." *Black World,* September 1971, pp. 15–29.

———. "Roots: A Commentary on West Indian Writers." *Bim,* 10, No. 37 (July–December 1963), 10–21.

Braithwaite, L. E. "Jazz and the West Indian Novel." *Bim,* January–June, 1968, pp. 115–26.

"British West Indies Poets and Their Culture."*Phylon,* First Quarter, 1953, pp. 71–73.

"The Calypso Tradition in West Indian Literature." *Black Academy Review,* Spring–Summer 1971, pp. 109–43.

Canton, E. Berthe. "A Bibliography of Caribbean Literature: 1900–1957." *Current Caribbean Bibliography,* Vol. 7.

"Caribbean Literature." *The Massachusetts Review,* 1974. Special issue.

"Caribbean Writers." *Présence Africaine,* 57(1966), 173–255; 397–428; 503; 555–559. Special issue.

Cartey, Wilfred G. O. "The Writer in the Caribbean." In *Social and Cultural Pluralism in the Caribbean. Annals of the New York Academy of Sciences,* 83 (January 20, 1960), 892–903.

"French Caribbean Novelists of Today." *Caribbean,* June 1959, pp. 110–13.

Herdeck, Donald E., ed. *Caribbean Authors.* Washington, D. C.: Inscape Corporation, 1977.

Koshland, Miriam G. "The Development of the Literary Idiom in Haiti." *Black Orpheus,* 7 (June 1960), 46–56.

———. "The Literature of the French West Indies." *Books Abroad,* Summer 1956, pp. 275–77.

Livingston, James T., ed. *Caribbean Rhythms: The Emerging English Literature of the West Indies.* New York: Washington Square Press, Pocket Books, 1974.

"Love in Haitian Literature." *Présence Africaine,* Fourth Quarter, 1966, pp. 159–71.

"Mayotte Capecia—Martiniquan Woman Writer," *CLA Journal,* 16, No. 4 (June 1973), 415–25.

Murray, Rudy G. "A Bibliography of Caribbean Novels in English." *Black Images,* (January 1972), pp. 15–25.

"The Novel in the British Caribbean." *Bim,* January–June 1968, pp. 75–78.

Parris, Dudley Eliot. "The Ideology of Creative Writers of the English-speaking Caribbean: 1950–1972." Los Angeles, 1973. (New York Public Library Microfilm R-1565.)

Porter, Dorothy. "African and Caribbean Creative Writings: A Bibliographic Survey." *African Forum,* Spring 1966, pp. 107–11.

"The Protest Tradition in West Indian Poetry." *Jamaica Journal,* June 1972, pp. 4–45.

Ramchand, Kenneth. *The West Indian Novel and Its Background.* London: Faber & Faber, 1970.

Ramsaran, J. A. *New Approaches to African Literature.* Ibadan, Nigeria: Ibadan University Press, 1970. Contains material on the Caribbean, pp. 87–122.

Revista/Review Interamericana. *Caribbean Literature(s).* Hato Rey, Puerto Rico, 1974, pp. 305–454. (New York Public Library [809.897–R].)

"Social Background of the West Indian Novel." *Black Orpheus,* 4 (October 1956), 46–50.

Sparer, Joyce L. "The Art of Wilson Harris." In *New Beacon Reviews, Collection One.* London: New Beacon Books, 1968.

Stoelting, Winfred L. "A Checklist of the West Indian Novel." *Black Books Bulletin,* 1, No. 3 (1972), 37.

Swanzy, Henry. "The Literary Situation in the Contemporary Caribbean." *Books Abroad,* Summer 1956.

"The Theme of Africa in West Indian Literature." *Phylon,* 26 (Third Quarter, 1965), 255–76.

"The Theme of the Past in Caribbean Literature," *Joliso,* 1, No. 3 (1973), 25–40.

"West Indian Drama in English (a Bibliography)." *Studies in Black Literature,* 6, No. 2 (Summer 1975), 14–16.

West Indian Literature: A Select Bibliography. Mona: University of the West Indies, 1964.

"West Indian Themes in Thirty-six Short Stories." *Caribbean Quarterly,* 2, No. 2, 12–23.

Wynter, Sylvia. "Reflections on West Indian Writing and Criticism." *Jamaica Journal,* 2, No. 4 (December 1968), and 3, No. 1 (March 1969), 26–42.

Fiction and Drama

Allfrey, Phyllis Shand. *The Orchid House*. New York: E. P. Dutton & Co., 1953.

Ashtine, Eaulin. *Crick-Crack! Trinidad and Tobago Folk Tales* (*Retold*). Trinidad: University of West Indies Press, 1966.

———. *Nine Folk Tales* (retold) Trinidad: University of West Indies Press, 1968.

Ashton, Helen. *Far Enough*. London: Ernest Benn, 1928.

Bell, Vera. "Joshua." In *Caribbean Anthology of Short Stories,* edited by Ernest A. Carr, et al. Kingston, Jamaica: Pioneer Press, 1953.

Bennett, Louise. *Jamaica Labrish*. Kingston, Jamaica: Songster's Book Stores, 1966.

———. and Ors. *Anancy Stories Dialect, Verse, and Proverbs,* 1950.

Bottome, Phyllis. *Under the Skin.* New York: Harcourt, Brace & Co., 1950. (A review of this novel appears in *Caribbean Quarterly,* 1, No. 4 [1950], 41.)

Chapman, Esther Hyman. *A Study in Bronze: A Novel of Jamaica.* London: Chantry Publications, 1953.

———. *Too Much Summer: A Novel of Jamaica.* London: Chantry Publications, 1953.

Chauvet, Marie. *Dance on the Volcano*. New York: William Sloane Associates, 1959.

Cousins, Phyllis. *Queen of the Mountain* (stories). London: Ginn and Company, 1967.

Duncan, Jane. *My Friends, the Mrs. Millers.* New York: St. Martin's Press, 1965.

Fleur, Anne Elizabeth. *Jeanne-Marie Goes to Market.* New York: Grosset & Dunlap, 1938.

Fonrose, Veronica. *The Evil Spirit* (a play). Port of Spain: University of the West Indies Extra-Mural Department, 1966.

Gimble, Rosemary. *Jonathan and Large.* London: André Deutsch, 1965.

Gould, Cora Smith. *The Caribbean Sea.* New York: National Americana Society, 1927.

Guy, Rosa. *Bird at My Window.* Philadelphia: J. B. Lippincott, 1966.

———. *The Friends.* New York: Holt, Rinehart & Winston, 1973.

Hodge, Merle. *Crick, Crack, Monkey.* London: André Deutsch, 1970.

Iremonger, Lucille. *The Cannibals, A Novel.* London: Hammond, Hammond & Company, 1952.

———. "Indian Pastoral." In *Caribbean Anthology of Short Stories,* edited by Ernest A. Carr, et al. Kingston, Jamaica: Pioneer Press, 1953.

———. *Creole.* London: Hutchinson & Company, 1951.

———. *Yes, My Darling Daughter.* London: Secker & Warburg, 1964.

Lina, Clara Rosa. *Tomorrow Will Always Come.* New York: Ivan Obolensky, 1965.

Lockett, Mary F. *Christopher.* New York: Abbey Press, 1902.

Lyons, Ruth. *The Island Lovers.* Garden City, N.Y.: Doubleday & Company, 1969.

Marr, Nancy. *Adam.* London: Museum Press, 1952.

———. *The Dark Divide: A Romance.* London: Museum Press, 1951.

———. *Nigger Brown.* London: Museum Press, 1953.

Marshall, Paule. *Brown Girl, Brownstones.* New York: Random House, 1959.

———. *The Chosen Place, the Timeless People.* New York: Harcourt, Brace & World, 1969.

———. *Soul Clap Hands and Sing.* New York: Atheneum Publishers, 1961.

Mathews, Gertrude S. *Treasure.* New York: Henry Holt & Company, 1917.

Maynard, Olga Winnefred. *Carib Echoes: A Collection of Short Stories and Poems.* Port of Spain: Yuille's Printerie [1927–] 34.

Mayo, Katherine. "Big Mary." *Atlantic Monthly,* January 1911.

———. "Sissa and the Bakru." *Atlantic Monthly,* October 1912.

Quayle, Ada. *The Mistress*. London: MacGibbon & Kee, 1957.

Riera, Pepita. *Prodigy*. New York: Pageant Press, 1956.

Rodway, James. *In Guiana Wilds: A Study of Two Women*. Boston: L. C. Page & Company, 1899.

Rovere, Ethel. "Only White People Cry." In *Caribbean Anthology of Short Stories,* edited by Ernest A. Carr, et al. Kingston, Jamaica: Pioneer Press, 1953.

———. "Spanish Jar." In *Caribbean Anthology of Short Stories,* edited by Ernest A. Carr, et al. Kingston, Jamaica: Pioneer Press, 1953.

Saher, Lilla Van. *The Echo*. New York: E. P. Dutton & Co., 1947.

———. *Macamba*. New York: E. P. Dutton & Co., 1949.

Tropica (pseudonym of Mary Adella Wolcott). *The Island of Sunshine*. New York: Knickerbocker Press, 1904.

Waite-Smith, Cicely. *Africa Sling-Shot* (a play). Port of Spain: University of the West Indies Extra-Mural Department, 1966.

———. *The Creatures* (a play). Port of Spain: University of the West Indies Extra-Mural Department, 1966.

———. *The Impossible Situation* (a play). Port of Spain: University of the West Indies Extra-Mural Department, 1966.

———. *Return to Paradise* (a play). Port of Spain: University of the West Indies Extra-Mural Department, 1966.

Wynter, Sylvia. *The Hills of Hebron*. New York: Simon & Schuster, 1962. (A review appears in *Negro Digest,* October 1962.)

Young, Rida Johnson. *Out of the Night*. New York: W. J. Watt & Company, 1925.

Selected Anthologies in Which Caribbean Women Are Represented

Cohen, J. M., ed. *Writers in the New Cuba*. Baltimore: Penguin Books, 1967.

Ana Marie Simo

Culmer, Jack, ed. *A Book of Bahamian Verse*. London: Bailey Brothers, 1930.

Julia Warner Michael
Margaret Joyce Scott
Iris Tree

Dathorne, O. R., ed. *Caribbean Verse*. London: William Heinemann, 1967.

Vera Bell (Jamaica)
Vera Margon (Jamaica)
Stella Mead (Jamaica)

Daisy Myrie (Jamaica)
Vivian Virtue (Jamaica)

Engber, Marjorie. *Caribbean Fiction and Poetry*. New York: Center for Inter-American Relations, 1970.

Figueroa, John. *Caribbean Voices*. (Vol. 1: *Dreams and Visions*. London: Evans Brothers, 1966.

———. *Caribbean Voices*. Vol. 2: *The Blue Horizons*. London: Evans Brothers, 1970.
Louise Bennett (Jamaica)
Gloria Escoffery (Jamaica)
Barbara Ferland (Jamaica)
Vivette Hendriks (Jamaica)
Una Marson (Jamaica)
Dorothy Phillips
Clovis Scott
Vivian Virtue (Jamaica)

Gray, Cecil, ed. *Response*. London: Thomas Nelson & Sons, 1969.

Howes, Barbara. *From the Green Antilles*. New York: Macmillan, 1966.

Hughes, Langston, and Bontemps, Arna. *The Poetry of the Negro, 1746–1949*. N.Y.: Garden City, Doubleday & Company, 1949.
Knolly S. La Fortune (Trinidad)
Mary Lockett (Jamaica)

Jarn, Nathaniel, ed. *Con Cuba: An Anthology of Cuban Poetry of the Last Sixty Years*. New York: Grossman Publishers, 1969.
Lydia Cabrera (Cuba)
Gloria Escoffery (Jamaica)
Barbara Ferland (Jamaica)
Vivette Hendricks (Jamaica)
Constance Hollar (Jamaica)
Una Marson (Jamaica)
Agnes Maxwell-Hall (Jamaica)
Stella Mead (Jamaica)
Florette Morand (Guadeloupe)
Arabel Moulton-Barrett
Phyllis May Myers
Daisy Myrie (Jamaica)
Stephanie Ormsby (Jamaica)
Millicent Payne (Barbados)
Monica Skeete (Barbados)
Flora Squires (Barbados)
Vivian Virtue (Jamaica)

McFarlane, John E. C., ed. *A Treasury of Jamaican Poetry.* London: University of London Press, 1949.
Clara Maud Garrett
Faith Goodheart
Constance Hollar
Ruth Hornor
Albinia C. Hutton
Lena Kent
Mary Lockett
Una Marson
Agnes Maxwell-Hall
Arabel Moulton-Barrett
Eva R. Nicholas
Stephanie Ormsby
Vivian L. Virtue
Dorothy Whitfield

Murphy, Beatrice M., ed. *Ebony Rhythm: An Anthology of Contemporary Negro Verse.* New York: Exposition Press, 1948.
Edna L. Harrison (Jamaica)

Onis, Harriet de. *The Golden Land: An Anthology of Latin America Folklore in Literature.* New York: Alfred A. Knopf, 1948.
Gertrudis Gómez de Avallaneda (Cuba)

Sergeant, Howard., ed. *New Voices of the Commonwealth.* London: Evans Brothers, 1968.
Vivian Virtue

Shapiro, Norman R., ed. *Negritude: Black Poetry from Africa and the Caribbean.* New York: October House, 1970.
Joselyn Etienne (Guadeloupe)
Marie-Therese Rouil (Martinique)

Poetry

Allfrey, Phyllis Shand (Dominica). *In Circles, Poems.* Middlesex, England: Raven Press, 1940.

Brown, Paula (St. John). *A Woman Singing, Poems & Drawings.* St. John Cruz Bay Arts, 1958.

Daniel, Edith (Trinidad). *Gems in Verse.* Ilfracombe, Devon, England: Arthur Stockwell, 1962.

Delaney, Lessie A. (Trinidad). *Verses from the Caribbean.* Ilfracombe, Devon, England: Arthur Stockwell, n.d.

Gray, Cecil, ed. *Response.* London: Thomas Nelson & Sons, 1969.

Hazell, Vivian (British West Indies). *Poems.* Ilfracombe, Devon, England: Arthur Stockwell, 1956.

Jones, Barbara Althea (Trinidad). *Among the Potatoes. A Collection of Modern Verses.* Ilfracombe, Devon, England: Arthur Stockwell, 1967.

Lee, Erica B. (St. Thomas). *Reflections; A Collection of Poems.* San Juan: Padilla Printing Works, 1939.

Lyons, Miriam (Jamaica). *Fugitive Poems.* London: Unicorn Press, 1933.

Marson, Una (Jamaica). *Towards the Stars; Poems.* Bickley, Kent: University of London Press, 1945.

Mead, Stella (Jamaica). *Splendor at Dawn—Poems.* London: University of London Press, 1943.

Michael, Julia Warner (Bahamas). *Native Nassau: A Memory of New Providence Island.* New York: H. Marchbank's Print Shop, 1909.

Normal, Alma (Jamaica). *Ballads of Jamaica.* London: Longmans, Green & Co., 1967.

Ormsby, Harriet (Jamaica). *Ideal Jamaica and Other Poems.* Ilfracombe, Devon, England: Arthur Stockwell, n.d.

Tree, Iris (Bahamas). *Poems.* New York: John Lane, 1919.

———. *The Traveller and Other Poems.* New York: Boni & Liveright, 1927.

Contributors

Robert Alvin Bell is a graduate student in comparative literature at Georgetown University, Washington, D.C. He has also done graduate work in England, and as undergraduate at Morehouse College in Atlanta, Georgia, he was involved in numerous cultural activities, including poetry, drama, and music festivals. He has published in the *Atlanta University Reader 2,* a poetry anthology featuring the works of Atlanta University Center students and faculty. Mr. Bell travels widely in First World countries and utilizes his experiences in his critical and creative works.

Melba Joyce Boyd was an assistant editor at Broadside Press between 1973 and 1975, and she has taught at Wayne State University, Shaw College, Wayne Community College, Eastside Street Academies, and Cass Tech High School in Detroit. Her poetry, book reviews, and photographs have appeared regularly in the Detroit *Sun* since April 1976; in *The Broadside Annual,* 1975 and 1976; in *Broadside Memories: Poets I Have Known;* in *Black Creation, Obatala, Black Books Bulletin,* and *Black World.* Mrs. Boyd lives and works in Detroit.

Mary Williams Burger, assistant provost in the Division of Arts and Humanities at the University of Maryland, College Park, was born in North Little Rock, Arkansas, and attended public school there. After receiving a B.A. in English from A.M.&N. College (University of Arkansas, Pine Bluff) she completed an M.A. at Colorado State University and a Ph.D. in Modern Literature from Washington University, St. Louis, Missouri. Coeditor of *Black Viewpoint* (1971), she also has written critical articles on Black American poetry and autobiography, and she is a frequent lecturer on the literature and experiences of Black women in America.

Dr. Iva Carruthers is associate professor and department chairman of Sociology at Northeastern Illinois University, Chicago. She and her family have traveled widely throughout Africa and the Caribbean and she has written several children's stories reflecting those experiences. She serves on the Editorial Advisory Board of the *Journal of Negro Education* and is active in the Association of African Historians. She is a wife and mother of three sons.

Leo Carty was born in New York City, where he won a scholarship to the Museum of Modern Art School for Children when he was eleven. He graduated from the High School of Music and Art, and attended Cooper Union and Pratt Institute. Mr. Carty has worked as a fashion illustrator, political cartoonist, teacher, and free-lance illustrator for the adventure magazines *Sir, Escape,* and *Target*. He has also been an illustrator with the New York City Department of Health. His exhibitions include among others, "Art: U.S.A." at Madison Square Garden, Marion Gallery, Market Place Gallery, and Fulton Art Fair. Presently, Leo Carty lives and works in St. Croix, Virgin Islands.

Daryl C. Dance, assistant professor of English at Virginia Commonwealth University, received the A.B. and M.A. degrees in English from Virginia State College, and the Ph.D degree in English from the University of Virginia. Her essays and reviews have appeared in *CLA Journal* and *Negro American Literature Forum.*

Gloria T. Hull is an assistant professor of English at the University of Delaware. Her critical work on Black American literature has appeared in numerous scholarly journals. She maintains active membership in CLA (College Language Association) and MLA (Modern Language Association).

Jacquelyn Furgus Hunter was born and educated in San Fernando, Trinidad, and furthered her studies in London. She is presently residing in Atlanta, Georgia, with her husband and daughter.

Gloria Joseph is a professor of Black Studies and Psychology at Hampshire College, School of Social Science, Amherst, Massachusetts. Her critical articles have appeared in various social science journals, and she is currently at work on a book which explores Black and white responses to the women's liberation movement.

Winifred Oyoko Loving was born in Boston and describes herself this way in her collection of poems, *Remember When* (1974): "Teacher. Philosopher. Traveller. Singer. Mother. Believer. Giver. Lover. Doer." Currently she lives and works in St. Croix with her daughter.

Haki R. Madhubuti (Don L. Lee) has been a consistently powerful and prolific writer and lecturer since his poems and essays began receiving wide acclaim in the sixties. His statements/poems have appeared in every major Black organ, among them the *Black Scholar, Black World,* and *Black Books Bulletin.* He is on the executive council of the Congress of Afrikan People, is writer-in-residence at Howard University, director of the Institute of Positive Education (which produces *Black Books Bulletin*), and editor of Third World Press in Chicago.

Paule Marshall was born of Barbadian parents in Brooklyn and is widely anthologized in Afro-American and Women's Studies Readers. She is the author of the novels *Brown Girl, Brownstones; Soul Clap Hands and Sing; The Chosen Place, the Timeless People.* Among her best known short stories are "Reena" (*Harper's Magazine,* October 1962); "Barbados" (*International Library of Negro Life and History,* 1969); "Some Get Wasted" (*Harlem, U.S.A.,* 1964); "To Da-da in Memoriam" (*Black Voices,* 1968). She has received both the Guggenheim and Ford Foundation fellowships.

Judy C. Mutunhu is a free-lance photographer. She is a graduate of Pace University, New York, but her photographic training was acquired from Cornell University, Ithaca, New York, and from a photography apprenticeship with the Ithaca *Journal,* where she later worked as a news photographer. Some of her photographs have been published in *A.A.U. News, Syncro-Info, My Weekly Reader, Eye,* and *Watu.* At present, she lives in North Carolina with her husband and two children.

Kenneth McClane was born in New York City in 1951, attended school there, and went to Cornell University, where he received a B.A. (with distinction in all subjects) and was elected to Phi Beta Kappa. He continued at Cornell and received an M.A. and an M.F.A. in creative writing. Now he teaches at Cornell. His publications include two books of poems, *Out Beyond the Bay* (1975), *Moons and Low Times* (1977), and poems in many magazines including *Beloit Poetry Journal, Northwest Review, Crisis, Epoch, Obsidian,* and *Pequod.*

Samuel Koomsom Otoo is an engineering student at Cornell University. Born in Ghana, he intends to combine his engineering and writing talents in a future career inspired by Wole Soyinka and Amos Tutuola.

Richard Powell is a native of Chicago. His works have appeared in such publications as *Tuesday Magazine, Southern Exposure, Black Books Bulletin,* and *The Massachusetts Review.* He received his B.A. from Morehouse College and holds an M.F.A. from Howard

University. He has recently completed a series of intaglio prints on American novelist Richard Wright, and a print-making session at Haystack School of Crafts, Deer Isle, Maine. He is presently a researcher at the Metropolitan Museum of Art in New York, on a Rockefeller Foundation Fellowship in Museum Education.

Andrea Benton Rushing is an assistant professor of Black Studies and English at Amherst College and has taught at Simmons College, University of Massachusetts/Boston, and Harvard University. She was born in New York City, received her B.A. from Queens College, her M.A. from Simmons College, and is currently a Ph.D. candidate (in English) at the University of Massachusetts/Amherst. Her writing and research center on images of Black women in African, Afro-American, and Caribbean literature.

Lynn Wheeldin Suruma is a Connecticut native, having graduated from the state's various schools, and then moving from there to New York City, where she worked with children's literature and films for the New York Public Library. At present she is an editor for the Institute of the Black World in Atlanta, Georgia, where she lives with her two sons.

Hortense Spillers presently teaches courses in literature and writing at Wellesley College, Wellesley, Massachusetts. A native of Memphis, Tennessee, she has also taught school in Kentucky and Arizona. She received a Ph.D. in English and American Literature at Brandeis University in 1974. Articles and stories of hers have been published by *Black Scholar, CLA Journal, Essence,* and *The Harvard Advocate.* An assistant editor of *Caliban: A Journal of New-World Thought and Writing,* and a 1976 recipient of the National Magazine Award for excellence in fiction and belles-lettres, she is at work on what she hopes to be a collection of short fiction and a revision of a manuscript on sermons. She lives in Boston.

Phyllis Thompson, from Philadelphia, is an artist and print maker who is presently working as an assistant professor of Art at Cornell University, Ithaca, New York. She received a B.S.A. degree from the Philadelphia College of Art in 1968, and in 1972, an M.F.A. degree from Tyler School of Art, Temple University, Philadelphia. Recent exhibitions of her work include a solo show at Keystone Junior College, La Plume, Pennsylvania, and group shows at Gallery Penn Limited, Washington, D.C., the Philadelphia College of Art, V. Hahn Gallery, Philadelphia, and the Johnson Museum, Ithaca, New York. Her work is included in the Philadelphia Museum of Art Prints & Drawings Collection.

Marie Linton-Umeh has an M.A. degree in English and one in African Studies. She has been an instructor of Third World literature at the State University of New York, Brockport, in Oneonta. Her research interests center around images of women in African nonvernacular literature. Mrs. Linton-Umeh is currently pursuing a doctorate at the University of Wisconsin, Madison.

Mary Helen Washington, assistant professor of Literature at the Center for Black Studies, University of Detroit, is the author of numerous critical articles appearing in scholarly journals devoted to Black issues. She is the editor of the highly successful anthology *Black-eyed Susans* (Doubleday, 1976). She lives in Detroit.

Paulette Childress White was born and educated in the public school system of Detroit, Michigan, the third of thirteen children. She attended art school for one year, and is currently a homemaker, the mother of five sons, and the wife of artist Bennie White. She has published one volume of poetry and is currently working on a novel.

Lorna Williams is an assistant professor of Romance Languages (Spanish and Portuguese) at Dartmouth College, Hanover, New Hampshire. Her short stories and articles have appeared in *Hispania, CLA Journal, Revista/Review Interamericana, Studies in Black Literature, The Journal of Ethnic Studies, Obsidian,* and *Bim.*

Marvin E. Williams, a 1977 graduate of Cornell University, was born and lives on St. Croix, Virgin Islands. He has published in various Crucian magazines and in *Watu,* Cornell's Black literary magazine, of which he is the present editor. *Ebony Field* was his first published book of poetry and two more are in preparation.